WORLD ON THE MOVE

WORLD ON THE MOVE

250,000 Years of Human Migration

Edward Liebow · James I. Deutsch
Daniel Ginsberg · Sojin Kim · Caitlyn Kolhoff

WILEY Blackwell

Copyright © 2025 by John Wiley & Sons, Inc. All rights reserved, including rights for text and data mining and training of artificial intelligence technologies or similar technologies.

Published by John Wiley & Sons, Inc., Hoboken, New Jersey.
Published simultaneously in Canada.

No part of this publication may be reproduced, stored in a retrieval system, or transmitted in any form or by any means, electronic, mechanical, photocopying, recording, scanning, or otherwise, except as permitted under Section 107 or 108 of the 1976 United States Copyright Act, without either the prior written permission of the Publisher, or authorization through payment of the appropriate per-copy fee to the Copyright Clearance Center, Inc., 222 Rosewood Drive, Danvers, MA 01923, (978) 750-8400, fax (978) 750-4470, or on the web at www.copyright.com. Requests to the Publisher for permission should be addressed to the Permissions Department, John Wiley & Sons, Inc., 111 River Street, Hoboken, NJ 07030, (201) 748-6011, fax (201) 748-6008, or online at http://www.wiley.com/go/permission.

The manufacturer's authorized representative according to the EU General Product Safety Regulation is Wiley-VCH GmbH, Boschstr. 12, 69469 Weinheim, Germany, e-mail: Product_Safety@wiley.com.

Trademarks: Wiley and the Wiley logo are trademarks or registered trademarks of John Wiley & Sons, Inc. and/or its affiliates in the United States and other countries and may not be used without written permission. "World on the Move: 250,000 Years of Human Migration" is a registered trademark of the American Anthropological Association. All other trademarks are the property of their respective owners. John Wiley & Sons, Inc. is not associated with any product or vendor mentioned in this book.

Limit of Liability/Disclaimer of Warranty
While the publisher and author have used their best efforts in preparing this book, they make no representations or warranties with respect to the accuracy or completeness of the contents of this book and specifically disclaim any implied warranties of merchantability or fitness for a particular purpose. No warranty may be created or extended by sales representatives or written sales materials. The advice and strategies contained herein may not be suitable for your situation. You should consult with a professional where appropriate. Further, readers should be aware that websites listed in this work may have changed or disappeared between when this work was written and when it is read. Neither the publisher nor authors shall be liable for any loss of profit or any other commercial damages, including but not limited to special, incidental, consequential, or other damages.

For general information on our other products and services or for technical support, please contact our Customer Care Department within the United States at (800) 762-2974, outside the United States at (317) 572-3993 or fax (317) 572-4002.

Wiley also publishes its books in a variety of electronic formats. Some content that appears in print may not be available in electronic formats. For more information about Wiley products, visit our web site at www.wiley.com.

Library of Congress Cataloging-in-Publication Data
Names: Liebow, Edward, author. | Ginsberg, Daniel (Anthropologist) author. | Kolhoff, Caitlyn, author. | Kim, Sojin, author. | Deutsch, James I., author.
Title: World on the move : 250,000 years of human migration / Edward Liebow, Daniel Ginsberg, Caitlyn Kolhoff, Sojin Kim, James Deutsch.
Description: Hoboken, New Jersey : Wiley-Blackwell [2025] | Includes index.
Identifiers: LCCN 2024039298 (print) | LCCN 2024039299 (ebook) | ISBN 9781394183302 (paperback) | ISBN 9781394183326 (adobe pdf) | ISBN 9781394183319 (epub)
Subjects: LCSH: Emigration and immigration–History–Exhibitions. | Human beings–Migrations–Exhibitions.
Classification: LCC JV6021 .L54 2025 (print) | LCC JV6021 (ebook) | DDC 304.809–dc23/eng/20241029
LC record available at https://lccn.loc.gov/2024039298
LC ebook record available at https://lccn.loc.gov/2024039299

Cover Design: Wiley
Cover Image: Photo courtesy of the Polynesian Voyaging Society and ʻŌiwi TV

Set in 10/12pt Bembo by Straive, Pondicherry, India

SKY10101556_033125

Contents

List of Figures — vi
Acknowledgments — vii

Section 1 Introduction and Overview — 1

1 Basic Concepts and Patterns of Migration and Displacement — 7
2 The Crossroads Concept — 34

Section 2 Where Do We Come From? — 61

3 Out of Africa — 63
4 The Peopling of Europe, Australasia, and the Pacific — 78
5 Peopling of the Americas — 92

Section 3 Why Do We Move? — 105

6 Movement and the Social Production of Vulnerability — 107

Section 4 How Does Migration Change Us? — 139

7 Language and Migration — 141
8 Economic Development and Gentrification — 159
9 Enslavement and Coercion — 194

Section 5 Where Are We Going? — 219

10 National and International Policy — 221
11 At A Crossroads — 255

Index — 257

List of Figures

1.1	Early dispersal routes out of Africa	15
1.2	SS *Vasari* alien passenger manifest, 20 April 1920	17
2.1	The Mediterranean basin	37
2.2	Pleistocene shoreline, northern circumpolar region	41
2.3	Countries of central Africa today	46
2.4	"The Goez Map Guide to the Murals of East Los Angeles"	50
3.1	The main geological time scale of eons, eras, periods, and epochs	72
4.1	Early dispersal routes out of Africa	79
4.2	Settlement of the Pacific Islands of Micronesia and Melanesia	80
5.1	Key paleoarchaeology sites in North America	93
10.1	Migration and the 2030 sustainable development agenda	223

Acknowledgments

This book has grown out of a collaboration between the American Anthropological Association and the Smithsonian Center for Folklife and Cultural Heritage. The tour of **a traveling exhibition** that is also a part of this project has been managed by the Public Programs Office of the American Library Association: Project Director Brian Russell and Program Coordinator Emily Gallaugher. The **exhibition development team** included James Deutsch, Daniel Ginsberg, Palmyra Jackson, Sojin Kim, Caitlyn Kolhoff, Nell Koneczny, Ed Liebow, John Powell, Melanie Welch, and Erin Younger. Meagan Shirley assisted with photo permissions. The work has benefited from **special content advisers** Suellen Cheng, Joel Darmstadter, Gilbert Estrada, William David Estrada, Harriet Evans, Quetzal Flores, Gilbert Hom, Munson Kwok, Betty Marín, Elizabeth Marino, Michael Atwood Mason, Eugene Moy, Kris Kelley Rivera, James Rojas, and Kim Walters. **Interns** involved in supporting the project include Deva Macias, Lucy Sprague, Meghan Ussing, and Hayat Zarzour.

Exhibition script and design review assistance was provided by Betty Belanus, Olivia Cadaval, Amalia Córdova, Eduardo Díaz, David Homa, Veronica Jackson, Deirdre Johnson, Somi Kim, Mary Linn, Jeff Meade, Magdalena Mieri, Sabrina Lynn Motley, Andrea Kim Neighbors, Stephanie Norby, Shannon Peck-Bartle, Philippa Rappoport, Margaret Salazar-Porzio, Rob Summers, and Ranald Woodaman. The exhibition's interactive activities were developed at workshops presented at the Smithsonian Folklife Festival. We also want to acknowledge the Washington DC Public Library's Capitol View and Tenley-Friendship Neighborhood Branches, whose after-school youth programs helped us to test interactive exhibition prototypes; and the Martin Luther King, Jr. Branch, which hosted the exhibition before it began its national tour and offered many useful suggestions on installation, hosting, and programming activities. Early in the exhibition planning stages, Randi Korn and associates facilitated the development of an evaluation planning framework. **Exhibition design** was managed by Smithsonian Exhibits, with special thanks to Project Manager Seth Waite and Lead Designer Paula Millett. **Exhibition fabrication** was completed by the Ravenswood Studio of Chicago.

The project unfolded over a lengthy incubation period, guided by the insights of an international **advisory board**, including Leo Chavez, Miguel Díaz-Barriga,

Margaret Dorsey, Matthew Durington, Judith Freidenberg, Sarah Green, Monica Heller, Antoinette Jackson, Laurel Kendall, Noel Salazar, Lynn Stephen, and Miguel Vilar.

Funding for this project was provided by the American Anthropological Association, the Smithsonian Center for Folklife and Cultural Heritage, the Wenner-Gren Foundation for Anthropological Research, and Dr. William Heaney.

We owe a deep debt of gratitude to Leith Mullings, without whose encouragement this project never would have been launched.

Section 1
Introduction and Overview

This book was conceived as a companion to a traveling exhibition developed by the American Anthropological Association and the Smithsonian Center for Folklife and Cultural Heritage. The exhibition, *World on the Move: 250,000 Years of Human Migration*, brings together the current state of knowledge about migration and displacement to reach a variety of audiences, including schoolchild and their families, educators, and community-based organizations. We aim to reframe the ways in which we think – and talk – about migration. *World on the Move* challenges people to consider the scale, composition, and time-depth of human population movements, the ways in which research on migration and displacement have been used (and misused) to support public policy, and the lived experiences of individuals, families, and communities on the move.

We hear a great deal of talk these days about how people move around much more than they used to. We also hear about what this moving does to our communities – and often it is not good news. Economic hardships, a shortage of affordable housing, religious persecution, war and conflict, the threat of disease, and even the effects of climate change may force people to move. People may also move in search of economic and educational opportunity. At the end of a migrant family's journey, sometimes the reception is a hearty embrace. But the reception is not always with open arms. In some places, there is concern that too many immigrants will take away jobs or change the character of a place beyond recognition.

Drawing on a wealth of case studies from across human history and its breadth of cultures, *World on the Move* aims to help people appreciate migration histories – their own and those of others. The exhibition has been designed to travel to public libraries, museums, and community centers around the world for a target audience of primary and secondary school-age visitors. As host institutions may not have educators or docents on hand to actively guide and interact with visitors, the exhibition design accommodates flexible self-navigation, with modular panel displays and accessible

World on the Move: 250,000 Years of Human Migration, First Edition. Edward Liebow, James I. Deutsch, Daniel Ginsberg, Sojin Kim, and Caitlyn Kolhoff.
© 2025 John Wiley & Sons, Inc. Published 2025 by John Wiley & Sons, Inc.

INTRODUCTION AND OVERVIEW

Refugees in transit charge their cell phones outside a train station in Budapest, Hungary. The city is a common transit point for migrants moving from Southwestern Asia to Central Europe. Source: Photo by Zoltan Balogh / MTI via AP.

interactive components. Host institutions can customize their presentations with displays that feature local stories and public programs.

This exhibition has been designed to inspire visitors to:

- Be curious about the long history of human migration.
- Appreciate the complexity and diversity of migration stories.
- Recognize that migration is a shared human experience.
- Feel safe to discuss issues surrounding migration.
- Share migration stories with family members, neighbors, and friends.
- Feel proud of their family's migration stories.
- Gain greater empathy toward migrants in their communities and elsewhere.
- Ask critical questions about migration.
- Consider their beliefs and opinions about migration.

One may notice that the overall goals for the visitors' experiences are as affective as they are cognitive. The exhibition does not directly ask visitors to identify the migration routes through which humans have come to populate the world or the types of evidence that have enabled researchers to recreate these routes, as a classroom teacher might do. Instead, we mean for visitors to *be curious, appreciate complexity, share stories,* and *feel proud.*

As a companion to the exhibition, this book fills in some of the gaps about migration routes and timing of dispersal of human populations around the world, along with the basic patterns, processes, causes, and consequences of such movements. This does not contradict the aims of the exhibition. Instead, it aims to answer some of the key questions that the exhibition raises and amplify the sense of curiosity with which we pursue greater understanding of this essential element of the human condition.

Prevailing Exhibition Narratives

World on the Move's narrative approach differs from the typical migration exhibition narrative structure. Most public exhibitions that focus on migration and displacement use a geographic reference frame involving places of origin and destination with a narrative that emphasizes the destination as the receiver and host of successive waves of new arrivals. At France's National Immigration Museum in Paris, for example, the central problem of the long-term exhibition on display is how to represent two centuries of immigration in France? The exhibition invites the visitor to follow along with immigrants' experiences when adapting to a new home in a sometimes welcoming, more frequently hostile, France.

At Britain's Migration Museum, the tone of the exhibition is set by the prologue label text, which quotes Robert Winder's *Bloody Foreigners: The Story of Immigration to Britain*: "Ever since the first Jute, the first Saxon, the first Roman and the first Dane leaped off their boats and planted their feet on British mud, we have been a migrant nation. Our roots are neither clean nor straight, they are impossibly tangled."

And in the United States, the Smithsonian's National Museum of American History presents *Many Voices, One Nation,* a long-term exhibition that takes visitors through a chronology of migrants "settling in" and "unsettling" America. It advances a narrative of diverse populations that blend or co-exist in service to the project of nation building.

As a traveling exhibition, *World on the Move* is not tied to a home institution nor committed to telling the story of any particular region. Instead, we take a more encompassing view that centers less on one specific place and more on the patterns and processes of migration and displacement. We feel it is necessary to complicate the orderly sense of place and time packed into this narrative structure. We resist the framing that begins with a privileged "we," which most typically corresponds to the imagined community of a nation-state, and the challenges presented by the arrival of a foreign "they." And we must call attention to the way such stories often rely heavily on a rational choice-making model of individual decision making to account for when, where, and why people move.

The linear narrative structure – people come from *there* (a place of origin) and move to *here* (a destination) – does not account for cyclical movement over seasonal, annual, lifetime, and intergenerational patterns. It cannot neatly account for agricultural and construction workers who shift locations with short-term employment prospects, for children who shuttle between rural and urban family members along with the yearly school calendar, for retirees and pensioners who divide their time between places, those who relocate for care-giving or cost of living accommodations, or for refugee and asylum seekers who retain a strong inclination to return – and may enable their children to return once conflict subsides.

The use of push–pull factors to explain migration dismisses altogether the coercive conditions of enslavement and trafficking, while discounting the widely prevalent circumstances in which the social production of vulnerabilities leaves individuals and families without any good options. Our decisions to move are usually influenced by forces beyond our control, such as where and when we were born and what the political, economic, and environmental conditions are like in our area. Migrants are often forced to choose between equally bad options. Stay and you may face difficulties and danger. Leave and you may face an uncertain future in a place you know nothing about and where you know no one.

Syrian and Iraqi refugees arrive in Lesvos, Greece from Turkey. Those who make it to the island are often fleeing poverty and violence and face an uncertain future. Source: Photo by Georgios Giannopoulos (Wikimedia Commons, CC BY-SA 4.0).

A narrative that involves the origin–destination binary, when coupled with the push–pull rational choice model, reinforces inequities that must be dismantled. It reinforces the structure of hierarchies – people from some places of origin and for selected reasons are more worthy than others of a welcome reception at their intended destination. In a world where just about everyone has a story of migration or displacement somewhere in their family history, we believe that it is time to change the narrative and public conversation to better understand our own stories and the stories of others.

The book is organized into five main parts. In the remainder of this introductory section, we describe some basic patterns and processes of migration over time; evidence that is used to measure migration, displacement, and their impacts; and the crossroads concept, a narrative device that informs the traveling exhibition. We feel this approach helps give observers a vantage point from which to see a variety of patterns in human movement.

Section 2, "Where Do We Come From?", presents an overview of major population movements over the course of human history. We begin with the first waves of movement out of Africa and describe the time horizons for the peopling of the major continents as well as the ways in which we use genetic, archaeological, linguistic, and cultural evidence to enrich and update our understanding of these movements. We discuss variations on the out of Africa hypothesis and cover highlights in the arrival of people in Australasia, Europe, the Americas, and the Pacific Islands. Through crossroads stories, we recreate the histories of the Mediterranean basin, Beringia, central Africa (and its connections to the transatlantic slave trade), and East Los Angeles as a site of settler colonialism, economic opportunity, and gentrification, all processes that readers may connect to similar locales around the globe.

Section 3, "Why Do We Move?" reviews the many reasons that propel the movement of human populations. Some move to attend college, to start a new job, or to be close to family and friends. Some move to build a better life or escape from poverty, conflict, persecution, or natural disasters. Some are forced to move through human trafficking and enslavement. And some are pushed aside to make room for economic development and urban renewal. Often people move for a combination of reasons, including forces beyond their control.

Section 4, "How Does Migration Change Us?" reviews the many ways in which migration affects us all, even if we haven't moved. Migration brings people from different backgrounds together. Newcomers adapt to new surroundings, new cultures, new languages, and new ways of life. Host communities adapt to new neighbors and the customs and traditions they bring. Those left behind adapt to life without their friends, family members, classmates, coworkers, and neighbors. These changes are part of moving. How we adapt to them affects everyone.

Section 5, "Where Are We Going?" is the book's final section. It focuses on international and national policies that concern immigration and displacement. Today, we are at a crossroads. The policies and decisions we make about migration now will affect the future of millions of people. Will we adapt to the changes that migration brings and find ways to live together? Or will we resist change and allow our differences to divide us? Even considering the tension between agency (the things we can influence) and structural forces beyond our control, by being informed citizens we can make a difference in where we are going, no matter where we are from.

Throughout, we have invited recognized experts to offer brief case studies that we call "Perspective" pieces. These Perspectives offer a more detailed summary of scholarship relevant to the section in which they appear. In Section 1, these include an introduction to mobility studies by Noel Salazar and a reflection on the concept of migrant deservingness by James Deutsch. In Section 2, Agustín Fuentes underscores the prevalence of mobility in evolutionary anthropology, and Jennifer Raff highlights genetic evidence that has reshaped our understanding of the peopling of the Americas. In Section 3, we present case studies about the motivations for migrants' movement from China (by Harriet Evans), from Central America (by Lynn Stephen), from Ethiopia (by Patricia Sunderland), and from northern Asia (by Laurel Kendall). In Section 4, Monica Heller offers a perspective on language and the preservation of Acadian culture, and case studies about the consequences of migration for communities are presented about the Mediterranean (by Sarah Green), Jewish people in Argentina (by Judith Freidenberg), gentrification and displacement in Baltimore (by Matthew Durington), and resilience in the aftermath of enslavement (by Antoinette Jackson). And finally, in Section 5, Leo Chavez offers a perspective on the policy of birthright citizenship; Susan Terrio reflects on policies that affect migrant mothers and their children; Miguel Díaz-Barriga and Margaret Dorsey summarize their scholarship on border walls and security policy; and Elizabeth Marino, Chantel Comardelle, and Dennis Davis report on climate change–driven migration in coastal Native communities.

Review Questions

1. As you start to read this book, what do you think are some of the main reasons people leave their place of residence for somewhere else? What are the "who, what, where, when, and why" of migration stories in your own family history?
2. Have you ever read a fiction or nonfiction immigrant narrative, such as *Americanah* or *The Beekeeper of Aleppo*, or seen a feature film like *Brick Lane* or *Moana*? If you haven't read or seen one of these works, think of one you are familiar with. How was the story structured – who were the characters, what were their motivations, whose perspective did the story follow, and what were the beginning, middle, and end of the plot? How does this compare to the storyline that informs the *World on the Move* exhibition and this book?

1
Basic Concepts and Patterns of Migration and Displacement

This chapter introduces key concepts and patterns of human population movement. Important patterns and processes of movement throughout history are discussed, including urbanization, colonization, enslavement and trafficking, and forced displacement due to environmental change. These patterns and processes emphasize how the movements of people are selective and have consequences for changing the demographic characteristics (size, composition, and growth potential) of their places of origin and destination.

Nigerian migrants pass through a boarding gate for Europe in the Port of Ceuta, a Spanish city on the north coast of Africa. Source: Photo by Silvia DiMeo.

World on the Move: 250,000 Years of Human Migration, First Edition. Edward Liebow, James I. Deutsch, Daniel Ginsberg, Sojin Kim, and Caitlyn Kolhoff.
© 2025 John Wiley & Sons, Inc. Published 2025 by John Wiley & Sons, Inc.

What is Migration? Defining Key Terms

The United Nations International Office on Migration (IOM) has compiled a lengthy list of key migration terms and their definitions (United Nations International Organization for Migration n.d.). For consistency, we will use these terms as defined by the authoritative sources cited by the IOM.

- **Asylum seeker** – An individual who is seeking international protection. In countries with individualized procedures, an asylum seeker is someone whose claim has not yet been finally decided on by the country in which they have submitted it. Not every asylum seeker will ultimately be recognized as a refugee, but every recognized refugee is initially an asylum seeker.
- **Chain migration** – A process by which migrants from a particular place follow other migrants over time to a particular destination, often with the assistance of those who arrived at the destination earlier.
- **Climate migration** – The movement of a person or group of persons who, predominantly for reasons of sudden or progressive change in the environment due to climate change, are obliged to leave their habitual place of residence (or choose to do so), either temporarily or permanently, within a nation-state or across an international border.
- **Displacement** – The movement of persons who have been forced or obliged to flee or to leave their homes or places of habitual residence as a result of or to avoid the effects of armed conflict, situations of generalized violence, violations of human rights, or natural or human-made disasters.
- **Emigration** – From the perspective of the country of departure, the act of moving from one's country of nationality or usual residence to another country; the country of destination effectively becomes their new country of usual residence.
- **Immigrant** – From the perspective of the country of arrival, a person who moves into a country other than that of their nationality or usual residence; the country of destination effectively becomes their new country of usual residence.
- **Internal migration** – The movement of people within a nation-state that involves the establishment of a new temporary or permanent residence.
- **Internally displaced persons (IDPs)** – Persons or groups of persons who have been forced or obliged to flee or otherwise leave their homes or places of habitual residence, as a result of or to avoid the effects of armed conflict, situations of generalized violence, violations of human rights, or natural or human-made disasters, and who have not crossed an internationally recognized nation-state border.
- **International migration** – The movement of persons away from their place of usual residence and across an international border to a country of which they are not nationals. Note that this definition excludes movements that are due to recreation, holiday or vacation, visits to friends and relatives, business, medical treatment, or religious pilgrimages.

- **Irregular migration** – The movement of persons outside the laws, regulations, or international agreements that govern the entry into or exit from the nation-state of origin, transit, or destination. Although a universally accepted definition of irregular migration does not exist, the term is generally used to identify persons moving outside regular migration channels. The fact that they migrate irregularly does not relieve nation-states from the obligation to protect their rights. Moreover, categories of migrants who may not have any other choice but to use irregular migration channels can include refugees, victims of trafficking, or unaccompanied migrant children. The fact that they use irregular migration pathways does not imply that nation-states are not, in some circumstances, obliged to provide them with some forms of protection under international law, including access to international protection for asylum seekers fleeing persecution, conflicts, or generalized violence. In addition, refugees are protected under international law against being penalized for unauthorized entry or stay if they have traveled from a place where they were at risk.
- **Labor migration** – The movement of persons from one country to another, or within their own country of residence, for the purpose of employment.
- **Lifetime migration** – The migration (or the number of moves) that one person has experienced between their birth and the time of a census or survey.
- **Migrant** – An umbrella term, not defined under international law, that reflects the common lay understanding of a person who moves away from their place of usual residence, whether within a country or across an international border, temporarily or permanently, and for a variety of reasons. The term includes: (1) a number of well-defined legal categories of people, such as migrant workers; (2) persons whose particular types of movements are legally defined, such as smuggled migrants; and (3) those whose status or means of movement are not specifically defined under international law, such as international students.
- **Migrant flow** – The number of migrants arriving at or departing from a defined place over a specified period of time.
- **Migrant stock** – The number of migrants present in a given place at a particular point in time.
- **Migration** – The movement of people from their place of usual residence. People may migrate from one country to another or within the same country. Migration can be temporary or permanent, voluntary or forced.
- **Migration stream** – A group of migrants that share a common origin and destination in a given time period.
- **Mover** – Anyone who has moved from one residential address to another.
- **Net migration** – The balance between immigration and emigration over a specific time period.
- **Place of origin (departure)** – The place or region away from which a migrant moves.
- **Place of destination (arrival)** – The place or region to which a migrant moves.

- **Place of transit** – In the context of migration, the country through which a person or a group of persons pass on any journey, either to the country of destination or from the country of destination, to the country of origin or habitual residence.
- **Refugee** – A person who, owing to a well-founded fear of persecution for reasons of race, religion, nationality, membership of a particular social group, or political opinion, is outside the country of their nationality and is unable or (owing to such fear) is unwilling to avail themselves of the protection of that country; or a person who, not having a nationality and being outside the country of their former habitual residence as a result of such events, is unable or (owing to such fear) is unwilling to return to it.
- **Remittances** – Private international monetary transfers that migrants make, individually or collectively. Remittances are primarily sent to people in the migrants' countries of origin with whom they maintain close links; although, in some cases, they are also sent to relatives in other countries of destination. Increasingly, the terms "social remittances" or "social capital transfer" are used in the context of transfers with non-monetary value that occur as a result of migration, such as the transfer of knowledge, know-how, networking, and skills.
- **Return migrant/migration** – A person who has left and then moved back to the area where they formerly resided.
- **Short-distance/local mover** – A person who has moved only within a political or administrative jurisdiction.
- **Xenophobia** – No universally accepted definition of xenophobia exists at the international level; it can be described as "attitudes, prejudices and behaviour that reject, exclude and often vilify persons, based on the perception that they are outsiders or foreigners to the community, society, or national identity" (Workshop Group on Migration and Trafficking 2001).

PERSPECTIVE: Mobilities, by Noel B. Salazar

Professor in the Department of Social and Cultural Anthropology and founder of the Cultural Mobilities Research cluster at KU Leuven (Belgium).

Human mobility lies at the core of migration. While migration entails mobility, most research on migration has privileged studying the causes and impacts of migration on points of departure and (settlement) destinations, so before or after the physical migratory movement. In the practice of migration policies, the term "mobility" often becomes synonymous with temporary migration and the multiplication of modes of migration. By examining patterns, routes, and modes of migration, mobility studies shed light on the mechanics of movement. This includes analyzing transportation systems, networks, and migration corridors. More generally, mobility studies delve into the movement of people (human migration, individual mobility, travel, transport), ideas (such as memes), and things (transport). Beyond mere movement, it also examines the broader social implications of these mobilities. As such, it enables a more comprehensive assessment of the complex dynamics involved in migration.

Mobility studies have evolved at the crossroads of academic disciplines, including anthropology, sociology, geography, political science, law, and economics. Increasingly, it incorporates insights from health studies, development studies, governance studies, and more. This interdisciplinary approach enriches our understanding of migration and displacement. The term "mobility turn" has been used to indicate a perceived transformation of the social sciences and humanities in response to the increasing societal importance of movement. In general, mobility has become a widely used perspective that takes many forms. The way scholars use the term, mobility entails, in its coinage, much more than mere physical motion. Rather, it can be understood as movement infused with both self-ascribed and attributed meanings (Salazar 2018).

Notwithstanding the many kinds of involuntary or forced movements (typically linked to situations of poverty, disaster, conflict, or persecution), most back-and-forth mobilities are positively valued. Mobility itself has become an important socially stratifying factor. Many people automatically link voluntary, geographical mobility to some type of symbolic climbing, whether economically (in terms of resources), socially (in terms of status), or culturally (in terms of cosmopolitan disposition). In other words, mobility is used as an indicator of the variable access to and accumulation of various types of symbolic capital. Migration or mobility are thus much more than objective empirical phenomena. There are always complex power dynamics at work (Salazar and Glick Schiller 2014).

Mobility is commonly perceived as a marker of freedom. It is a widespread idea that much of what is experienced as freedom lies in mobility. However, there lies an inherent paradox in the contemporary idealization of freedom of movement: the mobility of some has consequences for (or corresponds to) the immobility of others (Salazar 2021). To understand mobility, we need to pay close attention also to immobility, to the structures (which, once again, shift and move in their own right) that facilitate certain movements and impede others (Salazar and Smart 2011). Even those who do not move are affected by the movements of people in or out of their communities and by the resulting changes. Present-day news reports remind us of the commonplace restrictions on border crossing movements.

Important in this context is the concept of motility, or the potential for mobility (i.e., resources and access), and people's agency to be mobile and to choose whether to move or to stay put. The ability to move (freely) is spread very unevenly within countries and across the planet. Moreover, not everybody wants to be mobile. A persistent misconception is the assumption that free movement across borders equals more migration (in the sense of permanent settlement) instead of mobility (movements back and forth) (Abram et al. 2017). However, it may well be the other way around. Because restrictions on movement limit people's freedom to circulate, they may lead to a higher rate of permanent migration and discourage seasonal workers, for example, from returning (temporarily or not) to their country of origin. Mobility is formidably difficult for many in contemporary times; sometimes more so than in earlier historical periods.

Mobility, as a concept–metaphor, captures the common impression that our lifeworld is in flux, with people, cultures, objects, capital, businesses, services, diseases, media, images, information, and ideas circulating across (and even beyond) the planet. While analyzing mobile practices is not at all new, what emerges in the more recent scholarship on mobilities is a concern with mobility as an assemblage of phenomena of its own kind that requires specific methodologies and conceptual frameworks. *How* mobilities should be studied remains a challenge (Elliot et al. 2017). A fundamental issue is that of scale. In the study of mobility, scale often has to do with the presence, absence, and relative efficacy of overarching institutions, networks, and processes, rather than with a merely geographic or demographic scope. Scale, in this sense, requires researchers to simultaneously focus on the macro-processes through which the world is becoming increasingly, albeit unevenly, interconnected and how subjects mediate these processes.

Recent research has developed a range of innovative methodologies, including mobile technologies. A mobile perspective that follows migrants along their trajectories, for instance, offers a fruitful methodological approach for grasping ongoing long-term and long-distance migratory journeys (Zenteno Torres and Salazar 2023). Following has taken two main methodological forms. The first, perhaps more immediately intuitive, mode of engagement requires the researcher to travel alongside the moving subjects being studied. The second mode, or form, of methodological engagement draws on the researcher's observations, interviews, mapping, and other techniques of tracing aimed to capture the complex mobilities of the subject. In the latter case, following requires imaginative mobilities and methodological and analytical attention as much as it does physical travel. Though this approach may miss some details of the mobilities involved, for various practical reasons it can provide a solid option when being co-mobile is not possible or desirable. Although the value of remaining in place when studying movement has received increasing recognition, the first mode of engagement with mobility (built on the idea of following one's subject of study) often remains the most alluring methodological route. It is useful to ask how much following is necessary and whether too much of it detracts attention from the emplaced.

In sum, movement per se, including that involved in migration (but not exclusively), can be regarded as an essential characteristic of this day and age. Human mobilities – be they physical or imaginative – are molded by sociocultural knowledge and practices (Salazar 2014). Culturally rooted understandings of mobility – colored by media images as well as personal accounts – in interaction with physical movements are important in attempts to explain migratory phenomena. Mobility is a contested ideological construct that involves

> much more than mere movement but is socially embedded, manifesting in metacultural discourses and imaginaries (Seiger et al. 2020). We urgently need more systematic comparative studies of how migratory mobilities are generated in everyday life and facilitated as well as constrained by mobility circuits and institutions. An emerging area where the importance of a mobilities lens is proving crucial is the nexus between migration and climate change.
>
> Mobility studies do not refer to a new subject of scholarly investigation, much less a new discipline. Rather, these studies direct new questions toward traditional social science subjects (such as migration). People, objects, and ideas are moving all the time, but not all movements are equally meaningful and life shaping – neither for those who move nor for those who stay put. Individuals and groups may engage in multiple forms of mobility over their lifetimes, including migration, circulation, and immobility. This perspective leads to a more holistic understanding of migration and displacement, one that considers the social, cultural, and economic factors that influence decisions to move and movement experiences. Mobility gains meaning through its embeddedness within societies, culture, politics, and histories (which are themselves, to a certain extent, mobile). Importantly, migration is not only about migrants; it is an integral part of the way the world is imagined, and as such it impacts how individuals, communities, nation-states, and transnational formations imagine themselves and their (co)inhabitants.

Measurement and Data Sources

A central theme in this book is that human population movements are not new. Mobility is an essential element of the human condition, and movements have been taking place ever since there have been people on the planet. To estimate the timing, scale, locations, and composition of these movements requires a special set of methods, which are ever evolving, to yield new insights about migration and displacement. Here, we highlight two distinct types of methods for estimating migration, one that involves pre-historic and historic population movements and a second that involves contemporary movements.

Estimating migration in history and pre-history

Researchers from many fields of knowledge study human migration, including anthropologists, archaeologists, geneticists, historians, sociologists, demographers, geographers, linguists, and folklorists. Their work helps us understand when, how, and why people have moved throughout history. However, many unanswered questions remain, and new evidence continues to change what we once thought we knew.

Human genetic analysis provides considerable insight regarding the earliest movement of people around the world. Advances in genetic sequencing technology have accelerated since 2000, when mapping the human genome was first completed. The human genome is enormously complex, containing more than three billion elements that are divided into 24 linear molecules, or chromosomes (Nurk et al. 2022). Genetically speaking, most people are pretty much the same, however, on average we differ in just one element for every 1,000. Therefore, it is not necessary to examine every element, just the locations where there are known differences, which are also known as genetic markers (Hellenthal et al. 2014). These genetic markers are still present in skeletal remains and fossils long after people die, which makes it possible to include pre-historic as well as historic and contemporary populations in genetic analyses. By comparing genetic markers, it is possible to develop a picture of how different population groups are related to one another and how far back in time they might have diverged from one another (Hernández 2023; Dalal et al. 2023). This comparative analysis, in turn, has led in recent years to the development and significant revision of estimates for when the first groups of people arrived in distinct regions of the world and the routes they likely took to get there (Figure 1.1).

Archaeological data consist of the physical remains of past human activities, including pre-historic activities, which are activities that took place before there was a contemporaneous written record to document them. These data may include tools, human-made objects, burials, artwork, buildings, quarry sites, and other alterations of the landscape. In the absence of historical records, archaeologists use a variety of techniques to estimate the dates or time periods that these objects and features were made or used (Human Relations Area Files, 2021). These range from chemical analysis techniques (e.g., radiocarbon and archaeomagnetic dating and thermoluminescence) to plant-based techniques (e.g., tree-ring dating, or dendrochronology, and pollen analysis). Establishing the dates for archaeological materials adds important information about the arrival of people in an area, since we can assume that they brought with them a distinctive repertory of materials and activities. New discoveries and new techniques for revising earlier interpretations of dates and sequences of events are continuously updating our reconstruction of the timing and scale of population movements.

Information about languages and language change can also help us understand patterns and processes of human population movement (e.g., Vansina 1995; Sicoli and Holton 2014). Languages can be distinguished from one another based on their grammatical structure and vocabulary, and even people who speak the same language may speak different versions of it, each having different pronunciations of words or different words or phrases for the same meanings. These variations of the same language are called dialects. When people from different language backgrounds come together, they often create a combined-language form so that they have a way to communicate with one another. Linguists call this combined-language form a "creole," or if it is a specialized form for communicating about a limited subset of matters, like trade, it is called a "pidgin." An example of a creole is found in Louisiana, formed by speakers of French (who moved to the area by way of the Canadian maritime provinces) and a number of African languages when Louisiana was a French colony with thousands of enslaved former African residents and their descendants (Valdman and Klingler 1997). By carefully

BASIC CONCEPTS AND PATTERNS OF MIGRATION

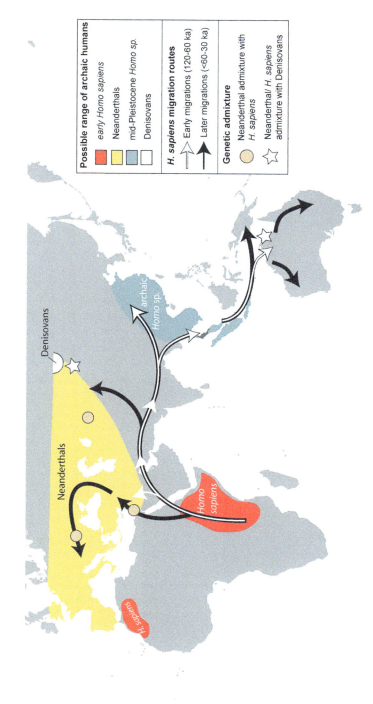

Figure 1.1 Early dispersal routes out of Asia. Source: Bae et al (2017). Human colonization of Asia in the Late Pleistocene: Introduction to Supplement 17. *Current Anthropology* 58(S17): S373–382. Reprinted with permission from the Wenner-Gren Foundation for Anthropological Research.

studying the features of Louisiana Creole, it is possible to enrich our understanding of the nature of contacts and interactions among the speakers of this combined-language form (Mufwene 2016).

Estimating migration in contemporary times

How do we estimate the size and composition of contemporary groups of people on the move? What methods and sources do we use to estimate historical population movements? As we have already noted, migration involves the movement of one's usual residence from one place to another. Some changes in residence are temporary, however, such as when someone takes a vacation or a business trip and then returns to their usual residence. These temporary movements are not generally considered a form of migration.

Data about contemporary migration can come from a variety of sources. **Six of the most common sources include:**

1 *Statistics collected on the occasion of movement across international borders, mostly as part of the administrative operations of border control.* When a person or family group crosses an international border with the intention of residing in the country where they have arrived, they are normally asked to complete documentation to create a record about their country of birth, the country from which their trip originated, their destination within the country where they have arrived, the transportation method that has brought them to the country, whether they have received an employment offer or been admitted to a college or university, and in some instances, whether they are seeking asylum or temporary protected status. The specific structure of the data record varies by country, but these general categories of information are fairly standard and provide data that can be compiled from individual ports of entry to form a cumulative snapshot and longitudinal record for the arrival country.

2 *Passenger statistics obtained from passenger manifests from air or sea travel.* A passenger manifest is a list that contains each passenger's name, the number and names of people accompanying the passenger, their relationship(s) to the passenger, the carrier (airline or ship), and the flight or passage identifier. (for example, Figure 1.2)

3 *Statistics from applications for visas and work permits.* Related to the data collected at border crossings, applications for visas and work permits request information about prospective migrants' places of origin and destination as well as the demographic characteristics of individuals and accompanying household members.

4 *Statistics obtained from population registers, voter registration rolls, and employment history data.* A population register may be an index of births, deaths, marriages and civil unions. Data from such a register may be used to corroborate individuals' demographic characteristics. Similarly, voter registration rolls and employment history records can be used to identify people of voting or working age, which can then be used to corroborate movements from one jurisdiction to another.

BASIC CONCEPTS AND PATTERNS OF MIGRATION

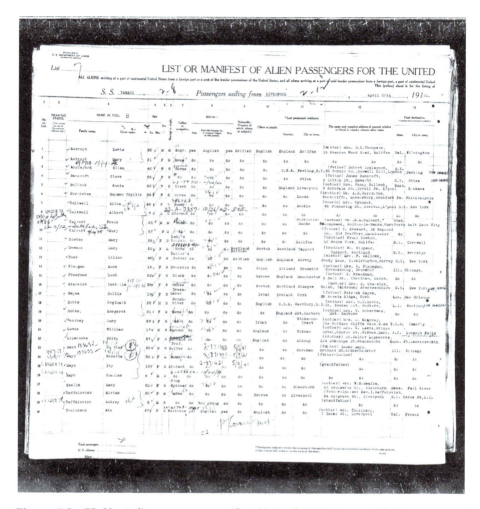

Figure 1.2 SS *Vasari* alien passenger manifest, 20 April 1920. Source: US Department of Labor (Wikimedia Commons).

5 *Statistics obtained in censuses or periodic national surveys based on questions about previous residence, place of birth, or citizenship.* Most countries conduct a periodic national census and sample population surveys that include questions about place of birth, previous residence, languages spoken at home, and other individual and household characteristics.

6 *Statistics collected in special surveys regarding migration, previous residence, place of birth, or citizens living outside their usual country of residence as well as employment histories.* An example of such a special survey is the International Passenger Survey, which has

been conducted on an ongoing basis in the United Kingdom since 1961. It consists of a face-to-face interview with a random sample of passengers to identify migrants as they enter or leave the United Kingdom. The survey covers all major airports, seaports, and the Channel Tunnel. The British government office that administers the survey estimates that about 90% of all passengers entering or leaving the United Kingdom have a chance of being selected for an interview. In the United States, in addition to international migration estimates from the decennial census (administered every 10 years), the American Community Survey (administered every five years) provides information about movements *within* the United States, from state to state, between metropolitan areas, and between counties in the country.

How to estimate documented migration between countries (international migration)?
The most common way to estimate international migration is by using a census of population and housing. These questionnaires include small number of items about an individual's country of birth, country of residence one or five years ago, and (if their earlier country of residence is not the same as where they are residing at the time of the census) the year they arrived in the country of their current residence.

To be considered an immigrant to a country, a person must:

- Enter the country by crossing the international border;
- Have been a usual resident of another country before entering, or must not be a usual resident of the one they are entering; and
- Stay or intend to stay in the country for at least one year.

To be considered an emigrant from a country, a person must:

- Leave the country by crossing an international border;
- Have been a usual resident of the country; and
- Stay or intend to stay in another country or abroad for at least one year.

Complicating the definition of who counts as an international migrant, based on a change in their usual place of residence, are some of the following circumstances:

- *Persons belonging to the diplomatic and consular corps*, who are likely to maintain dwellings in two countries and may consider their country of usual residence to remain their country of citizenship, since their presence in the country where they are posted is strictly temporary and they continue to work for their own government.
- *Members of the armed forces stationed outside their country of citizenship*, who are also unlikely to be viewed as changing country of usual residence, since they are usually posted abroad for limited periods and may not establish dwellings in the country of destination.

- *Nomads* who, by the very nature of their mode of life, do not have a fixed place of usual residence but likely have a regular pattern of movement that *might* take them across international borders. Thus, even if they cross international boundaries, they cannot be regarded as changing their country of usual residence.
- *Border workers who are granted permission* to be employed on a continuous basis in the receiving country provided they depart at regular, short intervals (daily or weekly) from that country. They should therefore not be treated as changing their country of usual residence.

Description of the categories of immigrating foreigners (United Nations International Organization for Migration n.d.; Sicoli and Holton 2014):

- **Foreign students**—Foreigners admitted under special permits or visas that allow them to undertake a specific course of study in an accredited institution of the receiving country. Their dependents, if admitted, are also included in this category.
- **Foreign trainees**—Foreigners admitted under special permits or visas that allow them to undertake training that is remunerated from within the receiving country. Their dependents, if admitted, are also included in this category.
- **Foreign migrant workers**—Foreigners admitted by the receiving nation-state for the specific purpose of exercising an economic activity remunerated from within the receiving country. Their length of stay is usually restricted, as is the type of employment that they can engage in. Their dependents, if admitted, are also included in this category.
- **Foreigners having the right of free establishment**—Foreign persons who have the right to establish residence in the receiving country because of special treaties or agreements between their country of citizenship and the receiving country. Their dependents, if admitted, are also included in this category.
- **Foreigners admitted for settlement**—Foreign persons granted permission to reside in the receiving country without limitations regarding their duration of stay or exercise of an economic activity. Their dependents, if admitted, are also included in this category.
- **Foreigners admitted for family formation or reunification**—This category includes the foreign fiancé(e)s and foreign adopted children of citizens, the foreign fiancé(e)s of other foreigners already residing in the receiving country, and all foreign persons allowed to join their immediate relatives already established in the receiving country.
- **Refugees**—Foreign persons granted refugee status, either at the time of admission or before admission. This category includes foreign persons granted refugee status while abroad and entering the receiving country to be resettled as well as persons granted refugee status on a group basis upon arrival in the country. In some cases, refugee status may be granted when the persons involved are still in their country of origin through in-country processing of requests for asylum.

- **Foreigners seeking asylum**—This category encompasses both persons who are eventually allowed to file an application for asylum (asylum seekers proper) and those who do not formally enter the asylum adjudication system but are nevertheless granted permission to stay until they can return safely to their country of origin (foreigners granted temporary protected status).
- **Foreigners whose entry or stay is not sanctioned**—This category includes foreigners who violate the rules of admission of the receiving country and are deportable as well as foreign persons attempting to seek asylum but who are not allowed to file an application and are not permitted to stay in the receiving country on any other grounds.

The two measures of international migration most commonly used are **flows** and **stocks** of international migrants (United Nations 2020). The term "inflow of migrants" is defined as the number of international migrants who arrive in a given country over the course of a specific time period, usually a calendar year. The outflow is equal to the number of international migrants who depart from a given country over the course of that period. The term "immigrant stock" is defined as the total number of international migrants present in a given country at a particular point in time, while the emigrant stock is equal to the total number of emigrants from a given country at a particular point in time. Migrant stock is a static measure of the number of persons who can be identified as international migrants at a given point in time.

How to estimate undocumented migration?
We often hear talk about migrants who cross international borders and remain in a new destination without official authorization to do so. Estimating the size of the undocumented immigrant population in a given country is difficult, but accurate and reliable estimates can be developed using what is known as the residual method (Baker 2017). This method involves taking reliable information about the total number of immigrants and subtracting estimates from administrative records of the size of the authorized immigrant population. The residual, or what is left over, is an estimate of the number of immigrants who are not authorized. For example, in the United States, an agency of the federal government called the US Bureau of the Census regularly surveys the national population through mechanisms such as the American Community Survey and the Current Population Survey. Both of these sample surveys ask a question about whether the respondents were born outside the United States. This allows for an estimate of the total foreign born resident population. It is also possible to estimate the lawful immigrant population from administrative records kept by the US Department of Homeland Security's Office of Immigration Statistics (and its predecessor at the Immigration and Naturalization Service). By subtracting the estimated lawful immigrant population from the total foreign born population, one can derive an estimate of the residual, or unauthorized, immigrant population (Passel and Cohn 2018).

PERSPECTIVE: "Deserving" and "Undeserving" Immigrants, by James I. Deutsch

Content Coordinator, Smithsonian Institution (USA)

The key terms from the United Nations International Office on Migration – such as asylum seeker, immigrant, and refugee – are generally neutral. However, many of those terms have also acquired shades of value, particularly to assess whether individuals on the move merit entry to their new locale. As framed not only by legal authorities but also by those who arrived earlier in that place, the question becomes whether the more recent arrivals deserve (or not) to stay in their new homelands.

In recent years, the question of "deserving" vs. "undeserving" immigrants has taken controversial political tones. One does not have to look far to hear politicians complaining that new arrivals are coming "from prisons, … mental institutions and insane asylums. We know they are terrorists. It's poisoning the blood of our country" (Wolf 2023). Or that the new arrivals "have no reason to stay" because they "broke the law the minute they set foot" in their new homes (Galbreath 2017, p. 8). Or that many of the new arrivals represent "a swarm of people" who are "not able to integrate" (Elgot 2016).

The question of deserving vs. undeserving immigrants is not entirely new, but the sheer volume of people on the move, combined with the increasing scarcity of resources to support them, has significantly raised the stakes and the concerns. According to one recent study of how immigration has transformed America, historically "there were no numerical limits on European immigration" until the 1920s. Most of those "immigrants came by boat, and most got through the ports of entry easily because they already had been screened, mainly for disease, by steamship companies before embarking. Of the more than 12 million immigrants who landed at Ellis Island between 1892 and 1954, only 2 percent were excluded from entry" (Foner 2022, p. 11).

However, the passage of immigration acts in 1921 (Emergency Quota Act, Pub. L. 67-5, 42 Stat. 5) and 1924 (Johnson–Reed Act, Pub. L. 68-139, 43 Stat. 153) by the US Congress, with their numerical quotas and restrictions, "created a new class of persons within the national body – illegal aliens – whose inclusion in the nation was at once a social reality and a legal impossibility" (Ngai 2014, p. 57). The new "deportation laws gave rise to an oppositional political and legal discourse, which imagined deserving and undeserving illegal immigrants and, concomitantly, just and unjust deportations" (Ngai 2014, p. 57).

It seems likely that the categories of deserving and undeserving immigrants came from earlier distinctions between the deserving and the undeserving poor. According to one political scientist,

> The "deserving poor" was largely a negative description, referring to those who were not lazy and shiftless, but rather hard-working or, if unemployed, hopelessly infirm. Certainly, they were not poor because they rejected the

virtues of hard work or the sanctity of private property.... [They] accepted the dominant business values, remaining poor through no real fault of their own (Halper 1973, p. 72).

In contrast, the "undeserving poor" were "shiftless" and "insufficiently motivated," and therefore "unworthy of compassion or significant material assistance" (Halper 1973, pp. 79–80).

When applied to migrants, the category of deserving often attaches itself to those who are members of a model minority, which refers to a group's success of assimilating into mainstream American society. According to one sociologist:

The model minority stereotype constructs distinctions between "deserving" and "undeserving" racial groups in the United States by highlighting "models" who embrace dominant American values such as hard work and self-reliance (e.g., Asian Americans) and distinguishing them from those who are unfairly and inaccurately perceived as rejecting those values (e.g., Latinos and African Americans). The stereotype largely ignores the structural factors (including racism) that shape outcomes for members of different racial and ethnic groups in different ways. Instead, those who embrace dominant values are seen as deserving of the full rights and responsibilities of US citizenship, while those who supposedly do not are viewed as unworthy, creating a hierarchy of deservingness that has often exacerbated conflict and divisions between racial and ethnic minority groups (Yukich 2013, p. 303).

One example of these inter-ethnic conflicts and divisions emerged in "emotionally charged" focus groups in which some participants—migrants themselves—"defensively asserted [their own deserving] character attributes that they considered respectable, such as honesty and kindness," while complaining about other "migrants and asylum seekers taking advantage of the migration and welfare system," whom they characterized "as dishonest, insincere and manipulative"—and thereby undeserving (Dhaliwal and Forkert 2016, pp. 52, 55).

Other tensions may arise based on the criteria used to evaluate deservedness. One study found debates among immigrant advocates regarding whether to determine deservedness based on "cultural assimilation" and "identification with the State" or based on "economic performance," even though "employment-based deservingness is not always attributed to workers themselves" (Chauvin and Garcés-Mascareñas 2014, p. 427).

The other type of deserving immigrants who have been welcomed, at least selectively, have involved refugees fleeing certain war and conflict zones. For example, in the lead up to World War II, hundreds of thousands of people fled Nazi persecution in Europe. Some of the most vulnerable were children. Between 1938 and 1940, the *Kindertransport* (children's transport) helped nearly 10,000 Jewish children escape Nazi-occupied Europe to the United Kingdom. Many of those evacuated were the children of those later sent to concentration camps during the Holocaust. Most of the evacuated children lived satisfactorily with British host families or in hostels.

At the same time, not all refugees and asylum seekers fleeing war and conflict are considered equally deserving. In the early 1990s, for example, a military coup in Myanmar (formerly known as Burma) violently persecuted a Muslim minority group called the Rohingya, forcing hundreds of thousands of Rohingya to flee for safety in nearby Bangladesh. The Bangladeshi government was decidedly not welcoming to these refugees and mobilized its military to force the Rohingya into squalid, prison-like encampments that created conditions barely less hostile than those the migrants were fleeing. The tensions remain heightened and have persisted well into the twenty-first century (Prasse–Freeman 2017).

Tensions between migrants from different cultural and ethnic groups, which raise issues of deserving versus undeserving, often appear in forms of American popular culture. One well-known example is *Crash* (2004), which received three Academy Awards for 2004: Best Picture, Best Original Screenplay, and Best Film Editing. Set in contemporary Los Angeles (LA), the film's opening lines explain the film's title and leading premise: "In LA, nobody touches you. We're always behind this metal and glass. I think we miss that touch so much that we crash into each other, just so we can feel something."

Throughout the film, characters collide into each other, both literally and metaphorically. Farhad (Shaun Toub), an immigrant shop owner from Iran mistaken for an Arab terrorist, seeks revenge against Daniel (Michael Peña), a Latino locksmith, in the mistaken belief that Daniel has cheated him. Jean Cabot (Sandra Bullock), married to the district attorney of LA, mistakenly believes that Daniel will sell the "key to one of his gang banger friends" after replacing the locks in the Cabot home. Mistakenly believing that everyone – including Maria, her Latina housekeeper – is deliberately trying to aggravate her, Jean is "angry all the time" and takes out her frustrations on those around her. Graham Waters (Don Cheadle), an LA police detective, is sleeping with his fellow detective Ria (Jennifer Esposito), but mistakenly believes her family is from Mexico. When Ria corrects him to say that her father is from Puerto Rico and her mother is from El Salvador, he observes, "Well, then I guess the big mystery is who gathered all those remarkably different cultures together and taught them all how to park their cars on their lawns?" Two Korean immigrants married to each other, Kim Lee (Alexis Rhee) and Choi Chin Gui (Greg Joung Paik), are both involved in car accidents with other characters in the film; Kim trades insults with Ria and Choi ends up in the hospital after viewers learn that he is involved in smuggling migrants from Cambodia.

Admittedly, the collisions of race in the film are perhaps even more significant than the collisions of immigrants. But *Crash* remains one of the best illustrations of how a major Hollywood production addresses immigration in the early twenty-first century, decidedly and optimistically categorizing its immigrant characters as deserving. The hard-working Farhad tries to shoot the hard-working Daniel, but the gun contains blanks, relieving Farhad of the murder and allowing him to feel great remorse for his actions. Daniel's daughter, Lara, believes that the "invisible cloak" protected her, allowing her to feel safer in their neighborhood.

> When Jean trips and tumbles down steps in her home, Maria is the only one to help, allowing Jean a transformative epiphany as she hugs Maria and tells her, "You're the best friend I've got." Ria is there to console Graham when he learns that his younger brother has been killed. Kim and Choi Chin console each other in the hospital, in spite of their wounds.
>
> Members of the Academy of Motion Picture Arts and Sciences may not have been thinking of deserving immigrants when they voted to award Best Picture and Best Original Screenplay to *Crash,* but many viewers of the film most likely left the theaters (or their home screens) feeling better about the world in which we live. Whether through cultural integration or economic achievement, the immigrant characters in *Crash* demonstrate their positive values by the film's end. They have learned from their mistakes, they have earned our compassion, and they have achieved some form of redemption, which most viewers may believe is well deserved.

Selective Movement

Migration is selective. In other words, not everyone is equally likely to leave one particular place and move to another. The population of those who move is concentrated in some specific categories of age, gender, education level, work specializations, and family status. The composition of a population of migrants is almost always different from that of their origin and destination (Elwood and Nathalie 2020). The specific nature of the differences has implications for the places of origin (i.e., who is left behind), destination (i.e., how new arrivals change the population composition), demand for public services and facilities, effects on labor force, and accumulation of human capital.

For example, the United Arab Emirates (UAE) rely heavily on migrant guest workers in the national workforce. Elessawy and Zaidan (2014) reported that the UAE population had increased by 800% between 1975 and 2005, almost completely due to migrant workers who are imported to work for a few years at a time on large-scale construction projects. These foreign workers were almost all men between the ages of 21 and 40 years, and they largely came from South Asia (India, Pakistan, and Bangladesh). With such a large surge in working-age men, the population of UAE residents has become heavily imbalanced with respect to age and gender.

Certain parts of the Mediterranean coast of Spain are heavily populated by retirees from England. In coastal areas like the Spanish province of Alicante, nearly 25% of the year-long residents are foreign nationals who have moved there at the end of their working years or in pursuit of service industry jobs, the demand for which has been elevated by the influx of retirees.

The Philippines are a place of origin for overseas migrant workers worldwide, with nearly two million Filipinos employed outside their home country. Known as

Migrant workers working on a building in Bur Dubai, UAE. Source: Photo by Gaurav Dhwaj Khadka (Wikimedia Commons, CC BY-SA 4.0).

overseas Filipino workers (OFWs) they are considered heroes, because they send home a portion of their earnings, or remittances. Total remittances account for 75% of the Philippines gross domestic product. Most OFWs are women, who typically work as cleaners, domestic helpers, and agricultural laborers. A majority of OFWs work in Asia, especially Saudi Arabia, the UAE, Hong Kong, Kuwait, Singapore, and Qatar (Eugenio 2023).

Urbanization and the growth of cities

For most of human existence, there were not any cities. People made their livelihoods from hunting and gathering activities, accompanied by fishing, shellfish harvesting, and sea mammal hunting in watersheds and coastal areas. This meant living in small, extended family groups and moving with the seasons, as vegetation changed and the birds, fish, and game animals moved. Sometimes one hears the term "nomad" to characterize this movement, which has the connotation of wandering aimlessly without a pattern. On the contrary, the seasonal rounds of hunter-gatherer groups followed predictable patterns and often saw larger groups come together during seasons when natural resources were more plentiful and more densely concentrated, while dispersing into smaller groups during seasons when resources were more spread out. Everyone obtained their own food, built their own houses, and made their own tools.

Recent archaeological research reports indicate that about 8,000 years ago, we began to see the emergence of fortified settlements among hunter-gatherer groups, even if it remains unclear whether these settlements were occupied year-round (Piezonka et al. 2023). Almost 6,000 years ago the world began to see the formation of cities in several places around the world, with people moving their place of permanent residence from more sparsely settled areas to settlements of greater size, density, and diversity. This movement, first observed in Mesopotamia (the valleys of the Tigris and Euphrates rivers in present-day Iraq), coincided with the rise of irrigated agriculture.

Building and maintaining the waterworks (especially canals, with gates to regulate the water flow) to divert water from the river helped to stabilize crop production and required specialized knowledge and work, which led to a more specialized division of labor among workers. Because some workers were not directly involved in producing their own food, this division of labor was accompanied by the exchange of goods or services for food. It also led to conflicts over territory and natural resources, and the rise of organized military forces to wage wars led, at least in some instances, to the creation of the city of Uruk, with walls and other defensive fortifications. Households moved from the hinterlands to inside these fortified settlements for protection.

At nearly the same time as the rise of Uruk in Mesopotamia, the cities of Harappa and Mohenjo-Daro appeared in the Indus Valley of Pakistan and western India (about 4,300–4,800 years ago). Less is known about these cities because deciphering the writing system in use at the time is still a work in progress, but the archaeological evidence points to a carefully planned grid layout with large-scale architecture features. These features suggest the presence of powerful leadership to plan and direct this urban development (Chandler and Fox 1974).

By around the time of Christ (2,100 years ago), cities emerged in Mesoamerica (central and southern Mexico and northern Central America), with Mayan urban centers flourishing in the tropical forest lowlands of southern Mesoamerica and Indigenous urban centers in the temperate highlands (Teotihuacan near Mexico City and Monte Albán in the Mexican state of Oaxaca). By around 1,200 years ago, the growth of population centers could be found throughout the region, with widespread commercial exchange and an exchange of ideas and cultural practices between these centers. These centers varied greatly in their size and composition as well as their prominence in larger trade networks. However, a considerable pattern of urban planning was found in most of these population centers.

By the early 2000s, nearly 60% of the world's population was living in urban areas, a proportion that is expected to increase to 68% by 2050, according to United Nations statistics (United Nations Department of Social and Economic Affairs 2018). Migrants make up more than half of the growth in urban areas. While the historical trend may have been for movement to follow a one-way pattern (rural to urban), not all migrants who arrive in the city remain permanently, and modern technological affordances make it possible for some city dwellers to leave an urban residence without giving up their livelihoods.

BASIC CONCEPTS AND PATTERNS OF MIGRATION

More than two dozen of the world's largest cities are in China, including Beijing, pictured here. Migrant workers provide the labor that builds and sustains China's urban development. Photo by TonyV3112 (Shutterstock).

Anthropological research shows that many people moving to the city go as temporary migrants who do not intend to stay. They move with the intention of accomplishing a specific objective, such as saving a sum of money. In some places, the main pattern is cyclical. Individuals move periodically between their rural homes and urban centers or may stay for longer in an urban area but return to a rural setting near the end of their lives.

Colonization and the concept of *terra nullius*

Colonization is a process by which the government of one country seizes control over a territory outside its boundaries, often by sending or enabling some of its residents to move to the territory it wishes to control. The Latin term *terra nullius* means "nobody's land." This principle has often been used as the basis for claiming ownership of land by occupying it and asserting that the land appeared unoccupied or at least not occupied by a recognizable government.

This principle was used by colonizing powers from Europe who settled in the Americas in the sixteenth century; in the North Atlantic, Africa, and the Indonesian archipelago in the seventeenth century; and in Australia and New Zealand in the eighteenth century. In all of these cases, the lands were already populated, even if land use and settlement patterns made it seem to the unfamiliar observer that the land was vacant. Outside settlers established themselves and (moving toward military, political, and demographic dominance) sought to take over land from the people who were already there. Settlers used a mixture of force, treaty negotiations, and legal instruments to marginalize previous inhabitants and push them into progressively smaller and less desirable tracts of land. These outside groups were often animated by the messianic sense that the land they were expropriating was destined to be theirs. If they acknowledged that the land being taken had previous occupants, the colonizers would further justify the taking by claiming that the groups who had inhabited it for centuries were inadequate to the task of cultivating it properly.

Colonialism has not always taken the form of settler colonialism. Large parts of colonial Africa, South Asia, and Southeast Asia, for example, were administered by European colonial powers in the absence of significant settler populations. Historically, where there were large settler populations—Algeria, Kenya, Zambia, Zimbabwe, and South Africa are examples—colonialism tended to generate more violent conflict. It was accompanied by more extreme kinds of supremacist ideology, involved greater displacement of native peoples, the development of mechanisms to separate natives from settlers, and enforced restrictions on the everyday movements of Indigenous populations perceived as threatening.

Enslavement and human trafficking

One notorious form of involuntary population movement is slavery, inevitably accompanied by slave trading. Enslavement involves the treatment of people as though they were property, compelling them to work against their will, and usually, transporting these involuntary workers in captivity away from their homelands. Evidence of enslavement dates to the distant past in Africa (Engmann 2023), Asia (Chakraborty and van Rossum 2020), Europe (Bradley 1985, Price 2020), and more recently, the Americas (Hannah-Jones 2021; Reséndez 2017; Donald 1997).

Nowadays, "human trafficking" is used as an umbrella term that refers to the act of recruiting, transporting, providing, or obtaining a person to exploit the labor or services of that person. A person may be coerced, forced, or defrauded by a trafficker into such exploitation. Coercion can include threats of force, debt manipulation, withholding of pay, confiscation of identity documents, psychological coercion, reputational harm, manipulation of the use of addictive substances, and threats to other people. According to the US State Department, widespread forms of forced labor include domestic servitude and forced child labor. Sex trafficking, where a person is coerced into engaging in commercial sex work, is another widespread form of contemporary forced labor.

Climate Migrants

Climate change is a global phenomenon whose cumulative impacts are growing more visible everywhere (Intergovernmental Panel on Climate Change 2022). Coastal areas, where a large percentage of the world's population resides, are increasingly vulnerable to storms. In polar regions like Alaska, Siberia, Greenland, northern Scandinavia, and the Canadian maritime provinces, sea ice that formed a shoreline buffer against strong winds and waves is melting, subjecting these unprotected shorelines to rapid erosion. In watersheds elsewhere, floods that were projected to occur once a century are now occurring every two years in some places. Formerly productive agricultural areas are now subjected to prolonged droughts. Changing habitats are allowing the appearance and prosperity of disease-bearing insect populations in places where these insects have never been seen before.

Climate change is also giving rise to a new category of migrants, climate refugees, people who are forced to move because of climate change impacts such as rising sea levels, increased risk of flood and storm hazards, decreasing crop productivity, and increased risk of water shortages (Bellizzi et al. 2023). Climate refugees may move to a different country – one estimate predicts that about 1.2 billion

People ride on rickshaws to cross a flooded street in Dhaka, Bangladesh. Almost 75% of Bangladesh is below the current sea level, and its low-lying geography makes it especially vulnerable to flooding. Source: Photo by Sk Hasan Ali (Shutterstock).

people could be displaced by 2050 due to natural disasters and climate change (Institute for Economics and Peace 2020). Even if they are not forced to move to a different country, the World Bank recently estimated that if no action is taken, by the year 2050 more than 143 million people in sub-Saharan Africa, South Asia, and Latin America will be forced to move within their countries due to climate change impacts (Rigaud et al. 2018).

Chapter Summary

In this chapter, we have introduced some key terms that are in common use among people who study migration, immigration, and related patterns and processes. These terms will be used throughout the rest of the book. We have introduced some important characteristics of human population movements that are frequently measured, along with the data sources that are used to complete these measurements. Finally, we have noted some widely prevalent patterns that will be discussed in later chapters. First, migration is selective. Not everyone in a given place is equally likely to move to another place. Second, the growth of cities in human history is largely a result of people moving from sparsely settled rural and frontier areas to create larger, more densely settled places. Other important processes of human population movement have included colonization, enslavement and human trafficking, and movements in response to changing environmental conditions, which many observers think will accelerate in scale and pace in the coming decades due to global climate change.

We have covered a good deal of ground here in presenting some important concepts and patterns of human population movement. And now we would like to present you with questions for reflection and discussion, to make these concepts and patterns a little less abstract and a little more directly related to your life.

Review Questions

1. Where is home for you? Is it where you were born? Where you grew up? Where you live now?
2. What would it take for you to move? Would you move to start a new job or to be closer to family? Would you move if conditions in your area suddenly changed? Think about how forces outside your control might influence your decision. Have you ever moved to be closer to family? Do you travel to see family members who live far away? How would you feel if you suddenly had to move to a new place where no one spoke your language?
3. To what extent do you agree with the notion of deservingness among migrants, meaning that some people are considered more deserving than others of a welcoming reception and supportive services in their new home? What are some of your reasons for this view?

References

Abram, S, B Feldman Bianco, S Khosravi, N Salazar, and N de Genova. 2017. The free movement of people around the world would be utopian. In *Identities: Global Studies in Culture and Power*. Vol. 24 (2). pp. 123–155. https://doi.org/10.1080/1070289X.2016.1142879.

Workshop Group on Migration and Trafficking. 2001. Declaration on racism, discrimination, xenophobia and related intolerance against migrants and trafficked persons,. www.hurights.or.jp/wcar/E/tehran/migration.htm, accessed 21 Dec 2023.

Baker, B. 2017. Estimates of the Unauthorized Immigrant Population Residing in the United States: January 2014. In *Population Estimates, US Department of Homeland Security, Office of Immigration Statistics*. https://www.dhs.gov/sites/default/files/publications/Unauthorized%20Immigrant%20Population%20Estimates%20in%20the%20US%20January%202014_1.pdf, accessed 27 Nov 2023.

Bae, Christopher J., Katerina Douka, and Michael D. Petraglia (2017). Human colonization of Asia in the Late Pleistocene: Introduction to Supplement 17. *Current Anthropology* 58(S17): S373–382. https://doi.org/10.1086/694420.

Bellizzi, S, C Popescu, C M Panu Napodano, M Fiamma, and L Cegolon. 2023. Global health, climate change and migration: The need for recognition of "climate refugees.". *Journal of Global Health* 13: 03011. https://doi.org/10.7189/jogh.13.03011.

Bradley, K. 1985. The early development of slavery at Rome. *Historic Reflections / Réflexions Historiques* 12(1): 1–8. https://www.jstor.org/stable/41298844.

Elwood, D C, and E W Nathalie, eds. 2020. *Comparative Demography of the Syrian Diaspora: European and Middle Eastern Destinations*. Springer Cham. https://doi.org/10.1007/978-3-030-24451-4.

Chakraborty, T, and M van Rossum. 2020. Slave trade and slavery in asia – new perspectives. *Journal of Social History* 54(1): 1–14. https://doi.org/10.1093/jsh/shaa004.

Chandler, T, and G Fox. 1974. *3000 Years of Urban Growth*. New York: Academic Press.

Chauvin, S, and B Garcés-Mascareñas. 2014. Becoming Less Illegal: Deservingness Frames and Undocumented Migrant Incorporation. *Sociology Compass* 8(4): 422–432. https://doi.org/10.1111/soc4.12145.

Crash. 2004. Directed by Paul Haggis. Santa Monica, CA: Lionsgate Films.

Dalal, V, N Pasupuleti, G Chaubey, N Rai, and V Shinde. 2023. Advancements and challenges in ancient DNA research: bridging the global North-South divide. *Genes* 14(2): 479. https://doi.org/10.3390/genes14020479.

Dhaliwal, Sukhwant, and Kirsten Forkert. 2016. Deserving and Undeserving Migrants. *Soundings: A Journal of Politics and Culture* 61: 49–61. https://muse.jhu.edu/article/609284.

Donald, Leland. 1997. *Aboriginal Slavery on the Northwest Coast of North America*. Berkeley: University of California Press.

Elessawy, Fayez, and Esmat Zaidan. 2014. Living in the move: Impact of guest workers on population characteristics of the United Arab Emirates (UAE). In *The Arab World Geographer*. Vol. 17. pp. 2–23. https://doi.org/10.5555/arwg.17.1.04502312v8g83u76.

Elgot, Jessica. 2016. How David Cameron's Language on Refugees Has Provoked Anger. In *Guardian*. https://www.theguardian.com/uk-news/2016/jan/27/david-camerons-bunch-of-migrants-quip-is-latest-of-several-such-comments.

Elliot, Alice, Roger Norum, and Noel B Salazar. 2017. *Methodologies of mobility: Ethnography and experiment*. Oxford: Berghahn.

Engmann, Rachel Ama Asaa. 2023. Slaving and Slave Trading in Africa. *Annual Review of Anthropology* 52: 491–510. https://doi.org/10.1146/annurev-anthro-05261-022531.

Eugenio, Laurinne Jamie. 2023. Overseas Filipino workers: the modern-day heroes of the Philippines. *Harvard International Review.* 11 Aug 2023. https://hir.harvard.edu/overseas-filipino-workers-the-modern-day-heroes-of-the-philippines/#:~:text=Overseas%20Filipino%20Workers%20(OFWs)%20is,Bagong%2DBayani'%20in%201988, accessed 14 Dec 2023.

Foner, Nancy. 2022. *One quarter of the Nation: Immigration and the Transformation of America.* Princeton: Princeton University Press.

Galbreath, Megan. 2017. An analysis of Donald Trump and Marine Le Pen. *Harvard International Review* 38(3): 7–9. https://link.gale.com/apps/doc/A503261035/AONE?u=anon~205e03af&sid=googleScholar&xid=04a0bd65.

Halper, Thomas. 1973. The poor as pawns: the new "Deserving poor" and the old. *Polity* 6(1): 71–86. https://doi.org/10.2307/3234182.

Hannah-Jones, Nikole. 2021. *The 1619 Project: A New Origin Story.* New York: Random House. https://1619books.com/.

Hellenthal, Garrett, George B J Busby, Gavin Band, et al. 2014. A genetic atlas of human admixture history. *Science* 343(6172): 747–751. https://doi.org/10.1126/science.1243518.

Hernández, Candela. 2023. Mitochondrial DNA in human diversity and health: from the golden age to the Omics Era. *Genes (Basel)* 14(8): 1534. https://doi.org/10.3390/genes14081534.

Human Relations Area Files. 2021. "Dating Methods" eHRAF workbook. https://hraf.yale.edu/wp-content/uploads/2023/07/eHRAF-Workbook-Dating-Methods-v2.pptx, accessed 20 Dec 2023

Institute for Economics and Peace 2020. Over one billion people at threat of being displaced by 2050 due to environmental change, conflict and civil unrest. https://www.economicsandpeace.org/wp-content/uploads/2020/09/Ecological-Threat-Register-Press-Release-27.08-FINAL.pdf, accessed 30 Nov 2023

Intergovernmental Panel on Climate Change. 2022. 2022. Climate change 2022: impacts, adaptation, and vulnerability. In H O Pörtner, D C Roberts, M Tignor, et al., eds. *Contribution of Working Group II to the Sixth Assessment Report of the Intergovernmental Panel on Climate Change.* Cambridge, UK: Cambridge University Press. https://doi.org/10.1017/9781009325844.

Mufwene, Salikoko S. 2016. The Emergence of Creoles and Language Change. In Nancy Bonvillain, ed. *The Routledge Handbook of Linguistic Anthropology.* London: Routledge. pp. 345–368. https://mufwene.uchicago.edu/publications/23.%20EMERGENCE%20OF%20CREOLES%20AND%20LANGUAGE%20CHANGE%20-%20HDBK%20OF%20LINGUISTIC%20ANTHROPOLOGY.pdf, accessed 20 Dec 2023.

Ngai, Mae. 2014. *Impossible Subjects: Illegal Aliens and the Making of Modern America.* Updated ed. Princeton: Princeton University Press.

Nurk, Sergey, Sergey Koren, Arang Rhie, et al. 2022. The complete sequence of a human genome. *Science* 376(6588): 44–53. https://doi.org/10.1126/science.abj6987.

Passel, Jeffrey S, and D'Vera Cohn. 2018. *US Unauthorized Immigrant Total Dips to Lowest Level in a Decade.* Washington, DC: Pew Research Center. https://www.pewresearch.org/hispanic/wp-content/uploads/sites/5/2019/03/Pew-Research-Center_2018-11-27_U-S-Unauthorized-Immigrants-Total-Dips_Updated-2019-06-25.pdf, accessed 27 Nov 2023.

Piezonka, Henny, Natalya Chairkina, Ekaterina Dubovtseva, et al. 2023. The world's Ooldest-known promontory fort: amnya and the acceleration of hunter-gatherer diversity in Siberia 8000 years ago. *Antiquity* 97(396): 1381–1401. doi:10.15184/aqy.2023.164.

Prasse–Freeman, Elliott. 2017. The Rohingya crisis. *Anthropology Today* 33(6): 1–2. https://doi.org/10.1111/1467-8322.12389.

Price, Nell. 2020. *Children of Ash and Elm: A History of the Vikings.* New York: Basic Books.

Reséndez, Andrés. 2017. *The Other Slavery: The Uncovered Story of Indian Enslavement in America*. Boston: Mariner Books.

Rigaud, Kumari, Alex Kanta, Bryan de Sherbinin, Jonas Bergmann Jones, Viviane Clement, Kayly Ober, Jacob Schewe, Susana Adamo, Mc Cusker Brent, Silke Heuser, and Amelia Midgley. 2018. *Groundswell: Preparing for Internal Climate Migration*. Washington, DC: The World Bank. http://hdl.handle.net/10986/36248, accessed 12 Feb 2024.

Salazar, Noel B. 2014. Migrating imaginaries of a better life… until paradise finds you. In Michaela Benson, and Nicholas Osbaldiston, eds. *Understanding lifestyle migration: Theoretical approaches to migration and the quest for a better way of life*. London: Palgrave Macmillan. pp. 119–138. https://doi.org/10.1057/9781137328670_6.

Salazar, Noel B. 2018. *Momentous mobilities: Anthropological musings on the meanings of travel*. Berghahn: Oxford. https://doi.org/10.3167/9781785339356.

Salazar, Noel B. 2021. Immobility: The relational and experiential qualities of an ambiguous concept. *Transfers* 11(3): 3–21. https://doi.org/10.3167/TRANS.2021.110302.

Salazar, Noel B, and Nina Glick Schiller. 2014. *Regimes of mobility: Imaginaries and relationalities of power*. London: Routledge.

Salazar, Noel B, and Alan Smart. 2011. *Anthropological takes on (im)mobility*. Theme issue, Identities: Global Studies in Culture and Power 18(6). https://doi.org/10.1080/1070289X.2012.683674.

Seiger, Fiona-Katharina, Christiane Timmerman, Noel B Salazar, and Johan Wets. 2020. *Migration at work: Aspirations, imaginaries and structures of mobility*. Leuven: Leuven University Press. doi:10.11116/9789461663443.

Sicoli, Mark A, and Gary Holton. 2014. Linguistic phylogenies support back-migration from Beringia to Asia. *PLoS ONE* 9(3): e91722. https://doi.org/10.1371/journal.pone.0091722.

United Nations Department of Social and Economic Affairs. 2018. 68% of the World Population Projected to Live in Urban Areas by 2050, Says UN. https://www.un.org/uk/desa/68-world-population-projected-live-urban-areas-2050-says-un, accessed 14 Nov 2024.

United Nations International Organization for Migration. n.d. Key Migration Terms. https://www.iom.int/key-migration-terms, accessed 21 Dec 2023.

United Nations. 2020. Handbook on measuring international migration through population censuses, draft E. *ST/ESA/STAT/SER.F/115*. https://unstats.un.org/unsd/demographic-social/Standards-and-Methods/files/Handbooks/international-migration/2017-draft-E.pdf, accessed 19 Dec 2023

Valdman, Albert, and Thomas A Klingler. 1997. The structure of Louisiana Creole. In A Valdman, ed. *French and Creole in Louisiana. Topics in Language and Linguistics*. Boston: Springer. pp. 109–144. https://doi.org/10.1007/978-1-4757-5278-6_5.

Vansina, Jan. 1995. New linguistic evidence and "the Bantu Expansion.". *The Journal of African History* 36(2): 173–195. https://www.jstor.org/stable/182309.

Wolf, J.D. 2023. Trump Echoes Hitler: Migrants 'Poisoning the Blood of Our Country.' *MeidasTouch Network*. October 3. https://www.meidastouch.com/news/trump-echoes-hitler-migrants-poisoning-the-blood-of-our-country

Yukich, Grace. 2013. Constructing the model immigrant: movement strategy and immigrant deservingness in the new sanctuary movement. *Social Problems* 60(3): 302–320. https://doi.org/10.1525/sp.2013.60.3.302.

Zenteno Torres, E, and B Salazar Noel. 2023. Searching for the "Chilean oasis": waiting and uncertainty in the migration trajectories of Venezuelan women. *Journal of Immigrant and Refugee Studies* 21(3): 335–348. https://doi.org/10.1080/15562948.2021.1980642.

2

The Crossroads Concept

Wherever we are, mobile phones are an essential affordance of our daily lives on the move. Source: Photo by Nell Haynes.

As we have noted, this book grows out of a traveling exhibition that ambitiously aims to shift the public conversation. The overarching theme of the book is that migration and displacement are an integral element of the human condition, not tied to any particular region. Instead, we take a more encompassing view that centers less on one specific place and more on the patterns and processes of migration and displacement. We feel it is necessary to complicate the orderly sense of place and time packed into

World on the Move: 250,000 Years of Human Migration, First Edition. Edward Liebow, James I. Deutsch, Daniel Ginsberg, Sojin Kim, and Caitlyn Kolhoff.
© 2025 John Wiley & Sons, Inc. Published 2025 by John Wiley & Sons, Inc.

this narrative structure. We resist the framing that begins with a privileged "we," which most typically corresponds to the imagined community of a nation-state, and the challenges presented by the arrival of a foreign "they." And we must call attention to the way such stories often rely heavily on a rational choice-making model of individual decision making to account for when, where, and why people move.

The Crossroads Narrative Device

For *World on the Move*, "crossroads" has been chosen as a provocation, a narrative device to tell the story of migration and displacement from a different perspective. Crossroads are intersections where people from different places meet. Crossroads also symbolize connections between cultures and moments when crucial decisions are made. Placing oneself at selected crossroads affords one a vantage point from which to observe the gatherings and movements of people at and through an intersection. It is also an accessible concept that can apply to communities and experiences that are not specifically called out in the narrative.

The four crossroads locations we have chosen to highlight are of particular historical salience and clearly illustrate patterns and processes of migration and displacement: the Mediterranean, Beringia, central Africa, and East Los Angeles. We could have selected others distributed around the globe, of course, and it is our hope that the traveling exhibition and classroom and online activities will expand to generate additional stories that illuminate local lived experiences. In selecting this set of four crossroads, we aimed to highlight settings in which we can observe human population movements from different geographic and temporal scales. And we specifically chose regions that cross the boundaries of nation-states. The Mediterranean and Beringia are expansive regions that encompass multiple political boundaries and continents. Central Africa spans countries within a single continent. East Los Angeles is an area that extends from a metropolitan area in a state, albeit a large one, within a single country. At its core, the usefulness of the crossroads interpretive framework is how it foregrounds the age-old social sciences debate about the combined explanatory power of agency and structure. The crossroads concept is a corrective for the current over-emphasis on individual agency in understanding migration. At each of the selected crossroads we are able to demonstrate a rich and variegated history of people on the move, for a variety of reasons, with profound changes resulting from encounters between peoples from different places and backgrounds, both setting and resetting the local and regional stage for changes yet to come.

The Mediterranean Basin

Throughout history, one could stand on the shores of the Mediterranean Sea and watch much of the world go by. The ancient Phoenician, Greek, and Roman civilizations rose and fell along the Mediterranean's shores. This region was also home to the

Ottoman Empire, which controlled much of North Africa, the Middle East, and southeastern Europe for nearly 600 years. Today, the Mediterranean basin remains a crossroads for people risking their lives to flee dangerous conditions in North Africa, South Asia, and the Middle East.

Where in the world is the Mediterranean?

The Mediterranean Sea is connected to the Atlantic Ocean at its western end through the narrow Strait of Gibraltar and to the Black Sea at its northeastern end through the Bosporus Strait. Several areas of water, such as the Aegean and Adriatic Seas, are part of the overall Mediterranean basin, which is otherwise surrounded by land; southern Europe forms its northern coastline, northern Africa forms its southern coastline, and Turkey and the Middle Eastern countries of Syria, Lebanon, Palestine, and Israel forms its eastern coastline. From west to east, the Mediterranean Sea extends about 4,000 km (2,500 miles), and at its widest point, it is about 800 km (500 miles) north to south (Figure 2.1).

The sea, the islands it surrounds, and the coastal basin that it forms have been major thoroughfares for trade, imperial conquest, and transcontinental cultural exchange for nearly 200,000 years. Data from the Misliya Cave, in what is now Israel, indicate human presence roughly 170,000–190,000 years ago (Hershkovitz et al. 2018). Archaeological evidence from coastal Greek sites shows human settlements 130,000–160,000 years ago (Harvati, Panagopoulou, and Runnels 2009). Knowing that Crete was separate from the mainland throughout the Pleistocene, evidence of human settlements on Crete during the late Middle or early Late Pleistocene (120,000–80,000 years ago) suggests that people were able to cross open water by then (Strasser et al. 2011).

Who lives in the Mediterranean now?

Looking at a map and starting from the west, the countries of the Mediterranean basin, in counterclockwise order, include Morocco, Algeria, Tunisia, Libya, Egypt, Israel, Palestine, Lebanon, Syria, Turkey, Greece, Albania, Montenegro, Bosnia and Herzegovina, Croatia, Slovenia, Italy, Monaco, France, and Spain. Cyprus and Malta are island countries surrounded by the Mediterranean Sea.

Who has passed through here? Where were they headed? And what remains to mark their presence here?

Although evidence of human settlement in the Mediterranean basin is found as long as 200,000 years ago, it must be emphasized that until the emergence of sedentary agriculture in the region between 8,000 and 9,000 years ago, livelihoods were made by hunting, fishing, and gathering plants. This means that *everyone* was on the move in well-established seasonal patterns, or what anthropologists call "annual rounds," shaped by variations in topography and weather (Headland et al. 1989).

THE CROSSROADS CONCEPT

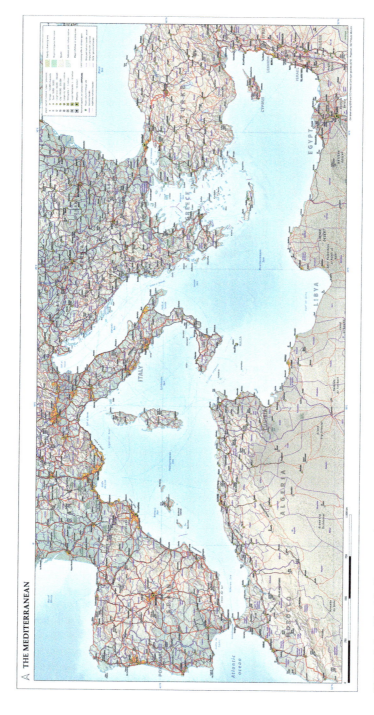

Figure 2.1 The Mediterranean basin. Source: Janwillemvanaalst, own work (Wikimedia Commons, CC BY 4.0).

With the advent of increasingly intensive forms of agriculture, larger and larger permanent settlements such as Alexandria were possible, drawing people to population centers, which led to distinct specialties in livelihood and centralized authorities for supporting, coordinating, and controlling the production, distribution, and exchange of goods and services — in short, civilization. Several civilizations emerged along the Mediterranean coasts, taking advantage of the sea for fishing as well as trade routes, colonization, and conquest.

These civilizations included the Phoenicians, the Egyptians, the Greeks, and the Romans. As the Roman Empire was in eclipse, the Byzantine Empire formed in the fourth century, and about three centuries later the rapid spread of Islam across the Mediterranean basin gave rise to the Arab Empire, which lasted well into the thirteenth century. Viking expansion from the north between the eighth and eleventh centuries extended its reach to include trade and settlement along the coast of Spain and southern Italy. By the fourteenth century, mercantile states like Genoa and Venice controlled much of the trade with central and eastern Asia that came by land over the Silk Road routes and further west around the Mediterranean basin by ship.

By the fifteenth century, the Ottomans expanded their control of Mediterranean shipping lanes, first by conquest of the Byzantine Empire and then making their way west to establish naval outposts along the coasts of France, Tunisia, and Algeria in the sixteenth century. Also, along the coast of North Africa, from western Libya to Morocco (called the "Barbary Coast" by the Greeks), bands of Berbers monitored the sea trade, taking cargo and enslaving crew and passengers. The so-called Barbary pirates also raided coastal towns in Italy, France, Spain, Ireland, and England, capturing residents and selling them in Ottoman slave markets. As many as one million people may have been enslaved between 1500 and 1800.

When the Suez Canal opened in 1869 it connected the Mediterranean with the Red Sea with a lockless waterway that cut weeks off the mercantile trip between Europe and east Africa and Asia. From these regions, people and cargo flowed into southern European ports in unprecedented numbers. Throughout the late nineteenth to mid-twentieth century, war and conflict in the Mediterranean basin displaced millions, pushing people from southern Europe to northern Europe and North America as well as Australia. In 1948, shortly after the end of World War II, the United Nations established the state of Israel in territory carved from the British colony of Palestine, displacing thousands of Palestinians and inviting Jewish people — who had been displaced by the Nazis and fascists and who had survived the Holocaust — to move to Israel.

Since the end of World War II, agricultural innovations, the off-shoring of industrial operations, the fall of the Soviet state, the increasing globalization of the production of goods and services, and ongoing conflicts over land and resources throughout the Balkans, the Middle East, and the African continent have combined to propel peoples' movements. They have moved from rural to urban areas, fleeing war and religious persecution or seeking economic and educational opportunities for themselves and their families that have been either temporarily or permanently foreclosed in their homelands.

In the twenty-first century, the Mediterranean has been the scene of a dramatic increase in refugees and asylum seekers crossing from North Africa to escape harsh economic conditions in sub-Saharan Africa as well as war and conflict in the Middle East. More than three million asylum seekers arrived in Europe between 2013 and 2019, and at its peak in 2015, more than one million migrants crossed the Mediterranean into Europe in a single year (Clayton and Holland 2015). Their reception in different European countries has ranged from warm and welcoming to outright hostility with strenuous efforts to block these new arrivals (Kyriakopoulos 2019).

> Lampedusa now bears an enormous burden of pain. We have had to go through the Prefecture to ask other boroughs for help in order to provide the last 11 corpses with a dignified burial as we have no more sites available. I know there will be others that we will bury, but I have one question which I must address to everyone: just how large exactly does the cemetery on my island need to be?
> *Open letter from the Mayor of Lampedusa to the European Union, November 15, 2012*

What other places in the world are like the Mediterranean?

As captured in Fernand Braudel's monumental history of the region (Braudel 1972), the Mediterranean is best understood as a complicated expanse of sea and the lands that border it. In many respects, the South China Sea has some striking similarities to the Mediterranean crossroads. The southern coast of China forms its northern boundary. To the east are Taiwan and the Philippines, and to the south are Borneo and Sumatra, parts of modern-day Indonesia. To the west is the Indochinese Peninsula, including Thailand, Laos, and Vietnam. A visitor standing on any of these shores would see an enormous amount of maritime shipping, highly productive fisheries, extensive mineral and petroleum reserves, and of course, a legacy of diverse cultural heritages that stretches back millennia. Archaeological evidence indicates early (60,000–70,000 years ago) human migration routes and settlement locations through what is now Thailand, Laos, Vietnam, and the Philippines on the way to Indonesia and Australia. Coastal navigation in outrigger boats and ocean-going catamarans may have begun about the time of the Phoenicians in the Mediterranean, and early agriculture emerged 4,000 years ago in the area.

Beringia

Encompassing the now-submerged Bering land bridge between Asia and North America, Beringia has long served as a passageway between continents. Throughout history, people have crossed Beringia by land and by sea under very different environmental conditions. New evidence suggests people crossed Beringia in successive waves starting as long as 36,000–19,000 years ago. Some made permanent settlements there, while others rapidly populated the entire Western Hemisphere.

Today, climate change threatens to force the region's residents to leave their homes or adapt to new ways of life.

Where in the world is Beringia?

Beringia is a geographic name that remains largely unknown to many people despite being one of the world's most pivotal crossroads by virtue of connecting the two continents of Asia and North America. One reason for its relative obscurity is that the name did not exist until 1937 when the Swedish botanist Eric Hultén coined the term in his study of plant species during and after periods of glaciation (Hultén 1937, p. 34). Another reason is that key sections of Beringia have been submerged below the Bering and Chukchi Seas for at least the past 12,000 years. As far as we know, there is no other place on earth that is comparable to Beringia in terms of both natural and human history.

The precise geographic boundaries of Beringia are (pardon the pun) fluid. Expanding Hultén's concept of "the immense unglaciated areas of Alaska and the adjacent regions of northwestern Canada and northeastern Russia," the current consensus is that Beringia encompasses "the entire region between the Lena River in northeast Russia and the Mackenzie River in northwest Canada" (Ickert-Bond et al. 2009, p. 26). One analysis of Beringian landscapes divides the crossroads area into three distinct ecologies. Western Beringia, in northeastern Russia, consists of "steep mountain ranges attaining heights of 2,000–3,000 m" through which traverse the "northward-flowing river basins of the Lena, Indigirka, and Kolyma" (Hoffecker and Elias 2007, p. 26). Central Beringia is now largely submerged, but it is where the Bering land bridge had "formed a broad connection between northeastern Siberia and western Alaska during Pleistocene glaciations," including a time when the "global sea level fell 120–130 m below modern sea level" (Hoffecker and Elias 2007, p. 28). Eastern Beringia covers portions of northern Alaska, Yukon Territory, and Northwest Territories (Figure 2.2). Its main geographic feature is the Arctic coastal plain, where the layer of permafrost may be more than 300 m deep and "the landscape is dotted with an abundance of shallow lakes, because soil drainage is inhibited by permafrost and little water evaporates in the cold arctic climate" (Hoffecker and Elias 2007, p. 32).

We do not know who the first people were to move across Beringia or why they chose to do so – other than to speculate that they were following herds of game animals, sea mammals, and migratory fish whose foraging ranges and spawning grounds were affected by environmental changes. However, we do know that "genetic and linguistic data suggest movements in both directions" (Hoffecker 2017, p. 305), and archaeological evidence suggests these movements were on land as well as coastal water routes. We also know that archaeologists have now updated previous views about the peopling of the Americas (Braje et al. 2017). Until recently, the prevailing wisdom was that the earliest arrivals to North America involved foot

THE CROSSROADS CONCEPT

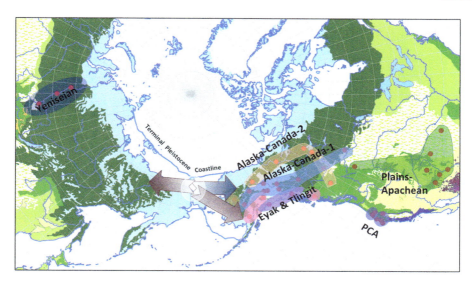

Figure 2.2 Pleistocene shoreline, northern circumpolar region. This polar projection map of Asia and North America shows the approximate terminal Pleistocene shoreline. The center of geographic distribution of Yeniseian and Na-Dené language is in Beringia. From this center, burgundy arrows extend toward the North American coast and into Siberia. A blue arrow indicates interior dispersals of Na-Dené. Source: Reprinted from Mark Sicoli and Gary Holton (2014) "Linguistic phylogenies support back-migration from Beringia to Asia", *PLoS ONE* 9(3): e91722.

traffic through glacial gaps. A growing body of evidence indicates that "maritime explorers voyaged by boat out of Beringia…about 16,000 years ago and quickly moved down the Pacific coast, reaching Chile by at least 14,500 years ago" (Wade 2017, p. 542). The radiocarbon dating of seeds found in a set of preserved footprints in New Mexico suggests that humans were present in the Americas even earlier, perhaps around 21,000–23,000 years ago (Bennett et al. 2021).

Because it is so rugged and remote, Beringia was "among the last regions on earth to be described by Western explorers and cartographers" and "remained a great blank on world maps well into the eighteenth century" (Fitzhugh and Crowell 1988, p. 9). That being said, Beringia has long been rich in opportunities for food and shelter, with an abundance of fish, migratory birds, sea mammals (including otters, seals, walruses, and whales), and land mammals (including bears, beavers, caribou, moose, and reindeer). One constant throughout human history is that the inhabitants of Beringia depended on fishing and hunting and move around seasonally for their subsistence. Their livelihoods depend on local knowledge and careful observation of changes in their environment. To this day, in the State of Alaska about one in six resident households live outside of urban areas, and practically all of these households depend on subsistence fishing and hunting (Alaska Department of Fish and Game 2018).

Traveling with a team of reindeer, 1922, Alaska. Source: *Reindeer team*, Frank and Frances Carpenter Collection, Library of Congress, Gift of Mrs. W. Chapin Huntington.

Who lives in Beringia now?

The present-day inhabitants of western Beringia are extremely varied and often inaccurately identified, due in part to Soviet-era scholars who asked questions "specific to their ideological situation" and placed Indigenous peoples "in a Marxist evolutionary framework" (Vitebsky and Alekseyev 2015, p. 439). Even today, the "census categories and figures are questionable," especially for identifiable groups of Indigenous peoples (Vitebsky and Alekseyev 2015, p. 440). Soviet anthropologists recognized 26 different Indigenous groups but "with increasing subdivision, more than 40 are recognized currently" (Vitebsky and Alekseyev 2015, p. 440). These include the Chukchi and Yupik people – numbering in the hundreds – who practice whaling in the Chukchi and Bering Seas; the Sakha (also known as Yakut) who practice horse and cattle herding in far western Beringia and who may number close to 500,000; and the Evenki and Even (also known as Lamut) whose culture and economy were formerly "based on reindeer herding and hunting" (Arutianov 1988, p. 36) but has shifted in post-Soviet times "from reindeer husbandry to reindeer hunting" (Takakura 2012, p. 42).

During the Soviet era, non-Indigenous peoples – primarily Russians, Belorussians, and Ukrainians – temporarily migrated to western Beringia due to "a combination of Soviet planned economic incentives and state-regulated migration" (Crate 2013, p. 6). However, the collapse of the Soviet Union brought an end to state subsidies and many large industrial projects, which triggered a return of those temporary migrants to their homes in Belarus, Ukraine, and western Russia. For instance, the population of the Chukotka Autonomous Okrug (the most northeasterly region in Russia) decreased 68.9% from 1989 to 2013 – which was the largest percentage drop of any region in the Russian north (Heleniak 2017, p. 71).

The present-day inhabitants of eastern Beringia are much better documented but also represent an extremely diverse group of peoples. Based on US Census returns from the 2010s (the latest official figures available), Alaska counted about 105,000 Native residents (or 14.8% of the state population). The primary cultural and linguistic groups were "Iñupiat, Yupik, Athabascan, Aleut, Tlingit, and Haida, organized into some 226 tribes," with many living in "more than 200 rural villages, most of which are remote settlements with fewer than 200 people each" (Hudson 2011, p. 378). Note that these statistics also include settlements in more densely populated southeastern Alaska, which means that (if restricted to Beringia) the percentage of those living in remote settlements would presumably be even higher. For northern Canada, one recent study estimated 20,100 Athabaskans and 44,700 Inuit but also concluded, "Despite the importance of [I]ndigenous people in the Arctic, there is no accurate estimate of their size and distribution" (Young and Bjerregaard 2019, pp. 1, 12).

In contrast to western Beringia, the overall population of eastern Beringia has increased during the past 30 years. One factor was the Cold War and Alaska's strategic far-north location across the Bering Strait from the Soviet Union. The result was a "militarized landscape" with soldiers and civilians "engaged in military construction and operations" (Hummel 2005, p. 50). When oil was discovered on Alaska's North Slope in 1968, the existing military infrastructure literally paved the way for energy companies to exploit the natural resources. The defense industry had been Alaska's "biggest employer and biggest spender from 1940s to 1970s" but was "overtaken by the oil industry when the North Slope fields started producing in 1977" (Hummel 2005, p. 58). Although northern Alaska is not experiencing a massive population boom as it did in the 1970s, its population – encompassing the North Slope Borough, Northwest Arctic Borough, and Nome Census Area – has been averaging a 4% annual increase from 2010 to 2019. This is the same rate as the southwest region and is topped only by the 5% rate for the region around Anchorage, where more than half the state's population resides (Alaska Department of Labor and Workforce Development 2020, p. 53).

Who has passed through here? Where were they headed? And what remains to mark their presence here?

Physical, tangible records of Beringia, and especially central Beringia's land bridge, remain elusive. One theory, which is based on genetic and botanical evidence, suggests that central Beringia "may have been a glacial refugium and postglacial center of dispersal for the people who first settled the Americas" (Hoffecker, Elias, and O'Rourke 2014, p. 979). However, folklorists and anthropologists who have studied the intangible record, such as myths and legends, see direct connections between the Native peoples who crossed Beringia and those who settled in interior North America. For instance, one study of oral traditions suggests that "verbal literature arguably preserves glimpses and echoes of the long-vanished Pleistocene world of our ancestors" (Echo-Hawk 2000, p. 273). More specifically, an origin story that refers to underground worlds from which "humans emerge to populate the earth" may be "a distorted remembrance of Beringia and the Arctic Circle" (Echo-Hawk 2000, p. 276). Other scholars recognize a wide range of "cultural ties" across the Bering Strait – from "plate and rod armor, the sinew-backed bow, wrist-guards, and sinew-twisters" to "raven mythology" and "beliefs about similarly named evil spirits (*kele, kala, kalag*) and similar deities of the sky and sea world" (Fitzhugh 1994, p. 33).

The melting of glaciers and rising sea levels from the start of the Holocene some 12,000 years ago are echoed today as climate change raises both temperatures and sea levels. For instance, Point Hope, Alaska in eastern Beringia "is the northwesternmost settlement in North America and one of the longest continuously inhabited places in the Western Hemisphere" (Sakakibara 2008, p. 457). As the Chukchi Sea rises, already having forced the village's Iñupiat inhabitants to move from Old Town to New Town, the stories that they tell not only reflect the environmental threats but also serve "as a way of maintaining connectivity to a disappearing place" (Sakakibara 2008, p. 473). We must hope that Point Hope will not physically disappear like central Beringia. But should that happen, the inhabitants' oral traditions and verbal literature will still indelibly mark their passages and crossroads.

An aerial view of Point Hope, Alaska in early spring (2017). Source: Photo by Dennis Davis.

What other places in the world are like this one?

Although there is no other place on earth quite like Beringia, there are many other places where climate change is causing sea levels to rise with the consequent loss of land and communities. One example is a community of Biloxi–Chitimacha–Choctaw Indians in Isle de Jean Charles, Terrebonne Parish, Louisiana, where "if nothing is done, the Isle will be gone before 2050" (Maldonado et al. 2013, p. 606). Not surprisingly, a multidisciplinary team of anthropologists, sociologists, and climate experts compared the situation in Louisiana with that of Beringia – specifically the communities of Kivalina and Newtok, Alaska – noting that these tribal communities "share a common fight to save their culture, ancestral land, and communities in the face of both the causes and effects of climate change" (Maldonado et al. 2013, p. 603). Comparisons might be made to the Ganges–Brahmaputra–Meghna delta in Bangladesh or island nations such as Tuvalu, Kiribati, the Maldives, and others.

Central Africa

At the heart of the world's longest inhabited continent, central Africa has always been a hub for movement. Merchants from across Africa traveled to and through the region to trade many things, including ivory, salt, copper, and oil. In the 1600s and 1700s, millions of people were taken from their homes in central Africa and sold into slavery. Central Africa remains a busy crossroads today as people move to, from, and through the region, fleeing conflict and seeking educational and economic opportunity.

Where in the world is central Africa?

Modern central Africa consists of eight countries: Cameroon, Equatorial Guinea, São Tomé and Principe, Congo Republic-Brazzaville, and Gabon on the Atlantic coast to the west as well as Chad, the Central African Republic, and the Democratic Republic of Congo in the interior. The region and contemporary national borders are shown in Figure 2.3.

Who lives in central Africa now?

Today, the seven mainland central African countries are inhabited by various ethnic groups that are largely descended from Bantu speakers. While their official languages reflect their colonial past (e.g., French, English, and Spanish) common Indigenous languages are derived from Bantu (Herbert and Bailey 2002, p. 53). Prior to the arrival of Portuguese explorers in the 1470s the island nation of São Tomé and Principe was uninhabited. Current inhabitants include descendants of Angolan slaves, people of mixed Portuguese and African ancestry, Portuguese settlers, and contract laborers from nearby countries. Unlike the other countries in central Africa, the common languages spoken on the islands are not of Bantu origins.

THE CROSSROADS CONCEPT

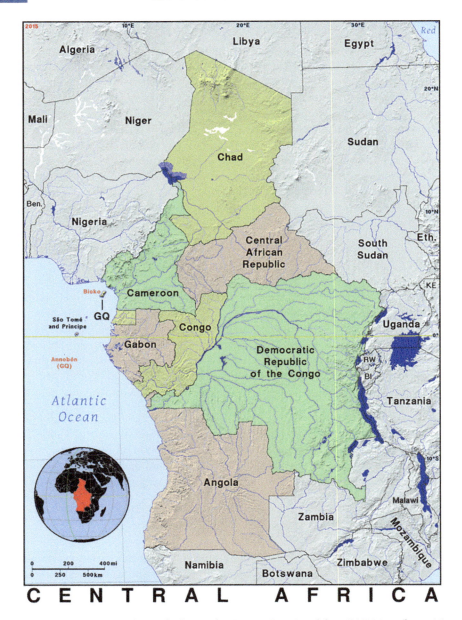

Figure 2.3 Countries of central Africa today. Source: Reprinted from PAT Maps (https://ian.macky.net/pat/map/afri/afri.html).

Who has passed through here? Where were they headed? And what remains to mark their presence here?

Africa has a rich migration history characterized by continuous waves of populations moving throughout the continent in pursuit of food, better shelter, and greater security (Aina 1995, p. 87). One of the more influential groups of migrants are the Bantu-speaking people who reshaped the ecological landscape of central and southern Africa. Classified by linguists as belonging to the Bantu, or Niger-Congo, language family (Michigan State University 2024), their patterns of movement followed a new expanse of savanna lands that stretched from present-day Cameroon and Nigeria to the western and southern regions of Africa (Grollemund et al. 2015, p. 1). Their legacy includes the hundreds of languages in the Bantu family that are now spoken throughout central and southern Africa, from Swahili, which is mainly spoken in Tanzania and Kenya, to the Bulu language of Cameroon and the Xhosa language of South Africa.

About 2,000 years ago, a wave of Bantu speakers commingled with existing communities of forest dwellers who subsided off of a hunter-gatherer diet in the rainforest and savannas of central Africa (Michigan State University 2024). Evidence of their merger is present in the genetic makeup and languages of the present-day inhabitants of the region. The cultivation of plants and the domestication of animals accompanied the Bantu speakers' arrival, which, along with metallurgy, led to the formation of more permanent sedentary settlements. Eventually, as early as the eighth century, the region's population became increasingly concentrated into larger communities that formed the basis of centralized governing systems to rule separate regions (Hiribarren 2016, p. 1). These kingdoms were positioned at strategic points along the salt, textile, and dried fish routes that spanned from the west and east coasts of Africa.

By the fifteenth century, long-distance trade routes linked China, northern India, Egypt, and Europe; the farthest southern tail of the route reached northern and western Africa (Newitt 2005, p. 2). However, unlike other parts of the continent, central Africa had very little contact with Muslim, Berber, and Arab traders (Michigan State University 2024). Insulation from the trade routes ended in 1483 when the Portuguese landed on the western shores of the Kingdom of Kongo (Michigan State University 2024). Driven by the potential of discovering new commercial routes from Africa to India, the source of the spice trade, Portuguese explorers began the search for a sea passage in the interior of Africa (Newitt 2005, p. 6). There, they encountered the Kingdom of Kongo, established in the thirteenth century, which spanned from present-day Gabon to Angola and the Democratic Republic of Congo. A trade relationship developed between the Portuguese and the Kingdom of Kongo as they exchanged material goods and enslaved people.

Central African goods were widely traded and highly prized abroad due the fine quality of workmanship in manufactured items (Gondola 2002, p. 14). Due to the advances in Native forge technology and textile production, central African-produced metals and cloths were of higher quality than that of their European counterparts (Gondola 2002, p. 14).

However, though cloth, ivory, and copper were actively traded, Portuguese merchants exchanged nearly all goods for enslaved persons (Heywood 2009, p. 10). Slavery, as an institution, had existed from the time that the Kingdom of Kongo emerged as a dominant power in west central Africa in the fourteenth century (Heywood 2009, p. 3). Based on oral traditions, it is believed that enslaved persons were captured during conflict with neighboring kingdoms. When the Portuguese and the Kingdom of Kongo began their trade relationship, foreign-born citizens of other African kingdoms were used as a commodity because they had high monetary value in Portugal (Heywood 2009, p. 5). However, by the late 1500s the political power of Kongo fragmented as rival contenders fought for the throne (Heywood 2009, p. 3). Without the protection of a king, Kongo citizens were exported to colonial territories (Heywood 2009, p. 3) as part of the transatlantic slave trade in which 12.5 million Africans were enslaved and forced to migrate to North America (Mintz n.d.).

After the invasion and wresting of political control by Belgian, German, and French colonial powers beginning in the late sixteenth century, with British colonists arriving later, internal migration in central Africa was limited to economic movements that supported colonial governments (Aina 1995, pp. 89–90). From 1884 to 1885 European colonists convened at the Berlin Conference, also known as the "Scramble for Africa," to partition central Africa into "spheres of influence, protectorates, and colonies" (Michalopoulos and Papaioannou 2016, p. 1802). Because European colonists had limited knowledge of local culture, environment, and geography, they imposed political borders that fractured kingdoms, clans, villages, language, and ethnic groups, setting the stage for civil and national wars as ethnic groups sought to regain control of ancestral lands (Michalopoulos and Papaioannou 2016, p. 1810). The imposition of these arbitrary colonial boundaries also precipitated economic decline and poverty. Existing trade routes were restricted or blocked by new political borders (Michigan State University 2024). New trade routes concentrated the movement of inland goods to coastal areas for shipment (Michigan State University 2024). Many central Africans were forced to migrate from landlocked countries to coastal ones to provide the labor that cleared the land and waterways for the harvesting and shipping of goods. This type of short-term, male-dominated, and seasonal migration following agricultural output of the coastal lands (Aina 1995, p. 90) replaced the free-moving migration patterns that characterized the land prior to colonial intervention.

Today, the legacies of European colonial control are present in the political borders of African countries and the lasting damage to and erasure of Indigenous languages and ethnicities. Although Africans began reclaiming their independence from European powers in the 1950s, the national borders drawn by colonists in the late 1800s have remained (Michalopoulos and Papaioannou 2016, pp. 1808-1809).

Most of the migration and displacement that persist throughout central Africa today is intra-continental, the result of deteriorating economic, social, political, and ecological conditions (Adepoju 2002, p. 4). Much of this movement is undocumented, resulting from a long history of policed borders that lack physical landmarks and blurred distinctions between countries and regions where the same language and customs are shared (Aina 1995,

p. 93). Some countries, such as Equatorial Guinea and São Tomé and Principe, have out-migration rates that far exceed global averages due to the large volume of students, skilled workers, and temporary workers migrating to international locations (Shimeles 2010, pp. 7–8). The movement of skilled workers, like healthcare professionals, out of the region is referred to as "brain drain" because it typically involves the relocation of highly educated citizens to former colonial powers for employment opportunities. In Equatorial Guinea, skilled workers who in the past might have emigrated to Spain for employment are today moving instead to Gabon, due to an economic boom (Adepoju 2002, p. 6; Shimeles 2010, p. 12). This type of migration is described as "brain circulation" and may characterize the future of central African migration (Adepoju 2002, p. 6). Another type of migration is caused by desertification and declining agricultural production. For example, workers in the northern region of Chad are being forced by environmental changes to pursue temporary and seasonal work in Cameroon, Congo, Gabon, and the Central African Republic (Adepoju 2002, p. 7).

What other places in the world are like this one?

Another crossroads region that has some similarities to central Africa is Central America. The rise and spread of Mayan culture throughout Central America was accompanied by increasing agricultural intensification, disruptions by the arrival of settler colonists, and the establishment of arbitrary colonial borders that all contributed to a familiar pattern. The colonial establishment of infrastructure that served the appropriation and export of mineral wealth and agricultural products left a legacy in the post-colonial era that has perpetuated economic inequities and the economic migration of many to large urban centers in the region or away from the region to flee conflict and violence and seek economic and educational opportunities elsewhere.

East Los Angeles

East Los Angeles (LA) is more than a neighborhood; it is a cultural hub and a powerful symbol of identity. This area has been shaped by interactions between diverse communities. It has witnessed ancient trade relations between Indigenous peoples, the arrival of Spanish colonists, Mexican independence, US statehood, and more recent waves of immigration. Today, East LA is home to one of the largest Mexican American populations in the US, as well as people from other parts of the world.

Where in the world is East LA?

East LA encompasses approximately 40–50 km^2 (15 to 20 miles^2) in Southern California. Located 225 km (140 miles) north of the international border with Mexico and on the Pacific rim of the North American continent and the Western United States, East LA is a crossroads within a crossroads.

The city that grew to be Los Angeles was established as a northern outpost of colonial New Spain on the western bank of a river, el Río de la Porciúncula, the only

Figure 2.4 "The Goez Map Guide to the Murals of East Los Angeles." A lithograph print produced in 1975 by Goez Publishing Co. in East LA. Source: Illustration, design, and research by Johnny González, David Botello, Robert Arenivar, and Lupe Botello.

year-round waterway in a drought-prone region. Now known as the Los Angeles River, the communities that developed along the eastern bank are described collectively as "East LA." It encompasses a cultural landscape—reductively imagined as an immigrant barrio plagued by poverty, substandard education, and crime—but also celebrated as an influential site of Chicano political activism and cultural production (Figure 2.4).

A total of six freeways and the sprawling East LA interchange configure a major transportation crossroads in the area. It is estimated that 1.7 million vehicles traverse these roads daily (Estrada 2005, p. 301), situating East LA at the intersection of south–north and west–east axes that reach from Mexico to Canada and the Pacific to the Atlantic, respectively.

Who lives in East LA now?

Today, East LA is a densely populated, largely working-class immigrant area supported by commercial corridors and edged by industrial zones. More than 90% of area residents are Latino, Mexican, and Chicano, the largest such community in the United States. This includes immigrants escaping precarious conditions in their homelands, American-born generations, and long-term residents.

The last few decades have seen increased immigration from Central America. And in more recent years, some East LA neighborhoods, especially Boyle Heights, have become destinations for upwardly mobile homebuyers and businesses attracted to the local culture, the relative affordability of property, and the amenities enabled by commercial and public investment. The result has been conflicts over gentrification.

Who has passed through here? Where were they headed? And what remains to mark their presence here?

East LA's boundaries and pathways have been redefined by different population movements, political and commercial interests, and national regimes, including pre-historic Native trade relationships, Spanish conquest and settlement, Mexican independence, US statehood, and new immigration and redevelopment in the twenty-first century.

Historical sources and contemporary Indigenous mapping projects acknowledge the villagers of Apachiangna as the early stewards of what is now East LA (Welts 1962; Torres et al. n.d.; Metzli Projects, n.d.). The Tongva—or Gabrieleño, as they refer to themselves today—moved into the area as long as 7,000 years ago, eventually displacing the people who had preceded them. It is surmised that these Uto-Aztecan speakers had moved from the Great Basin regions of Utah and Nevada (800–1,200 km to the northeast) due to drought and food scarcity. Hunter-gatherers, they adapted effectively to the local environment and prospered, developing an extensive network across which tangible (food, trade goods) and intangible cultures (stories, songs, ceremonies) were exchanged over land and along the seacoast.

In the 1700s the Spanish moved into the region to expand their colonial settlement. They relied on Native knowledge and labor to establish a successful and self-sustaining northern outpost of Spain's empire. The Tongva were either absorbed into, displaced by, or excluded from the growing pueblo, which developed on the western edge of the Los Angles River. Lands on the east side of the river were primarily used for cattle grazing and agriculture through the period of Mexican independence that began in 1822 and ended in 1848, after the US–Mexico War established American rule in California.

In 1848 "the world rushed in[to]" California after gold was discovered near present-day Sacramento (Holliday 1981). Los Angeles cattle ranchers prospered, and the city grew as a regional trading center, provisioning fortune-seeking miners from across the globe. Among these were the men who invested in the first residential subdivisions of land that would become East LA.

Since the late nineteenth century, East LA has been a place of possibility but also in persistent flux and sometimes upheaval. The city around it expanded into a metropolitan center with the arrival of the railroad in the 1870s, which increased land speculation and industrialization. Initially an affluent suburb, the communities east of the river would become more heterogeneous and working-class as wealthy residents moved to newer, more homogeneously "Anglo" areas.

From the 1920s through the 1950s East LA had one of Southern California's most diverse populations. Newly arriving households were driven here by wars in their homelands and extreme poverty, attracted to the jobs in nearby downtown industries and excluded from other parts of the city by restrictive housing covenants. These communities built institutions, including places of worship, dance halls, language schools, mutual aid societies, hospitals, and cemeteries – some of which remain today. Among the distinctive and particularly visible populations during this period were Mexicans uprooted by the Mexican Revolution of 1910–1917; the largest concentration of Jewish people west of the Mississippi River; Russian Molokans, Christian pacifists escaping mandatory conscription and religious persecution in Russia; one of the largest concentrations of Japanese Americans in Southern California; and African Americans, Armenians, Syrians, Chinese, and Italians.

At the time, some observers were intrigued by the possibility of diverse community building at this crossroads. Pauline Young described "a strange conglomerate of immigrant peoples living side by side though speaking a veritable babel of tongues" (Young 1932, p. 19). Ralph Friedman characterized one eastside neighborhood, Boyle Heights, as "a United Nations in microcosm" (Friedman 1955, p. 12). Others considered this diversity a liability – especially with respect to a working-class, heavily immigrant population. Thus, the area was vulnerable to policy interventions that destabilized and disenfranchised residents, often forcing them from the area (Sanchez 2010). In the 1930s, thousands of local Mexicans were deported in response to racial scapegoating that stemmed from the economic strain of the Great Depression. Later in the decade, discriminatory home loan policies appraised East LA communities as high risks due to the area's racially heterogeneous population, which devalued property, curtailed local home ownership, and paved the way for destructive urban renewal projects. During World War II, the city's entire Japanese American population was removed and incarcerated in inland camps. Starting in the 1940s, Los Angeles's investment in suburban expansion came disproportionately at the expense of East LA residents. The freeways routed through the area degraded the quality of life, separated families and entire communities, and displaced at least 10,000 residents.

The experiences of those who have settled and passed through East LA have been recorded in the land. Archaeological findings provide evidence of the wide-reaching trade networks of the Tongva. Some of Southern California's municipal boundaries and major thoroughfares correspond with ancient pathways and former Spanish- and Mexican-era rancho boundaries (Nelson et al. 1964). In the built landscape, bygone people and events are still visible in monuments, buildings, place names, and public art.

Traces of earlier generations are also buried here. East LA's many old cemeteries are religiously or ethnically specific, marking the passage of earlier generations of the region's Catholic, Jewish, Chinese, Russian Molokan, and Serbian residents. Evergreen Cemetery, the city's oldest nondenominational burial ground, is an East LA landscape that embodies both the urge to remember and the ease of forgetting those who came before. This site is the final resting place of city leaders, veterans of conflicts that date back to the US–Mexico War of 1848, indigent people, and regular folks who are memorialized on headstones in Armenian, English, Japanese, and Spanish.

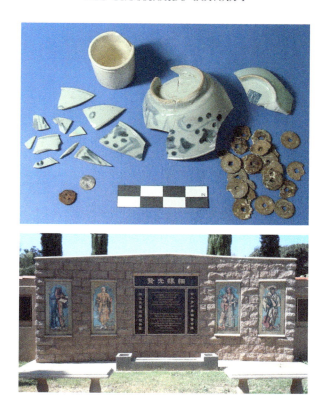

Urban archaeology in East LA. In 2005, while preparing for a street-widening project alongside the cemetery, archaeologists working for LA's transportation authority discovered the graves of 174 people whose burial in a former potter's field had been covered over under 14 feet of dirt. DNA analysis of the human remains and examination of the headstones and materials recovered from the graves revealed that most were Chinese, likely railroad workers who had settled in the city in the late 1800s (Gust, Glover, and Houck 2007; Goldstein et al. 2012). *Top*, excavated Chinese materials. Source: Photo by and courtesy of Cogstone Resource Management, Inc. *Bottom*, trilingual memorial wall in English, Spanish, and Chinese for the excavated potter's field. Source: Photo by Laura Dominguez, courtesy of the Los Angeles Conservancy.

The influence and legacies of previous East LA generations animate enduring social and cultural practices – from musical styles engendering hybridity to foodways. Current residents also evoke with pride the history of local grassroots efforts to resist and organize for social justice. Today's activists build on this lineage and memorialize it creatively in song, place names, formal historic designations, and community events.

Public art in East LA. Today, a powerful reminder of East LA's ongoing struggles over space and newer gentrification threats is expressed as a mural on the public housing complex Ramona Gardens, sponsored by the local councilman's office. Completed in 2008 by Raul González, Ricardo Estrada, and Joséph "Nuke" Montalvo, the mural, titled *Conoce Tus Raíces,* depicts Toypurina, a 24-year-old Indigenous woman who led a nearby rebellion against LA's Spanish colonizers in 1784. Source: Photo by Alan Nakagawa.

What other places in the world are like this one?

With its history of ethnic succession and reputation as an immigrant enclave, East LA resembles other places where the interactions of diverse populations have shaped distinct heritages and surfaced structural inequalities. It resembles international cities, centers of trade, and urban districts from São Paulo to New Orleans and Singapore's Kampong Glam neighborhood to New York City's Lower East Side. Like these, it is a transnational space where the movement of people expands the scope of communities beyond neat political borders.

East LA is similar to many old urban centers that were historical ports of entry or way stations – places en route to somewhere else, possibly somewhere better. Like ethnic enclaves around the world, East LA is a place formed from policies designed to exclude and segregate populations but that has also served as a site of refuge and deliberate long-term settlement. Even after former residents have moved away, such places often continue to be an anchor for identity and belonging.

Today, as investors and people move back into city centers, East LA also resembles places worldwide where gentrification has become a pressing concern. These communities, which once suffered from neglect or direct assault, are now reimagined for material investment and consumption. As in the past, East LA residents are organizing for environmental justice, housing rights, educational equality, and the right to stay. These advocacy efforts join international and national conversations that spotlight the increasing tensions between ongoing migration, displacement, and globalization.

Chapter Summary: Why the Crossroads Narrative Device Works

People have always been on the move, and we can expect this will not change. The people, places, and patterns may change, but the underlying experiences remain the same.

In both senses – intersections where people meet and crucial moments for decisions – we believe that humanity is at a crossroads. Today, roughly one in seven people on earth, or more than one billion people, are estimated to have migrated at least once in their lives. Of these, 763 million people are internal migrants who have moved within the country where they were born, and 272 million people are international migrants who have moved from one country to another. Many of the forces that drive migration today are the same as those that mobilized our ancestors, including poverty, conflict and violence, persecution, political instability, labor shortages, competition for resources, natural disasters, and more gradual environmental changes. By 2050 there may be as many as 405 million international migrants around the world and as many as one billion climate migrants.

The spread of COVID-19 that began in 2020 shows us how interconnected places are to one another, regardless of how distant and disconnected they might have seemed. The inevitability of people on the move in such an interconnected world means greater numbers of people encountering more people of diverse backgrounds, which heightens the need to make the world safe for cultural difference. The decisions we make about migration and displacement now will affect the future of millions of people. Will we adapt to the changes that migration brings and find ways to live together? Or will we resist change and allow our differences to divide us?

Review Questions

1. What are some of the different meanings of "crossroads"? How does this concept suggest ways that we can consider the patterns and outcomes of human population movements?
2. What different patterns can you observe among the four crossroads featured in the exhibition?
3. What are other examples of places or regions that are crossroads? Explain how and why.

References

Adepoju, A. 2002. Fostering Free Movement of Persons in West Africa: Achievements, constraints, and prospects for intraregional migration. *International Migration* 40(2): 3–28. https://doi.org/10.1111/1468-2435.00188.

Aina, Tade Akin. 1995. Internal Non-Metropolitan Migration and the Development Process in Africa. In Jonathan Baker, and Tade Akin Aina, eds. *The Migration Experience in Africa*. Uppsala: Nordic Africa Institute. pp. 41–53. https://www.diva-portal.org/smash/get/diva2:272934/FULLTEXT01.pdf.

Alaska Department of Fish and Game, Division of Subsistence 2018. *Subsistence in Alaska: A Year 2017 Update*. https://www.adfg.alaska.gov/static/home/subsistence/pdfs/subsistence_update_2017.pdf, accessed 8 February 2024.

Alaska Department of Labor and Workforce Development. 2020. *Alaska Population Overview: 2019 Estimates*. Juneau: Department of Labor and Workforce Development.

Architectural Resources Group, Inc 2014. *Historic Resources Survey Report: Boyle Heights Community Plan Area*. Prepared for City of Los Angeles, Department of City Planning, Office of Historic Resources. https://planning.lacity.org/odocument/b31b12ce-5c90-4165-bd8e-a899ce940b64/BoyleHeights_SurveyReport.pdf, accessed 8 February 2024.

Arutianov, S A. 1988. Even: Reindeer Herders of Eastern Siberia. In William W Fitzhugh, and Aron Crowell, eds. *Crossroads of Continents: Cultures of Siberia and Alaska*. Washington, D.C.: Smithsonian Institution Press. pp. 35–38. https://library.si.edu/digital-library/book/crossroadsofcont00wash, accessed 5 Apr 2024.

Avila, Eric. 2004. *Popular Culture in the Age of White Flight: Fear and fantasy in suburban Los Angeles*. Berkeley: University of California Press.

Bennett, Matthew R, David Bustos, Jeffrey S Pigati, et al. 2021. Evidence of humans in North America during the Last Glacial Maximum. *Science* 373(6562): 1528–1531. https://doi.org/10.1126/science.abg7586.

Braje, Todd J, Tom D Dillehay, Jon M Erlandson, et al. 2017. Finding the first Americans. *Science* 358(6363): 592–594. https://DOI.org/10.1126/science.aao5473.

Braudel, Fernand. 1972. *The Mediterranean and the Mediterranean World in the Age of Phillip II*. Vol. 2. Translated by Siân Reynolds. Re-issued in 2023. 2nd ed. Berkley: University of California Press.

Clayton, J. and Holland, H. 2015. Over One Million Sea Arrivals Reach Europe in 2015. *United Nations High Commission on Refugees* (30 December). https://www.unhcr.org/news/latest/2015/12/5683d0b56/million-sea-arrivals-reach-europe-2015.html, accessed 8 Feb 2024.

Crate, Susan A. 2013. *Climate Change and Human Mobility in Indigenous Communities of the Russian North*. Washington, DC: Brookings Institution. https://www.brookings.edu/articles/climate-change-and-human-mobility-in-indigenous-communities-of-the-russian-north/, accessed 9 Feb 2024.

Delgadillo, Natalie. 2017. The Neighborhood that Went to War Against Gentrifiers. In *Bloomberg CityLab* (3 January 2017) https://www.bloomberg.com/news/articles/2017-03-01/the-gentrification-battles-of-east-l-a-s-boyle-heights, accessed 4 Feb 2024.

Echo-Hawk, Roger C. 2000. Ancient History in the New World: Integrating oral traditions and the archaeological record in deep time. *American Antiquity* 65(2): 267–290. https://doi.org/10.2307/2694059.

Estrada, Gilbert. 2005. If You Build It, They Will Move: The Los Angeles freeway system and the displacement of Mexican East Los Angeles, 1944-1972. *Southern California Quarterly* 87(3): 287–315. https://doi.org/10.2307/41172272.

Ethington, Phillip J. 2010. *Ab Urbis Condita*: Regional regimes since 13,000 Before Present. In William Deverell, and Greg Hise, eds. *A Companion to Los Angeles*. Wiley-Blackwell: Malden, MA. pp. 177–215.

Fitzhugh, William W. 1994. Crossroads of Continents: Review and prospect. In William W Fitzhugh, and Valérie Chaussonnet, eds. *Anthropology of the North Pacific Rim*. Washington, DC: Smithsonian Institution Press. pp. 27–51.

Fitzhugh, William W, and Aron Crowell. 1988. Crossroads of Continents: Beringian oecumene. In William W Fitzhugh, and Aron Crowell, eds. *Crossroads of Continents: Cultures of Siberia and Alaska*. Washington, DC: Smithsonian Institution Press. pp. 8–16. https://library.si.edu/digital-library/book/crossroadsofcont00wash, accessed 5 Apr 2024.

Friedman, Ralph. 1955. UN in Microcosm: Boyle Heights: An example of democratic progress, In *Frontier: The Voice of the New West*, March: 12.

Goldstein, S, S Sekhon, N I Bautista, et al. 2012. *Evergreen in the City of Angels: A history of a Los Angeles cemetery*. Los Angeles: Studio for Southern California History.

Gondola, Ch Didier. 2002. *The History of Congo*. New York: Bloomsbury Academic.

Gottlieb, Robert. 2007. *Reinventing Los Angeles: Nature and community in the global city*. Cambridge, MA: MIT Press. https://doi.org/10.7551/mitpress/7398.001.0001.

Gouriévidis, Laurence, ed. 2014. *Museums and Migration: History, memory, and politics*. London and New York: Routledge. https://doi.org/10.4324/9781315774596.

Grollemund, Rebecca, Simon Branford, Koen Bostoen, et al. 2015. Bantu expansion shows that habitat alters the route and pace of human dispersals. *Proceedings of the National Academy of Sciences* 112(43): 13296–13301. https://doi.org/10.1073/pnas.1503793112.

Gumprecht, Blake. 1999. *The Los Angeles River: Its life, death, and possible rebirth*. Baltimore: Johns Hopkins University Press. https://doi.org/10.56021/9780801860478.

Gust, Sherri, A Glover, and K Houck. 2007. *The Historic Los Angeles Cemetery (CA-LAN-3553), Los Angeles Metro Gold Line Project, East Portal Area, Los Angeles, CA*. Final Report by Cogstone Resource Management Inc. for the Metropolitan Transportation Authority. http://libraryarchives.metro.net/dpgtl/archaeology/2007-historic-los-angeles-cemetary-final-report/2007-historic-los-angeles-cemetery-final-summary-report.pdf, accessed 1 Feb 2024.

Harvati, Katerina, Eleni Panagopoulou, and Curtis Runnels. 2009. The Paleoanthropology of Greece. *Evolutionary Anthropology* 18: 131–143. https://doi.org/10.1002/evan.20219.

Headland, Thomas N, Lawrence A Reid, M G Bicchieri, et al. 1989. Hunter-Gatherers and Their Neighbors from Prehistory to the Present [and Comments and Replies]. *Current Anthropology* 30(1): 43–66. https://doi.org/10.2307/2743304.

Heleniak, Timothy. 2017. Boom and Bust: Population Change in Russia's Arctic Cities. In Robert W Orttung, ed. *Sustaining Russia's Arctic Cities: Resource politics, migration, and climate change*. New York: Berghahn Books. pp. 67–87. https://doi.org/10.3167/9781785333156.

Herbert, Robert K, and Richard Bailey. 2002. The Bantu Languages: Sociohistorical perspectives. In Rajend Mesthrie, ed. *Language in South Africa*. Cambridge: Cambridge University Press. pp. 50–78. https://doi.org/10.1017/CBO9780511486692.

Hershkovitz, Israel, Gerhard W Weber, Rolf Quam, et al. 2018. The earliest modern humans outside Africa. *Science* 359(6374): 456–459. https://doi.org/10.1126/science.aap8369.

Heywood, Linda M. 2009. Slavery and its Transformation in the Kingdom of Kongo: 1491-1800. *Journal of African History* 50(1): 1–22. https://doi.org/10.1017/S0021853709004228.

Hiribarren, Vincent. 2016. Kanem-Bornu Empire. In Nigel R Dalziel, and John M MacKenzie, eds. *The Encyclopedia of Empire*. https://doi.org/10.1002/9781118455074.wbeoe014.

Hoffecker, John F. 2017. *Modern Humans: Their African origin and global dispersal*. New York: Columbia University Press.
Hoffecker, John F, and Scott A Elias. 2007. *Human Ecology of Beringia*. New York: Columbia University Press. https://doi.org/10.7312/hoff13060.
Hoffecker, John F, Scott A Elias, and Dennis H O'Rourke. 2014. Out of Beringia? *Science* 343(6174): 979–980. https://doi.org/10.1126/science.1250768.
Holliday, J S. 1981. *The World Rushed*. In *The California Gold Rush Experience*. Norman: University of Oklahoma Press.
Hudson, Heather E. 2011. *Digital Diversity: Broadband and indigenous populations in Alaska*. Anchorage, AK: Institute of Social and Economic Research, University of Alaska, Anchorage. https://iseralaska.org/static/legacy_publication_links/DigitalDiversityAlaskaHudson.pdf, accessed 8 Feb 2024.
Hultén, Eric. 1937. *Outline of the History of Arctic and Boreal Biota during the Quaternary Period*. Stockholm: Bokförlags Aktiebolaget Thule.
Hummel, Laurel J. 2005. The U.S. military as geographical agent: The case of Cold War Alaska. *Geographical Review* 95(1): 47–72. https://doi.org/10.1111/j.1931-0846.2005.tb00191.x.
Ickert-Bond, Stefanie M, David F Murray, and Eric DeChaine. 2009. Contrasting patterns of plant distribution in Beringia. *Alaska. Park Science* 8(2): 26–32. https://www.nps.gov/articles/aps-v8-i2-c3.htm, accessed 8 Feb 2024.
Kyriakopoulos, Irene. 2019. *Europe's Responses to the Migration Crisis: Implications for European integration*. Washington, DC: Institute for National Strategic Studies, National Defense University. https://inss.ndu.edu/Media/News/Article/1824758/europes-responses-to-the-migration-crisis-implications-for-european-integration/, accessed 8 Feb 2024.
Maldonado, Julie Koppel, Christine Shearer, Robin Bronen, Kristine Peterson, and Heather Lazrus. 2013. The impact of climate change on tribal communities in the US: Displacement, relocation, and human Rights. *Climatic Change* 120(3): 601–614. https://data.globalchange.gov/article/10.1007/s10584-013-0746-z#.
Metzli Projects, https://www.meztliprojects.org/, accessed 8 Feb 2024.
Michalopoulos, Stelios, and Elias Papaioannou. 2016. The Long-Run Effects of the Scramble for Africa. *American Economic Review* 106(7): 1802–1848. https://www.aeaweb.org/articles/pdf/doi/10.1257/aer.20131311.
Michigan State University. 2024. Exploring Africa: Module 18 – Central Africa. https://exploringafrica.matrix.msu.edu/curriculum/unit-four/module-eighteen/module-eighteen-activity-two/, accessed 9 Mar 2024.
Mintz, Steven. n.d. *Historical Context: Facts about the Slave Trade and Slavery*. New York: Gilder Lehrman Institute of American History. https://www.gilderlehrman.org/history-resources/teacher-resources/historical-context-facts-about-slave-trade-and-slavery, accessed 21 Nov 2024.
Nelson, Howard J, Cornelius Loesser, Eugene McMillian, et al. 1964. Remnants of the Ranchos in the Urban Pattern of Los Angeles. *California Geographer* 5: 1–11. https://scholarworks.calstate.edu/concern/publications/0p096b38n, accessed 8 Feb 2024.
Newitt, Malyn. 2005. *A History of Portuguese Overseas Expansion, 1400-1668*. New York: Routledge. https://doi.org/10.4324/9780203324042.
Romo, Ricardo. 1983. *East Los Angeles: History of a barrio*. Austin: University of Texas Press.
Sakakibara, Chie. 2008. 'Our Home Is Drowning': Iñupiat storytelling and climate change in Point Hope. *Alaska. Geographical Review* 98(4): 456–475. https://doi.org/10.1111/j.1931-0846.2008.tb00312.x.

Sanchez, George J. 1993. *Becoming Mexican American: Ethnicity, culture, and identity in Chicano Los Angeles, 1900–1945*. New York: Oxford University Press.

Sanchez, George J. 2010. Disposable People, Expendable Neighborhoods. In William Deverell, and Greg Hise, eds. *A Companion to Los Angeles*. Malden, MA: Wiley-Blackwell. pp. 129–146.

Shimeles, Abebe. 2010. *Migration Patterns, Trends and Policy Issues in Africa*. Tunis: African Development Bank Group. Working Paper Series No. 119. https://core.ac.uk/download/pdf/6220444.pdf, accessed 18 Nov 2024.

Sicoli, M. A. and Holton, G. (2014). Linguistic phylogenies support back-migration from Beringia to Asia. PLoS ONE 9(3): e91722. https://doi.org/10.1371/journal.pone.0091722

Strasser, Thomas F, Curtis Runnels, Karl Wegmann, et al. 2011. Dating Paleolithic sites in southwestern Crete. Greece. *J Quaternary Science* 26(5): 553–560. https://doi.org/10.1002/jqs.1482.

Takakura, Hiroki. 2012. The Shift from Herding to Hunting among the Siberian Evenki: Indigenous knowledge and subsistence change in northwestern Yakutia. *Asian. Ethnology* 71(1): 31–47. https://asianethnology.org/downloads/ae/pdf/a1738.pdf, accessed 8 Feb 2024.

Torres, Craig, Cindi Alvitre, Allison Fischer-Olson, Mishuana Goeman, and Wendy Teete, n.d. "Perspectives on A Selection of Gabrieleño/Tongva Places," https://www.arcgis.com/apps/MapJournal/index.html?appid=4942348fa8bd427fae02f7e020e98764, accessed 8 Feb 2024

Vitebsky, Piers, and Anatoly Alekseyev. 2015. Siberia. *Annual Review of Anthropology* 44: 439–455. https://doi.org/10.1146/annurev-anthro-092412-1555546.

Wade, Lizzie. 2017. On the Trail of Ancient Mariners. *Science* 357(6351): 542–545. https://doi.org/10.1126/science.357.6351.542.

Welts, Alan W. 1962. *The Gabrielino Indians at the Time of the Portola Expedition*. Los Angeles: Southwest Museum.

Young, Pauline V. 1932. *The Pilgrims of Russian-Town*. Chicago: University of Chicago Press.

Young, T Kue, and Peter Bjerregaard. 2019. Towards estimating the indigenous population in circumpolar Regions. *International Journal of Circumpolar Health* 78: 1–14. https://doi.org/10.1080/22423982.2019.1653749.

Section 2

Where Do We Come From?

We all share common ancestors, if you go back in history far enough. But that does not mean that we all share the same journeys. Some communities have lived continuously in the same area for thousands of years. Their traditional stories describe their ancestors' origins in these places. Other people live in places where they or their ancestors have arrived more recently. In Section 2, we present an overview of major population movements over the course of human history, beginning with the first waves of movement out of Africa. We also describe the time horizons for the peopling of the major continents, along with the ways in which we use genetic, archaeological, linguistic, and cultural evidence to enrich and update our understanding of these movements. We discuss variations on the Out of Africa hypothesis and cover highlights in the arrival of people in Europe, Australasia, and the Americas. Through crossroads stories we recreate the histories of the Mediterranean basin, Beringia, central Africa (and its connections to the transatlantic slave trade), and East Los Angeles as a site of settler colonialism, economic opportunity, and gentrification, all processes that readers may connect to similar locales around the globe.

World on the Move: 250,000 Years of Human Migration, First Edition. Edward Liebow, James I. Deutsch, Daniel Ginsberg, Sojin Kim, and Caitlyn Kolhoff.
© 2025 John Wiley & Sons, Inc. Published 2025 by John Wiley & Sons, Inc.

Africa is the cradle of humankind. Scientists studying DNA have discovered that Africa's population has more genetic variation than people from other parts of the world. This is because people have lived there for longer than anywhere else on earth. Source: Illustration by Arthimedes (Shutterstock).

3
Out of Africa

If you go back in history far enough, we all share common ancestors, but that does not mean we all share the same journeys. Some communities have lived continuously in the same area for thousands of years. Their traditional stories describe their ancestors' origins in these places. Other people live in places where they or their ancestors have arrived more recently.

In this chapter, we will introduce the idea of the origin story, and contrast the folkloric forms of origin stories with the scientific origin story for humans the world over. Nearly all communities and cultural groups have a well-developed and widely shared narrative about where they come from. This narrative usually involves movement of some sort, whether from chaos to order, darkness to light, or dispersing from one place to many. Anthropologists, folklorists, and literary scholars often call these narratives "origin stories" or "creation myths" to convey the sense that they carry deep symbolic meaning and inspire a sense of place by noting landscapes, landmarks, and other features of nature.

These narratives are not necessarily to be taken literally, but they must be understood as immensely valuable. In addition to naming places and imbuing them with meaning, they often include lessons on what living a good life looks like for that culture, including ideal relationships with the natural, social, and spiritual worlds.

Origin Stories

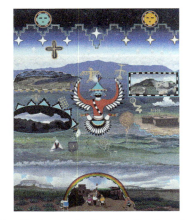

Many creation stories from Aboriginal groups in Australia involve heroic spirits, *Wandjina*, who journey across the land to establish important places. Some ancient rock art in northern Australia depicts Wandjina as if traveling among clouds in the sky. Source: Photo by Graeme Churchard (Creative Commons).

The Zuni people live in the American Southwest. Their creation stories tell how they emerged from an underground world and traveled through deserts and canyons to arrive at their home in the Middle Place. Source: Painting by Ronnie Cachini, © Denver Museum of Nature & Science.

Decades ago, Mircea Eliade (1964) offered what is still useful guidance about these narratives. He reviewed a very broad sampling of stories recorded or reported throughout the world and sorted them into five main categories.

1   **Creation out of nothing (*ex nihilo*)** – The origin of the peoples' world derives from the thoughts, words, dreams, or bodily secretions of a divine being. The Abrahamic (Islam, Judaism, Christianity) Genesis narrative is of this sort: In the beginning, the divine creator made the world out of a dark, formless, void. Among the Bantu-speaking Bushongo people in the contemporary, central African Democratic Republic of Congo, the first creator was called Mbombo (or Bumba). Alone in a world of darkness and water, he became ill from his loneliness until he vomited up the sun, providing light and drying up the water. Successive waves of vomiting yielded the moon and stars, animals, and eventually people. Bumba's sons finished fashioning the world, creating trees, plants, and finally, fire (Schipper 2007).
2   **Creation from a diver** – A child or an animal sent by a creator dives into the depths of an ancient sea to bring up mud or sand that becomes the terrestrial

world. One example of this narrative is told in the *Vishnu Purana*, the Hindu sacred text in which the creator Brahma took the form of a boar and dove down through the ancient waters covering the world to raise up the earth to where it floats now (Leeming 2010, pp. 24–25).

3. **Emergence stories**—In these, the first cohort of people pass through a series of worlds until they reach the present world. For example, the people of the Zuni Pueblo in contemporary New Mexico, USA have an origin narrative that involves humans living underground in the dark before emerging to the surface through a series of caverns. The world had been covered by water, and two brothers—holding a magic shield, a rainbow, and arrows of cosmic lightning—ignited a fire that dried the earth and turned threatening creatures into helpers that would serve the people instead of devouring them.
4. **Creation from dismembering an ancient being**—For example, the Aztecs of Mexico have a narrative in which a terrifying sea monster, Cipactli, was destroying the world until the gods stepped in, chopping Cipactli into three parts. Her head became the heavens, her mid-section became the earth, and her tail became the underworld (Tate 2008).
5. **Creation by dividing or rearranging an ancient unity**—For example, in the traditional Maori narrative from Aotearoa (New Zealand), the origin of the people is accounted for in the movement from nothingness and darkness, from which emerge the sky father, Ranginui, and the earth mother, Papatūānuku. They are joined together, and the resulting children separate them, allowing light to flow into the world. The children of the earth and sky then organize the elements of the natural and social worlds (Leeming 2010, pp.183–185).

A Scientific Origin Story: Out of Africa

An altogether different narrative about where we come from is constructed from the systematic observations of genetic, archaeological, and paleontological evidence of human population movements, what we will call a "scientific origin story." Unlike the folkloric narrative form, which is relatively fixed, the scientific narrative is never-ending, as science is always subject to correction. In its simplest terms, the scientific narrative structure follows a path of prediction, observation, and revision. With new observations come new revisions.

And what a series of recent revisions we have witnessed! As new evidence is discovered, it constantly changes our interpretation of the patterns and processes constructed from earlier observations. What we know about the very earliest prehistoric human population movements—movements well before there were contemporaneous written records made of these movements—comes from a variety of skeletal, genetic, archaeological, and paleontological evidence. Rather than relying on one single observation, scientists have pieced together observations of several different types.

First, there is **skeletal evidence** from fossilized human remains. The anatomically modern human skeleton has a characteristic braincase, brow ridges that have central and side portions, a flat and retracted mid-face, a chin on the lower jaw, specific tooth formations (dentition), and a narrow pelvis.

In addition to the anatomical and physiological characteristics of these human remains, it is possible to conduct **genetic analysis** on some of these remains. Such analyses may help estimate the relatedness of individuals found in different locations, and comparisons of modern and ancient DNA, especially single nucleotide polymorphisms (SNPs) can further confirm the proper characterization of remains as belonging to anatomically modern humans (Reich et al. 2011).

Next, accompanying the fossilized human remains, there are sometimes **archaeological artifacts** such as tools. For example, there may be a characteristic set of slicers, scrapers, chippers, projectile points (arrowheads and spearheads) as well as the stone cores from which these tools were made. Other accompanying artifacts sometimes include engravings, beads, and incised egg or clam shells.

Finally, evidence of **ancient environmental conditions**, especially markers of paleoclimate change, provides a solid basis from which to infer movements.

PERSPECTIVE: In, Out, Around, and All Over: Our Ancestors were Already on the Move, by Agustín Fuentes

Professor of Anthropology, Princeton University (USA)

We humans come from a long line of travelers. Emerging just under three million years ago in sub-Saharan Africa, various bands of our lineage (the genus *Homo*) immediately began journeying around Africa, spreading across the east and south of the continent. By at least two million years ago, some groups of *Homo* moved a bit north, setting out into Eurasia. Some stayed in central Eurasia, and others pushed eastward, eventually reaching the Pacific Ocean and the Sunda region (Southeast Asia). Over the last two million years, small groups in our genus moved from one place to another, sometimes over great distances, other times just into the next valley, often staying in those places for eons, other times returning or moving on to new locales. Sometimes these voyaging groups came into places where there were already *Homo* living, and at least some of encounters resulted in merging, forming new groups. For more than 2,000 millennia small bands of our genus moved, stayed, mixed, expanded, and disappeared repeatedly across Africa and much of Eurasia.

Then, about 300,000 years ago in Africa, a new slightly new variant of *Homo* developed. This cluster of *Homo* did not come from one single line of ancestors, rather they emerged from the mixing and movement of many, many ancestral groups. We call this variant *sapiens*, us, and we are the product of our ancestors' journeying habits. Groups of this new *sapiens* blend of *Homo* spread across the continent of Africa, encountering, mixing with, and sometimes even replacing other groups in the *Homo* lineage. Stretching across the continent, our species repeated the earlier *Homo* pattern with some groups leaving Africa going north, west, and east; others staying in place; and yet others moving to new places around the continent. Over a few hundred thousand years, groups of *Homo sapiens* spread far and wide: leaving behind the ancestral continent, other groups came back into it, and still others left anew. By about 50,000 years ago our species ranged from the southern Cape to the western coast, across the Horn, and into the north of Africa as well as across the entire coastline of the Mediterranean Sea; north to the Baltic Sea; east across Central and South Asia, reaching the Pacific; and south, across waters and onto the paleocontinents of Sahul and Australinea. In the last 30,000 years or so, groups of *H. sapiens* journeyed into the Americas and voyaged into the Pacific realms of Oceania, Melanesia, and Polynesia. During some of these journeys, across the past few hundred thousand years in particular, these earlier *sapiens* encountered groups of other lineages in the genus *Homo* (such as those we call Neanderthals and Denisovans) and, at least some of the time, shared genes and culture.

The human legacy is that of a species who moves across land, water, and whatever obstacles the world presents; frequently mixes and melds; and occasionally fights with other groups they encounter. Above all, it has the remarkable ability to make home wherever they go. But how did we get this way? No other primate, or mammal for that matter, comes close to the particular journeying capacity and tendency that we see in humans. How is it possible that a relatively naked, bipedal, ape-like primate turned out to be a journeyer extraordinaire? The answers are in our evolutionary history.

The genus *Homo* most likely emerged from a cluster of hominin lineages lumped into the group called Australopithecines. The Australopithecines lived in small groups with relatively complex social lives, including the creation and use of simple stone and bone tools and probably extended care of their young. There were many varieties of Australopithecines across different local regions in southern and eastern Africa, with the variations probably reflecting the modification of basic biology and structure of bodies when a population does not move too much or too far from a given locale. But these same bodies and lives–being relatively large (and complex) brained, tool making, bipedal apes–set the stage for the evolution and development of a slightly different version of hominin (and eventually us). With the emergence of our genus (*Homo*) legs got a little longer, feet a little better for extended walking, and brains a bit larger and more complex. Expanding on the core hominin (Australopithecine-version) way of being, early *Homo* began to experiment a bit more with culture, materials, and movement. By about two million years ago groups of the genus *Homo* pushed the exploratory envelope–spreading across, out of, and back into, the continent of Africa. A pattern that repeats itself again and again across the history of our genus.

The earliest adventurers
It is not clear how many populations of early *Homo* contributed to the expansion of movement starting around two million years ago. But it was more than one. We know this by the variations in fossils found outside of the African continent. Between one and two million years ago, a variety of slightly different looking members of the genus *Homo* show up in locations across central Eurasia and eastern and southeastern Asia. Their behavior—aside from the movement part—was also likely variable, as we find different types of tools in association with these fossils at different times and places across these early expansions of the *Homo* range. There was also substantial movement around the continent of Africa, with evidence of members of the genus *Homo* showing up in more and more locations. We do not yet know how many times groups left and then returned to the African continent, but we can expect that there was quite a bit of back and forth and all around (and there has been ever since). However, it is likely that most of these early adventures, and adventurers, are not direct ancestors of contemporary humans (us). These adventuring groups stayed small in number, frequently, successfully moving into new areas and facing a variety of new challenges but eventually, mostly, dying out. These early movements and their often long-lived (but ultimately temporary) successes enable us to better understand the suite of changes in bodies and behavior over the last million years that came to characterize us (*H. sapiens*). Movement is deep in our evolutionary history, and we kept getting better at it.

The evolution of a human niche
Compared to the Australopithecines, the genus *Homo* underwent specific changes in bones, muscles, and physiologies alongside less easily measurable but significant, behavioral and cognitive shifts across the last two million years. It is during this time period that much we take for granted as being thoroughly human emerged: hyper-cooperation, complex collaboration in social interactions, and increasingly complex material technologies. Our ancestors developed ways to more effectively work together, assist each other day in and day out, and expand the intensity of mutual care, the depth of social bonds, and reliance on each other. This enabled the development of more intricate and diverse foraging and hunting patterns as well as a range of increasingly complex collaborative behavior and communication. Key necessities for a lineage (and a species) that moves far and wide.

In the last million years, *Homo* developed increased neurobiological complexity, necessitating a longer growth and development period; *Homo* childhood extended to be the longest, and most community-involved, developmental process for any primate (or mammal). By at least 800,000 years ago groups began to experiment with fire: to create it; to use it to reshape bone, wood, and stone; and to cook a plethora of different foods. By 300,000–400,000 years ago *Homo* was developing more social connections across different groups and places, followed by the emergence of exchange networks across longer and longer distances. Then, in the past few hundred thousand years, engravings, carvings, and eventually, art began to show up consistently and ubiquitously. And all of this was accompanied by increasingly complex communication and information sharing, eventually resulting in that amazing system called language. This human niche, this way of being in the world, was the baseline for (and emerged in concert with) a lineage and eventually, a single species (us) that is frequently on the move.

There are a few major insights from our evolutionary history for contemporary humanity. And they are truly related to our deep-seated tendency and remarkable capacity to wander.

First, humans today are identical in more than 99% of our DNA. In fact, there is more genetic diversity within most human groups than there is between them. Yet, humans across the planet look and act differently in many, many ways. This amazing and distinctive human pattern of substantial genetic homogeneity and huge physical and cultural diversity is a result of the habitual movement and mixing in humans across the last tens of thousands of years. On the one hand, the extensive movement combined with the sharing of genes (and a lot more) keeps the species as biologically cohesive and unified as we are. On the other hand, the great distances between places where humans live as well as the hyper-rapid pace at which humans alter their environments and their cultural ways of being produce the massive diversity in bodies and lives. It is also clear that moving around and mixing it up via migration and mating is on par for humans across our entire history and deep into our ancestry. This does not mean that all humans move all the time. In fact, most humans do not move that much or too far in any given lifetime, but on average, across many, many generations, human groups (or at least parts of those groups) do move. This means that the contemporary movement of people—as well as the challenges and successes of navigating the melding of cultures, lives, and ways of being—is nothing new. It is one of the oldest traditions of humanity. Thus, despite the complexity in the contemporary moment related to movement, our species has the toolkit and experience to make migration and immigration work. We have done it since before we were even us. The human story is one of movement, adventures, failures, and successes in the past, and in the present. And if we pay serious attention to what we already know and are capable of, we can likely tip the scales toward success in the future.

Once fossil or archaeological evidence is gathered, the story is not complete until an approximate date can be assigned to the finding. As we noted in Chapter 1, methods used to estimate origin dates and time ranges get less precise the farther back in history we go. **For this earliest period of human history, some of the methods that have been used with reasonable success include:**

- Uranium series and electron spin resonance techniques to date tooth enamel samples.
- Uranium–thorium dating to determine the age of the sediment stuck to fossils.

- Thermoluminescence to measure the age of burned tools found close to a fossilized skeletal piece.
- Paleoclimatic reconstructions using speleothems, the oxygen content of deep-sea cores (marine isotope stages), and pollen analysis.
- References to environmental changes due to key events (e.g., volcanic eruptions) with well-established dates.

Because the fossil record from this early period is limited, each new observation of skeletal or genetic phenomena is just as likely to challenge previous notions as it is to confirm them. Until recently, scientists believed that the anatomically modern human species, *H. sapiens*, was likely to have first appeared between 300,000 and 200,000 years ago in eastern Africa (Lahr and Foley 1994). The consensus view was that humans then began moving off to spread through the Middle East, Europe, western and central Asia, and beyond. For example, at the Misliya Cave complex in contemporary Israel, a *H. sapiens* jaw bone accompanied by stone tools are dated to 240,000–150,000 years ago, indicating one of the earliest instances of humans outside of Africa (Hershkovitz et al. 2018; Zaidner and Weinstein-Evron 2020).

However, in 2017 Jean-Jacques Hublin and colleagues reported a finding from Jebel Irhoud in contemporary Morocco that pushes back the earliest, anatomically modern human to between 350,000 and 300,000 years ago (see also Stringer and Galway-Witham 2017 and Richter et al. 2017). These reports are interesting because they rely on fossilized skeletal findings that were initially encountered along with very old stone tools in the 1960s when Morocco was ramping up mining operations. Shortly after they were found, an initial interpretation suggested that these remains were around 40,000 years old and represented a form of Neanderthals, related to but distinct from *H. sapiens*. Bones from animals assumed to have been hunted by the occupants of this old site were also found, but the excavation in the 1960s was imprecise, the location where remains were found was not precisely detailed, and there was great uncertainty about the geological age of the rock layers in which they were found. More recent excavations have made it possible to provide a more accurate estimate of the local geology, and new skeletal remains were also found. Altogether, a picture has emerged that the site's occupants were not Neanderthals from 40,000 years ago but anatomically modern humans from more than 300,000 years ago (Hublin et al. 2017; Richter et al. 2017).

This finding from western Africa means that there would have been considerable movement *within* Africa between the eastern and western parts of the continent, perhaps for as long as 100,000 years, *before* the movement of some people away from Africa, into the Middle East and beyond. The movement and mixing of people within Africa across many, many generations is supported by genetic evidence (Rito et al. 2019; Schlebusch et al. 2012; Schlebusch et al. 2017; Montinaro et al. 2021; Bergström et al. 2021).

This pattern of movement and mixing of people within Africa is further supported by Eleanor Scerri and her colleagues (Scerri et al. 2018), who point to a range of morphological diversity within the fossilized skeletal materials that have been found to date. When combined with archaeological and genetic evidence, Scerri et al. suggest that it is useful to think of the earliest human populations in Africa as having been divided into small groups that lived in multiple regions and were connected by sporadic gene flow, rather than remaining in a single region. There was also probably mating from time to time with other hominins (e.g., Neanderthals, Denisovans) that lived in different regions.

Further evidence of movement within Africa is presented by Eva Chan and her colleagues (Chan et al. 2019) as well as Mahmoud Abbas and his colleagues (Abbas et al. 2023). Both teams have taken a detailed look at environmental circumstances — especially the locations of watersheds, savannas, and grasslands—to point to likely pathways for movement. Genetic data combined with environmental data, especially climate data, suggest that a southern African homeland for anatomically modern humans was quite stable for many thousands of years and followed by increased humidity, which Chan et al. suggest "opened green corridors first to the northeast and then to the southwest" (Chan et al. 2019, p. 188).

However, a big evidence gap makes it difficult to construct a definitive timeline and leaves considerable uncertainty among scientists about when people began moving beyond their African places of origin. **Some of the models currently supported include:**

- An early beginning to several waves of movement, each associated with favorable climate conditions, that began about 180,000–200,000 years ago with notable surges about 130,000 years ago (Groucutt et al. 2015; Petraglia et al. 2010; Petraglia et al. 2015; Zaidner and Weinstein-Evron 2020).
- An early southern route across the Arabian Peninsula, beginning between 130,000 and 106,000 years ago, with evidence from fossilized skeletons and toolkits (e.g., Armitage et al. 2011; Usik et al. 2013).
- Somewhat later dispersals across the southern Arabian Peninsula over a series of waves that began about 70,000 years ago, followed by northern routes starting about 50,000 years ago (Abbas et al. 2023).

Remember that peoples' subsistence depended on a livelihood strategy that anthropologists call "hunting and gathering." Hunter-gatherers depend on wild foods for their subsistence, rather than growing their food (Ingold 2000). As a result, hunter-gatherers tend to move in small groups according to the changes in seasons, as the vegetation they would gather and the game animals that also fed on this vegetation would typically change with the seasonal cycles of weather and sunlight.

In addition to these seasonal rounds, longer-term changes in environmental conditions are likely to affect the abundance and diversity of vegetation and wildlife. These paleoenvironmental changes are now much better understood than previously, facilitated by the development of new analytical tools. Determining ancient surface water regimes (lakes, rivers, sea levels, and coastlines) is especially important as the locations of rivers, lakes, and seacoasts are essential to identifying migration corridors.

Since we are talking about ancient environmental changes that happened relatively slowly over a long period of time a very long time ago, it is useful to take a small side trip to the world of geological nomenclature. As shown in Figure 3.1, scientists have divided the history of the earth into different units based on the life forms that existed during times since the planet was created. These general units, from the longest to the shortest, are eons, eras, periods, and epochs.

Eon	Era	Period	Epoch	MYA	Life Forms	North American Events
Phanerozoic	Cenozoic (CZ)	Quaternary (Q)	Holocene (H)	0.01	Extinction of large mammals and birds; Modern humans	Ice age glaciations; glacial outburst floods
			Pleistocene (PE)	2.6		Cascade volcanoes (W); Linking of North and South America (Isthmus of Panama)
		Tertiary (T) Neogene (N)	Pliocene (PL)	5.3	Spread of grassy ecosystems	Columbia River Basalt eruptions (NW); Basin and Range extension (W)
			Miocene (MI)	23.0		
		Paleogene (PG)	Oligocene (OL)	33.9		
			Eocene (E)	56.0	Early primates	Laramide Orogeny ends (W)
			Paleocene (EP)	66.0	Mass extinction	
	Mesozoic (MZ)	Cretaceous (K)			Placental mammals; Early flowering plants	Laramide Orogeny (W); Western Interior Seaway (W); Sevier Orogeny (W)
		Jurassic (J)		145.0	Dinosaurs diverse and abundant	Nevadan Orogeny (W); Elko Orogeny (W)
		Triassic (TR)		201.3	Mass extinction; First dinosaurs; first mammals; Flying reptiles	Breakup of Pangaea begins; Sonoma Orogeny (W)
				251.9	Mass extinction	
	Paleozoic (PZ)	Permian (P)		298.9		Supercontinent Pangaea intact; Ouachita Orogeny (S)
		Pennsylvanian (PN)		323.2	Coal-forming swamps; Sharks abundant; First reptiles	Alleghany (Appalachian) Orogeny (E); Ancestral Rocky Mountains (W)
		Mississippian (M)		358.9	Mass extinction; First amphibians; First forests (evergreens)	Antler Orogeny (W); Acadian Orogeny (E-NE)
		Devonian (D)		419.2		
		Silurian (S)		443.8	First land plants; Mass extinction	
		Ordovician (O)		485.4	Primitive fish; Trilobite maximum; Rise of corals	Taconic Orogeny (E-NE); Extensive oceans cover most of proto-North America (Laurentia)
		Cambrian (C)		541.0	Early shelled organisms	
Proterozoic					Complex multicelled organisms	Supercontinent rifted apart; Formation of early supercontinent Grenville Orogeny (E)
		Precambrian (PC, W, X, Y, Z)		2500	Simple multicelled organisms	First iron deposits; Abundant carbonate rocks
Archean				4000	Early bacteria and algae (stromatolites)	Oldest known Earth rocks
Hadean				4600	Origin of life; Formation of the Earth	Formation of Earth's crust

Figure 3.1 The main geological time scale of eons, eras, periods, and epochs. Source: Reprinted from the US National Park Service (https://www.nps.gov/subjects/geology/time-scale.htm).

We are currently in the Cenozoic Era, the Age of Mammals. The Cenozoic Era began roughly 65 million years ago and is further subdivided into the Tertiary Period and the more recent Quaternary Period. The Quaternary Period is further divided into the Pleistocene Epoch, when anatomically modern humans emerged, and the Holocene Epoch, in which human populations dispersed across the globe (Cohen and Gibbard 2019).[1]

As it concerns early human population movements, a related timescale of the earth's ancient climate has been developed. This timescale is called the marine isotope stage (MIS) timescale, and it was developed from taking deep-sea core samples and extracting oxygen isotope values that indicate temperature changes (Lisiecki and Raymo 2005). Oxygen isotopes (^{16}O and ^{18}O) are helpful in reconstructing ancient climate conditions because they come from the shells of marine organisms, and shells from colder water contain more ^{18}O relative to ^{16}O than do shells secreted in warmer water. By measuring this ratio of ^{18}O to ^{16}O in deep-sea core samples, scientists have been able to graph changes in ocean water temperatures over long periods of time and correlate these temperature changes to the storage of water in large ice sheets on land (Elias 2013).

The MIS timescale is directly relevant to the discussion about the timing of human population dispersal out of Africa. When fossilized human remains and accompanying artifacts are found in rock layers, the MIS stage of a particular layer helps date the fossilized remains and tie them to particular environmental conditions. This synthesis of archaeological and paleoclimatological data led Nicholson et al. (2021) to conclude that a wave of rapid population expansion from Africa and across Arabia resulted from the northward expansion of a monsoon rain belt, a wide availability of water resources, and the formation of grasslands. As Abbas and colleagues observed, this combination of conditions "provided an opportunity for humans, herbivores, and carnivores to expand and survive over time" (Abbas et al. 2023, p. 3).

Were all of these dispersals from Africa a success? As more observations accumulate, it appears from genetic and archaeological evidence that some early waves of movement out of Africa were ultimately ill-fated (Fu et al. 2013), and that due to variations in environmental conditions, patterns of population dispersal were mixed and discontinuous, rather than some smooth and steady incoming spread of population groups (Rabett 2018).

---

[1] Earth scientists have been discussing whether to declare the Anthropocene as the latest geologic epoch, one that would succeed the roughly 12,000 year–old Holocene Epoch (Prillaman 2023). Decisions about a new epoch are made by a committee formed by the International Commission on Stratigraphy and involve a determination about which set of rock layers best illustrate a specific change in the planet's geology. The Anthropocene is the label given to the time interval in which human activity has begun to alter the planet with industrial and radioactive emissions. A specific location is chosen to represent the boundary rock layer, and news reports indicate that Crawford Lake in Canada (Carrington 2023) was the scientific committee's choice. However, in March 2024, the Commission rejected this choice (Witze 2024), and further discussion is likely.

The overall impression is that people were highly adaptive, using a variety of inland and coastal routes. It is also likely that later surges in population movement wiped out evidence of earlier movements along the same routes. Since the evidence is skimpy, each new discovery can significantly modify scientists' thinking (Schroeder and Rogers Ackermann 2023).

Chapter Summary

Origin stories are well-developed and widely shared narratives about where communities and cultural groups come from. This narrative usually involves some pattern of movement. Found among almost all communities and cultural groups, origin stories carry deep symbolic meaning and inspire a sense of place by noting landscapes, landmarks, and other features of nature. In addition to naming places and imbuing them with meaning, they often include lessons on what living the good life looks like, including ideal relationships with the natural, social, and spiritual world.

Unlike the folkloric form of origin story, which is relatively fixed and unchanging, the scientific narrative is a never-ending story, as science is always subject to correction. We set up scientific questions so they can be either confirmed or challenged by new evidence. Evidence of when and where humans first moved out of Africa is scarce enough that it leaves room for multiple interpretations. The re-examination of fossilized skeletal remains and recent innovations in genetic analyses of ancient DNA suggest that there may have been considerable movement *within* Africa between the eastern and western parts of the continent (perhaps for as long as 100,000 years) before the movement of some people away from Africa, into the Middle East (beginning about 200,000 years ago), and then beyond. Paleoclimate data, which relies on the chemical composition of ancient seafloor core samples, help us reconstruct periods of higher humidity, greater rainfall, and lower sea levels, which would have opened routes for dispersal and expansion either overland or across a narrow, shallow strait from the Horn of Africa to the Arabian Peninsula. It is also likely that later surges in population movement wiped out evidence of earlier movements along the same routes. Since the data record is thin, each new discovery may significantly modify scientists' thinking.

Review Questions

1. How are human origins in traditional stories told by and in communities? What might these stories add to the understanding that we take away from more scientific explanations?
2. What are some of the key scientific findings that have helped chart the pathways followed by anatomically modern humans out of Africa to the Middle East and points beyond?

3. Recent evidence indicates that the earliest anatomically modern humans that moved into Europe and Central Asia were not moving into empty lands along these migration routes. Who were the occupants of the land at that time? How does this encounter compare to more recent examples of colonization and conquest?

References

Abbas, Mahmoud, et al. 2023. Human dispersals out of Africa via the Levant. *Science Advances* 9(40): 1–9. https://doi.org/10.1126/sciadv.adi6838.

Armitage, Simon J, Sabah A Jasim, Anthony E Marks, et al. 2011. The southern route "out of Africa": Evidence for an early expansion of modern humans into Arabia. *Science* 331(6016): 453–456. https://doi.org/10.1126/science.1199113.

Bergström, Anders, Chris Stringer, Mateja Hajdinjak, Eleanor M L Scerri, and Pontus Skoglund. 2021. Origins of modern human ancestry. *Nature* 590: 229–237. https://doi.org/10.1038/s41586-021-03244-5.

Carrington, Damian. 2023. Canadian Lake Chosen to Represent Start of Anthropocene. *The Guardian* (11 Jul 2023). https://www.theguardian.com/environment/2023/jul/11/nuclear-bomb-fallout-site-chosen-to-define-start-of-anthropocene.

Chan, Eva K F, Axel Timmermann, Benedetta F Baldi, et al. 2019. Human origins in a southern African palaeo-wetland and first migrations. *Nature* 575: 185–189. https://doi.org/10.1038/s41586-019-1714-1.

Cohen, K M, and P Gibbard. 2019. Global chronostratigraphical correlation table for the last 2.7 million years, version 2019 QI-500. *Quaternary International* 500: 20–31. https://doi.org/10.1016/j.quaint.2019.03.009.

Eliade, Mircea. 1964. *Myth and Reality (Religious Traditions of the World)*. London: Allen & Unwin.

Elias, Scott. 2013. Introduction. In Scott Elias, and Cary Mock, eds. *Encyclopedia of Quaternary Science*. 2nd ed. Elsevier. pp. xi–xii. https://doi.org/10.1016/B978-0-444-53643-3.09982-9.

Fu, Qiaomei, Alissa Mittnik, Philip L F Johnson, et al. 2013. A Revised Timescale for Human Evolution Based on Ancient Mitochondrial Genomes. *Current Biology* 23(7): 553–559. https://doi.org/10.1016/j.cub.2013.02.044.

Groucutt, Huw S, Michael D Petraglia, Geoff Bailey, et al. 2015. Rethinking the dispersal of *Homo sapiens* out of Africa. *Evolutionary Anthropology* 24: 149–164. https://doi.org/10.1002/evan.21455.

Hershkovitz, Israel, Gerhard W Weber, Rolf Quam, et al. 2018. The earliest modern humans outside Africa. *Science* 359(6374): 456–459. https://doi.org/10.1126/science.aap8369.

Hublin, Jean-Jacques, Abdelouahed Ben-Ncer, Shara E Bailey, et al. 2017. New fossils from Jebel Irhoud, Morocco and the pan-African origin of *H. sapiens*. *Nature* 546: 289–292. https://doi.org/10.1038/nature22336.

Ingold, Tim. 2000. *The Perception of the Environment: Essays on livelihood, dwelling, and skill*. London and New York: Routledge. https://leiaarqueologia.files.wordpress.com/2017/08/the-perception-of-the-environment-tim-ingold.pdf, accessed 27 Jan 2024.

Lahr, Marta Mirazon, and Robert Foley. 1994. Multiple Dispersals and Modern Human Origins. *Evolutionary Anthropology* 3(2): 48–60. https://doi.org/10.1002/evan.1360030206.

Leeming, David A. 2010. *Creation Myths of the World*. 2nd ed. Santa Barbara, CA: ABC-CLIO. https://publisher.abc-clio.com/9781598841756/1, accessed 13 Feb 2024.

Lisiecki, Lorraine E, and Maureen E Raymo. 2005. A Pliocene-Pleistocene stack of 57 globally distributed benthic $\delta^{18}O$ records. *Paleoceanography* 20: PA1003. https://doi.org/10.1029/2004PA001071.

Montinaro, Francesco, Vaisili Pankratov, Burak Yelmen, Luca Pagani, and Mayukh Mondal. 2021. Revisiting the out of Africa even with a deep learning approach. *The American Journal of Human Genetics* 108: 2037–2051. https://doi.org/10.1016/j.ajhg.2021.09.006.

Nicholson, Samuel L, Rob Hosfield, Huw S Groucutt, et al. 2021. Beyond arrows on a map: The dynamics of *H. sapiens* dispersal and occupation of Arabia during Marine Isotope State 5. *Journal of Anthropological Archaeology* 62: 101269. https://doi.org/10.1016/j.jaa.2021.101269.

Petraglia, Michael D, Michael Haslam, Dorian Q Fuller, Nicole Boivin, and Chris Clarkson. 2010. Out of Africa: new hypotheses and evidence for the dispersal of *Homo sapiens* along the Indian Ocean rim. *Annals of Human Biology* 37: 288–311. https://doi.org/10.3109/03014461003639249.

Petraglia, Michael D, Ash Parton, Huw S Groucutt, et al. 2015. Green Arabia: Human prehistory at the Crossroads of Continents. *Quaternary International* 382(2015): 1–7. http://dx.doi.org/10.1016/j.quaint.2015.05.071.

Prillaman, Mc Kenzie. 2023. Are we in the Anthropocene? Geologists could define a new epoch for Earth. *Nature* 613: 14–15. https://doi.org/10.1038/d41586-022-04428-3.

Rabett, Ryan J. 2018. The success of failed *Homo sapiens* dispersals out of Africa and into Asia. *Nature Ecology and Evolution* 2(2): 212–219. https://doi.org10.1038/s41559-017-0436-8.

Reich, David, Nick Patterson, Martin Kircher, et al. 2011. Denisova admixture and the first modern human dispersals into Southeast Asia and Oceania. *American Journal of Human Genetics* 89(4): 516–528. https://doi.org/10.1016/j.ajhg.2011.09.005.

Richter, Daniel, Rainer Grün, Renaud Joannes-Boyau, et al. 2017. The age of the hominin fossils from Jebel Irhoud, Morocco, and the origins of the Middle Stone Age. *Nature* 546: 293–296. https://doi.org/10.1038/nature22335.

Rito, Teresa, Daniel Vieira, Marina Silva, Eduarto Conde-Sousa, Luisa Pereira, Paul Mellars, Martin B Richards, and Pedro Soares. 2019. A Dispersal of *Homo sapiens* from Southern to Eastern Africa immediately preceded the out-of-Africa migration. *Scientific Reports* 9(4728): 1–10. https://doi.org/10.1038/s41598-019-41176-3.

Scerri, Eleanor, Mark G Thomas, Andria Manica, et al. 2018. Did our species evolve in subdivided populations across Africa, and why does it matter? *Trends in Ecology and Evolution* 33: 582–594. https://doi.org/10.1016/j.tree.2018.05.005.

Schipper, Mineke. 2007. Stories of the Beginning Origin Myths in Africa South of the Sahara. In Markham Geller, and Mineke Schipper, eds. *Imagining Creation, IJS Studies in Judaica*. Vol. 5. pp. 103–138. https://doi.org/10.1163/ej.9789004157651.i-424.25.

Schlebusch, Carina M, Helena Malmström, Torsten Günther, et al. 2017. Southern African ancient genomes estimate modern human divergence to 350 000 to 260 000 years ago. *Science* 358: 652–655. https://doi.org/10.1126/science.aao62.

Schlebusch, Carina M, Pontus Skoglund, Per Sjödin, et al. 2012. Genomic variation in seven Khoe-San groups reveals adaptation and complex African history. *Science* 338: 374–379. https://doi.org/10.1126/science.1227721.

Schroeder, Lauren, and Ackermann Rebecca Rogers. 2023. Moving beyond the adaptationist paradigm for human evolution, and why it matters. *Journal of Human Evolution* 174: 103296. https://doi.org/10.1016/j.jhevol.2022.103296.

Stringer, Chris, and Julia Galway-Witham. 2017. On the origin of our species. *Nature* 546: 212–214. https://doi.org/10.1038/546212a.

Tate, Carolyn E. 2008. Landscape and a Visual Narrative of Creation and Origin at the Olmec Ceremonial Center of La Venta. In John Staller, ed. *Pre-Columbian Landscapes of Creation and Origin*. New York: Springer. pp. 31–65. https://doi.org/10.1007/978-0-387-76910-3_2.

Usik, Vitaly I, Jeffrey Ian Rose, Y H Hilbert, et al. 2013. Nubian complex reduction strategies in Dhofar, southern Oman. *Quaternary International* 300: 244–266. https://doi.org/10.1016/j.quaint.2012.08.2111.

Witze, Alexandra. 2024. Geologists reject the Anthropocene as Earth's new epoch – after 15 years of debate. *Nature* (06 Mar 2024). https://www.nature.com/articles/d41586-024-00675-8.

Zaidner, Yossi, and Mina Weinstein-Evron. 2020. The Emergency of the evallois technology in the Levant: a view from the Early Middle Paleolithic site of Misliya Cave Israel. *Journal of Human Evolution* 144. https://doi.org/10.1016/j.jhevol.2020.102785.

4

The Peopling of Europe, Australasia, and the Pacific

As we reported in the preceding chapter, scientists are uncertain about the precise timing of the earliest human population movements out of Africa. The archaeological, genetic, and paleoclimate data are thin but growing. With each new observation point and the development of new analytical methods to revisit earlier observations, scientists are filling in the substantial gaps in our understanding about groups of people on the move during the Upper Pleistocene and lower Holocene Periods.

In the *World on the Move* exhibition, we captured the general flows and approximate timeframes for the earliest human settlements around the world (Figure 4.1). Previous conventional wisdom held that early modern humans dispersed from Africa and outcompeted other indigenous hominin populations due to superior intellectual capacities that were assumed to accompany a larger brain (e.g., Stringer and Andrews 1988). This replacement view has given way, based on new and improved genetic analyses of ancient DNA, to one of assimilation and hybridization due to interbreeding with other hominin species, Neanderthals and Denisovans in particular.

The best combination of evidence suggests that population dispersal and expansion first went from Africa to the Arabian Peninsula. From there, further expansion went north and westward onto the European continent and, at the same time, eastward along coastal routes through the Indian subcontinent and toward Southeast Asia (or Sunda, a pre-Ice Age land mass). One flow of expansion from Southeast Asia then went further south and east across Indonesia to the combined, Pleistocene landmass of Australia and New Guinea (or Sahul). At the same time, another flow moved northeast through present-day China and eventually, further northward toward Siberia. Movement to the east across Beringia followed, and then, within a relatively compressed timeframe, settlements appeared all along the Pacific coast of the Americas.

World on the Move: 250,000 Years of Human Migration, First Edition. Edward Liebow, James I. Deutsch, Daniel Ginsberg, Sojin Kim, and Caitlyn Kolhoff.
© 2025 John Wiley & Sons, Inc. Published 2025 by John Wiley & Sons, Inc.

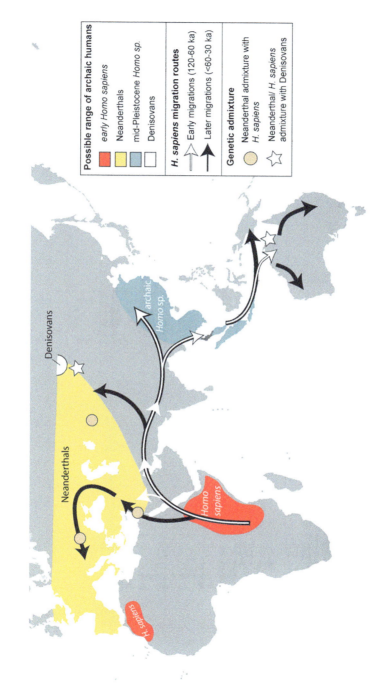

Figure 4.1 Early dispersal routes out of Africa. Source: Bae et al. 2017a, reprinted courtesy of the Wenner–Gren Foundation for Anthropological Research.

THE PEOPLING OF EUROPE, AUSTRALASIA, AND THE PACIFIC

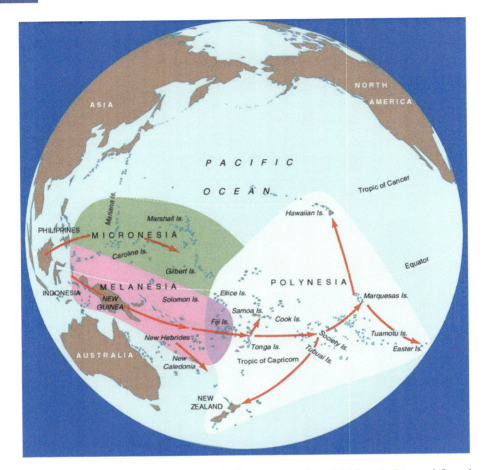

Figure 4.2 Settlement of the Pacific Islands of Micronesia and Melanesia. Dispersal flowed along routes from Southeast Asia across vast stretches of open water. Source: Map courtesy of David Eccles (Wikimedia Commons, CC BY 4.0).

The most recent places to be settled in this global migration flow were from Southeast Asia to the Pacific Island regions of Melanesia, Micronesia, and Polynesia (Figure 4.2).

Into the Arabian Peninsula

A growing body of evidence indicates two main routes into the Arabian Peninsula: (1) a northern land route along the western shore of the Red Sea, across the Sinai Peninsula to the southern Levant, then to the Arabian Peninsula; and (2) a southern route that involved crossing the Bab el-Mandeb Strait in Djibouti and Eritrea, then eastward to Yemen (Petraglia et al. 2018).

Armitage et al. (2011) point to the Jebel Faya archaeological site, in the current United Arab Emirates (the eastern coast of the Arabian Peninsula), as evidence of early human movement along the southern coast of the Arabian Peninsula about 125,000 years ago. This site is located near the Strait of Hormuz, which separates the Persian Gulf from the Gulf of Oman at the north end of the Indian Ocean. A rock shelter and its accompanying stone tools, first excavated between 2003 and 2010, were assigned these early dates based on the tools' appearances. No fossilized skeletal remains were found at the site. The site appears to have been occupied through multiple eras from 38,000 to 15,000 years ago. Through careful analysis of ancient sea-level heights, evidence of wet and dry humidity cycles, and fluctuations in oxygen isotopes captive in sea floor core samples, the authors suggest that the initial expansion of anatomically modern humans occurred at this early date (125,000 years ago). At this point the sea level was extremely low, and it was possible to cross the Bab el-Mandeb Strait at the southern end of the Red Sea (from what is now Djibouti and Eritrea) into Yemen. Armitage and colleagues further suggest that once groups of people had crossed into southern Arabia, they "would have experienced decreased predation and competition for resources. Southern Arabia may have become a secondary center for human population growth" (2011, p. 455). Two stretches of time when the climate in southern Arabia was much wetter (135,000–120,000 years ago and 82,000–78,000 years ago) may have made it possible to move through the interior of the Arabian Peninsula as well as the along the coastline (Rosenberg et al. 2011). Lower sea levels between 75,000 and 14,000 years ago would have provided a land connection between southeastern Arabia and Iran (Hill et al. 2022). A corridor at the southern end of the Persian Gulf would have opened up for humans and game animals, and very old sites like those at Jebel Faya might have been reoccupied after having remained vacant for long stretches of time (Erlandson and Braje 2015).

Breeze et al. (2016) discuss a northern land route out of Africa and onto the Arabian Peninsula. Their observations rely on *Homo sapiens* fossils found distributed in the Levant region (modern day Middle East) along with stone tools. Combining the geographical distribution of these sites with paleoenvironmental records, they suggested that freshwater was available to provide several opportunities for people and game animals to move along corridors through otherwise hostile desert areas. In addition, some permanent watercourses in the Nile and Euphrates River corridors would have supported movement along possible dispersal routes through much of the Pleistocene Period (2016, p. 174).

After Breeze and colleagues published their comprehensive study, an important report about an even earlier occupation (between 177,000 and 194,000 years ago) was published by Hershkovitz et al. (2018). They reported finding a human jawbone associated with a characteristic set of stone tools that they believe represent the earliest fossil evidence of *H. sapiens* out of Africa. Because of the Misliya Cave complex's location in the Levant (in modern day Israel), this further supports the view put forth by Breeze and colleagues for a northern land-based route, conditions permitting, along the western side of the Red Sea and across the Sinai Peninsula into the Levant.

Misliya excavation site and cave. Source: Photos by Mina Weinstein-Evron, University of Haifa.

Into Europe

Groups of people moved from the Levant at the eastern end of the Mediterranean basin into Europe beginning at least 45,000 years ago (Mylopotamitaki et al. 2024; Pederzani et al. 2024). There were other hominins living in this European region earlier, most notably Neanderthals. Neanderthals persisted until at least 40,000 years ago (leaving as much as a 5,000-year overlap after the first *H. sapiens* arrived) with strong genetic evidence that the first European humans interbred with Neanderthals during this time (Hajdinjak et al. 2021). Hajdinjak and her colleagues note that the skeletal remains of anatomically modern humans have been found together with archaeological artifacts distributed across Europe from western England to Poland, Bulgaria, and Ukraine. These remains can be dated with confidence to the period more than 40,000 years ago. Additional sites with modern humans in the period from 30,000 to 39,000 years ago are found in Italy, Belgium, Germany, and western Russia (Hajdinjak et al. 2021, p. 254). The geographic range of Neanderthal archaeological sites completely overlaps with the range of sites that involve *H. sapiens* (Hajdinjak et al. 2021, p. 256).

Importantly, recent research reports correct an earlier view held by scientists about the movement of humans into Europe in a single wave. As reported in a news story, new evidence from a site in Germany called "Ranis", when added to human remains found in Bulgaria and the Czech Republic, "suggests that rather than a single wave, small groups of modern humans moved from Africa into Europe *piecemeal* (emphasis added) starting about 48,000 years ago, overlapping with Neanderthals for many millennia" (Curry 2024, p. 469).

In other words, although earlier forays into Europe were recorded, genetic evidence suggests that they did not leave a significant contribution to later populations. There is a time gap of some 20,000 years before the more stable settlement of Europe and western Asia began. The Persian plateau is now thought to be the region in which a population settled for this 20,000-year period before multiple population waves began moving westward into Europe and eastward into South and East Asia (Vallini et al. 2024).

Into South and East Asia

As we learn from the scholars who assembled at a special 2016 symposium on the human colonization of Asia in the Late Pleistocene (Bae et al. 2017a, 2017b), Asia is an important but understudied region in our quest to understand the early population movements that eventually led to the peopling of Australia, the Americas, and the South Pacific Islands. In the first two decades of the twenty-first century, researchers have found an extensive presence of Neanderthals beyond Europe into Siberia (Krause et al. 2007) as well as other archaic hominins such as Denisovans (Stoneking and Delfin 2010) and *H. floresiensis* (Brown et al. 2004). Archaeological evidence, along with at least one fossilized skeletal part, suggests that *H. sapiens* arrived in China while Neanderthals were still there (Liu et al. 2015; Michel et al. 2016; Yang et al. 2017). There is also clear genetic evidence that the arriving *H. sapiens* immigrants interbred with these other hominins (Fu et al. 2014).

The initial dispersal routes that brought people into Asia from the Arabian Peninsula are thought to have seen movement in a series of separate waves (Shriner et al. 2016) and likely followed a coastal route along the northern shore of the Indian Ocean (Armitage et al. 2011). The archaeological and genetic evidence available to confirm these routes and their timing is thin, and it grows even thinner as one moves further east into China. Wang et al. (2021) report that only two pre-Ice Age, fossilized human remains have been found in East Asia, one from 40,000 years ago in Tianyuan Cave, China (Yang et al. 2017) and one from 35,000 years ago in Salkhit, Mongolia (Massilani et al. 2020).

With relatively little fossil evidence between the mouth of the Euphrates River in southern Iraq and these two individuals (many thousands of miles to the east in China and Mongolia), the question of what ancient routes were taken to cover this distance is important to answer, as it will direct researchers where to look for further evidence to confirm or challenge our current understanding.

For example, Clarkson et al. (2020) have acknowledged that the fossil record is non-existent for a key time period around an important volcanic eruption known as the Toba event (Petraglia et al. 2007). The Toba volcano, located on what is today the Indonesian island of Sumatra, erupted about 74,000 years ago. It is said to have been the largest volcanic eruption of the past 100,000 years, with an atmospheric release of roughly 1,000 times the volume of material in the 1980s eruption of Mount St. Helens (Robcock et al. 2009). The widely deposited ash layer from this eruption provides a clear dating benchmark for archaeological materials. Clarkson et al. (2020) report on an assemblage of stone tools in the Middle Son River Valley of Madhya Pradesh in northern India that began before this eruption and lasted until well afterward. This tool assemblage is taken as clear evidence of *H. sapiens* in the region as early as 80,000 years ago. Petraglia et al. (2007) report on a similar stone tool assemblage at the Jwalapuram archaeological site in the Jurreru River Valley of Andhra Pradesh in southern India.

To repeat for emphasis, almost all scientific judgments about the appearance of *H. sapiens* in the Indian subcontinent are based on stone tool assemblages and other archaeological materials, not fossilized skeletal remains (Bar-Yosef and Belfer-Cohen 2013). While the stone tool assemblages found in northern and southern India are much earlier, the earliest definitive *H. sapiens* skeletal remains on the Indian subcontinent were found in a Sri Lankan cave site and dated to between 36,000 and 28,000 years ago, according to Blinkhorn and Petraglia (2017, p. S468).

There seems to be a fork in the road of dispersal routes beyond India to the north and south. Wang et al. (2021) used a combination of genetic and linguistic evidence to investigate population splits and gene flows over time. They conclude that "much of East Asian ancestry can be derived from... two ancient populations: one from the same lineage as the ~40,000-year-old Tianyuan [individual] and the other from the same lineage as Indigenous Andaman Islanders (Onge)" (Wang et al. 2021, p. 414).

The present-day Andaman Islanders live in a remote Bay of Bengal archipelago that is about 80 miles (130 km) off the coast of Myanmar. While no skeletal remains have been found that date to this early period, genetic analyses conducted by Endicott and colleagues suggest that the isolated Andaman Islander group is descended from some of the earliest people arriving in South Asia, perhaps as long as $63,000 \pm 6,000$ years ago (Endicott et al. 2003, p. 182).

The Japanese archipelago, east of mainland China, is at the terminus of one dispersal route for early human populations on the move. As summarized by Nakazawa (2017), the fossil record in Japan contains only modern *H. sapiens*, with specimens dated to between 40,000 and 38,000 years ago. In addition, a considerable record of archaeological sites throughout the main islands of contemporary Japan indicate that early humans began arriving at about this time.

How they got there is still subject to discussion. Nakazawa summarizes research that hypothesizes several possible routes from Korea, from the Russian Far East, and from China (either directly or through Taiwan). All of these routes require advanced nautical skills and boat construction knowledge, even during the Pleistocene Ice Age period when the sea level had dropped by 100 meters (330 feet) or more. Ikeya (2015) provides a detailed analysis of obsidian tools brought from an offshore island as early as 38,000 years ago, an indication that marine transportation was active then. He suggests that dugout canoes and leather-clad canoes would be superior for navigating inter-island ocean currents compared with rafts (2015, p. 372).

Into Southeast Asia and Indonesia

Moving further to the southeast from India and China, fossil data have recently established that people were present on the Indochinese Peninsula as early as 70,000 years ago (Demeter et al. 2017; Westaway et al. 2017). Stone tools and shell fish hooks have been dated on the Indonesian island of East Timor to 42,000 years ago (Marwick et al. 2016). Carro and her colleagues summarize two distinct models that have been used to explain how early human population groups arrived in Southeast Asia: the two-layer and regional continuity models (Carro et al. 2019, p. 2). In the first model

(McColl et al. 2018), archaeological, fossil, and linguistic data are used to suggest that there was an early wave of colonists found in territory extending from China and Japan all the way to Australia, followed by a much later wave of people in the same area who share genetic characteristics with people living in the region today. This second wave of movement would have been possible due to the Pleistocene Ice Age (between 26,000 and 15,000 years ago) when there was a drop in the sea level of up to 135 meters (442 feet). Such a dramatic drop in sea levels would have facilitated movement along what is today the Indonesia archipelago. In addition, it is assumed that the Ice Age also changed the plant cover, wildlife, and fisheries, which likely propelled further movement of people.

The regional continuity model uses morphological, genetic, and archaeological data to suggest that the northern and southern regions of Eastern Asia remained quite separate from one another, rather than indicating that the southern regions were initially populated by intrusion or replacement from the northern region (Pietrusewsky 2010). In other words, the fork in the road – that had some population groups go north into mainland China and on to Japan, far eastern Siberia, and Beringia, while others headed to the southeast and on to Indonesia, New Guinea, and Australia – happened much longer ago than previously thought, with people arriving in Sumatra between 73,000 and 63,000 years ago (Westaway et al. 2017).

Into Australia

Australia and New Guinea were once part of the same landmass as Antarctica, forming a large continent that geologists call "Gondwana" (Torsvik et al. 2013). Fossilized remains of dinosaurs and ancient marsupials have been found in both Australia and Antarctica. Gondwana began to split about 85 million years ago, and by about 30 million years ago, Australia and New Guinea formed the landmass called "Sahul," which was completely separate from other land masses.

New Guinea and Australia remained connected by land until about 10,000 years ago, when the glacial ice retreated and rising sea levels separated Australia from New Guinea and Tasmania. For the whole time that people have been on the planet, mainland Australia has been an island continent (or part of an island continent, together with New Guinea and Tasmania), with at least 70 km (40 miles) of water separating it from the next nearest land. Archaeological and fossilized skeletal remains found at several locations in northern, western, and southern Australia suggest that anatomically modern humans arrived on the continent between 72,000 and 51,000 years ago (Malaspinas et al. 2016; Clarkson et al. 2017). By about 47,000 years ago, genomic evidence from Indigenous Australians indicates a divergence from Papua New Guinean and Eurasian groups (Silcocks et al. 2023).

Balme (2013) makes a convincing argument based on paleogeological and environmental evidence that, even with significantly lower sea levels than we have observed in later periods, people crossing the water some 50,000 years ago would have required boats. These boats were probably made of wood or bamboo lashed together with cordage made of stripped bamboo or other plant fibers. Since these materials would not be preserved over tens of thousands of years, it is difficult to establish with any certainty what kind of boats there were or whether they were powered by sails, paddles, or both. Balme reports that although the archaeological evidence from the time of the very earliest arrivals is limited, it does not appear that these earliest immigrants subsisted on marine resources (2013, p. 71). And although the boats made of wood and plant fibers would not likely have been preserved from 50,000 years ago, Balme points to symbolic marine objects found at these early sites that suggest the maritime origins of these first immigrants would have been treasured (2013, p. 72). Evidence of the use of netting at inland lakes as long as 30,000 years ago, accompanied by depictions of netting in rock art, is further support of a seafaring heritage (2013, p. 73).

Into the Pacific Islands

The last stop on our quick tour of the human settlement of the Old World involves the Pacific Islands east of New Guinea and Australia. Perhaps the most comprehensive summary of the history of human settlement in the Pacific Islands remains Patrick Kirch's book, *On the Road of the Winds: An Archaeological History of the Pacific Islands Before European Contact* (Kirch 2000). Kirch's scholarship has since been updated (Kirch and Rallu 2007; Matisoo-Smith 2012; Kirch 2017), and Matisoo-Smith (2015) adds an excellent overview of evidence from ancient DNA.

Australia, New Guinea, and the Solomon Islands off the northeast coast of New Guinea are referred to as "near Oceania," and were probably settled between 65,000 and 30,000 years ago, as we have noted above. "Remote Oceania," a term first coined by Ralph Green (1991), includes all the islands east of the Solomons and extends to Micronesia and Polynesia, as far east as Hawai'i. As Kirch (2017) and Matisoo-Smith (2012) have observed, human settlement in the near Oceania region is much more recent. A cultural group referred to as the Lapita—characterized by pottery designs, domesticated plants and animals, and buildings on stilts—appeared in the Bismarck archipelago around 3,500 years ago and then across a large stretch of open ocean to Samoa and Tonga.

It is not clear precisely where the Lapita cultural complex originated, but based mainly on linguistic evidence, Robert Blust (1996) offers support for the view that Indigenous Taiwanese language is the source of the languages found throughout the Pacific, so this may also be the source of Lapita culture. Movement across the water continued from Samoa and Tonga to the rest of Polynesia, including Hawai'i by around 1,200 years ago and Rapa Nui (Easter Island) and Aotearoa (New Zealand) by around 800 years ago.

Although human remains are relatively scarce due to the wet tropical environment of the Pacific, the introduction of ancient DNA evidence in 2015–2016 (Matisoo-Smith 2015; Skoglund et al. 2016; Friedlaender and Tucci 2020) has helped researchers piece together the sequence of island-to-island navigation and settlement. And what navigation skills have been involved! Settling these remote islands and actively maintaining social and economic relationships among them involved advanced nautical expertise many centuries before seafaring Europeans and Africans took to the seas out of the sight of land.

THE PEOPLING OF EUROPE, AUSTRALASIA, AND THE PACIFIC

Pacific Islanders navigated their open-ocean voyages without compass, sextant, or other instruments, using instead their observations of the stars, the sun, ocean currents, birds, and other signs from nature to fix their position and course toward a destination. The local knowledge accumulated into oral traditions committed to memory, but by the early nineteenth century much of this traditional navigational knowledge had been lost (Kirch 2017, p. 204). In the mid-twentieth century some observers, most notably Thor Heyerdahl (1952) and Andrew Sharp (1956), proposed that the Polynesians had drifted on ocean currents with prevailing winds, arriving at the islands they settled mostly by chance.

Even at the time, researchers did not take these claims of unintentional drift seriously, and a comprehensive account of Lapita seafaring has been the life's work of archaeologist Geoffrey Irwin (e.g., Irwin 1992, 1998, 2008). Although the actual design of seafaring canoes is difficult to know in the absence of archaeological evidence, Irwin is convinced by experiment and ethnographic analogy that the canoes were probably equipped with outriggers, and they were big enough, safe enough, and fast enough to support movements across large expanses of open ocean. What enabled effective long-distance nautical exploration was a predictable pattern of winds at certain latitudes near the equator, with prevailing east-to-west trade winds that reliably reverse at certain times of the year (the summer monsoon and episodes of El Niño). Sailing vessels could sail on the westerlies to the east and then return on the prevailing trade winds. The band of trade-wind latitudes could be gauged by the sun during the day, stars at night, and surface markers of ocean currents. As long as the sailors stayed in the proper latitude range, they did not need to know their longitude.

Master navigator Mau Pialug and the Hōkūle'a. Micronesian master navigator Mau Piailug teaches his son Stan how to navigate using the stars as a compass, 1983. Piailug helped revive traditional ocean voyaging among young people in the Pacific. In 1976 Mau Pialug guided the traditional Hawaiian double-hull canoe *Hōkūle'a* (star of gladness) on a 2,300-mile voyage without navigation instruments. *Left,* photo by Steve Thomas; *right,* photo by Na'alehu Anthony, courtesy of the Polynesian Voyaging Society and 'ŌIWI TV.

Chapter Summary

In this chapter we have reviewed the archaeological, genetic, and paleoenvironmental evidence that points us to the routes that human population groups followed in dispersing from Africa, first to the Arabian Peninsula and then to Europe, Asia, Australia, and the Pacific Islands. This dispersal and geographic expansion appear to have taken place in waves rather than all at once. The timing of these waves of movement coincides with major global climate changes that changed the ranges of vegetation and wildlife and caused fluctuations in sea levels that, in turn, made it possible to cross territories that were submerged at times. It is also likely that humans became accomplished seafarers as long as 50,000 years ago, which enabled them to cross open waters and settle in Australia and the Japanese archipelago by 30,000 years ago. Later nautical accomplishments enabled the exploration and settlement of vast stretches of the Pacific Islands, well before the Mediterranean and transatlantic voyages of recorded history.

The earliest arrivals of anatomically modern humans in Europe and Central Asia were between 70,000 and 45,000 years ago, and during this period, people were not moving into empty lands along these dispersal routes. Instead, a growing body of evidence indicates that they encountered populations of archaic hominins, Neanderthals and Denisovans in particular. Interbreeding is apparent from recent analyses of ancient DNA, which leads us to reconsider an earlier view that humans replaced these archaic hominin groups. It is now evident that mixing between humans and our predecessor species was more common than scientists previously thought.

Review Questions

1. Compared to the initial migration of humans out of Africa, there is less evidence available to confirm the migration routes that brought people into Asia from the Arabian Peninsula, and the record grows even thinner as one moves further east into China. Why do you think that is?
2. What are the main global environmental changes that have caused gradual but dramatic changes in sea levels over many thousands of years? How do scientists think that changes in ancient sea levels affected human population movements into Southeast Asia, Indonesia, Melanesia, and Australia?
3. What is the difference between Thor Heyerdahl's hypothesis for how the islands of the southern Pacific were first populated and the view of other observers such as Geoffrey Irwin? What evidence is used to support these differing perspectives?

References

Armitage, Simon J, Sabah A Jasim, Anthony E Marks, et al. 2011. The southern route "Out of Africa": Evidence for an early expansion of modern humans into Arabia. *Science* 331: 453–456. https://doi.org/10.1126/science1199113.

Bae, Christopher J, Katerina Douka, and Michael D Petraglia. 2017a. Human colonization of Asia in the late pleistocene: Introduction to supplement 17. *Current Anthropology* 58(S17): S373–S382. https://doi.org/10.1086/694420.

Bae, Christopher J, Katerina Douka, and Michael D Petraglia. 2017b. On the origin of modern humans: Asian perspectives. *Science* 358: eaai9067. https://doi.org/10.1126/science.aai9067.

Balme, Jane. 2013. Of boats and string: the maritime colonization of Australia. *Quaternary International* 285: 68–75. https://doi.org/10.1016/j.quaint.2011.02.029.

Bar-Yosef, Ofer, and Anna Belfer-Cohen. 2013. Following Pleistocene road signs of human dispersals across Eurasia. *Quaternary International* 285: 30–43. https://doi.org/10.1016/j.quaint.2011.07.043.

Blinkhorn, James, and Michael D Petraglia. 2017. Environments and cultural change in the Indian subcontinent: Implications for the dispersal of *Homo sapiens* in the Late Pleistocene. *Current Anthropology* 58(S17): S463–S479. https://doi.org/0.1086/693462.

Blust, Robert. 1996. Austronesian culture history: The window of language. *Transactions of the American Philosophical Society* 86(5): 28–35. https://doi.org/10.2307/1006619.

Breeze, Paul S, Huw S Groucutt, Nick A Drake, et al. 2016. Palaeohydrological corridors for hominin dispersals in the Middle East ~250–70,000 years ago. *Quaternary Science Reviews* 144: 155–185. https://doi.org/10.1016/j.quascirev.2016.05.012.

Brown, Peter, Thomas Sutikna, Mathew W Morwood, et al. 2004. A new small-bodied hominin from the Late Pleistocene of Flores, Indonesia. *Nature* 431: 1055–1061. https://doi.org/10.1038/nature02999.

Carro, Sofia C, Felicity Gilbert Samper, David Bulbeck, et al. 2019. Somewhere beyond the sea: Human cranial remains from the Lesser Sunda Islands (Alor Island, Indonesia) provide insights on Late Pleistocene peopling of Island Southeast Asia. *Journal of Human Evolution* 134: 102638. https://doi.org/10.1016/j.jhevol.2019.07.002.

Clarkson, Chris, Clair Harris, Bo Li, et al. 2020. Human occupation of northern India spans the Toba super-eruption ~74,000 years ago. *Nature Communications* 11: 961. https://doi.org/10.1038/s41467-020-14668-4.

Clarkson, Chris, Zenobia Jacobs, Ben Warwick, et al. 2017. Human occupation of northern Australia by 65,000 years ago. *Nature* 547: 306–310. https://doi.org/10.1038/nature22968.

Curry, Andrew. 2024. In Europe, an early, cold dawn for modern humans. *Science*. 383(6682): 468–469. https://doi.org/10.1126/science.ado3858.

Demeter, Fabrice, Laura Shackelford, Kira Westaway, et al. 2017. Early modern humans from Tam Pà Ling, Laos: Fossil review and perspectives. *Current Anthropology* 58(S17): S527–S538. https://doi.org/10.1086/694192.

Endicott, M, Thomas Gilbert, Chris Stringer, et al. 2003. The genetic origins of the Andaman Islanders. *American Journal of Human Genetics* 72(1): 178–184. https://doi.org/10.1086/345487.

Erlandson, Jon M, and Todd J Braje. 2015. Coasting out of Africa: The potential of mangrove forests and marine habitats to facilitate human coastal expansion via the Southern Dispersal Route. *Quaternary International* 382: 31–41. https://doi.org/10.1016/j.quaint.2015.03.046.

Friedlaender, Jonathan S, and Serena Tucci. 2020. Human migrations: Tales of the Pacific. *Current Biology* 30(24): 4846–4856.e6. https://doi.org/10.1016/j.cub.2020.11.008.

Fu, Qiaomei, Heng Li, Priya Moorjani, et al. 2014. Genome sequence of a 45,000-year-old modern human from western Siberia. *Nature* 514(7523): 445–449. https://doi.org/10.1038/nature13810.

Hajdinjak, Mateja, Fabrizio Mafessoni, Laurits Skov, et al. 2021. Initial Upper Palaeolithic humans in Europe had recent Neanderthal ancestry. *Nature* 592: 253–257. https://doi.org/10.1038/s41586-021-03335-3.

Hershkovitz, Israel, Gerhard W Weber, Rolf Quam, et al. 2018. The earliest modern humans outside Africa. *Science* 359: 456–459. https://doi.org/10.1126/science.aap8369.

Hill, Jon, Alexandros Avdis, Geoff Bailey, and Kurt Lambeck. 2022. Sea-level change, palaeotidal modelling and hominin dispersals: The case of the southern Red Sea. *Quaternary Science Reviews* 293: 107719. https://doi.org/10.1016/j.quascirev.2022.107719.

Ikeya, Nobuyuki. 2015. Maritime transport of obsidian in Japan during the Upper Paleolithic. In Yousuke Kaifu, Masami Izuho, Ted Goebel, Hiroyuki Sato, and Akira Ono, eds. *Emergence and diversity of modern human behavior in Paleolithic Asia.* College Station: Texas A&M Press. pp. 362–375. https://www.researchgate.net/publication/309346744_Maritime_Transport_of_Obsidian_in_japan_during_the_Upper_Paleolithic, accessed 6 Feb 2024.

Irwin, Geoffrey. 1992. *The Prehistoric Exploration and Colonization of the Pacific.* Cambridge: Cambridge University Press. https://doi.org/10.1017/CBO9780511518225.

Irwin, Geoffrey. 1998. The colonization of the Pacific: Chronological, navigational, and social issues. *Journal of the Polynesian Society* 107: 111–143. http://www.jstor.org/stable/20706789.

Irwin, Geoffrey. 2008. Pacific seascapes, canoe performance, and a review of Lapita voyaging with regard to theories of migration. *Asian Perspectives* 47(1): 12–27. https://doi.org/10.1353/asi.2008.0002.

Kirch, Patrick V. 2017. *On the Road of the Winds: An archaeological history of the Pacific Islands before European contact.* 2nd ed. Berkeley: University of California Press. https://www.jstor.org/stable/10.1525/j.ctv1xxsng.

Kirch, Patrick V, and Jean-Louis Rallu, eds. 2007. *The Growth and Collapse of Pacific Island Societies: Archaeological and demographic perspectives.* Honolulu: University of Hawai'i Press. https://www.jstor.org/stable/j.ctt6wqwnc.

Krause, Johannes, Ludovic Orlando, David Serre, et al. 2007. Neanderthals in Central Asia and Siberia. *Nature* 449(7164): 902–904. https://doi.org/10.1038/nature06193.

Liu, Wu, María Martinón-Torres, Yan-Jun Cai, et al. 2015. The earliest unequivocally modern humans in southern China. *Nature* 526(7575): 696–699. https://doi.org/10.1038/nature15696.

Malaspinas, Anna-Sapfo, Michael C Westaway, Craig Muller, et al. 2016. A genomic history of Aboriginal Australia. *Nature* 538(7624): 207–214. https://doi.org/10.1038/nature18299.

Marwick, Ben, Chris Clarkson, Sue O'Connor, and Sophie Collins. 2016. Early modern human lithic technology from Jerimalai, East Timor. *Journal of Human Evolution* 101: 45–64. https://dx.doi.org/10.1016/j.jhevol.2016.09.004.

Massilani, Diyendo, Laurits Skov, Mateja Hajdinjak, et al. 2020. Denisovan ancestry and population history of early East Asians. *Science* 370(6516): 579–583. https://doi.org/10.1126/science.abc1166.

Matisoo-Smith, Elizabeth. 2012. On the Great Blue Highway: Human migration in the Pacific. In M Crawford, and B Campbell, eds. *Why Do We Migrate? An Interdisciplinary Exploration of Human Migration.* New York: Cambridge University Press. pp. 388–416. https://doi.org/10.1017/CBO9781139003308.022.

Matisoo-Smith, Elizabeth. 2015. Ancient DNA and the human settlement of the Pacific: A review. *Journal of Human Evolution* 79: 93–104. https://doi.org/10.1016/j.jhevol.2014.10.017.

McColl, Hugh, Fernando Racimo, Lasse Vinner, et al. 2018. The prehistoric peopling of Southeast Asia. *Science* 361: 88–92. https://doi.org/10.1126/science.aat3628.

Michel, Veronique, Hélène Valladas, Guanjun Shen, et al. 2016. The earliest modern *Homo sapiens* in China? *Journal of Human Evolution* 101: 101–104. https://doi.org/10.1016/j.jhevol.2016.07.008.

Mylopotamitaki, Dorothea, Marcel Weiss, Helen Fewlass, et al. 2024. *Homo sapiens* reached the higher latitudes of Europe by 45,000 years ago. *Nature*. https://doi.org/10.1038/s41586-023-06923-7.

Nakazawa, Yuichi. 2017. On the Pleistocene population history in the Japanese Archipelago. *Current Anthropology* 58(S17): S539–S552. https://doi.org/10.1086/694447.

Petraglia, Michael D, Paul S Breeze, and Huw S Groucutt. 2018. Blue Arabia, Green Arabia: Examining human colonization and dispersal models. In N Rasul, and I Stewart, eds. *Geological setting, palaeoenvironment and archaeology of the Red Sea*. New York: Springer. pp. 675–683. https://doi.org/10.1007/978-3-319-99408-6_30.

Petraglia, Michael, Ravi Korisettar, Nicole Boivin, et al. 2007. Middle Paleolithic assemblages from the Indian subcontinent before and after the Toba super-eruption. *Science* 317: 114–116. https://doi.org/10.1126/science.1141564.

Pietrusewsky, Michael. 2010. A multivariate analysis of measurements recorded in early and more modern crania from East Asia and Southeast Asia. *Quaternary International* 211(1-2): 42–54. https://doi.org/10.1016/j.quaint.2008.12.011.

Robcock, Alan, Caspar M Ammann, Luke Oman, et al. 2009. Did the Toba volcanic eruption of ~74ka B.P. produce widespread glaciation? *Journal of Geophysical Research: Atmospheres* 114(D10): D10107. (9pp.). https://doi.org/10.1029/2008JD011652.

Rosenberg, Thomas M, Frank Preusser, Dominik Fleitmann, et al. 2011. Humid periods in southern Arabia: Windows of opportunity for modern human dispersal. *Geology* 39: 1115–1118. https://doi.org/10.1130/G32281.1.

Shriner, Daniel, Fasil Tekola-Ayele, Adebowale Adeyemo, and Charles N Rotimi. 2016. Ancient human migration after Out-of-Africa. *Scientific Reports* 6: 26565. https://doi.org/10.1038/srep26565.

Silcocks, Matthew, Ashley Farlow, Azure Hermes, Gimuy Walubara Yidinji, et al. 2023. Indigenous Australian genomes show deep structure and rich novel variation. *Nature* 624(7992): 593–601. https://doi.org/10.1038/s41586-023-06831-w.

Skoglund, Pontus, Cosimo Posth, Kendra Sirak, et al. 2016. Genomic insights into the peopling of the Southwest Pacific. *Nature* 538: 510–513. https://doi.org/10.1038/nature19844.

Stoneking, Mark, and Frederick Delfin. 2010. The human genetic history of East Asia: Weaving a complex tapestry. *Current Biology* 20: R188–R193. https://doi.org/10.1016/j.cub.2009.11.052.

Stringer, Chris B, and Peter Andrews. 1988. Genetic and fossil evidence for the origin of modern humans. *Science* 239: 1263–1268. https://doi.org/10.1126/science.3125610.

Torsvik, Trond H, L Robin, and M Cocks. 2013. Gondwana from top to base in space and time. *Gondwana Research* 24(3-4): 999–1030. https://doi.org/10.1016/j.gr.2013.06.012.

Vallini, Leonardo, Carlo Zampieri, Mohamed Javad Shoaee, et al. 2024. The Persian Plateau served as hub for *Homo sapiens* after the main Out of Africa dispersal. *Nature Communications* 15: article #1882. https://doi.org/10.1038/s41467-024-46161-7.

Wang, Chuan-Chao, Hui-Yuan Yeh, Alexander N Popov, et al. 2021. Genomic insights into the formation of human populations in East Asia. *Nature* 591: 413–419. https://doi.org/10.1038/s41586-021-03336-2.

Westaway, K E, J Louys, R D Awe, et al. 2017. An early modern human presence in Sumatra 73,000-63,000 years ago. *Nature* 548: 322–325. https://doi.org/10.1038/nature23452.

Yang, Melinda A, Xing Gao, Christoph Theunert, et al. 2017. 40,000 year-old individual from Asia provides insight into early population structure in Eurasia. *Current Biology* 27(20): 3202–3208.e9. https://doi.org/10.1016/j.cub/2017.09.030.

5

Peopling of the Americas

Just as archaeologists, geneticists, linguists, and other scientists continue to debate the chronology and circumstances by which our human ancestors left the continent of Africa and migrated into Europe, Australasia, and the Pacific (see Chapters 3 and 4), so too the chronology and circumstances remain uncertain for the peopling of the Americas. However, what we do know is that humans arrived in the Americas many thousands of years after they had already settled the other world continents. "Apart from Antarctica, the Americas were the last of Earth's major land masses to be glimpsed by human eyes" (Andersen 2021, p. 75).

This chapter will provide an overview of the major research and scholarship that has shaped our emerging understanding of when and how people arrived in what is North and South America today. Admittedly, new discoveries in the twenty-first century continually revise our understanding of how people arrived and spread. What is becoming increasingly clear is that the peopling of the Americas was not a single, straightforward journey but rather a series of events that occurred multiple times via multiple routes.

As noted in our *World on the Move* exhibition, archaeologists once thought the earliest humans to the Americas came on foot across a now-submerged Bering land bridge that connected the two continents of Asia and North America and is part of the crossroads region known as Beringia (Meltzer 2021). However, a series of archaeological excavations in the late twentieth and early twenty-first centuries have completely upended what we thought we knew about the peopling of the Americas. As a result, most researchers now believe that the first migrants to the Americas were maritime explorers from northeastern Asia who (perhaps as long as 20,000 years ago) made their way by boat south along the Pacific coast, even reaching southernmost Chile around 14,500 years ago. A growing list of ancient coastal sites in both North America and South America supports this theory (Figure 5.1).

World on the Move: 250,000 Years of Human Migration, First Edition. Edward Liebow, James I. Deutsch, Daniel Ginsberg, Sojin Kim, and Caitlyn Kolhoff.
© 2025 John Wiley & Sons, Inc. Published 2025 by John Wiley & Sons, Inc.

PEOPLING OF THE AMERICAS

Figure 5.1 Key paleoarchaeology sites in North America. Source: *Wade* 2017.

Of course, the seafaring theory does not refute the existence of the Bering land bridge, which dominated the thinking of scientists and researchers for several centuries and may account for even more migrants to the Americas than by various sea routes, particularly to the interior of the continent. Precisely when this land bridge existed remains a matter of debate, with estimates ranging from 50,000 to 15,000 years ago – though recent sources suggest 36,000 to 19,000 years ago (Farmer et al. 2022). We do not know who the first humans were to migrate by foot across Beringia or why they chose to do so – other than the speculation that they were following game animals in an expanded range or seeking new regions to explore. However, we do know that the migration was not just in one direction. According to John Hoffecker's wide-ranging study of global dispersal, the "genetic and linguistic data suggest movements in both directions" between northeast Asia and Alaska (Hoffecker 2017, p. 305).

Whether by land or by sea, the peopling of the Americas resulted from climate change "triggered by the retreat of the massive glaciers that had covered most of northern North America, opening up a coastal and – somewhat later – an interior route southward after 15,000 years ago" (Hoffecker 2017, p. 305). Those first migrants were the ancestors of today's Native Americans – the Indigenous peoples of the Americas – and their achievements were extraordinary. "In only a few thousand years, they ripped down from the polar cold of northeastern Eurasia through two continents of terra incognita, which encompassed every known terrestrial biome," wrote *The Atlantic*'s senior editor for science, health, and technology. "This feat of exploration surely ranks among humanity's greatest, but the route and identity of those who achieved it remain matters of fierce dispute" (Andersen 2021, p. 74).

PERSPECTIVE: A Genetic History of the Americas, by Jennifer Raff

Associate Professor in the Department of Anthropology, University of Kansas (USA)

Genetics is a powerful tool in helping us reconstruct past population movements. In the Americas, studies of the genetic variation of contemporary Native Americans and their ancestors have revealed a complex history.

The very first people in the Americas may have entered the continents quite early – perhaps sometime before the Cordilleran and Laurentide ice sheets fused, blocking any movement out of present-day Alaska from about 23,000 years ago until after 17,000 years ago. Evidence of this potential early migration is scarce and controversial, although human footprints at the White Sands Locality 2 site in New Mexico (dated to 21,000–23,000 years ago) support an early human presence during the Last Glacial Maximum (LGM). Furthermore, many Indigenous communities have origin narratives that place them in their lands in the deep past (Bennett et al. 2021; Pigati et al. 2023). We have no direct genetic evidence from the people who made the footprints at White Sands (or any other potentially very early populations), so their biological affinities and the degree to which they contributed genetic ancestry to later Indigenous populations remain open questions in the field at present. Nevertheless, the presence of people (Ancient North Siberians, represented by the genomes of two young boys) above the Arctic Circle by 32,000 years ago at the Yana Rhinoceros Horn site raises intriguing questions about possible early migration events (Sikora et al. 2019; Pitulko et al. 2004). This is an area of active research in both archaeology and paleogenomics.

Complete genomes recovered from ancient individuals across the Americas, Siberia, and East Asia offer a biological history of the First Peoples of the Americas that begins in the Upper Paleolithic. They show us that between 25,000 and 20,000 years ago an ancient population from East Asia interacted with people related to the Ancient North Siberians, perhaps as the result of population movements related to climatic upheavals during the LGM. This gene flow event – or potentially multiple events – gave rise to the ancestors of Native Americans as well as a group that is ancestral to present-day Indigenous peoples of northeastern Siberia (Raghavan et al. 2014a).

Our best-supported genetic models suggest that ancestors of Native Americans were then isolated from all other populations for a few thousand years. We do not know where this isolation took place, as we currently have no archaeological evidence that directly links any population to this group. During the LGM people across the world retreated into climatic refugia in response to cold and arid environmental conditions. It seems reasonable to infer that the Ancestral Native American population did as well, and archaeological evidence suggests that Siberia was depopulated during this time. So where might the ancestors of Native Americans have gone? Archaeologists have suggested various locations, including southern Siberia, northern Beringia, the southern coast of central Beringia, and even within North America itself (if the White Sands site represents a pre-LGM migration of Native American ancestors). Current genetic data cannot definitively settle this question, and there are challenges to testing some areas directly. For example, paleoenvironmental data suggest that the southern region of central Beringia would have had a relatively mild climate and more resources than other portions of northern Siberia and Beringia. It also would have provided conditions necessary for the population isolation that geneticists infer from their models. However, it is difficult to explore archaeologically as this area is currently underwater. A number of candidate sites in eastern Beringia have been offered as evidence that humans were in the region during the LGM, but none so far have been widely accepted as definitive[1] (Graf and Buvit 2017).

---

[1] The earliest, firm archaeological evidence for humans in Alaska dates to 14,400 years ago, which is several thousand years after the First Peoples had already entered the Americas. This reflects the inconsistent preservation of the archaeological record and the difficulties archaeologists must contend with when developing models of human history.

However difficult it may be to identify where the ancestral population was isolated during the LGM, genetics offers hints as to what people were doing during this period, showing us that this population subdivided into several branches. What exactly caused this subdivision is unknown, but one reasonable explanation is that the population was spread across a region with some geographic barriers (or simply large distances) that slowed gene flow between groups and allowed subtle genetic differences to emerge over time.

One branch, called "Unsampled Population A," emerged while the ancestors of Native Americans were isolated about 24,700 years ago, at the same time or almost immediately after the merging of the Ancient East Asian and Ancient North Siberian populations. Unlike the Ancient Beringians, no genomes have been sequenced from any member of this group. Instead, it was indirectly identified by geneticists through its contribution to the ancestry of present-day Mixe people of Mesoamerica. It has not (yet) been identified in any North American populations (Moreno-Mayar et al. 2018a).

Another group, which geneticists have termed the "Ancient Beringians," split from other Native American populations between 23,300–21,200 years ago (Moreno-Mayar et al. 2018a). Researchers have identified individuals belonging to the Ancient Beringian population at two Late Pleistocene/Early Holocene sites in Alaska: the 11,500 year old Upward Sun River (Xaasaa Na') site and the 9,000 year old Trail Creek Caves site (Moreno-Mayar et al. 2018a, 2018b). No present-day people have yet been identified as belonging to this branch, nor have any other ancient individuals outside of Alaska. Current genetic evidence shows that contemporary Indigenous peoples of the Arctic trace their ancestry to the Holocene migrations of peoples from Siberia (Raghavan et al. 2014b; Flegontov et al. 2019), but much more work is necessary to fully understand the genetic histories of these populations.

To date, all of the genetically identified Ancient Beringians have been linked to the Denali Complex, one of several cultural traditions present in the archaeological records across the North American arctic during the Late Pleistocene and Early Holocene (Potter et al. 2014; Lee and Goebel 2016). More genetic and archaeological work is needed to draw broader conclusions about the lives and histories of Ancient Beringians, particularly whether the association between this genetically identifiable branch of Native Americans and Denali complex material culture implies an Ancient Beringian–associated cultural identity observable in the archaeological record.

The third genetically identifiable group that emerged during the LGM is ancestral to Native Americans south of the ice sheets. Members of this Ancestral Native American group form three genetically recognizable and geographically patterned lineages after about 21,000 years ago, which likely reflects early population movements south of the ice sheet (Willerslev and Meltzer 2021). The first lineage, which diverged from other Native Americans between 21,000 and 16,000 years ago, is represented by a single genome from an individual at the Big Bar site in British Columbia. The second two lineages, Northern Native Americans (NNA) and Southern Native Americans (SNA) split from each other between about 17,500 and 14,600 years ago. The NNA lineage includes Algonquian, Na-Dené, Salishan, and Tsimshian-speaking populations as well as ancient individuals from the northwest coast. SNA includes all living and ancient Indigenous peoples in North America south of Canada, Central America, and South America. Both the estimated date of divergence and the fact that NNA and SNA are equally related to the Ancient Beringians suggests that their split from each other likely took place after their shared ancestral population had moved south of the ice sheet (Moreno-Mayar et al. 2018a; Willerslev and Meltzer 2021; Rasmussen et al. 2014). Genetic evidence from ancient and contemporary members of SNA indicates that they spread very rapidly throughout North, Central, and South Americas (Moreno-Mayar et al. 2018a; Posth et al. 2018).

This genetic evidence, along with archaeological sites in the Americas dating to as early as 15,500 years ago, supports a model of initial migration by boat along the west coast by the First Peoples sometime after 17,000 years ago. Although no boats this old have been found, traveling by boat would have allowed people to expand their range southward (and return northward for visiting, conducting trade, performing ceremonies, and to find marriage partners) much faster than migrating by land. In addition, coastal resources would have been plentiful and consistently familiar to people moving into new regions, facilitating their exploration. The alternative route into the Americas, through an ice-free corridor that opened between the Laurentide and Cordilleran glaciers, would not have been available to the First Peoples until after 15,000 years ago and would have resulted in much slower movements not consistent with currently observed patterns of genetic variation (Willerslev and Meltzer 2021; Braje et al. 2020).

Currently there are many questions regarding the initial peopling of the Americas that require additional genetic data to answer. One of the most pressing is whether there was a migration prior to the LGM. Some ancient and contemporary genomes from South America have some shared genetic ancestry with Australasians, present in patterns of variation that cannot be explained by a transpacific migration (Skoglund et al. 2015). One hypothesis for this shared ancestry is a pre-LGM migration of a population that subsequently mixed with SNA peoples who moved into South America about 17,000 years ago (Moreno-Mayar et al. 2018a). Additional ancient genomes from across the Americas will be necessary to test this – and many other – hypotheses (Raff 2022). But even more important is the work that scientists in this field must do to repair relationships and regain the trust of Indigenous communities after decades of harmful research practices (Fleskes et al. 2022).

Evidence is mixed about the primacy of land versus sea routes (Potter et al. 2018). Data are not altogether conclusive, and the dispute relates in part to what archaeologists have labeled the "Clovis-first theory." For much of the twentieth century – based on the discovery of some 10,000 Clovis points found "scattered in 1,500 locations throughout most of North America" – archaeologists linked the human migration across the Bering land bridge and beyond to those points. Named for their initial discovery in Clovis, New Mexico, near the Texas Panhandle – and thus far from any sea routes – the Clovis artifacts are what *Smithsonian Magazine* has termed "slender, finger-long spear points, … sleek and often beautifully made" that "trace back 13,500 years" (Mann 2013).

Starting in the late 1930s, the Clovis-first theory hypothesized that the peopling of the Americas "began when the Clovis people made their exodus across the grassland steppe that then connected Siberia and Alaska. After the rollback of two ice sheets opened a new corridor east of the Rockies, they raced down into the North American interior" (Andersen 2021, p. 75). Using their distinctive Clovis points to hunt large mammals for sustenance, the Clovis people quickly spread throughout the heart of the Americas. The Clovis-first theory was "for decades … our anchor to understanding the peopling of the New World" and "a touchstone for archaeologists, a rare 'truth' and comfort regarding the unknowable archaeological past" (Stanford and Bradley 2012, p. 31).

One of the first cracks in the Clovis-first theory emerged in the late 1970s with the Monte Verde excavations of human habitations in southern Chile, roughly 30 miles (50 km) inland from the Pacific Ocean; a project led by Vanderbilt University archaeologist Tom Dillehay. Thanks to a peat bog covering the site, much of the archaeological evidence – including huts, wooden foundations, fire pits lined with clay, and even the remains of partially eaten food – was remarkably well-preserved. Notably absent were any Clovis points. A recent report points to archaeological evidence, including "*in situ* stone artifacts, faunal remains, and burned areas that suggests discrete horizons of ephemeral human activity radiocarbon dated between ~14,500 and possibly as early as 19,000 cal BP [years ago]" (Dillehay et al. 2015, pp. 2–3). Those early dates reinforce the likelihood that the Monte Verde inhabitants arrived there by sea and not by land.

Another important archaeological site in South America is Huaca Prieta, on Peru's Pacific coast, roughly 380 miles (600 km) north of Lima. In the 1940s archaeologist Junius Bird from the American Museum of Natural History in New York had excavated "a large preceramic mound site located on the southern tip of an ancient terrace in the present-day delta of the Chicama River Valley," which indicated the "long presence of maritime foragers and part-time horticulturalists initially radiocarbon dated between ~5,500 and 4,200 cal yr BP" (Dillehay et al. 2012, p. 418). However, subsequent archaeological work (again led by Dillehay) dug deeper beneath the surface to uncover evidence of simple stone tools made from quartzite and basalt, charred wood in fire pits, and the bones of deer, sea lions, and various birds – but no Clovis points. According to one analysis, "the new evidence from Huaca Prieta establishes that people were present on a prominent landform on a low-gradient alluvial plain between the Andean foothills and the seashore in northern Peru by ~14,200–13,300 cal yr BP" (Dillehay et al., 2012, p. 422).

The discoveries at both Monte Verde and Huaca Prieto strongly suggest that human migrants had reached those places by boat from along the Pacific coast, but a third site on the Atlantic coast of Argentina complicates the story. Known as Arroyo Seco 2, the site sits on a grassy knoll that overlooks a deep lake. It is 325 miles (520 km) south of Buenos Aires in the Pampas region, some 40 miles (65 km) from the Atlantic Ocean. Although archaeological excavations began in 1977, the work done in 2015 – by a team led by Gustavo Politis from the Universidad Nacional del Centro de la Provincia de Buenos Aires – has consolidated earlier findings. In particular, they demonstrated the presence of tools made of chert and quartzite, with which humans "hunted/scavenged an extinct horse (*Equus neogeus*) and giant ground sloth (*Megatherium americanum*)," using the stone tools to butcher and break the animal bones (Politis et al. 2016, p. 21). The earliest date for Arroyo Seco 2 is 14,064 years ago, which once again demonstrates the presence of human hunters throughout the southernmost part of South America well before the arrival of the Clovis people in the Americas. Arroyo Seco's proximity to the Atlantic coast suggests that boats may have made the passage around the southernmost tip of South America. However, archaeologists have also determined that humans may have traveled from "Pacific coastal locations and possibly to deglaciated passes through the Andes to the Argentine steppes" (Dillehay et al. 2015, pp. 21–22).

The stone tools and butchered bones found at Arroyo Seco provide solid archaeological evidence for human habitation, but even more solid evidence has emerged from Paisley Cave in southern Oregon – located some 250 miles (400 km) east of the Pacific coast, though also potentially accessible via the Klamath River. In the cave, a team led by University of Oregon archaeologist Dennis Jenkins discovered Western stemmed projectile points and human coprolites that may be 14,300 years old. The projectile points are significant because "In the American Far West, the Western Stemmed Tradition (WST) is recognized as the oldest non-fluted lithic technology" (Jenkins et al. 2012, p. 223). Because stemmed points "are morphologically and technologically distinct from the generally broader, concave-based, fluted Clovis points," archaeologists believe that the two forms "were contemporaneous and parallel – not unilinear – North American technological developments" (Jenkins et al. 2012, pp. 224, 227).

Three labs – one in Germany, one in England, and one in the United States – determined that the DNA extracted from the coprolites in the Paisley Cave were 14,300 years old, which makes this the earliest genetic evidence of human habitation in the Americas. "For the first time, we are actually radiocarbon dating human remains that are pre-Clovis," Jenkins explained. "There are older radiocarbon dates on sites in North America, but not directly on human remains" (Curry 2008, p. 44).

Even older radiocarbon dates for charcoal and bone materials – estimated at 15,500 years ago – exist at Cooper's Ferry in western Idaho, northeast of Paisley Cave. Ten years of excavations, led by Oregon State University archaeologist Loren Davis, "uncovered dozens of stone spear points, blades, and multipurpose tools called bifaces, as well as hundreds of pieces of debris from their manufacture" (Wade 2019, p. 848). Moreover, many of the spear points belong to the WST, rather than to the Clovis shape. Although Cooper's Ferry is some 300 miles from the Pacific coast, Dean believes that seafaring people could have found their way there via the Salmon, Snake, and Columbia Rivers. "As people come down the coast, the first left-hand turn to get south of the ice comes up the Columbia

River Basin," Dean told *Science* (Wade 2019, p. 849). Because "Bayesian age modeling and archaeological evidence … indicate that humans were initially present at the Cooper's Ferry site 16,560–15,280 [years ago]," this adds further evidence to the peopling of the Americas by sea, rather than by land (Davis et al., 2019, p. 895).

Pushing the oldest date for the peopling of the Americas back even further are the human footprints found imprinted in what once was a lake but is now a desert – the White Sands National Park in New Mexico (Bennett et al. 2021). According to "radiocarbon dating of seeds from the aquatic plant *Ruppia cirrhosa*," a team of researchers, led by US Geological Survey geologist Jeffrey Pigati, estimates that humans left the footprints "between ~23,000 and 21,000 years ago" (Pigati et al. 2023, p. 73). Aside from the debate surrounding the dates, the footprints reinforce the human dimensions of these archaeological discoveries. Kim Charlie, an enrolled member of the Pueblo of Acoma, not far from White Sands in New Mexico, told *Science* that she feels a strong connection "with the people who made them. 'These tracks trace back to us, back to the Indigenous people of North America'" (Wade 2023). Looking at a cluster of multiple footprints, Charlie observed, "'This was a family' [and] their footprints are 'like a photograph' … It's something they left us, saying, '*We were here*'" (Wade 2023).

Archaeological and genetic evidence are not the only sources for tracing the movements of peoples across the Americas. Linguists have analyzed the typological features of languages to demonstrate patterns of migration. For instance, linguists Mark A. Sicoli and Gary Holton compared typological features of Ket and Kott (two Yeniseian languages of Siberia) with 37 Na-Déné languages of North America that encompass the Pacific coast Athabascan, Tlingit, Eyak, and Haida. They determined that the migration of these languages was not simply from central or western Asia to North America, as might be expected, but rather "radiation out of Beringia with back-migration into central Asia" (Sicoli and Holton 2014, p. 1). As Sicoli explained to *Smithsonian Magazine*, "Growing up, I'd look at maps showing migrations to the Americas, and they'd always just show arrows going in one direction: straight across from Asia to North America… What we see now is something more complicated, because some of those arrows go back to Siberia, and it wasn't a non-stop trip" (Stromberg 2014).

In that same interview, Sicoli observed how his linguistic study "makes it look like Beringia wasn't simply a bridge, but actually a homeland – a refuge, where people could build a life" (Stromberg 2014). Indeed, building a life has long been one of the most crucial factors to explain why people are always on the move. As our exhibition *World on the Move* demonstrates, people move for many reasons – whether to start a new job, relocate closer to family or friends, or escape from forces beyond their control, such as natural disasters, urban renewal, persecution, or climate change.

As noted previously, the changes in climate that occurred tens of thousands of years ago allowed for the peopling of America – both with the emergence of a land bridge that reliably connected Asia and North America and then with the melting of glaciers that opened new migration routes along both sea and land. More climate change in the twenty-first century and beyond may profoundly affect human migration. According to a series of articles made possible by a partnership between *ProPublica* and the *New York Times Magazine*, with support from the Pulitzer Center, the outlook is grim:

> Once you accept that climate change is fast making large parts of the United States nearly uninhabitable, the future looks like this: With time, the bottom half of the country grows inhospitable, dangerous and hot. Something like a tenth of the people who live in the South and the Southwest – from South Carolina to Alabama to Texas to Southern California – decide to move north in search of a better economy and a more temperate environment (Lustgarten 2020).

In the words of another observer: "Nobody wants to migrate away from home, even when an inexorable danger is inching ever closer. They do it when there is no longer any other choice" (Lustgarten 2020).

Chapter Summary

As we have seen, the work of some of the archaeologists, geneticists, linguists, and other scientists cited here has certainly complicated – in a positive way – our understanding of migration patterns. Further research is needed to uncover archaeological sites in areas of Beringia where models predict that pathways of dispersal might be found (Graf and Buvit 2017). New discoveries in the years ahead will further complicate the chronology and circumstances by which our human ancestors peopled the Americas, and changing circumstances ahead will determine how twenty-first-century humans will exist on the globe. The fact remains that we have never stopped moving and, presumably, will remain on the move.

Review Questions

1. What has changed in recent years about our understanding of how and when migrants first came to the Americas? What evidence is this most recent understanding based on?
2. What is the relationship between prehistoric climate change and the peopling of the Americas? Given where most major population centers are currently concentrated in the Americas, how might contemporary changes in climate patterns affect the migration or displacement of people in the twenty-first century?
3. In the "Perspectives" piece by Jennifer Raff, three distinct and genetically identifiable groups appear to have emerged during the LGM. What are these groups, and why does this subdivision of groups interest scientists who are focused on reconstructing prehistoric population movements?

References

Andersen, Ross. 2021. America's Atlantis: did people first come to this continent by land or by sea? *Atlantic* 328(October): 72–81. https://www.theatlantic.com/magazine/archive/2021/10/prehistoric-america-atlantis/619819/.

Bennett, Matthew R, David Bustos, Jeffrey S Pigati, et al. 2021. Evidence of humans in North America during the last glacial maximum. *Science* 373: 1528–1531. https://doi.org/10.1126/science.abg7586.

Braje, Todd J, Jon M Erlandson, Torben C Rick, et al. 2020. Bladmark + 40: what have we learned about a potential Pacific coast peopling of the Americas? *American Antiquity* 85(1): 1–21. https://doi.org/10.1017/aaq.2019.80.

Curry, Andrew. 2008. Ancient excrement: an unexpected source of human DNA resets the clock on the settlement of the Americas. *Archaeology* 61(4): 42–45. https://archive.archaeology.org/online/features/coprolites/.

Davis, Loren G, David B Madsen, Lorena Becerra-Valdivia, et al. 2019. Late upper paleolithic occupation at Cooper's Ferry, Idaho, USA,~16,000 Years Ago. *Science* 365(6546): 891–897. https://doi.org/10.1126/science.aax9830.

Dillehay, Tom D, Duccio Bonavia, Steve L Goodbred Jr, et al. 2012. A late Pleistocene human presence at Huaca Prieta, Peru, and early Pacific Coastal adaptations. *Quaternary Review* 77(3): 418–423. https://doi.org/10.1016/j.yqres.2012.02.003.

Dillehay, Tom D, Carlos Ocampo, José Saavedra, et al. 2015. New archaeological evidence for an early human presence at Monte Verde, Chile. *PLoS ONE* 10(12): e0145471. https://doi.org/10.1371/journal.pone.0141923.

Farmer, Jesse R, Tamara Pico, Ona M Underwood, and Daniel M Sigman. 2022. The Bering Strait was flooded 10,000 years before the Last Glacial Maximum. *Proceedings of the National Academy of Sciences* 120(1). https://doi.org/10.1073/pnas.2206742119.

Flegontov, Pavel, N Ezgi Altinişik, Piya Changmai, et al. 2019. Palaeo-Eskimo genetic ancestry and the peopling of Chukotka and North America. *Nature* 570: 236–240. https://doi.org/10.1038/s41586-019-1251-y.

Fleskes, Raquel E, Alyssa C Bader, Krystal S Tsosie, et al. 2022. Ethical guidance in human paleogenomics: new and ongoing perspectives. *Annual Review of Genomics and Human Genetics* 23: 627–652. https://doi.org/10.1146/annurev-genom-120621-090239.

Graf, Kelly E, and Ian Buvit. 2017. Human dispersal from Siberia to Beringia: assessing a Beringian standstill in light of the archaeological evidence. *Current Anthropology* 58(S17): S583–S603. https://doi.org/10.1086/693388.

Hoffecker, John F. 2017. *Modern Humans: Their African Origin and Global Dispersal*. New York: Columbia University Press.

Jenkins, Dennis L, Loren G Davis, Thomas W Stafford Jr, et al. 2012. Clovis age western stemmed projectile points and human coprolites at the Paisley Caves. *Science* 337(6091): 223–228. https://doi.org/10.1126/science.1218443.

Lee, Craig, and Ted Goebel. 2016. The slotted antler points from Trail Creek Caves, Alaska: new information on their age and technology. *PaleoAmerica* 2(1): 40–47. https://doi.org/10.1080/20555563.2015.1136727.

Lustgarten, Abrahm. 2020. Climate Change will Force a New American Migration. *ProPublica*. September 15. https://www.propublica.org/article/climate-change-will-force-a-new-american-migration

Mann, Charles. 2013. The Clovis Point and the Discovery of America's First Culture. *Smithsonian Magazine* 44(7): 58–65. https://www.smithsonianmag.com/history/the-clovis-point-and-the-discovery-of-americas-first-culture-3825828/.

Meltzer, David J. 2021. *First Peoples in a New World*. 2nd ed. Cambridge: Cambridge University Press. https://doi.org/10.1017/9781108632867.

Moreno-Mayar, J Victor, Lasse Vinner, Peter De Barros Damgaard, et al. 2018a. Early human dispersals within the Americas. *Science* 362(6419): eaav2621. https://doi.org/10.1126/science.aav2621.

Moreno-Mayar, J Víctor, Ben A Potter, Lasse Vinner, et al. 2018b. Terminal Pleistocene Alaskan Genome Reveals First Founding Population of Native Americans. *Nature* 553: 203–208. https://doi.org/10.1038/nature25173.

Pigati, Jeffrey S, Kathleen B Springer, Jeffrey S Honke, et al. 2023. Independent Age Estimates Resolve the Controversy of Ancient Human Footprints at White Sands. *Science* 382(6666): 73–75. https://doi.org/10.1126/science.adh5007.

Pitulko, Vladimir V, Pavel A Nikolsky, Evgeny Yu Girya, et al. 2004. The Yana RHS site: humans in the Arctic before the Last Glacial Maximum. *Science* 303(5564): 52–56. https://doi.org/10.1126/science.1085219.

Politis, Gustavo G, María A Gutiérrez, Daniel J Rafuse, and Adriana Blasi. 2016. The Arrival of *Homo Sapiens* into the Southern Cone at 14,000 Years Ago. *pLoS ONE* 11(9): e0162870. https://doi.org/10.1371/journal.pone.0162870.

Posth, Cosimo, Nathan Nakatsuka, Iosif Lazaridis, et al. 2018. Reconstructing the deep population history of Central and South America. *Cell* 175(5): 1185–1197.e22. https://doi.org/10.1016/j.cell.2018.10.027.

Potter, Ben A, James F Baichtal, Alwynne B Beaudoin, et al. 2018. Current Evidence Allows Multiple Models for the Peopling of the Americas. *Science Advances* 4(8): eaat5473. https://doi.org/10.1126/sciadv.aat5473.

Potter, Ben A, Joel D Irish, Joshua D Reuther, and Holly J McKinney. 2014. New insights into Eastern Beringian mortuary behavior: a terminal Pleistocene double infant burial at Upward Sun River. *Proceedings of the National Academies of Science* 111(48): 17060–17065. https://doi.org/10.1073/pnas.1413131111.

Raff, Jennifer. 2022. *Origin: A Genetic History of the Americas*. New York: Twelve Books.

Raghavan, Maanasa, Michael DeGiorgio, Anders Albrechtsen, et al. 2014a. The genetic prehistory of the New World Arctic. *Science* 345(6200): 1255832. https://doi.org/10.1126/science.1255832.

Raghavan, Maanasa, Pontus Skoglund, Kelly E Graf, et al. 2014b. Upper Palaeolithic Siberian genome reveals dual ancestry of Native Americans. *Nature* 505: 87–91. https://doi.org/10.1038/nature12736.

Rasmussen, Morten, Sarah L Anzick, Michael R Waters, et al. 2014. The genome of a Late Pleistocene human from a Clovis burial site in western Montana. *Nature* 506: 225–229. https://doi.org/10.1038/nature13025.

Sicoli, Mark A, and Gary Holton. 2014. Linguistic Phylogenies Support Back-Migration from Beringia to Asia. *PLoS ONE* 9(3): e91722. https://doi.org/10.1371/journal.pone.0091722.

Sikora, Martin, Vladimir V Pitulko, Vitor C Sousa, et al. 2019. The population history of northeastern Siberia since the Pleistocene. *Nature* 570(7760): 182–188. https://doi.org/10.1038/s41586-019-1279-z.

Skoglund, Pontus, Swapan Mallick, Maria Cátira Bortolini, et al. 2015. Genetic evidence for two founding populations of the Americas. *Nature* 525: 104–108. https://doi.org/10.1038/nature14895.

Stanford, Dennis J, and Bruce A Bradley. 2012. *Across Atlantic Ice: The Origin of America's Clovis Culture*. Berkeley: University of California Press.

Stromberg, Joseph. 2014. Ancient Migration Patterns to North America Are Hidden in Languages Spoken Today. *Smithsonian Magazine*. March 14. https://www.smithsonianmag.com/science-nature/ancient-migration-patterns-north-america-are-hidden-languages-spoken-today-180950053/

Wade, Lizzie. 2017. On the trail of ancient mariners. *Science* 357(6351): 542–545. https://doi.org/10.1126/science.357.6351.542.

Wade, Lizzie. 2019. Ancient site in Idaho implies first Americans came by sea: 16,000-year-old occupation predates possible land route. *Science* 365(6456): 848–849. https://doi.org/10.1126/science.365.6456.848.

Wade, Lizzie. 2023. New footprint dates Bolster claim that humans lived in Americas during Ice Age. *Science*. (October 5) https://doi.org/10.1126/science.adl2172.

Willerslev, Eske, and David J Meltzer. 2021. Peopling of the Americas as inferred from ancient genomes. *Nature* 594: 356–364. https://doi.org/10.1038/s41586-021-03499-y.

Section 3

Why Do We Move?

People move for many reasons. Some move to attend college, to start a new job, or to be close to family and friends. Some move to build a better life or escape from poverty, conflict, persecution, or natural disasters. Some are forced to move through human trafficking and enslavement. And some are pushed aside to make room for economic development and urban renewal. Often people move for a combination of reasons, including forces beyond their control.

A family from Florida stops in North Carolina on their way to New Jersey in 1940. From 1916 to 1970, six million African Americans moved from the rural American South to cities in the North, Midwest, and West in an attempt to escape poverty and racial oppression. Source: Photo by Jack Delano, Farm Security Administration, Office of War Information Photograph Collection (Library of Congress).

World on the Move: 250,000 Years of Human Migration, First Edition. Edward Liebow, James I. Deutsch, Daniel Ginsberg, Sojin Kim, and Caitlyn Kolhoff.
© 2025 John Wiley & Sons, Inc. Published 2025 by John Wiley & Sons, Inc.

6

Movement and the Social Production of Vulnerability

This chapter reviews and complicates the conventional social demographic models that inform much of migration scholarship by highlighting patterns of cyclical movement over seasonal, annual, lifetime, and intergenerational intervals. It also highlights the widely prevalent circumstances in which the social production of vulnerabilities leaves individuals and families with no good options, which makes us skeptical about relying solely on rational choice, decision-making models for explaining migration. Using examples ranging from the formation of twentieth century megacities to the World War II exclusion and incarceration of West Coast Japanese Americans and the refugees and asylum seekers in contemporary South Asia, North America, and western Europe, we highlight how our decisions to move are usually influenced by forces beyond our control, such as where and when we were born and what political, economic, and environmental conditions are like in our area. Migrants are often forced to choose between equally bad options. Stay and you may face difficulties and danger. Leave and you may face an uncertain future in a place you know nothing about and where you know no one.

Conventional Models of Migration

Places of origin and destination and push–pull factors

The most common way to describe patterns of movement involves sender regions, also known as places of origin, and receiver regions, or places of destination. This origin–destination binary requires an assumption that movement follows a linear

World on the Move: 250,000 Years of Human Migration, First Edition. Edward Liebow, James I. Deutsch, Daniel Ginsberg, Sojin Kim, and Caitlyn Kolhoff.
© 2025 John Wiley & Sons, Inc. Published 2025 by John Wiley & Sons, Inc.

pattern, with individuals, households, or whole communities that leave point A and arrive at point B, a new destination where they settle into residence. Analysis of this point A-to-B mobility and its impacts then looks at the magnitude of out-migration (how many people, or what percentage of the place-of-origin's population), selectivity (who leaves and who remains), and how their arrival in a new destination affects the size, composition, and density of the population that hosts them. This linear pattern of movement has an underlying assumption that people usually move from point A to point B, and once they get to point B, they stay there. What is discounted or dismissed altogether are the places that people pass through while on the move, variable lengths of stay at interim and ultimate destinations, and cyclical patterns of return to places of origin.

Usually accompanying the over-simplified origin–destination pattern of movement is an explanation for the causes of individual and population movements that refers to push and pull factors. Push factors are reasons that people may move away from their homes, including poverty, lack of social mobility, violence, or persecution. Pull factors are reasons that people might be drawn to settle in a particular locale away from their former homes. These factors might include higher wages, a more affordable cost of living, the availability of social services such as education or health care, or the prospect of a greater tolerance for diverse lifestyles.

In addition to assuming that people usually move from a place of origin to a place of destination and stay there, the linear pattern of movement further assumes that such a move is governed by a rational choice model of decision making. In other words, it is often assumed that people make an active choice to move, they have accurate information available about the advantages and disadvantages of moving, and they make a choice after weighing the information they have considered.

What we observe, however, are deficits in the information available and its accuracy; family, household, and community groups having difficulty reaching a consensus choice; and many non-linear patterns of movement. We also see how people may talk about their move in a rational way after the fact, but the actual determinants of movement may be quite different than how the decision to move has been reconstructed (Glick Schiller 2021).

Movement of people may be cyclical, the result of seasonal changes in educational opportunities, the demand for labor, non-seasonal low-wage labor, and a pattern of movement of professionals and transnational entrepreneurs. Movement cycles may be intergenerational, with children of immigrant households returning to the place of their parents' origin.

Movement may be involuntary, as in the case of enslavement and the forced relocation of people out of the way of roads, dams, and other infrastructure development projects. Forced relocation has also been prompted as a matter of public policy, as in the case of the internment of Japanese American citizens living in coastal areas of the western United States during World War II and Native American communities forcibly relocated to make way for Euroamerican settlers. The partitioning of lands has also been an attempt to reduce long-standing conflicts, for example, forcing people to resettle on the Indian subcontinent or in Israel and Palestine.

Information is often incomplete and not altogether accurate, the range of feasible choices may be highly restricted, and the reasons for picking a particular destination to move to are often based on social ties rather than an objective analysis of cost versus rewards.

Recognizing that movement is socially selective and not random, a different perspective about the causes and consequences of mobility places the focus on **vulnerability**, which itself is the result of exposure, sensitivity, and adaptive capacity (Engle 2011; Smit and Wandel 2006; Wisner et al. 2003). These characteristics, in turn, vary with race, ethnicity, income, and other elements of socioeconomic status (Mah et al. 2023).

From this perspective, movement is often an adaptive response to vulnerability, in particular, an attempt to reduce exposure to sources of potential harm – environmental conditions, war and conflict, religious persecution, and gender-based violence, among others.

Once again, access to resources and the ability to avoid such threats are not randomly distributed across society. Rather, they result in uneven vulnerability based on social differences. If we better understand the reasons that uneven vulnerability exists, we may gain some useful insights into how to reduce inequitable vulnerability.

The social production of vulnerability is a term that describes the process whereby vulnerability to threats and disasters is not simply a product of risks and hazards to which everyone is equally exposed but is also shaped by social factors such as inequality, discrimination, and marginalization. It recognizes that certain groups of people are more likely to experience vulnerability than others due to their social position and the resources they have available to them.

For example, people living in poverty are more likely to be vulnerable to threats to their livelihoods and safety because they may live in hazardous areas, have inadequate housing, and lack access to transportation and healthcare. People with disabilities may also be more vulnerable because they may need additional assistance to evacuate or access essential services during acute events such as storms, floods, wildfires, or armed conflict.

The social production of vulnerability is important to understand because it can help us to identify and address the root causes of vulnerability. By understanding the social factors that make certain groups of people more vulnerable, we can develop policies and programs to reduce their risk of being harmed by hazards and disasters.

Here are some examples of the social construction of vulnerability:

- **Race and ethnicity** – People of color are more likely to live in hazardous areas and to have less access to resources in the aftermath of a disaster. This is due to a history of systemic racism and discrimination that limited choices of where people of color were permitted to live and the limited ability of people of color to effectively influence the siting of hazardous facilities.
- **Socioeconomic status** – People living in poverty are more likely to live in hazardous areas and to have less access to resources in the aftermath of a disaster.
- **Gender** – Women are more likely to be poor and to live in hazardous areas. They are also more likely to be caregivers for children and the elderly, which can make it difficult to evacuate during a disaster.

- **Disability** – People with disabilities may need additional assistance to evacuate or access essential services during a disaster.
- **Age** – Older adults and children are more vulnerable to the health impacts of disasters.

Vulnerability is not fixed. It can change over time and in different contexts. For example, a person who is vulnerable to a natural hazard may not be as vulnerable to a technological disaster. Additionally, people can develop resilience to vulnerability, which is the ability to cope with and recover from hazards and disasters.

The social production of vulnerability is a complex topic, but it is important to understand because it can help us to create a more just and equitable society. By addressing the root causes of vulnerability, we can reduce the risk of harm to all people.

Climate change is not the only source of hazards that may prompt movement, but it may be the most straightforward to demonstrate how socially produced vulnerabilities are created. Thomas et al. (2019) present a simple model of exposure, sensitivity, and adaptive capacity. Exposure refers to conditions of the physical environment and the social contexts that place people in harm's way. Not everyone lives in flood-prone areas or on hillsides susceptible to mudslides after heavy rain. The reasons that certain people live in these places may be linked to both historic systemic inequality that put them there as well as social and economic limits to mobility that keep them in place.

Sensitivity refers to the degree to which exposure to a hazard adversely affects an individual, household, or community. Thomas et al. (2019) gives an example of residents in a coastal fishing area. A marginalized community dependent on fishing for their livelihoods would likely be more sensitive to the impact of coastal flooding or sea-level rise than an affluent community of retirees or second-home owners. The latter may have another home elsewhere and the resources to rebuild if their coastal residence were affected. In contrast, the fishing community may suffer a loss of livelihood, security, and having no other home to which they could retreat, they would more likely suffer health risks or loss of life.

Adaptive capacity refers to the characteristics and assets of an individual, household, or community that shape their ability to prepare for, cope with, or respond to impacts. Moving out of harm's way, either temporarily or for a longer duration, is one response that depends on adaptive capacity.

What is the role of culture in shaping vulnerability? Culture frames how individuals perceive and explain sources of risk and harm as well as judgments about the likely consequences of adaptive actions, such as moving out of harm's way. Because threats of harm are experienced where people live, many aspects of exposure, sensitivity, and adaptive capacities are context specific.

Urbanization and Megacities

The first cities appeared around 9,000 years ago in areas where the land was well suited to growing crops (such as the cities of Eridu, Uruk, and Ur) in the historic region known as Mesopotamia. These cities were among the many settlements that were established between the Euphrates and Tigris Rivers in what is today a part of Iraq. Cities also formed along the Nile River in Egypt, the Indus River Valley on the Indian subcontinent, and the Yellow (or Huang) River in China, as people began to cultivate crops and settle in communities. Agricultural production in these broad, flat river valleys first complemented and then replaced hunting and gathering, which involves seasonal movements to follow changes in vegetation and the game animals that feed on this vegetation. Sedentary agriculture also made it possible to build up food surpluses that made food available well past the harvest season and additional food that could be traded for other things of value. The rivers along which settlements were situated also made it easier to transport people and large volumes of trade goods.

More agricultural and trade centers were established and grew around the world, especially in broad, flat river valleys and coastal areas sheltered from storms. Some of these centers grew gradually over long periods of time, and some seemed to sprout in a very short period of time. Some of the cities that were once among the most populous in the world, like the largest cities of Mesopotamia, no longer exist, and others have experienced a decline in population. For instance, in the first century before the Christian era (BCE), Rome is estimated to have had one million residents, making this Mediterranean basin imperial center perhaps the world's largest city at the time. By the Middle Ages, however, Rome's population had declined to just 20,000 people. By 2023, Rome's metropolitan area had more than 4.3 million people (United Nations World Urbanization Prospects 2023).

Throughout history, people have been drawn to cities as centers of trade, culture, education, and economic opportunity, but the resulting urban population growth has not always been steady. Indeed, urbanization is a relatively recent phenomenon; until recent years, most people lived in rural areas. For instance, at the beginning of the nineteenth century, more than 90% of the global population lived in rural areas (United Nations World Urbanization Prospects 2009). Only by 2008, for the first time in human history, did more people live in cities worldwide than in rural areas. The US Census Bureau indicates that more than 94% of the US population lived in rural areas in 1800; by 1900 this number had dropped to 60%. As of the 2020 US Census, 20% of the US population lived in rural areas (United States Bureau of the Census 2022).

One of the main forces that propelled the growth of cities was the process of large-scale industrialization, which featured technologically innovative and mechanized ways of manufacturing goods in factories for trade and consumption. The eighteenth-century Industrial Revolution began in England, spread to other parts of Europe, then to the United States, and globally to the far reaches of the British Empire. Technological innovations like the steam engine, cotton gin, industrial scale textile looms, sugar mills, and mechanized timber mills drew workers from agricultural and fishing areas to factories in growing population centers. Over the next century, millions of people in North America and western Europe moved from farms to cities. As other parts of the world industrialized, they too became more urban. Due in part to the Industrial Revolution, London, England, grew from a population of one million in 1800 to over six million a century later. In the United States, the New York City metropolitan area grew to become the largest urban area in the world by 1950, with a population of 12.5 million.

More than half the world's population today lives in urban areas, and by 2050, nearly 70% of people will live in cities (United Nations Department of Economic and Social Affairs 2018). A portion of this growth is due to natural increase, more people being born than dying among people living in cities, but the larger portion of projected urbanization will be due to people moving into urban areas from rural areas, particularly in Africa and Eastern Asia.

PERSPECTIVE: Care and Precarity in China's Massive Urban Movement, by Harriet Evans

Professor of anthropology and Chinese studies, University of Westminster (United Kingdom)

China's vast migrant population is the human backbone of China's "great urban transformation" (Hsing 2010) and has literally provided the muscle for the massive construction of urban space and infrastructure since the early 1990s. By 2022, some 20% of China's 1.4 billion population was migrant.

This movement is of a globally unprecedented scale and has diverse and multiple drivers. Across time and space, these include state and global interests in capital accumulation, along with a hegemonic political discourse that urbanization holds the solution to rural poverty. These explanations are widely accompanied by the view that people migrate in pursuit of a decent economic livelihood and access to a wider range of cultural and social opportunities than life in rural areas affords. But migrants are not a homogenous group, so such explanations only scratch the surface of why rural residents move away from the lives they are familiar with. Indeed, the notion of a decent living is contingent and involves a range of desires, commitments, and principles obscured by the prevalent image of the young broker of modernity who wants to escape rural life in search of a modern life in the cities (Fengjiang 2021, p. 313).

The experiences I turn to now are based on fieldwork I conducted over many years in Dashalar, a small neighborhood in central Beijing that is destined to be engulfed by the spatial reconstruction of the capital (Evans 2020). Li Fuying and his wife Zhang Yuanchen arrived in Beijing in 1997 after a tortuous journey from their poor rural village in the northwest. Forced out of their village by the routine violence of local gangs and the corruption of the local cadres, they spent 10 years moving from place to place trying to eke out a living before deciding to move to Beijing, a city they had never been to. There, their existence was shaped by a relentless struggle for basic survival, motivated by a desire that they never spelled out but over time I came to understand: to finance their children, particularly their son, through higher education. The couple endured extensive periods of homelessness, detention, forcible repatriation, police brutality, and the routine disdain of their Beijing neighbors in the dilapidated neighborhood where they lived. Their desires for another future were thus punctuated – but never destroyed – by physical endurance, extreme poverty, and emotional heartache as core elements of a precarious migratory condition. They were sustained by a deep commitment to each other and their children as well as by strong principles of honesty and dignity. Their attachment to their goal was rooted in a commitment to observing ethics of care as an inseparable aspect of their everyday emotional and physical interactions.

Care involves acts, objects, and attention oriented toward people, things, and goals that may involve complex and emotionally charged relationships. Following Michael Lambek (2010), it is inseparable from the ethical disposition that is intrinsic to the acts and words of tacit, unspectacular, ordinary everyday relationships. Of particular significance to the story below is the conceptualization of an ethics of care oriented to protecting close kin relationships in conditions of mobility and spatial separation that threaten the continuity and cohesiveness of the family as a unit of reciprocal social, material, and welfare responsibilities (Ran 2025). As the experiences I narrate below reveal, parental decisions to migrate in search of labor and a livable life may be motivated, fundamentally, by desires to sustain – care for – children's welfare in the future, implicitly in return for expectations of those children's filial reciprocity to their parents when the need arises. In this sense, an ethics of care may be enmeshed in and generative of feelings of tension, conflict, resentment, and guilt as effects of acts of self-sacrifice and care expected and experienced across generational divides.

The first time I met Li and Zhang in their tiny room in Dashalar in January 2006 was also the first time I met their son. Young Li was then 25 and was studying graphic design in Hebei Province. Li's pride in his son was evident from the outset, including in his remark that his son was now taller than he himself was. Young Li was also very handsome. He sat quietly, listening attentively as his father shared with me the story of his first years in Beijing. At that time, I knew little about the family's circumstances, but the strong bond of affection and respect between the son and his parents was readily apparent. The son's filial respect and care was later exemplified in a single instance of care; when the couple were repatriated back to their hometown in the northwest, the son's first act upon greeting his exhausted parents was to wash their feet.

By 2010, Young Li, then nearly 30 years old, showed few signs of wanting to marry and have children, as his parents wanted. His parents shared their deep anxieties about the situation with me, conveying their concerns about their son's as well as their own future. Since 2008 he had had an on–off relationship with a girlfriend, also from the countryside, but his parents were far from enthusiastic about the relationship. They felt that she was not sincere, and that she resented the time Young Li wanted to spend with his parents and sister. So, his parents were relieved when the two decided to split up in 2010. But by 2012 they were back together again and marriage was in the cards. Li and Zhang were worried that the wife-to-be was trying to drive a wedge between Young Li and his family, and that she might refuse to care for them when they could no longer work – that her rejection of normative expectations for a daughter-in-law's filial responsibilities would threaten the unity of the family. When I left Beijing in the autumn of 2012 without any resolution to this dilemma, Li Fuying and his wife were facing what they imagined would be total estrangement from their son.

I was thus more than surprised, when I returned to Beijing the following year, to hear Li Fuying tell me on the phone that his son's wife had given birth to a baby boy and that he, Li, and his wife were living with the young couple in their apartment. But, as soon as Li appeared at the station in the northern suburbs where we had agreed to meet, the distress on his face told another story. It turned out that he was not living with his son after all because the plan to live together had not worked out, and the daughter-in-law did not want her in-laws to help look after the baby. Nevertheless, despite my reluctance, Li and his wife still wanted to take me to their son's apartment to see the young couple and the baby.

The scene in the apartment was one of abject misery. The daughter-in-law kept herself in a bedroom adjacent to the living room trying to keep her baby quiet, while Young Li, looking exhausted and unkempt, rushed between me and his parents and his wife. The wife did not even come out to say goodbye to us when we left.

The next day I went to visit Li and his wife in their new accommodations. This was a single room in a chaotic development zone in a rural suburb not far from their son's apartment. Their room was just one in long rows of windowless, concrete-walled buildings in a zone crossed by unpaved, muddy tracks. It opened onto a walkway alongside a wide ditch that served as an open sewer. A hole in the ground surrounded by wooden boards was the shared toilet at the end of the walkway. There was little evidence of any plumbing except for a cold-water tap.

The material misery of this place mirrored Li's distress at his son's behavior: "A first grandson should be a happy occasion, but we cried when we heard he was born. I even thought of going to see a lawyer to demand 30 years of expenses back from my son, the expenses for having brought him up. We are no longer a family."

Li and Zhang eventually returned to their village sometime in 2015, heartbroken at the estrangement from their son. Sometime later I received an email from the son saying that they were well, and he was in touch with them.

This story highlights an ethical dilemma that retrospectively puts into sharp relief the deep concerns that were hidden by the everyday hardship and toil of the parents' precarious experience as migrants. The clash between the parents' anticipation of a future of dependency on their son's filial support and their son's decision to follow his own independent path together with his wife and child revolved around the parents' assumptions of their son's filial reciprocity. The father's despair when confronted with his son's betrayal was total, as if he had lost some essential aspect of his own interior self. I think this was what explained his conviction that it was the daughter-in-law who was responsible for his son's estrangement, as if this was a way to protect himself from total collapse.

> For his part, the son was caught in a dilemma wherein going along with his parents' hopes and expectations would have meant abandoning his ethical obligations of care to his wife and child. His decision, therefore, may be understood not so much as abandoning his filial commitment to his parents, but rather, in part at least, as a product of the new socioeconomic context created by his parents' and his own migratory experience.
>
> While the couple's initial decision to leave their village was determined by the violent situation in which they found themselves, ultimately it was sustained by their commitment to an ethics of care to enable their children to access a quality of life in the future that they had not been able to enjoy. The physical, psychological, and emotional labor they invested in pursuing this aim pinned them to an existence of precarious suspension across the rural–urban divide (Xiang 2021). And far from presenting itself as a solution to their conditions of deprivation and distress, urbanization became the site of even greater brutality and lawlessness than they had experienced in the village they had left. So where might their story, and other similar ones we have not yet heard, figure into the statistics of those who no longer live in the place of their household registration?

Urbanization in recent years has fueled the growth of ever-larger cities and a new type of city: the **megacity**, which is defined as having a population of 10 million or more. The metropolitan areas of New York City, USA and Tokyo, Japan became the world's first megacities in the 1950s; by 2023 there were 38 megacities across the globe. As of 2023 Tokyo, with more than 37 million residents, is the world's largest urban area; Delhi, India has almost 33 million. Other cities with more than 20 million residents include Shanghai, Dhaka, São Paulo, Mexico City, Cairo, Beijing, and Mumbai (World Population Review 2023).

Due largely to migration, more metropolitan areas are joining the ranks of megacities every decade, particularly in India, China, and on the African continent. The ability to meet the rapidly growing demand for housing and publicly provided facilities and services is severely challenged. Informal settlements established by recently arrived immigrants often lack water, sanitation, and wastewater treatment infrastructure and are sources of serious threats to public health and safety. The promise of education and employment opportunities is often foreclosed and, as difficult as life may have been in rural settings, a move to the city does not necessarily improve one's material circumstances (Selod and Shilpi 2021).

Forced Relocation: War and Conflict

Forced relocation is also known as forced migration or displacement. It is when people move away from their homes involuntarily, not by their own choice. The forces compelling them to move may involve war and conflict, natural disaster, gentrification, or a government that requires movement to accommodate social policies or economic development projects.

Japanese Americans in World War II

After the Japanese attack on the US naval fleet at Pearl Harbor, Hawai'i in December 1941, the US government began arresting Japanese Americans as alleged security risks. By the end of December, thousands of people were in custody, and widespread press reports alleged that Japanese Americans were suspect as spies and enemy agents. More arrests followed, and Japanese Americans up and down the Pacific coast were forced out of jobs and attacked in public places.

President Franklin Roosevelt issued Executive Order 9066 (7 FR 1407) in February 1942, authorizing the US military to evacuate Japanese Americans from so-called military areas. The next month, the US Army issued Civilian Exclusion Orders, which required that "all Japanese persons, both alien and non-alien" be removed from a number of areas along the Pacific coast and confined to relocation camps further inland. By November 1942 all of California, some of southern Arizona, and the portions of Washington and Oregon west of the Cascade Mountain crest had been declared military areas, and more than 100,000 Japanese Americans had been forcibly removed, regardless of their citizenship status.

Once the exclusion orders were issued, affected households were given a week to register with the military, gather whatever possessions they could carry, and report to an assembly center. They were required to sell their houses, farms, stores, and restaurants with no advance warning, often for far less than they were worth. The assembly centers were converted fairgrounds and racetracks where people were crammed together in stables, livestock stalls, or slept in the open air while waiting to be transported to the inland concentration camps.

The camps were located in Utah, Idaho, Arizona, Wyoming, Colorado, Arkansas, and inland California. These locations were chosen because of their remoteness, and they were like prisons, surrounded by barbed wire fences with watchtowers.

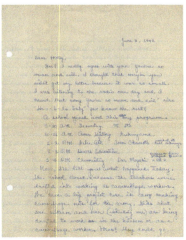

Letter from Sandie Saito to Mollie Wilson. Relocated from Los Angeles to the Gila River, Arizona internment camp, Sandie Saito sent a letter and a signed photo of her wearing their high school letter sweater to Mollie. Source: Photos courtesy of Japanese American National Museum (Gift of Mollie Wilson Murphy, 2000.273.3).

Eventually, routines were established, with children attending school and camp newspapers, farms, sports teams, and concerts put in place.

A 1982 congressional report, *Personal Justice Denied*, found that the incarceration was due to "race prejudice, war hysteria and a failure of political leadership." This congressional study found that the exclusion and forced imprisonment of Japanese Americans by the US government was based on the false premise of military necessity. There was no documented evidence of Japanese American espionage or sabotage during the war. Through efforts of many within and outside the Japanese American community, the Civil Liberties Act of 1988 (Pub. L. 100-383, 102 Stat. 903) was formalized. President Reagan acknowledged the ethically unjust and unconstitutional nature of the Japanese American incarceration period during World War II through an official government apology and redress.

PERSPECTIVE: Guatemalan Indigenous Women Fleeing Violence and Seeking Asylum in the United States, by Lynn Stephen

Phillip H. Knight Chair and Distinguished Professor of Arts and Sciences, University of Oregon (USA)

Human movement is intimately linked to extraction, capitalism, war, and global warming. US foreign policy, development policy, climate policy, and immigration policy all work together to influence how and why people are in diaspora. Communities in western Guatemala, such as the departments of Huehuetenango and Quiche, are places where genocide was perpetrated against Indigenous communities by the Rios Mont and other governments supported by the United States in the 1980s. During Guatemala's internal conflict (1960–1996), more than 100,000 Indigenous women were raped. The US government's foreign and development policy in Central America in the past and present continues to influence patterns of diaspora and refugees that arrive on the US–Mexico border.

During fiscal year 2023 the US Customs and Border Patrol recorded more than 2.4 million encounters at the southwest border (United States Customs and Border Patrol 2023). People from Mexico and Central America represented about 49% of these encounters, down significantly from 2020 when they accounted for almost 90% of encounters. For Indigenous Guatemalan women fleeing multiple forms of violence as well as the effects of climate change, poverty, unemployment, lack of access to healthcare and other services, the possibility of asylum in the United States can offer hope for the future. These forms of violence are not disparate acts that happen to individuals. They are structural, cumulative, intergenerational, and widely shared.

To signal the ways that historically rooted and intersecting structures of violence overlap and intertwine in peoples' bodies, biographies, and daily lives, I use the concept *of gendered embodied structures of violence*. This concept signals that misogynistic, racist, classist structures are not individually distinct relics of the past but rather overlapping and ongoing structures that are reproduced and experienced in people's bodies and in their daily lives. Gendered violence, in this view, is not a time-bound event or merely interpersonal; it is ongoing, intergenerational, and experienced at the collective and individual levels. When Guatemalan women seek asylum in the United States, often in relation to different forms of gendered violence, they are treated as individuals subject to discrete acts of violence. As of November 2022, there were 111,184 pending asylum cases from Guatemala, about 48% of which were women (TRAC 2022). The average time to get a hearing in migration court is 4.5 years.

Asylum protocols evaluate refugees primarily as individuals, rather than as members of groups or categories. United Nations declarations – the 1951 United Nations Convention Relating to the Status of Refugees and the United Nations 1967 Protocol Relating to the Status of Refugees – remain rooted in Cold War logic. These documents define applicant worthiness according to a well-founded fear of persecution in their country of origin on five grounds: (1) membership in a particular social group, (2) religion, (3) race, (4) nationality, or (5) political opinion. This legal framework disguises structural patterns of harm that intersect in refugees' lives.

In what follows, I discuss stories from two Mam women that I am connected to through my work as a volunteer expert witness for asylum cases. The Mam is an Indigenous Mayan group who live in Guatemala's western highlands. The details of these stories suggest ways that asylum could be reconfigured to better fit the reality of refugees today.

Maria Eugenia grew up in a small, rural, Mam village in Huehuetenango. From the time she was 10 years old, she went to work at 4:30 a.m. with her father in the fields. She experienced daily beatings by her father, little food, and constant work. When she was 19, a local man attempted to attack her physically and shot at her three times as she ran away. Against her father's wishes, Maria Eugenia reported the assault, but the perpetrator was only jailed overnight before he was released. Two years later, Maria Eugenia became intimately involved with a man who abandoned her when she became pregnant. After her child was born, her father beat her regularly, blaming her for placing an economic and social burden on the household by having a child outside of a partnership. Rather than offering her emotional and logistical support, the relatives that she turned to for help told her that she needed to put up with her situation and move forward. Ultimately, she left the house to protect herself and her child.

Maria Eugenia then went to live with relatives in a larger town and found work. Things were going well until members of a local gang started to stalk her, likely targeting her because she was seen as up for grabs, being a single woman without male protection. One night after work, several gang members followed her, assaulted her, and raped her. When she told her female relatives what happened, they told her not to report the assault to the police for fear of gang reprisals. She spent months in fear, not leaving her home. She became depressed and worried that she had no way to support her daughter. Out of desperation, she borrowed money and hired a coyote to take her and her daughter to the United States. She was picked up by the US Border Patrol in late 2016. She was detained. Elvira filed an application for asylum as she was deemed to have credible fear in her conversation with an asylum officer. She is still waiting for her immigration court date, which was postponed during the COVID-19 pandemic.

Josefina, also born in Guatemala, grew up in a small, Mam hamlet west of the city of Huehuetenango. Her parents had a small plot of land, and she worked there as a child, also harvesting coffee for part of the year. She speaks Mam and Spanish, which she learned while attending elementary school. Josefina had a child at age 21, and the father decided not to support her and her daughter, so she is a single mother. After extortion attempts – because it was known that she had siblings and cousins working in the United States who sent her financial support – and then threats to kill her if she did not pay, Josefina made the difficult decision to set out for the United States along with her infant daughter in late 2018. She came to the West Coast, where she had family. Her passage cost about $10,000, which she borrowed to pay to a coyote. Because she could carry her infant daughter, she was not charged for her passage. She came because of poverty, lack of work, and threats against her life.

When she arrived, she lived with her brother and his family for a while and then moved into an apartment with two other families, occupying the living room with her daughter. She sought whatever work was available, usually laboring as a farmworker and moving from job to job. She must send regular payments back to pay off her $10,000 debt.

Josefina has two brothers in the Pacific Northwest region of the United States. Her oldest brother and his wife received asylum, as did their two children. Josefina managed to make it to the Northwest undetected but was not able to file an application for asylum until 2023. Her brother and sister-in-law are an important support system for her.

About two hundred people from her community all live in a small city in the Northwest. Some nuclear families have asylum but a majority do not. Although this reconstituted community is composed of extended family groups who support one another, they do not have equal access to asylum or the resources to seek it. Most members are working, many as farm workers that put food on the tables of the Northwest.

In interviews with members of this community, as part of the COVID-19 Farmworker Study (COFS) in Oregon, they have shared stories of struggles through the COVID-19 pandemic, including a loss of wages and difficulty paying their rent, feeding their families, and sending money back to their home community to help their extended families, who are also suffering economic loss and sickness. Juana and others in her community, both with and without asylum, are also actively constructing networks of care, here in the United States and in Guatemala (see Stephen 2023).

> **What kinds of solutions can we think of to accommodate the ever-increasing numbers of refugees seeking asylum in the US, such as Maria Eugenia and Josefina?**
>
> - The United States could expand the number of refugees permitted into the country to at least 250,000 and give official refugee status to all of them. After the fall of Saigon in 1975 President Ford and Congress facilitated the legal resettlement of more than 300,000 Southeast Asians (Jordan 2021).
> - The United States can grant asylum to whole communities and groups of people, greatly expanding the number of refugees admitted.
> - The United States can grant asylum for the multiple reasons that people flee, including climate violence and trauma. While most climate migrants are internal to countries today, by 2050 some predict that 1.2 billion people could be displaced globally due to climate change and natural disasters (Institute for Economics and Peace 2020). Climate disasters often combine with political conflict and violence.
> - The supply of US workers is shrinking and will continue to contract between now and 2050. Immigration and refugee policy can be part of the solution by greatly increasing the number of permanent employment-based visas for all kinds of work.
> - We can lift up and support organizations, networks, and communities in diaspora in the United States as crucial resources for refugees of all kinds and as a source of models for effective ways of helping people – this is a community-based approach to assistance that can take us outside of what some have called the "industrial humanitarian complex."
> - Finally, we can explore the right to not migrate and the right to stay in place. People fleeing to the United States and other countries know what is required to stay in place and live a dignified and fulfilling life.

Settler colonialism

Two glaring examples of forced relocation to accommodate outside settlers' interests involve the US government's nineteenth century interventions on behalf of settlers encroaching on Native American lands. In the 1830s the catastrophic episode widely known as the Trail of Tears was a policy response to settler pressure for expanded farmlands and the discovery of gold in the southern Appalachians. The policy removed around 60,000 members of the Five Civilized Tribes (Cherokee, Muscogee [Creek], Seminole, Chickasaw, and Choctaw Nations) from their ancestral homelands in the southeastern United States to the newly created Indian Territory west of the Mississippi River (what is today the state of Oklahoma).

Between 1863 and 1866 settler encroachment and armed conflict in the American Southwest led to a military intervention. In this three-year period more than 10,000 Navajo (Diné) were forcibly removed to the Bosque Redondo area in present-day New Mexico, anywhere from 250 to 450 miles (400–725 km) from their homelands.

In these instances, the lands taken from the original occupants for the benefit of newcomers were never returned. The Eastern Band of Cherokees resisted forcible relocation and were eventually able to carve out a tiny portion of their original homelands, which is now held in trust by the US government for the Eastern Band's beneficial use. The Oklahoma Territory became a state in 1907 and assumed jurisdiction over all the lands within its boundaries except the Osage Reservation and seven very small areas in the northeast corner of the state. A 2020 US Supreme Court Decision (*McGirt v. Oklahoma* 2020) ruled that the tribal areas had not been extinguished by Oklahoma statehood, but the enforcement of this decision remains uncertain. The Navajo who had been captured and relocated to Bosque Redondo were able to move back to areas from which they had been removed, and an 1868 treaty resulted in the establishment of the Navajo Nation, albeit on a much-diminished portion of the land area they previously used (Denetdale 2007).

Palestinian resettlement or *Nakba* (catastrophe)

While the history of relations between Palestinian Arabs and Jews is long, complex, and hotly disputed, it is clear that as a result of a war in 1947 about 750,000 Palestinians were forcibly removed from their lands and resettled to what are known today as the Occupied Territories of the West Bank of the Jordan River, East Jerusalem, and the Gaza Strip along the Mediterranean Sea. The area now known as Israel was controlled by the Ottoman Empire until it was defeated in World War I, and its provinces outside the Arabian Peninsula were divided among the French and the British. The British took control of Palestine, and as elsewhere in the British Empire, local populations mobilized to end British occupation. In 1946 Britain agreed to withdraw from Palestine, and the newly formed United Nations established a special committee that proposed a partition of Palestine to set aside lands for Palestinians and a homeland for Jewish refugees from Nazism, whom the West largely refused to take in. In 1947 civil war between Arabs and Jews broke out in the territory. Hundreds of Arab villages were destroyed, and many Palestinians lost their homes to Jewish families (Kimmerling and Migdal 2003, pp. 162–163). The mass exile and dispossession of these Palestinians was consolidated in March 1948 with Plan Dalet (a plan for taking control of Mandatory Palestine, creating a Jewish nation-state, and securing its borders). In mid-1948, after the declaration of the nation-state of Israel, the region experienced the flight and forceful expulsion of up to 750,000 Palestinians (out of a Palestinian population of 900,000) from the portion of Palestine that became Israel (Gordon 2008, p. 5; Sa'di and Abu-Lughod 2007). Some were pushed to the West Bank (then a part of Jordan), while others were pushed to the Gaza Strip (then a part of Egypt) (Albanese and Lilly 2019).

In 1967 Israel captured the Gaza Strip from Egypt and the West Bank from Jordan. A period of Israeli military supervision ensued until 1993, when the agreements known as the Oslo Accords were reached between Israel and the Palestine Liberation Organization. The Oslo Accords aimed to fulfill the "right of the Palestinian people to self-determination," and the next year, Palestinians took control as the governmental authority of Gaza and the West Bank.

What has followed since 1994 are cycles of armistice punctuated by Palestinian uprisings in response to Israeli government policies and practices that continue to support Israeli settlements in Palestinian territory and limit Palestinians' mobility in the region. The latest of these uprisings, which began in October 2023, involved a violent attack by the Hamas militia against Israelis living near the Gaza Strip. The Israeli military responded with unprecedented force, resulting in significant loss of Palestinian lives, property destruction, and the forced displacement of at least half the Palestinian residents of Gaza. Evidence from history suggests that it is difficult to envision a future without armed conflict and further involuntary displacement if Israeli government policies and practices continue to support Israeli settlement in Palestinian territory.

Partitioning of Pakistan and India

The Indian subcontinent was subject to British imperial rule for more than 200 years, until just after the end of World War II. Home to numerous cultural groups, each with distinctive languages and many with specific spiritual practices, the Hindu and Muslim religions formed the largest of the coalitions comprising these groups. Beginning in the 1920s a model of two nations emerged, one that would be established as a Hindu state and the other as a Muslim state. As World War II was ending, Great Britain made plans to withdraw as an imperial occupier and grant independence to the Indian government. As the agreed-upon 1947 independence date approached, political support for partitioning the country heightened, and two newly formed states were established. Massive population movements (about 14.5 million people) took place as Hindu and Muslim believers moved to where they would be part of a religious majority. The population of undivided India in 1947 was about 390 million. After partition there were 330 million in India, 30 million in West Pakistan, and 30 million in East Pakistan (now Bangladesh). Movement continued for decades after, propelled by religious persecution.

Rohingyas displacement from Myanmar

The former British colony of Burma, in Southeast Asia, proclaimed its independence in 1948 and later changed its name to Myanmar. Seven ethnic minority states were established in the 1974 constitution, including the western coastal state of Rakhine (also known as Arakan). In 1974 about a third of the Rakhine population was Muslim (Rohingya), with 60% Buddhist and the rest from smaller religious communities (Mohajan 2018). Rohingyas were descendants of Arab settlers who arrived in Southeast Asia in the ninth century (Tha 2007).

In 1982 the Myanmar government enacted a citizenship law that excluded the Rohingya from qualifying for citizenship, citing their "non-indigenous ancestry" (Abdelkader 2013, p. 396). This prevented them from owning property, marrying, attending university, or moving freely about the country. Increasing violence, land confiscation, destruction of mosques, forced labor, and other violations of human rights forced hundreds of thousands of Rohingya to flee the country (Faye 2021).

MOVEMENT AND THE SOCIAL PRODUCTION OF VULNERABILITY

Rohingya refugee girls at the camp learning center, Cox's Bazar, Bangladesh. Source: Photo by Mostofa Mohiuddin (Shutterstock).

More than 500,000 Rohingyas fled for Bangladesh from the early 1980s to the early 1990s (Ullah 2011), and despite negotiations between the governments of Myanmar and Bangladesh to accommodate the Rohingyas in Bangladesh, more than 200,000 were repatriated to Myanmar in 1992 (Ullah 2011). Depredations by the Myanmar military government continued for the next two decades, even though a series of interventions from the international community sought to stop actions that a filing in the International Court of Justice termed "genocidal in character" (Fahim 2022, p. 8). Another large wave of refugees seeking asylum in Bangladesh began in 2017 with more than 700,000 crossing the international border in one year (Fahim 2022, p. 8). Without international assistance the immense surge in demand for housing and public services posed by such a large influx of displaced persons has been nearly impossible for the impoverished nation of Bangladesh to absorb.

Jewish refugee children and the *Kindertransport*. *Left,* Jewish refugee children arrive in Great Britain on the first *Kindertransport* from Germany, December 1938. Source: United States Holocaust Memorial Museum, courtesy of Instytut Pamięci Narodowej. *Right,* Beate Siegel (*far right*) and two other girls look out a train window as they leave Germany on a *Kindertransport* to Great Britain, June 1939. Source: United States Holocaust Memorial Museum, courtesy of Bea Siegel Green.

Forced Relocation: Economic Development

One of the common narratives about migration focuses on individuals and families that leave one place for another in the search for economic opportunities, but this narrative also has a dark, coercive side. Financial assistance from wealthy countries to poor countries, in the form of outright grants, trade agreements, and loans, has inadvertently become a source of forced relocation as the infrastructure built to support post-colonial economic development has taken land and other resources that supported traditional livelihoods. In other words, actions taken in the national interest have imposed local burdens, including the forced displacement of some vulnerable communities in developing economies.

Some deeper historical context is necessary here. The two twentieth-century world wars were total wars, waged by industrial means against civilians as well as between armies, with devastating results. In the interval between them came the Great Depression, which was the worst global financial collapse in the history of capitalism. The chaos of war amidst financial ruin pushed the United States and western European governments into a more active interventionist role. In 1944 a conference that took place at Bretton Woods, New Hampshire (USA) reached a consensus to adopt heavily modified versions of economic ideas for a new world order that had been proposed by British economist John Maynard Keynes.

The International Bank for Reconstruction and Development (now known as the World Bank) and the International Monetary Fund were established to help the post-war reconstruction of Europe. Along with the United Nations, the Bretton Woods conference laid down the basic structure of multilateral financial agencies, which has remained in place to this day. They were faced with an overwhelming crisis of debt, and rather than simply passing out grants, these two institutions added conditions that must be complied with to be eligible to receive funds. These conditions were designed to bring down public sector deficits, impose anti-inflationary measures, free up controlled prices and interest rates, reduce trade barriers, and privatize state enterprises.

Under these conditions, the infrastructure of borrowing countries could be overhauled to upgrade railroads, roadways, ports, electrical grids, water delivery and wastewater treatment systems, flood control, and so forth. But the initial focus of the World Bank–financed development loans was to promote national economic growth and reduce income disparities among countries, not within countries (Christoffersen 2021, p. 4). The social and economic benefits and burdens of these early World Bank–financed development projects were not evenly distributed. For example, the Aswan High Dam on the Nile River in southern Egypt created an enormous reservoir that displaced more than 100,000 Nubian people from their traditional farming and fishing areas (Mohamed 2019). Sardar Sarovar Dam on India's Narmada River, one of the largest dams in the world, was built to bring water and electricity to four states in western India. Due to its construction and the reservoir flooding traditional villages, more than 200,000 people were involuntarily relocated.

By the 1990s, the World Bank estimated that 10 million people were displaced in developing countries by activity in three economic sectors (hydropower, urban, and transport), which escalated in the first decade of the twenty-first century to 15 million people per year. The pace of displacements was only projected to accelerate (Cernea and Maldonado 2018, p. 4).

The World Bank began to recognize the burdens that its financing of development projects created (along with the benefits) and created a set of policies in the 1980s designed to reduce forced displacement and its potentially disruptive effects. Social scientist Michael Cernea led a World Bank team that first cataloged the social issues associated with involuntary resettlement in World Bank–financed projects (1980). They then set about developing a set of policies for investment-project financing that would avoid involuntary resettlements when possible and mitigate the most severe adverse impacts when involuntary resettlement was unavoidable.

Most recently updated in 2017 (World Bank Group 2017), Environmental and Social Standard (ESS)5 specially deals with involuntary resettlement. The ESS5 acknowledges that "project-related land acquisition or restrictions on land use may cause physical displacement (relocation, loss of residential land or loss of shelter), economic displacement (loss of land, assets or access to assets, leading to loss of income sources or other means of livelihood) or both." The standard places a priority on avoiding involuntary resettlement, but if it is unavoidable, it advocates providing timely compensation, adequate housing and access to services and facilities, and enabling displaced persons to benefit directly from the project.

These World Bank standards are important because they become the model for regional development banks and national government investments. Monitoring their implementation going forward will be necessary to protect vulnerable households and communities from becoming even more vulnerable.

Gentrification

We will discuss gentrification at greater length in Chapter 8, but here is a brief introduction to this pattern of economic development at the local level that can also result in the displacement of individuals, families, and communities. Gentrification is a process by which low-income, central-city neighborhoods experience investment and renewal accompanied by an in-migration of middle- and upper middle–class residents (Smith 1998, p. 198). It involves developers, businesses, and institutions as well as relatively well-off households, and it results in the physical, demographic, and cultural transformation of a low-income area into a middle- or upper-class neighborhood. The displacement of low-income residents is often a consequence of gentrification, as property values, housing prices, and accompanying taxes escalate and are no longer affordable to previous residents. Government laws and regulations are almost always complicit in facilitating this displacement, either directly through targeted redevelopment incentives, land use and zoning ordinances, and infrastructure investments or indirectly through such mechanisms as school attendance policies, rules governing tenant–landlord relationships, and even alcohol sales and distribution licenses.

But which neighborhoods are most likely to experience gentrification? Work by Hwang (2020) shows one under-explored mechanism that shapes patterns of uneven development and residential selection: immigrant replenishment. In other words, the urban neighborhoods most likely to be gentrified are neighborhoods with a higher likelihood of newly arriving immigrants. How might this work? The neighborhoods to which arriving immigrants move limits residential selection in gentrification and shifts pressures to low-cost Black neighborhoods. The rise of immigration after 1965 brought pioneers to many low-income, central-city neighborhoods, spurring gentrification in some neighborhoods and forming ethnic enclaves in others. New immigrants repopulated areas that lost population, as a result of deindustrialization and suburbanization, and established commercial businesses in affordable and vacant storefronts (Lin 1998; Muller 1993; Wilson 1987; Winnick 1990). Some of these neighborhoods eventually became established ethnic enclaves, which have only begun to face gentrification pressures in recent decades as gentrification became rapid and widespread (Hackworth and Smith 2001; Hum 2014; Wilson and Grammenos 2005); however, the neighborhoods to which most of these immigrants arrived were not ethnic enclaves at the time, even in traditional immigrant destination cities (Waldinger 1989). Many settled in affordable areas that were previously white and middle class, and others settled in affordable areas that were predominantly Black and low income (Bogen 1987; Oliver and Johnson 1984; Waldinger 1989). Through this demographic renewal, new immigrants revitalized declining areas by increasing housing demand in emptying neighborhoods and populating previously vacant residences and commercial storefronts (Winnick 1990), thereby creating more desirable economic and social neighborhood conditions that could attract gentrification.

Poor, minority neighborhoods in US cities have proven durable over the last quarter of the twentieth century, despite major urban transformations. Gentrification has generated highly contentious debates surrounding racial and socioeconomic inequality that have generally centered on the direct displacement of low-income minorities living in neighborhoods that gentrify, but the findings show that few predominantly Black neighborhoods and ethnic enclaves actually experienced gentrification in this early period. This highlights the extent to which low-income, minority neighborhoods generally remained isolated and often disadvantaged amid the expansion of gentrification that took place during this period. These neighborhoods were left particularly vulnerable to gentrification in recent decades, especially in cities with tight housing markets. Thus, policy makers face challenges to both increase the affordable housing supply to meet demand and to ensure that sustained reinvestment occurs in areas beyond gentrifying neighborhoods. As some low-income neighborhoods with particular characteristics garner investment, others tend to remain left behind, which perpetuates and increases neighborhood inequality (Tehrani et al. 2019). Nevertheless, these results reveal the potential of global neighborhoods to transform low-income neighborhoods that are in decline.

PERSPECTIVE Things That Were Carried: Three Storytelling Objects in a Museum Collection, by Laurel Kendall

Curator of Asian Ethnology, Curator-in-Charge of African and Pacific Ethnology, and Professor, Richard Gilder Graduate School, American Museum of Natural History (USA)

What do you grab when you run with your family from a burning house? What do you carry with you into another life? What do you collect because it resonates with generational memories made personal within a larger history of displacement? When might the gifting of an object to a museum be an act of memorialization? Sometimes a story accompanies the object, which may be preserved in an archive, a thickening of object identity. More often, objects enter anthropology and history collections as generic types, witnesses in the general sense of their use and meaning in a time and place, but without the personal stories once embodied in them. Sometimes, the tool, pot, or textile exhibited in a museum case provokes a flicker of recognition, like the "my mother used one of those," "my grandmother had one like that," and "I remember when I was a child…" comments overheard in our exhibition halls. The following three examples are objects that connect a museum accession record, personal and family experiences, and larger histories of human movement. These are case histories, if you will, and there are others.

The Armenian best dress

In an alcove in the Gardner D. Stout Hall of Asian Peoples at the American Museum of Natural History (AMNH) in New York City, a mannequin sculpted to resemble a young woman wears a long velvet dress in deep maroon color (catalog no. 70.3/2604), a testimony to the fine dyeing that has held up for well more than a century, including some recent decades spent under exhibition lights.[1] The alcove, celebrating the history and traditions of Armenia, came into being through the efforts and generosity of diasporic Armenians in the United States. The dress was a gift from Mrs. Nora Ordjanian (1903–2004) and had belonged to her grandmother. Nora's own daughter, Armen Susan, modeled for the mannequin. The existence of the Armenian alcove was a personal mission for Nora, who volunteered her services and worked for three intense years with the AMNH exhibition team, garnering support for the project through her contacts and with stories in Armenian community newspapers. Between 500,000 and 1.2 million people of Armenian ancestry live in the United States,

---

[1] Anahid Ordjanian and Armen Susan Ordjanian Elliott, interview by Laurel Kendall, Katherine Skaggs, and Moira Sullivan Page, November 11, 2021, transcript, Hall of Asian Peoples, Division of Anthropology Archive, American Museum of Natural History, New York City, NY. For more about the Armenian installation see https://archaeology.columbia.edu/facing-the-mannequin/armenia.

with almost 100,000 living in the New York City area. Nora commissioned an Armenian sculptor, Grigor Gevorkian, to make mannequins for the exhibition case; collected objects from the community for a significant Armenian collection at the museum; and consulted with experts to ensure the appropriateness of the material and the accuracy of the label commentary. Nora's other daughter Anahid recalls a common response among those who gave family objects and textiles, "I have these things and I'd like to hand them down to my children, to my grandchildren, but quite honestly I don't know if they would even appreciate [them], if they would know what they are, so maybe it's better for me to donate it to the Museum,[…] and many people will get to see it." This had been Armen Susan's own reaction when her mother asked how she felt about giving the museum the dress that would one day have come to her, "I'm like, of course, this is going to be seen by millions of people over the world, and I was thrilled."

An old studio photograph shows Anahid and Armen Susan's great grandmother Arousiag wearing the dress – almost certainly a best dress donned for the portrait – and posed with her husband and children around 1900. The family had lived in Kars, an Armenian area in eastern Turkey. In the genocide that accompanied the collapse of the Ottoman Empire during World War I, Arousiag's husband would be killed, and she would flee with her surviving family to Iran. Living in Tabriz, her daughter Arax (Nora's mother), would eventually marry a fellow Armenian, Grigor Acopian, whose family had precipitously left Tbilisi, Georgia (then part of the Soviet Union) to circumvent his likely arrest by Stalin's police. In Iran, the couple both became dentists and sent their children to the United States for college. There, Nora studied art at Rutgers University, graduated, and married fellow Armenian Dr. Nikit Ordjanian; born in Rustov-on-Don in southern Russia, he would parlay his research in mining engineering into a successful business in the United States. Attaining a settled life, Nora sent for her parents, reuniting the family on the East Coast. The dress in the museum exhibition had accompanied three generations of women, passed from mother to daughter, as a signifying object in a family history that spanned a once comfortable life in Ottoman Kars, the flight from Turkey to Iran, and settlement in the United States and drew in ties through marriage to a larger Armenian diaspora. Nora saw her work as presenting an Armenian story to the audience of a major American museum with the exhibit a source of pride for younger generations of Armenian Americans. The mannequin in the dress bears witness to this history.

Japanese Girls' Day dolls

On the third of March each year, Japanese families with young daughters celebrate the *Hina Matsuri* (doll festival), arranging a set of dolls that represent an imperial wedding with an emperor and empress on the top shelf, a hierarchical array of courtiers, and some tiny lacquer furniture at the base. Festival rice cake is prepared for the decorated display and little girls visit each other's houses to celebrate. Then, like fragile Christmas tree ornaments, the dolls are carefully packed away until the next year's Festival.

In 2012 I received a telephone call from Kanako Honda (Kana), a Japanese expatriate living in Hoboken, New Jersey who was about to return to Japan after many years of expat life owing to her husband's work. She had seen an emperor and an empress on exhibit in the Hall of Asian Peoples at AMNH and wondered if the museum would be interested in acquiring her set of dolls. This curator had long desired a full set of dolls for the collection and was more than interested. Counter to custom, Kanako had kept her dolls visible all year long in her New Jersey living room as a daily connection to her family in Japan. She had a special set of shelves made so the dolls would be protected behind glass panes, and she had replicated the seasonal rice cake offerings with more durable play dough. Upon her return to Japan, however, the dolls would necessarily stay packed away and Kanako did not have a daughter or granddaughter to celebrate the festival. She considered all of this "a little sad" and wanted to find the dolls a home.

The story of this particular set of dolls is the story of two families, Honda and Samejima, linked together by adoption. Bunpei and Ri-Ichi were cousins, and particularly close friends. As a young man, Ri-Ichi Samejima went to Tokyo to study medicine and became a successful dentist, establishing a lucrative practice installing prestigious gold fillings in the teeth of *geisha* (women who are performing artists and entertainers) in the Nihonbashi neighborhood. Kana describes the dolls as having been financed by the teeth of geisha, a luxury indulged by their patrons. Upon the birth of his eldest daughter Kazue in 1926, Ri-Ichi's family could afford a fine set of dolls from a named craftsman, accompanied by miniature furniture from a prominent Tokyo department store. During World War II Ri-Ichi's family left Nihonbashi and retreated to the coastal city of Shizuoka to escape the American firebombing of Tokyo, bringing the precious doll set with them. Whatever personal possessions they had left behind in Tokyo were subsequently destroyed in the bombing. At the end of the war Ri-Ichi's family relocated to Yokohama. Because Kazue and Noriko had outgrown the Girl's Day festival, the family gave the dolls to Bunpei's household so that his daughters, including Chizuko (Kana's mother), could enjoy them. In time, the dolls came to Kana and her sister and then were packed away for many years when the girls outgrew them.

When Kana's sister had a daughter, Kana's parents bought a new set of dolls, bigger and more resplendent dolls, following fashion and an indication of better material conditions. For the new granddaughter's first festival, the two sets were set up side-by-side. Kana recalls that when she saw the old dolls again, she became reacquainted with them and realized how nice they were. She asked if she could take the old dolls with her when she followed her husband to foreign postings, first in Hong Kong and then in New Jersey. She developed a careful system of wrapping the dolls for travel, which we documented as a part of their history: a pad of cotton in a paper twist to protect the face, tissue over the hands, marked paper packets for each of the removable accoutrements, a piece of paper for the base, another (folded like a hood) to cover the body, and then more padding inside the box. She had preserved the original boxes, which were labeled with her grandmother's handwriting.

When Kana informed Noriko, now in her nineties, that the dolls she had used in her childhood were going to "a famous museum in New York" her news was greeted with "something like a ripple of joy through the family" (K. Honda, AMNH Division of Anthropology Archive, Accession file 2013–1).

Embroidered Miao clothing and necklace
In 2008 Bee Vang co-starred with Clint Eastwood in the film *Gran Torino*, portraying a young Hmong American in Detroit whose family, like his own, had fled Laos in the 1970s after the end of the Indochina Wars.[2] More distant ancestors had migrated from China to highland Southeast Asia in the nineteenth century. When the filming was done, Bee made a trip to southwest China where, like many other Hmong Americans, he sought out ethnic cousins belonging to China's Miao minority. Before Bee traveled, anthropologist Louisa Schein accompanied him to the AMNH, where they examined Miao clothing in the collection. Recognizing familiar embroidery patterns on several of the garments, he hoped he would find speakers of the same dialect used in his family in the clothing's source community. Instead, visiting a wide assortment of Miao villages in Guizhou province, he found a cacophony of different dialects and even more varied clothing styles, all included among his Miao ancestors' traditions.

During his travels, Bee purchased a set of men's clothing, indigo dyed and brightly embroidered. Dressed, turbaned, and wearing a silvery necklace, a smiling Bee posed with his similarly attired hosts for a photograph that would appear on his web page. Eager to share the surprising Miao diversity he had encountered in China with fellow members of the diaspora and eventually with wider audiences, Bee decided to offer the costume to AMNH (accession 2013–1). Today, Bee combines acting with activist and communications work that includes the War Legacies Project, which addresses the harms of Agent Orange sprayed by the United States during the war in Laos. As a regular spokesperson for the Hmong American community, he has built on his frank critique of the *Gran Torino* film project, more recently directing his advocacy toward denouncing anti-Asian racism, especially as it intensified during the COVID-19 pandemic. Bee Vang's personal journey continues, grounded in an awareness of his long diasporic past and oriented toward a future of social change.

[2] Wikipedia, "Bee Vang," last modified 30 September 2024, 21:13 (UTC), https://en.wikipedia.org/wiki/Bee_Vang. (This section reviewed and updated by Vee Vang and Louisa Schein.)

Circular Migration

Circular migration is a pattern of movement that involves a departure from a place of origin followed by at least one return to that place. This is a pattern that may be repeated multiple times in one's lifetime or just once. The move may be motivated by educational or work opportunities, and the return may be the result of those opportunities not being realized, the opportunities being restricted in time, official policies requiring periodic return as a condition of entry, or reaching a stage of life in which the search for educational or work opportunities is no longer relevant.

For example, Antonijević, Grubišić, and Rašić (2021) reported on a massive longitudinal study of guest workers who left Serbia, in the former Yugoslavia, for work in Germany and Austria during the 1960s and 1970s. Until well into the 2000s, immigration laws in Germany and Austria made it difficult and time consuming for immigrant workers to become naturalized citizens. Without the benefits of full citizenship, the prevailing pattern has been for people to stay for a period of several years, send some of their earnings home in the form of remittances, accumulate some savings, and then, as they approach the end of the working years, return to their home communities in Serbia. A variation of this pattern, observed in the context of Italian workers in England, is an oscillating movement (Ganga 2006, p. 1406) of workers who, upon reaching retirement age, aim to maintain dual residency. This means that they move back and forth between home places in their original place of residence and the country where they were working.

PERSPECTIVE: Becoming an Ethiopian Refugee—"Not Once in a Life, But Twice," by Patricia Sunderland

Principal, Cultural Research Associates (USA)

Michael was born in Ethiopia in 1956 and left in 1976 after Emperor Haile Selassie was overthrown and the Dergue, a brutal military regime, had taken power. At the time Michael was in his first year of university, and as he tells it, if you were a student during that time, you basically had four choices: (1) join the Dergue, (2) join an opposition guerilla movement, (3) escape the country as a refugee, or (4) be killed. Michael chose the course of running (or more literally, walking) out of the country, escaping on foot across the Sudan border. He spent about eight months in Sudan, four months in Spain, and a year in Italy until finally making it to the United States in 1980.

The journey to the Sudan, a neighboring country, was fully supported by his parents, as they were concerned for their son's safety. Michael had already made a few feeble attempts to leave—for instance, boarding a train to Djibouti with a friend—only to be stopped by government authorities, which led to spending a few days in jail before, luckily, being sent home. His parents arranged to have an older man who knew the route act as a guide for Michael. They then awakened Michael one evening, told him what they had arranged, and sent him on his way. They had not told him earlier of their plans as they were concerned that he would tell his friends, which they feared could eventually lead to disclosure to the authorities.

What Michael remembers most about Sudan is the heat, the sand, and the hospitality of the people. He and other Ethiopians were able to survive there because of that hospitality. People often ate outdoors, and if one passed by, they would routinely ask if you would join them in having something to eat. Michael was also able to survive there as he had an aunt who lived in Khartoum, the capital city, and she had heard that he was in the country. Getting word to him via other Ethiopians, she invited him to stay at her home and would routinely pass along a bit of spending money. Days were spent hanging out with other Ethiopian refugees, punctuated by the main purpose in life: going to embassies and begging for a visa to get out of the country, for Michael, ideally to the United States but anywhere that would take him was a first step.

After about eight months, these efforts finally materialized into a travel document and visa with which Michael was able to travel to Spain. The visa had not been easy to come by. Were it not for a fellow refugee, an Ethiopian woman who threw herself to the ground and wrapped her arms around the legs of an ambassador, it would not have happened. Once in Spain, day-to-day life became much harder for Michael. Life was more expensive and there was no aunt. Things there reached a catalyzing turn on the day when Michael's older sister, who had gone to the United States to study before the turmoil in Ethiopia, wired him some money. Once he picked it up from the bank, he lost it all to the hands of a watchful, waiting pickpocket. This led Michael to ask for help from a church. There he met the clergyman Tom Goslin, a name never forgotten. Michael learned from him that it was an anomaly – and illegal – that he was even in Spain, as Spain normally issued refugee visas only to those from Cuba. Michael was thus offered help from the church to leave and asked whether he preferred to go to France or Italy. He chose Rome, as he knew that Ethiopian Airlines had flights to Rome and his brother, a pilot, sometimes flew there.

For Michael, the year in Rome ended up being a good one. It was not only because he sometimes actually enjoyed food made by his mother, brought to him by his brother on flights to Rome. Day-to-day life was made enjoyable because he spent that year at a dormitory for Protestant students studying in Rome. Students there would invite him to their family homes on breaks and holidays, and he also became a roommate with Paul, an American graduate student in theology in Rome on a Fulbright scholarship and since then, a lifelong friend. With the help of Paul's sponsorship as well as a flight and further sponsorship from the World Council of Churches, Michael was finally able to make it to the United States.

Once in the United States, he moved in with his sister in New York City (NYC) and was surprised on the first evening when she made him pasta for dinner. He was waiting for what would come next, as in Rome he had become accustomed to the dormitory's large midday meals that consisted of "*primo, secondo, terco, frutta e caffè*." In Michael's mind, there was a hierarchy among countries, and in that economic and social hierarchy, he situated the United States many rungs above Italy. Thus, he had imagined that if one ate delicious multi-course meals in Italy, it must be even better in the United States. He had yet to learn that in the United States, spaghetti and sauce could constitute a whole meal, especially when money is tight.

Michael soon began college at the State University of New York at New Paltz. Financially it was not always easy, and a few times he wondered if he should have taken the offer he had received while in Italy to study medicine in Norway. There, his tuition would have been covered by the university, and he would have been offered housing as well. Not so in the United States, but through a variety of jobs – doing everything from working in the library to delivering liquor and taxi driving in NYC – he finished college and eventually, a graduate degree in mathematics.

Michael worked at New York University and had made his life in NYC. However, in the early 1990s, after the Dergue regime in Ethiopia had finally been replaced by a federal democratic government, he started to wonder if he should return to Ethiopia as his sister and some other Ethiopians living in the United States had already done. Nonetheless, he remained at his job and in 1996 married an American woman. It was not until about 10 years later that it seemed that perhaps he could start a business in Ethiopia, and he thought about living half of the year in the United States and the other half in Ethiopia. As is true for many refugees, a large part of his heart was still in Ethiopia.

And so, in the mid-aughts, he purchased a bulldozer, imported it to Ethiopia, and began to lease it to the government for the building of roads. This was a business that seemed as if it could also serve in the betterment of Ethiopia, and as a business, it did work for several years. After this, Michael and his wife purchased a home in Ethiopia and began to make plans to live in Ethiopia for six months a year and continue to live and work in the United States during the other six months. This also worked, more or less, from 2015 to 2020. Then, in 2020 political events in Ethiopia took a turn that made Michael feel that once again he had been forced to become a refugee. As he said it, "not once in a life, but twice."

The post-Dergue government was formed by the victorious Tigray People's Liberation Front (TPLF) and its allies and had been led by Prime Minister Meles Zenawi until his illness and death in 2012. By 2020 the Ethiopian government was led by Prime Minister Abiy Ahmed. He was fundamentally against the system of ethnic federalism that had been set up by the TPLF and allies. He set about dismantling that system, which escalated to a war with the northern Tigray region and a systematic attempt to destroy the people of the region. People living in Tigray became the targets of drone and person-to-person attacks. Tigrayans living in the capital Addis Ababa were rounded up and put into prison. As an ethnic Tigrayan, it was no longer safe for Michael to be in Addis. Many ethnic Tigrayans became refugees, with many fleeing on foot to the Sudan as Michael had done in 1976. Within Tigray, others became internally displaced persons (IDPs), with approximately three million (roughly half of the total population) living in IDP camps. The war is estimated to have taken more than 800,000 Tigrayan lives, through direct killing during the war and in its aftermath through shortages of food and medicines.

By 2023 a peace agreement had been signed between the federal government and the Tigray regional authorities, and the genocidal campaign against Tigrayans was paused. Michael could return to Ethiopia and, once again, to his part-time house in Addis Ababa. It is still an open question whether his plan to retire in Ethiopia will be possible.

The circular pattern is also reported – among many others – to involve Portuguese construction workers who move to Spain in the early 2000s (Queirós 2019); Mexican agricultural workers in the United States (Holmes 2013); Native Americans moving between reservation and city homes (Hackenberg and Wilson 1972); South Asian workers and the Gulf Cooperation Council states of Kuwait, Saudi Arabia, Bahrain, Qatar, United Arab Emirates, and Oman (Babar and Gardner 2016); and between Ghana and Italy (Adamba and Quartey 2016). This last example is interesting because it is an instance of managed circular migration, where potential migrants are chosen from a larger pool of prospects, given an orientation, and then sent to the receiving country on a temporary basis. This approach is said to have benefited: (1) the sending country (Ghana) by encouraging entrepreneurship development, (2) the receiving country (Italy) by providing workers and reducing the trend of undocumented migration, and (3) the workers themselves.

Chapter Summary

People move for many reasons, and these reasons have remained constant for thousands of years. Some people move to pursue an education, to start a new job, or to be closer to family and friends. Some move to build a better life or escape from poverty, conflict, persecution, or changing environmental conditions. Some are forced to move through human trafficking and enslavement. And some are pushed aside to make room for economic development and urban renewal. Often people move for a combination of reasons, including forces beyond their control.

> *no one leaves home unless*
> *home is the mouth of a shark.*
>
> *you only run for the border*
> *when you see the whole city*
> *running as well.*
>
> An excerpt of "Home" by Warsan Shire, British-Somali poet

Our decisions to move are often influenced by forces such as where and when we were born as well as what conditions are like in our area. Migrants are often forced to choose between several bad options. Stay and you may face difficulties and danger. Leave and you may face an uncertain future in a place you know little about and where you know practically no one.

Review Questions

1. What are some examples of social circumstances and aspects of identity that contribute to differences in vulnerability?
2. What are some examples of different types of forced relocation in recent history?
3. The "Perspective" pieces in this chapter describe a range of reasons for migrating (from rural to urban China, from Guatemala to the United States, and out of Ethiopia and back again). What expectations did people have when making these moves? How did their experiences align with these expectations?

References

Abdelkader, E. 2013. The Rohingya Muslims in Myanmar: Past, present, and future. *Oregon Review of International Law* 15(3): 395–410. https://api.core.ac.uk/oai/oai:scholarsbank.uoregon.edu:1794/17966, accessed 13 Feb 2024.

Adamba, Clement, and Peter Quartey. 2016. Circular Migration and Entrepreneurship Development in Ghana. In C Solé, S Parella, T Martí, and S Nita, eds. *Impact of Circular Migration on Human, Political and Civil Rights*. United Nations University Series on Regionalism. Vol. 12. Cham, Switzerland: Springer. https://doi.org/10.1007/978-3-319-28896-3_12.

Albanese, Francesca, and Damian Lilly. 2019. The Palestinian refugee question: Root causes and breaking the impasse. *Forced Migration Review* 62: 82–84. https://www.fmreview.org/return/albanese-lilly.

Antonijevi, Dragana, Ana Banić Grubišić, and Miloš Rašić. 2021. A decade of studying guest workers through the projects of the Serbian ethnological and anthropological society. *Etnoantropološki Problemi Issues in Ethnology and Anthropology* 16(4): 981–1012. https://doi.org/10.21301/eap.v16i4.1.

Babar, Zahra, and Andrew Gardner. 2016. Circular migration and the Gulf states. In C Solé, S Parella, T Martí, and S Nita, eds. *Impact of Circular Migration on Human, Political and Civil Rights*. United Nations University Series on Regionalism. Vol. 12. Cham, Switzerland: Springer. https://doi.org/10.1007/978-3-319-28896-3_3.

Bogen, E. 1987. *Immigration in New York*. New York: Praeger.

Cernea, Michael M, and Julie K Maldonado. 2018. Challenging the Prevailing Paradigm of Displacement and Resettlement. In M Cernea, and J Maldonado, eds. *Challenging the Prevailing Paradigm of Displacement and Resettlement: Risks, Impoverishment, Legacies, Solutions*. London: Routledge. pp. 1–42. https://doi.org/10.4324/9781315163062.

Christoffersen, Leif E. 2021. The important contribution of social knowledge to international development. In M Koch-Weser, and S Guggenheim, eds. *Social Development in the World Bank*. Cham, Switzerland: Springer. pp. 3–25. https://doi.org/10.10007/978-3-030-57426-0_1.

Denetdale, Jennifer Nez. 2007. Discontinuities, remembrances, and cultural survival: History, Diné/Navajo memory, and the Bosque Redondo memorial. *New Mexico Historical Review* 82(3): 295–316. https://digitalrepository.unm.edu/nmhr/vol82/iss3/2.

Engle, N L. 2011. Adaptive capacity and its assessment. *Global Environmental Change* 21: 647–656. http://doi.org/10.1016/j.gloenvcha.2011.01.019.

Evans, Harriet. 2020. *Beijing from Below: Stories of Marginal Lives in the Capital's Center*. Durham, NC: Duke University Press.

Fahim, M H K. 2022. Forced migration of Rohingya refugees from Myanmar to Neighboring countries: A humanitarian crisis unresolved. *Society & Sustainability* 4(1): 1–10. https://doi.org/10.38157/society_sustainability.v4i1.373.

Faye, Malang. 2021. A forced migration from Myanmar to Bangladesh and beyond: Humanitarian response to Rohingya refugee crisis. *Journal of International Humanitarian Action* 6: 13. https://doi.org/10.1186/s41018-021-00098-4.

Fengjiang, Jiazhi. 2021. "To be a little more realistic": The ethical labour of suspension among nightclub hostesses in Southeast China. *Pacific Affairs* 94(2): 307–328. https://doi.org/10.5509/2021942307.

Ganga, Deianira. 2006. From potential returnees into settlers: Nottingham's older Italians. *Journal of Ethnic and Migration Studies* 32(8): 1395–1413. https://doi.org/10.1080/13691830600928789.

Glick Schiller, Nina. 2021. Migration, displacement, and dispossession. In Mark Aldenderfer, ed. *Oxford Research Encyclopedia of Anthropology*. New York: Oxford University Press. https://doi.org/10.1093/acrefore/9780190854584.013.205.

Gordon, Neve. 2008. *Israel's Occupation*. Berkeley: University of California Press.

Hackenberg, Robert, and C Roderick Wilson. 1972. Reluctant emigrants: The role of migration in Papago Indian adaptation. *Human Organization* 31(2): 171–186. https://www.jstor.org/stable/44125263.

Hackworth, J, and N Smith. 2001. The changing state of gentrification. *Tijdschrift Voor Economische En Sociale Geografie* 92: 464–477. https://doi.org/10.1111/1467-9663.00172.

Holmes, Seth. 2013. *Fresh Fruit, Broken Bodies: Migrant Farmworkers in the United States*. Berkeley: University of California Press.

Hsing, You-Tien. 2010. *The Great Urban Transformation: Politics of Land and Property in China*. Oxford: Oxford University Press.

Hum, T. 2014. *Making a Global Immigrant Neighborhood: Brooklyn's Sunset Park*. Philadelphia: Temple University Press.

Hwang, Jackelyn. 2020. Gentrification without segregation? Race, immigration, and renewal in a diversifying city. *City & Community.* 19(3): 538–572. https://doi.org/10.1111/cico.12419.

Institute for Economics and Peace. 2020. *Over one billion people at threat of being displaced by 2050 due to environmental change, conflict and civil unrest*. Press Release about the Ecological Threat Register. https://www.economicsandpeace.org/wp-content/uploads/2020/09/Ecological-Threat-Register-Press-Release-27.08-FINAL.pdf, accessed 18 Nov 2024.

Jordan, Miriam. 2021. 50 Years After Vietnam, Thousands Flee Another Lost American War. *New York Times* August 21. https://www.nytimes.com/2021/08/21/us/refugees-history-afghanistan.html

Kimmerling, Baruch, and Joel S Migdal. 2003. *The Palestinian People: A History*. Cambridge, MA: Harvard University Press.

Lambek, Michael, ed. 2010. *Ordinary Ethics: Anthropology, Language and Action*. New York: Fordham University Press.

Lin, Jan. 1998. Globalization and the revalorizing of ethnic places in immigration gateway cities. *Urban Affairs Review.* 34: 313–339. https://doi.org/10.1177/107808749803400206.

Mah, J C, J L Penwarden, H Pott, O Theou, and M K Andrew. 2023. Social vulnerability indices: A scoping review. *BMC Public Health* 23(1): 1253. https://doi.org/10.1186/s12889-023-16097-6.

McGirt v. Oklahoma, 140 S.Ct. 2452-2459 (2020). https://www.supremecourt.gov/opinions/19pdf/18-9526_9okb.pdf, accessed 18 Nov 2024.

Mohajan, Haradan Kumar. 2018. History of Rakhine state and the origin of the Rohingya Muslims. *Indonesian Journal of Southeast Asian Studies* 2: 3–20. https://doi.org/10.22146/ikat.v2i1.37391.

Mohamed, Nader Noureldeen. 2019. Negative Impacts of Egyptian High Aswan Dam: Lessons for Ethiopia and Sudan. *International Journal of Development Research* 9(08): 28861–28874. https://www.journalijdr.com/sites/default/files/issue-pdf/16178.pdf, accessed 18 Nov 2024.

Muller, Thomas. 1993. *Immigrants and the American City*. New York: NYU Press.

Oliver, M L, and J H Johnson. 1984. Interethnic Conflict in an Urban Ghetto: The case of Blacks and Latinos in Los Angeles. In R Ratcliff, and L Kriesberg, eds. *Research in Social Movements, Conflicts, and Change*. Greenwich, CT: JAI Press. pp. 57–94.

Queirós, João. 2019. Working Class Condition and Migrant Experience: The Case of Portuguese Construction Workers. In C Pereira, and J Azevedo, eds. *New and Old Routes of Portuguese Emigration*. IMISCOE Research Series. Springer. https://doi.org/10.1007/978-3-030-15134-8_8.

Ran, Peter Guangpei. 2025. The placing of care: Ordinary ethics of mobility in the Sino-Tibetan borderlands. *Journal of the Royal Anthropological Institute* 31(3). https://doi.org/10.1111/1467-9655.14237.

Sa'di, Ahmad H, and Lila Abu-Lughod. 2007. *Nakba: Palestine, 1948, and the Claims of Memory*. New York: Columbia University Press.

Selod, H, and F Shilpi. 2021. Rural-urban migration in developing countries: Lessons from the literature. *Regional Science and Urban Economics* 91: 103713. https://doi.org/10.1016/j.regsciurbeco.2021.103713.

Smit, B, and J Wandel. 2006. Adaptation, adaptive capacity and vulnerability. *Global Environmental Change* 16: 282–292. http://doi.org/10.1016/j.gloenvcha.2006.03.008.

Smith, N. 1998. Gentrification. In W V Vliet, ed. *The Encyclopedia of Housing*. London: Taylor and Francis. pp. 198–199.

Stephen, Lynn. 2023. Vulnerabilities and collective care: Indigenous Guatemalan and Mexican farmworkers in diaspora confronting COVID-19 in the Western United States. *Mexican Studies* 39(1): 117–144. https://doi.org/10.1525/msem.2023.39.1.117.

Tehrani, Shadi O, Wu Shuling, and Jennifer D Roberts. 2019. The color of health: Residential segregation, light rail transit developments, and gentrification in the United States. *International Journal of Environmental Research and Public Health* 16(19): 3683. https://doi.org/10.3390/ijerph16193683.

Tha, MATB. 2007. A Short History of Rohingya and Kamans of Burma. *Kaladan News*, 5–10.

Thomas, Kimberley, R Dean Hardy, Heather Lazrus, et al. 2019. Explaining differential vulnerability to climate change: A social science review. *Wiley Interdisciplinary Reviews of Climate Change* 10(2): e565. https://doi.org/10.1002/wcc.565.

TRAC. 2022. A Sober Assessment of the Growing U.S. Asylum Backlog. Dec. 29, 2022. https://trac.syr.edu/reports/705, accessed 11 Feb 2024.

Ullah, Akm Ahsan. 2011. Rohingya refugees to Bangladesh: Historical exclusions and contemporary marginalization. *Journal of Immigrant & Refugee Studies* 9(2): 139–161. https://doi.org/10.1080/15562948.2011.567149.

United Nations Department of Economic and Social Affairs. 2018. 68% of the world population projected to live in urban areas by 2050, says UN. https://www.un.org/development/desa/en/news/population/2018-revision-of-world-urbanization-prospects.html, accessed 18 Nov 2024.

United Nations World Urbanization Prospects. 2009. cited in Royal Geographical Society with IBG. N.d., 21st Century Challenges: Urbanisation. https://21stcenturychallenges.org/urbanisation-2, accessed October 6, 2023.

United Nations World Urbanization Prospects, 2023. https://worldpopulationreview.com/world-cities/rome-population, accessed Oct 5, 2023.

United States Bureau of the Census. 2022. Nation's Urban and Rural Populations Shift Following 2020 Census, Press Release Number CB22-CN.25 December 29, 2022. https://www.census.gov/newsroom/press-releases/2022/urban-rural-populations.html, accessed Oct 5, 2023.

United States Customs and Border Patrol. 2023. Total CPB Enforcement Actions https://www.cbp.gov/node/380448/printable/print, accessed 11 Feb 2024.

Waldinger, R. 1989. Immigration and urban change. *Annual Review of Sociology* 15: 211–232. https://doi.org/10.1146/annurev.so.15.080189.001235.

Wilson, David, and Dennis Grammenos. 2005. Gentrification, discourse, and the body: Chicago's Humboldt Park. *Environment and Planning D: Society and Space* 23: 295–312. https://doi.org/10.1068/d0203.

Wilson, W. J. 1987. *The Truly Disadvantaged: The Inner-City, the Underclass, and Public Policy*. Chicago: University of Chicago Press.

Winnick, Louis. 1990. *New People in Old Neighborhoods: The Role of Immigrants in Rejuvenating New York's Communities*. New York: Russell Sage Foundation. https://www.russellsage.org/sites/default/files/NewPeopleOldN.pdf, accessed 13 Feb 2024.

Wisner, Ben, Piers Blaikie, Terry Cannon, and Ian Davis. 2003. *At Risk: Natural Hazards, People's Vulnerability and Disasters*. 2nd ed. New York: Routledge.

World Bank. 1980. *Operational Manual Statement 2.33. Social Issues Associated with Involuntary Resettlement in Bank-Financed Projects*. Washington, DC: World Bank.

World Bank Group. 2017. *The World Bank Environmental and Social Framework*. Washington, DC: The World Bank Group. https://thedocs.worldbank.org/en/doc/837721522762050108-0290022018/original/ESFFramework.pdf, accessed 18 Nov 2024.

World Population Review, 2023. https://worldpopulationreview.com/world-cities, accessed Oct 6, 2023.

Xiang, Biao. 2021. Suspension: Seeking agency for change in the hypermobile world. *Pacific Affairs* 94(2): 233–350. https://doi.org/0.5509/2021942233.

Section 4
How Does Migration Change Us?

Migration affects us all, even if we have not moved. Migration brings people from different backgrounds together. Newcomers adapt to new surroundings, new cultures, new languages, and new ways of life. People from common points of origin also stay in touch with one another across distances. Host communities adapt to new neighbors and the customs and traditions they bring. Those left behind adapt to life without their friends, family members, classmates, coworkers, and neighbors. These changes are part of moving. How we adapt to them affects everyone.

A mariachi musician crosses the road in Boyle Heights, Los Angeles, 2012. Photo by Raphael Cardenas.

World on the Move: 250,000 Years of Human Migration, First Edition. Edward Liebow, James I. Deutsch, Daniel Ginsberg, Sojin Kim, and Caitlyn Kolhoff.
© 2025 John Wiley & Sons, Inc. Published 2025 by John Wiley & Sons, Inc.

7

Language and Migration

This chapter focuses on three threads of scholarship about the relationship between language and migration and, in particular, how a closer look at languages and language change can help us understand the patterns and processes of human population movement. The first scholarship thread is concerned with linguistic evidence of past population movements. The second thread concerns the place of language in international immigrants' quest for social services, education, employment, and citizenship in their new home countries. The third thread concerns the role of language as a marker of identity and cultural heritage, which in turn affects the ways in which the arrival of immigrants may alter the character of their destination.

Mardi Gras in Cajun Country, Tee Mamou, Louisiana. Source: Photo by Natalie Maynor.

World on the Move: 250,000 Years of Human Migration, First Edition. Edward Liebow, James I. Deutsch, Daniel Ginsberg, Sojin Kim, and Caitlyn Kolhoff.
© 2025 John Wiley & Sons, Inc. Published 2025 by John Wiley & Sons, Inc.

PERSPECTIVE: Acadie, by Monica Heller

Professor Emerita, Ontario Institute for Studies in Education, Department of Social Justice Education, University of Toronto (Canada).

Acadie has geographical dimensions, but it isn't a place on a map. Derived from the idea of the nation-state, it has flags and anthems, genealogies and cuisine, dictionaries and a literary canon but no official capital city or elected state representatives. It is a space people feel they belong to without having to – or being able to – delimit its entirety with territorial boundaries, although it has points of mooring in mapped places. People who call themselves "Acadians" are far-flung – sprung from mobilities, it is (in many ways) mobility that keeps them together. Mobility is key to its founding myths, to its material history, and to the ability of those who claim Acadie to connect to each other as well as construct the discursive spaces and the concrete moorings that make it real.

The idea of Acadie comes from the days of the French empire, when France, England, Russia, and Spain fought over control of what is now North America. (The origin of the name is not clear; one theory links it to European references of Greek Arcadia, another to Indigenous words that reference fertile or settlement grounds as written by Europeans.) New France extended over much of what is now Canada as well as significant portions of what is now the United States, especially down the Mississippi River to the Gulf of Mexico. Pieces of it were claimed over the course of about 200 years (the sixteenth to eighteenth centuries) by mobile emissaries of the French crown and the Catholic Church. The crown recruited the poor or landless of western and northern France to settle in fertile valleys or key military outposts and trade nodes, to safeguard France's territorial claims, and to stave off potential social unrest within France. These settlements, while initially built by men seeking land, depended of course on transatlantic mobilities (of goods, soldiers, priests, nuns, and more settlers, especially women) for survival. One such settlement was established in 1604 near the Atlantic in Mi'kmaq territory, successfully displacing (and perhaps at times incorporating) the Indigenous population. The area, already referred to during the imperial conquest process as "Acadie," is now the Annapolis River Valley in the Canadian province of Nova Scotia (the current names already provide a hint of what is to come).

All of New France was involved in broader imperial struggles for power, especially against the British. In 1713, at the end of one of the many wars of the period, France ceded Acadie to Britain. The British were prepared to leave the settlers alone as long as they swore allegiance to the British Crown. When the majority refused to do so, the British rounded them up and burned the settlement down. Some of the settlers were killed in the fire, many others died in the ensuing manhunt. Others escaped, fleeing deeper into New France or into places the British Army would find hard to reach. Most were deported on makeshift boats, some to Britain, some to France, some to the British colonies of the Atlantic seaboard, and many to the French territory of Louisiana at the mouth of the Mississippi (though not everyone survived the trip). These were often only first destinations, as Acadians continued to move around the nodes of this network. Famously, the American poet Henry Wadsworth Longfellow provided a romantic fictive version of this mobility in the epic poem *Evangeline* (published in 1847). The poem recounts the trauma of what came to be called *Le Grand Dérangement* (the great unsettling) of 1713 and follows the tragic story of Évangéline, who is separated during those events from her lover, Gabriel. She wanders down the Atlantic coast, searching for him until she finally finds him at death's door, under a live oak tree, allegedly in what is now St. Martinville, Louisiana.

Later in the eighteenth century the rest of New France was ceded to Britain and Louisiana to Spain. After a brief return to French control, Louisiana became part of the United States in 1803. The northern British colonies became the Dominion of Canada in 1867. Acadians found themselves dispersed to various political jurisdictions whose boundaries reduced the possibility of movement and which sought to attach their loyalties to their new home countries. They also found themselves in spaces where their signs of difference (language, religion, culture, economic practices) intersected with the varied gendered and racial logics of social difference and inequality as colonialism and nation-building proceeded in both the United States and Canada. Évangéline, ultimately, is a condensation symbol of the feminization of a minority group that, however, also lays claim to whiteness and so to a relatively (if only relatively and certainly precariously) privileged position in the ethno-racial hierarchies of the emerging states.

Statue of Évangéline, heroine of the Acadian deportation to Saint Martinville, Louisiana. The headstone reads, "Old Cemetery of St Martin, Memory of Acadians Exiled in 1755."
Source: Wikimedia Commons, CC BY-SA 3.0.

Of course, efforts were made to inscribe Acadians, like other minorities, into these English-speaking and mainly Protestant states, notably by forbidding the use of French as a language of instruction in schools and limiting the powers of the Catholic church. While these efforts were legitimated by a discourse of assimilation as progress, their focus on linguistic and cultural difference also served to inscribe Acadians (among other francophone North Americans) in a particular niche as laborers in an economy of resource extraction and related industrial development. This niche has long necessitated worker mobility, sometimes seasonal or involving long-range shifts (fish, lumber, oil, construction), sometimes for longer periods, even lifetimes (urbanization linked to industrialization, domestic service for women). More recently, tourism has provided more opportunities for mooring, while being dependent on the mobilities of both tourists and other service providers.

But conditions (albeit different in each country) have also long allowed a wide variety of forms of resistance, organized first in large part by the Catholic church and the lay élite it trained in its seminaries and convents. Since about the 1960s it has been organized by the lay élite on its own, now trained in public institutions that evolved out of those run by the church. This resistance has mirrored the United States and Canadian emphasis on nation-building—from the late nineteenth century on, efforts have been devoted to the construction of Acadie as a nation in religious, cultural, linguistic, political, and economic forms. There is a flag, there is an anthem. There are political associations. There was once, briefly, a movement to found an independent, territorially bound state.

Instead, in the face of its impossibility, Acadians have constructed monolingual institutional spaces over which they have some control. Some have themselves been mobile; for example, the Convention nationale acadienne, which assembled members of the clerical and lay élite between 1881 and 1979 in different locations across what had become the Maritime provinces. More recently, the Congrès mondial acadien has met every five years in a different part of the Acadian world since 1994 as a space for Acadian individuals, families, associations, and institutions to meet, to renew ties, to share culture, and to plan economic, social, and political activities.

The other institutions (mainly educational and cultural) can be understood as points of mooring that cluster Acadian institutional control in a few (albeit dispersed) centers in Canada (Moncton, Caraquet, Pointe-de-l'Église, Halifax, Chéticamp, Abram-Village, Charlottetown) and Louisiana (Lafayette). These universities serve today as particularly important nodes of mooring, attracting students and recruiting faculty from across Acadian and, more broadly, the francophone world; annual music, theater, literary and art festivals also play a key role, with music as a particularly important site of the discursive construction of Acadie.

These points of mooring are also necessarily dependent on mobility—teachers come from Europe, Québec, or New Brunswick; religious institutions depend more and more on Catholics from francophone Africa; Acadians go to France, Ottawa, Québec, or Montréal to study and work; Louisiana Cajuns and Canadian Acadians move back and forth for cultural and educational exchanges and programs.

> Many of these points of mooring have taken shape as a transnational and transatlantic network exactly at the time of general globalization, when older imaginaries of the nation-state were beginning to be called into question. They also emerge as these same conditions turn Acadian space into a space of recruitment—as the birth rate falls and immigration rises—and as upward mobility and the culture industries made Acadie cool. Indeed, in the early twentieth century the impossibility of territorial boundaries started to look less like a disadvantage and more like a form of avant-garde opportunity. A mobile, diverse, networked Acadie might be the future.
>
> **Acknowledgments: Annette Boudreau, Isabelle LeBlanc, and Mireille McLaughlin offered thoughtful suggestions.**

Linguistic Evidence of Past Population Movements

Evidence of language change over time adds another layer of understanding about human population movements, alongside genetic, archaeological, and environmental evidence. This is because all languages are always changing, and (along with differences in language learning, and social differentiation) a main source of change is people on the move, which brings people from different speech communities into contact with one another. As a result, new words may be borrowed or invented, the meanings of words may change, and pronunciations may change, as may grammar and spelling. After the passage of time, as these changes build up, the original language may be hardly recognizable.

Think, for example, of the history of the English language. The best-known work of Old English literature is the epic poem "Beowulf," written around the year 1000. Anyone who isn't a scholar of Old English has to read it in translation because English has changed so much since that time. The poem begins:

Hwæt. We Gardena in geardagum,
þeodcyninga, þrym gefrunon,
hu ða æþelingas ellen fremedon

The first line literally translates to:

What! We spear-Danes in year-days

But since it is a work of poetry, translators make it understandable to modern readers as a Modern English poem, not a literal word-for-word gloss. Consider Headley's 2020 translation, which begins:

Bro! Tell me we still know how to speak of kings! In the old days,

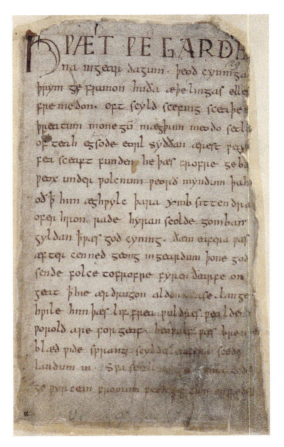

The first folio of the heroic epic poem Beowulf, written in the West Saxon dialect of Old English. Source: British Library Collection (Wikimedia Commons).

Why has our language changed so much over the past thousand years? Of course, language does change over time, but why did English change in these specific ways, and why did it change so much more than others? For example, Icelandic is another language of a small island in the North Atlantic but one whose modern-day speakers can still understand literature from around the time of "Beowulf." The answer is language contact—that is, people on the move.

In the year 1066 England was invaded by the Norman French, who came across the English Channel and established settlements in Britain. As a result of their influence, over the next few hundred years English grammar became more like French, relying more on word order and less on grammatical word endings. English also adopted a huge number of new words, so that now most English words are French or Latin in origin. For example, Geoffrey Chaucer's poem "Troilus and Criseyde" was written in Middle English in the 1380s—closer in time to "Beowulf" than to today—but the language is more similar to ours:

> *Ye knowe ek that in forme of speeche is chaunge*
> *Withinne a thousand yeer, and wordes tho*
> *That hadden pris, now wonder nyce and straunge*
> *Us thinketh hem, and yet thei spake hem so,*
> *And spedde as wel in love as men now do*

Just as Modern English evolved from Old English, entire families of languages are said to evolve from common ancestors (for example, the Romance languages French, Spanish, Italian, and Romanian all began as dialects of Latin), adapting to local variations in speech communities and subject to randomly introduced changes. Linguists and anthropologists have long been interested in developing a theory of language change to help them understand and describe these processes. One approach that was popular in the early to mid-twentieth century—but is now considered to rely on mistaken assumptions—thought of language change with an analogy to Darwinian evolution. Languages observed at any one time could be compared with one another to gauge the extent to which they shared common features, and it is assumed that languages that share a number of features are part of a family. The formal analysis of shared features followed a set of procedures known as *glottochronology*, from the Greek for "language study over time" (Swadesh 1952; Dyen 1956; Gudschinsky 1956). To complete this form of analysis it was assumed that certain features of any language change more slowly than others, especially a core vocabulary of "terms for pronouns, numerals, body parts, geographical features," among others (Gudschinsky 1956, p. 177). These core terms were assumed to change at the same rate in all languages, and the length of time since two languages of the same family began to diverge from one another could be estimated from the percentage of these core vocabulary items that remained the same.

As new techniques were developed to compare languages, glottochronology was discredited, as its main assumptions were not supported by new observations. The so-called Swadesh list of core vocabulary items was judged to be filled with cultural biases. It also became clear that the rate of change is not the same for all languages, as we saw in the case of English and Icelandic, nor is the rate of change uniform for any single language, as the Old English versus Middle English comparison showed.

Glottochronology is one specific analysis technique that fits in a larger category called **phylogenetic** approaches to language change (Dunn 2015). With the advent of increased computational capacity and the refinement of Bayesian statistics, it has become possible to analyze a larger number of observed features of languages, infer the missing pieces where insufficient data are available for rare languages, and refine our classification of language family groupings by lumping some languages previously thought to belong to different families, while splitting others apart that previous analyses had thought to belong together (Wichmann et al. 2010; Rama and Wichmann 2020; Pellard et al. 2024).

Tracing language family lineages, for example, has led to the recognition that the Athabascan-speaking tribes of interior Alaska and First Nations of northwestern Canada are related to the Diné (Navajo) and Apache tribal nations of the American Southwest (Campbell 1997, p. 110ff.). Similarly, the Bantu family of about 600 languages spoken by more than 300 million people in modern-day sub-Saharan Africa (e.g., Swahili, Zulu, Xhosa, Shona) had spread from its initial origin point in the Nigerian–Cameroonian border area to the east and south over a period of 5,000 years (Van de Velde et al. 2019).

This spread of languages is driven mainly by migration, conquest, and trade, which bring people from different speech communities in contact with one another (Kerswill 2006; Capstick 2020). Contact under these circumstances forces people to find a way of communicating with one another by necessity. When speakers of unrelated languages are forced into contact and the resulting new language becomes the first language of their children, this is called a "creole language". There are many creole languages around the world, often created in circumstances of colonialism and human trafficking. One of the more well-known and well-studied is Haitian Creole, which combines the vocabulary of French with the grammar of the West African languages spoken by people who were enslaved and brought to Haiti.

When the French settled the colony of Saint-Domingue (present-day Haiti), in the seventeenth century, the main industries were cotton and tobacco farming, and they brought indentured servants from France as well as enslaved people from West Africa to work the land. Around the turn of the eighteenth century, however, the sugar crop came to dominate under the control of a few large landowners. Growing sugar is intense and dangerous work; many enslaved people died in the fields, and many more were trafficked and brought to the Caribbean. As a result, "in 1739, Haiti's white population was 2.3 times what it had been in 1681; the population of color was 52 times what it had been" (Singler 1996, p. 215).

In this environment enslaved people needed to find a way to communicate with one another. A majority were speakers of languages in the Gbe family, such as the Fon language of present-day Benin, but the community as a whole was linguistically diverse, including descendants of earlier generations of enslaved people who had more exposure to French colonizers and the French language. Enslaved people did not typically have access to language classes; instead, searching for some way of communicating with one another, they developed a new language that we now know as Haitian Creole.

French speakers who hear Haitian Creole can understand much of it and may believe it to be a broken dialect of French, but this is incorrect. Rather, it is a distinct language with its own grammar, vocabulary, and community of speakers. To some extent, it reflects what would happen if speakers took the grammar of Fon and used it to combine French words. **For example, here is "Mary caught sight of the thief," in French, Fon, and Haitian Creole (examples from Lefebvre 1996):**

1. French
   Marie   a   vu   le   voleur
   Mary   has   seen   the   thief

2. Fon
   Mari   kò   mɔ̀   àjɔ́tɔ́   ɔ́
   Mary   PAST   see   thief   the

3. Haitian
   Mari   te   wè   volè   a
   Mary   PAST   see   thief   the

In these examples, the similarities between Haitian and French vocabulary are noticeable: Haitian *volè* and French *voleur* both mean "thief," and French *vu* is a form of the verb "to see," *voir,* which is pronounced something like "vwa" and resembles Haitian *wè*. At the same time, the similarity between Haitian and Fon grammar is also apparent, as both languages have a past-tense marker that precedes the verb "see" as well as a definite article, "the," that follows the noun "thief." We might conclude that the Haitian language is the historical result of speakers of Fon and related languages who tried to learn French without a textbook or teacher, made their best guesses based on the evidence available, and passed that language on to their children.

Today, the linguistic legacy of French colonialism in Haiti is clear. Haitian Creole is the preferred language of some 95% of Haitians, and Article V of the Haitian Constitution of 1987 states, "Creole is the only language that unites all Haitians. Creole and French are the official languages of the Republic of Haiti."[1] And yet, French is the preferred language of government and official business. For example, once a child has completed the lower elementary grades, the use of Haitian Creole in school is forbidden (DeGraff 2021), a policy that entrenches the privilege of French-speaking, upper-class families (DeGraff, Frager, and Miller 2022). In response, programs such as the MIT-Haiti Initiative (https://mit-ayiti.net) seek to promote the use of technology, active learning methods, and the Haitian Creole language in order to achieve educational and linguistic justice.

One additional language form that emerges from human population movements is what linguists call a "trade jargon" (Bakker 2008). One historically significant trade jargon was a simplified Romance language used on ships and in the Mediterranean port cities of medieval times, where people from various linguistic backgrounds (Greek, Turkish, Arabic, Sicilian, Venetian, French, Catalan, Castillian, and so forth) needed a way to converse with one another (Mallette 2014). The name of the language was *lingua franca,* literally meaning "Frankish language," where "Frank" was the word used in the Middle

---

[1] The Haitian Constitution has also been produced in Creole (Konstitisyon Repiblik Ayiti 1987).

Ages by people from the eastern Mediterranean to refer generically to people from Europe. Nowadays, the term "lingua franca" is used to describe any language that is regularly used for communication among people who do not share a native language.

The Chinook jargon is another trade language that developed to facilitate commerce among the Native peoples of the Pacific coast of North America, from the Columbia River in the United States north to British Columbia and Alaska. It was the language that European settlers used when they first arrived in the region in the eighteenth century, and it was the language used to negotiate the treaties of 1855 between the United States and numerous tribal representatives throughout the Columbia River Plateau and Puget Sound regions. Significantly, when contested treaty protections for tribal fishing rights were reviewed by the US Supreme Court in the 1970s (*Washington v. Fishing Vessel Association* 1979), the Court acknowledged that the English-language translation of the treaties was far more elaborate than the language actually used in the treaty negotiations, due to the restricted nature of the Chinook jargon in which the negotiations took place. Remember, this was no one's native language but a mixture of several unrelated Native languages, French, and English that was primarily used for international commerce. The Court insisted that the proper interpretation of the treaties was not according to the technical meaning of the translated words as understood by the "learned lawyers, but in the sense in which the words would naturally be understood by the Indians" at the time (*Washington v. Fishing Vessel Association* 1979).

Nowadays, many people regard English as a lingua franca (Jenkins, Cogo, and Dewey 2011; Melitz 2016). It is widely used as a common language used among people who speak different first languages, often for instrumental purposes such as air traffic control, international monetary exchanges, and other business transactions. In addition, because English is in such wide use around the world, it is often taught as a second language in countries from which international immigrants originate and may increase the chances of immigrants preferring to move to English-speaking destinations because they have some basic working knowledge before they move (Adserà and Pytliková 2016, p. 347).

Air traffic controller, Schiphol Tower (Netherlands). Source: Photo by Mark Brouwer (Wikimedia Commons CC-BY-SA-2.5).

Place of Language in Citizenship, Education, Employment and Social Services

The second scholarship thread in exploring the relationship of language and migration involves the ways that, especially for international immigrants, language is woven into policies for citizenship, education, employment, and the delivery of social services. Among the 27 member states of the European Union (EU), for example, the first two decades of the twenty-first century saw a surge in international immigrants from war and conflict zones in the Middle East and the African continent. This surge has propelled nationalist movements in many EU countries, with a contested focus on which (if any) of these international immigrants ought to be admitted and thereby gain access to social services, work, and the rights of citizenship.

The eligibility requirements for entry, residence, and citizenship vary from country to country, but the EU as a whole has incorporated in its Common Basic Principles for Immigrant Integration Policy the notion that language is an essential element in the process of integrating international immigrants into member states (European Union 2004, Item 12, p. 18). As Wodak (2013, p. 174) shows, in furtherance of these common basic principles, 7 countries require immigrants to pass a language proficiency test just to enter the country, 14 countries require immigrants to pass a language proficiency test to gain long-term residence, and all but 2 countries (Finland and Norway) require proficiency in the national language to gain citizenship (and such a requirement is under discussion in these remaining 2 countries).

In Mexico, Canada, and the United States, people applying for citizenship are required to demonstrate a proficiency in Spanish (Mexico), English or French (Canada), or English (United States). Indian citizenship requires a language certificate that proves proficiency in one of the Indian languages specified by the national constitution. South Africa has a requirement that foreigners applying for citizenship pass a test demonstrating proficiency in at least one of the country's 11 official languages. Australia requires applicants for citizenship to pass a test that assesses their English-language skills. Japan does not have a formal language test to acquire citizenship, but all written application procedures are conducted in Japanese.

If an acceptable proficiency in the national language is a prerequisite for immigrants to enjoy the full rights of citizenship, this policy reflects a belief that a common language is necessary for the establishment of a national identity — a belief that is contradicted by experiences in the Global South, particularly South Asia and southern Africa, where multilingual societies are often the norm (Rabbi and Canagarajah 2021). Yet, at least in Europe and North America, most countries that have such a requirement also recognize a responsibility to support language learning for both adults and children (European Commission/EACEA/Eurydice 2019). Most countries also make it a matter of policy to accommodate a certain level of language diversity, recognizing that acquisition of the national language in the host country will not happen overnight.

For example, the Language Policy Division of the Council of Europe was established in 2008 to provide technical assistance to the EU member states in assessing language learning needs, developing programs to meet those needs, and evaluating the effectiveness of these programs. Guided by principles that prioritize evidence-based high quality instructional programs, independent learning, giving incentives precedence over compulsion in language learning, and valuing the migrants' languages of origin, the Council of Europe recognizes that "languages are vital for building intercultural understanding and social cohesion" (Council of Europe 2014, p. 12).

A comprehensive survey of immigrant and refugee language policies by Li and Sah (2019) points to several trends that have emerged among the countries of Europe, North America, and Australia that are the most likely hosts for the twenty-first century surge in migrants fleeing war and conflict as well as economic hardship. The first trend they note is that communication barriers continue to contribute to immigrants' difficulties in accessing necessary social services, placing themselves on a path to economic self-sufficiency, and overcoming racial prejudice and other exclusionary policies and practices. In the words of another observer, despite the work of institutions like the Council of Europe's Language Policy Division, the cumulative result of social exclusion is that the experiences of many immigrants and refugees are described as "living in an open prison" (Seukwa 2013, p. 12).

With few exceptions, the approach to language learning adopted by most countries hosting a large influx of immigrants and refugees appears to be:

> an assimilation approach characterized by an exclusive focus on learning destination language and culture while neglecting the language resources that newcomers bring from home countries. The policies and programs also aim for basic skills training for rapid employment and fail to cater to the newcomers' population, which is heterogenous in education levels, employment experiences, host language proficiency, and personal needs (Li and Sah 2019, p. 327).

This approach is complicated by the fact that, while insisting on learning the host country's language to expedite societal integration, these host countries also point with pride to their cultural pluralism (Baynham 2020, p. 417). If learning the host language is a requirement – either formal or informal – for full participation in the new society, retaining one's native language may be seen as an act of resisting integration. Such resistance, as Prins and Toso (2012, p. 447) point out, can lead to emphasizing differences or the "othering" of language learners and heightened economic and social exclusion. Conversely, generations later, descendants of immigrants are typically monolingual speakers of the national language but may be stigmatized by being treated as though they were "foreign" speakers (Rosa 2016). Being perceived as foreign is sometimes a greater barrier to communication than actual linguistic proficiency.

Language as a Marker of Identity and Cultural Heritage

The final scholarly thread to be taken up in this chapter on language and migration focuses on the ways that migrants create language communities that, in turn, draw migrants to them, strengthening community identity and preserving cultural heritage. What do we mean by migrants creating language communities? Since communication is such an essential ingredient in providing social and material support, international immigrants who do not speak the host country's language upon arrival are limited in their ability to participate civically in their new place and are also challenged in gaining access to information and services. In the United States, the US Census Bureau uses the term "linguistic isolation" to describe the circumstances households face when their English-language abilities are limited, even if they are located in areas and embedded in communities where their language is widely spoken. While many immigrants speak English quite well, a substantial portion are living in linguistic isolation. When facing these circumstances, they usually turn to one another, which strengthens social ties in a self-reinforcing way.

The contemporary character of East Los Angeles, for example, was formed by restrictive housing covenants from the 1920s to the 1960s. These restrictions prevented households newly arriving in Southern California from settling elsewhere in Los Angeles and drove these households to seek housing in the geographically separated area east of the Los Angeles River. Once a more linguistically and ethnically diverse place, East Los Angeles today is predominantly Mexican American, with descendants of Mexicans who had been uprooted by the Revolution of 1910–1917 joined by much more recent arrivals because of the institutions that had been built in earlier decades. These institutions include places of worship, mutual aid societies, language schools, hospitals, and cemeteries.

In effect, the formation of a language community like what we find today in East Los Angeles is the result of the phenomenon called "chain migration." As briefly touched on in Chapter 1, chain migration is a pattern where migrants from one particular place or cultural background follow other migrants to a specific destination, taking advantage of family members, relatives, or other social network ties to try to establish themselves in a new and usually unfamiliar setting. As Avila (2007) points out in his essay about the history of East Los Angeles as captured in public art murals, a complex web of formal and informal racialized restrictions imposed on who could live where, combined with a federally initiated guest-worker program that brought about four million Mexican farm workers to the United States, pushed a widely diverse population of early twentieth century immigrant families out of Boyle Heights and led to the formation of the Mexican American barrio in the 1950s. Then the US government's ambitious interstate highway building project began in earnest, and the narratives depicted in public art as well as oral histories (Estrada 2005) chronicle the household moves under threat of displacement that pushed people into increasingly concentrated remaining pockets of the barrio.

In a sense, the opposite of concentrating language communities into restricted spaces is the emergence of diaspora languages (Adachi 2020). *Diaspora* is a word that comes from the Greek "to scatter," and it refers to people who are spread across many places away from their original homeland, usually by forced displacement (Dufoix 2017, p. 28). Rather than resettle in a single place, a diasporic settlement pattern involves dispersal among many places. When people disperse from their original homelands, they bring their language with them and often use their homeland language in their efforts to hold onto their cultural identity.

Some examples of diasporic communities include Africans enslaved beginning in the seventeenth century; Armenians who fled the Ottoman genocide in the early twentieth century; Jews, who have a long history of forced displacement but recently escaped the twentieth century Holocaust in Europe and, even more recently, the 1979 Islamic Revolution in Iran; and the South Asian diaspora at the hands of British colonial powers (see Ember, Ember, and Skoggard (2005) for a more comprehensive list and detailed case studies). Several decades ago, some migration scholars took up the issue of return migration (e.g., Brettell 1979; Gmelch 1980), and posited an ideology of return that retains the possibility of going back to the homeland from which they were displaced. Researchers have more recently observed that "dispersed populations do not necessarily expect or desire a diasporic return" (Canagarajah and Silberstein 2012, p. 81). Where a fixation on the homeland language might have cemented connections with the homeland and among community members, nothing stands still, including the homeland language. This changing nature is made more visible thanks to the global reach of internet-assisted telecommunications and more affordable travel.

Members of diasporic communities are also participants in the economic and social institutions of the places where they now live, and as Canagarajah and Silberstein observe, their "diaspora identity is one among many layered identities they enjoy" (2012, p. 82). This means that one might expect to observe multilingualism among the members of a diasporic community as well as switching back and forth between one's heritage language and the language of the dominant society in which they are now embedded. The heritage language may serve, under these circumstances, as "a strategic resource as it helps members negotiate their layered identities and group relationships" (Canagarajah and Silberstein 2012, p. 82).

Chapter Summary

We have reviewed three important threads of scholarship about the relationship between language and migration. First, we have summarized some key ways in which the evidence of language change over time adds to our understanding about migration, as people from different speech communities encountering another is one of the main ways in which language changes are brought about. Earlier attempts to trace language family trees by examining the degree of resemblance between two related languages has given way to computationally sophisticated phylogenetic approaches to language change. Other observed consequences of people on the move coming together and trying to communicate with one another include the development of creoles, trade jargons, and lingua francas.

A second scholarship thread in exploring the relationship between language and migration has to do with how language is woven into policies for citizenship, education, employment, and the delivery of social services. For international migration in particular, most countries see that as a matter of policy some level of proficiency in the host country's language is necessary for full participation as citizens, and many countries have made investments in language learning to accommodate the need for developing this proficiency.

A final scholarship thread discussed here has been the ways that migrants create language communities and, through language, strengthen community identity and preserve migrants' cultural heritage. Creation of these communities is often done out of a necessity for mutual assistance in the face of limited access to support services from the place of destination. In the special case of diaspora communities, migration scholars have come to see that diasporic language communities may create a place of respite and refuge as migrants move back and forth between the dominant society, which is often unwelcoming in subtle (or not so subtle) ways, and a community with whom a common language inscribes a shared identity and heritage.

Review Questions

1. What does language change over time tell us about past population movements? What are creoles and trade jargons? What is the relationship between these language forms and migration?
2. What is your opinion about the requirement that international immigrants must demonstrate a proficiency in the host country's official language to gain long-term residence or citizenship?
3. Without consulting any outside references, what do you think the official language of your home country is? Now, do a search online to see if you were correct. How do you feel about the result?
4. Many observers have noted that migrants may create language communities and, through language, strengthen community identity and preserve migrants' cultural heritage. Why do you think the creation of a language community is sometimes a necessity?

References

Adachi, Nobuko. 2020. Diaspora Language. In James Stanlaw, ed. *The International Encyclopedia of Linguistic Anthropology*. Oxford: Wiley-Blackwell. https://doi.org/10.1002/9781118786093.iela0441.

Adserà, Alicia, and Mariola Pytliková. 2016. Language and Migration. In Victor Ginsburgh, Shlomo Weber, and Ancy Dedman, eds. *The Palgrave Handbook of Economics and Language*. London: Palgrave Macmillan. pp. 342–372. https://doi.org/10.1007/978-1-137-32505-1_13.

Avila, Eric. 2007. East side stories: Freeways and their portraits in Chicano Los Angeles. *Landscape Journal* 26(1): 83–97. https://www.jstor.org/stable/43323756.

Bakker, Peter. 2008. Pidgins versus Creoles and Pidgincreoles. In Silvia Kouwenberg, and John Victor Singler, eds. *The Handbook of Pidgin and Creole Studies*. Oxford: Wiley. pp. 130–157. doi: 10.1002/9781444305982.ch6.

Baynham, Mike. 2020. Language and Migration. In Mike Baynham, and James Simpson, eds. *The Routledge Handbook of Applied Linguistics*. 2nd ed. New York: Routledge. pp. 413–427. https://doi.org/10.4324/9781003082637-4.

Brettell, Caroline. 1979. *Emigrar para voltar*: A Portuguese ideology of return migration. *Papers in Anthropology* 20(1): 1–20.

Campbell, Lyle. 1997. *American Indian Languages: The Historical Linguistics of Native America*. New York: Oxford University Press. https://amerindias.github.io/referencias/cam00americanindian.pdf.

Canagarajah, Suresh, and Sandra Silberstein. 2012. Introduction: Diaspora identities and language. *Journal of Language, Identity, and Education* 11: 81–84. https://doi.org/10.1080/15348458.2012.667296.

Capstick, Tony. 2020. *Language and Migration*. New York: Routledge. doi: 10.4324/9781351207713.

Council of Europe. 2014. *The Linguistic Integration of Adult Migrants: From one country to another, from one language to another*. Strasbourg: Council of Europe, Language Policy Division. https://rm.coe.int/16802fd54a, accessed 27 Mar 2024.

DeGraff, Michel. 2021. What Does Justice Sound Like? Theorizing the contemporary, *Fieldsights*, December 22. https://culanth.org/fieldsights/what-does-justice-sound-like

DeGraff, Michel, William Scott Frager, and Haynes Miller. 2022. Language policy in Haitian education: A history of conflict over the use of Kreyòl as language of instruction. *Journal of Haitian Studies* 28(2): 33–95. doi: 10.1353/jhs.2022.a901944.

Dufoix, Stéphane. 2017. *The Dispersion: A History of the word 'diaspora'*. Leiden: Brill. doi: 10.1163/9789004326910.

Dunn, Michael. 2015. Language Phylogenies. In Claire Bowern, and Bethwyn Evans, eds. *The Routledge Handbook of Historical Linguistics*. London: Routledge. pp. 190–211. https://doi.org/10.4324/9781315794013-10.

Dyen, Isidore. 1956. Language distribution and migration theory. *Language* 32(4): 611–626. https://doi.org/10.2307/411084.

Ember, Melvin, Carol R. Ember, and Ian Skoggard. 2005. *Encyclopedia of Diasporas: Immigrant and refugee cultures around the world*. Dordrecht: Kluwer Academic Publishers. https://doi.org/10.1007/978-0-387-29904-4.

Estrada, Gilbert. 2005. If you build it, they will move: The Los Angeles freeway system and the displacement of Mexican East Los Angeles, 1944-1972. *Southern California Quarterly* 87(3): 287–315. http://www.jstor.com/stable/41172272.

European Commission/EACEA/Eurydice. 2019. The Teaching of Regional or Minority Languages in Schools in Europe. *Eurydice Report*. Luxembourg: Publications Office of the European Union. https://eurydice.indire.it/wp-content/uploads/2019/09/minority_languages_en.pdf, accessed 4 Apr 2024.

European Union. 2004. *Common Basic Principles for Immigrant Integration Policy in the EU*. https://migrant-integration.ec.europa.eu/sites/default/files/2008-08/docl_1274_415560448.pdf, accessed 26 Mar 2024.

Gmelch, George. 1980. Return migration. *Annual Review of Anthropology* 9: 135–159. http://www.jstor.org/stable/2155732, Accessed 28 Mar 2024.

Gudschinsky, Sarah C. 1956. The ABC's of lexicostatistics (glottochronology). *Word* 12(2): 175–210. https://doi.org/10.1080/00437956.1956.11659599.

Headley, Maria Dahvana. 2020. *Beowulf: A New Translation*. New York: Farrar, Straus and Giroux.

Jenkins, Jennifer, Alessia Cogo, and Martin Dewey. 2011. Review of developments in research into English as a Lingua Franca. *Language Teaching* 44(3): 281–315. https://doi.org/10.1017/S0261444811000115.

Kerswill, Paul. 2006. Migration and Language. In Klaus Mattheier, Ulrich Ammon, and Peter Trudgill, eds. *Sociolinguistics/Soziolinguistik. An international handbook of the science of language and society*. Vol. 3. 2nd ed. Berlin: De Gruyter. https://doi.org/10.1515/9783110184181.3.10.2271.

Konstitisyon Repiblik Ayiti. 1987. https://original-ufdc.uflib.ufl.edu/AA00000626/00001/6j, accessed 6 Mar 2024.

Lefebvre, Claire. 1996. The tense, mood, and aspect system of Haitian creole and the problem of transmission of grammar in creole genesis. *Journal of Pidgin and Creole Languages* 11(2): 231–311. https://doi.org/10.1075/jpcl.11.2.03lef.

Li, Guofang, and Pramod Sah. 2019. Immigrant and Refugee Language Policies, Programs, and Practices in an Era of Change: Promises, contradictions, and possibilities. In Steven J Gold, and Stephanie J Nawyn, eds. *Routledge International Handbook of Migration Studies*. 2nd ed. Routledge. pp. 325–338. https://doi.org/10.4324/9781315458298.

Mallette, Karla. 2014. Lingua Franca. In Peregrine Horden, and Sharon Kinoshita, eds. *A Companion to Mediterranean History*. Oxford: Wiley Publishing. pp. 330–344. https://doi.org/10.1002/9781118519356.ch21.

Melitz, Jacques. 2016. English as a Global Language. In Victor Ginsburgh, Shlomo Weber, and Ancy Dedman, eds. *The Palgrave Handbook of Economics and Language*. London: Palgrave Macmillan. pp. 583–615. https://doi.org/10.1007/978-1-137-32505-1_21.

Pellard, Thomas, Robin J Ryder, and Guillaume Jacques. 2024. The Family Tree Model. In Adam Ledgeway et al., eds. *The Wiley Blackwell Companion to Diachronic Linguistics*. John Wiley & Sons, Limited. (preprint available here).

Prins, Esther, and Blair Wilson Toso. 2012. Receptivity towards immigrants in rural Pennsylvania: Perceptions of adult English as second language providers. *Rural Sociology* 77(3): 435–461. https://doi.org/10.1111/j.1549-0831.2012.00081.x.

Rabbi, Shakil, and Suresh Canagarajah. 2021. Cosmopolitanism and Plurilingual Traditions: Learning from South Asian and Southern African practices of intercultural communication. In Enrica Piccardo, Aline Germain-Rutherford, and Geoff Lawrence, eds. *The Routledge Handbook of Plurilingual Language Education*. New York: Routledge. pp. 82–95. https://doi.org/10.4324/9781351002783.

Rama, Taraka, and Søren Wichmann. 2020. A test of generalized Bayesian dating: A new linguistic dating method. *PLoS One* 15(8): e0236522. doi: 10.1371/journal.pone.0236522.

Rosa, Jonathan. 2016. From Mock Spanish to Inverted Spanglish: Language ideologies and the racialization of Mexican and Puerto Rican youth in the United States. In H Samy Alim, ed. *Raciolinguistics: How Language Shapes Our Ideas about Race*. Oxford: Oxford University Press. pp. 65–80. https://doi.org/10.1093/acprof:oso/9780190625696.003.0004.

Seukwa, Louis Henri. 2013. General Introduction. In Louis Henri, ed. *Integration of Refugees into the European Education and Labour Market*. Bern: Peter Lang Publishing. pp. 7–16. https://www.peterlang.com/document/1047544#BigPicturePanel, accessed 27 Mar 2024.

Singler, John Victor. 1996. Theories of creole genesis, sociohistorical considerations, and the evaluation of evidence: The case of Haitian Creole and the relexification hypothesis. *Journal of Pidgin and Creole Languages* 11(2): 185–230. https://doi.org/10.1075/jpcl.11.2.02sin.

Swadesh, Morris. 1952. Lexicostatistical dating of prehistoric ethnic contacts. *Proceedings of the American Philosophical Society* 96: 452–463. https://www.jstor.org/stable/3143802.

Van de Velde, Mark, Koen Bostoen, Derek Nurse, and Gérard Phillipson, eds. 2019. *The Bantu Languages*. 2nd ed. London: Routledge. https://doi.org/10.4324/9781315755946.

Washington v. Fishing Vessel Association. 1979. 443 U.S. 658. https://supreme.justia.com/cases/federal/us/443/658, accessed 26 Mar 2024.

Wichmann, Søren, Eric W Holman, André Müller, Viveka Velupillai, Johann-Mattis List, Oleg Belyaev, Matthias Urban, and Dik Bakker. 2010. Glottochronology as a heuristic for genealogical language relationships. *Journal of Quantitative Linguistics* 17(4): 303–316. https://doi.org/10.1080/09296174.2010.512166.

Wodak, Ruth. 2013. Dis-citizenship and migration: A critical discourse-analytical perspective. *Journal of Language, Identity, and Education* 12(3): 173–178. https://doi.org/10.1080/15348458.2013.797258.

8
Economic Development and Gentrification

As we have discussed in earlier chapters, there are many reasons why people move. One of the driving factors is economic opportunity. The movement of people is often tied to economic factors; it can take many different shapes from families moving to a new city for career opportunities to individuals temporarily crossing borders due to seasonal labor patterns. Communities that have thriving and robust job markets attract new people. For example, as technology giants like Apple and Oracle developed in Silicon Valley, California, the orange groves of the 1950s were replaced by their offices. While this change in industries led to an influx of technological workers and capital in the region, it also resulted in higher property and living costs (Kwon and Sorenson 2023). **Economic development** occurs when policies and programs foster the economic growth of a community and a restructuring of its institutions through activities such as job creation and innovation.

In the case of Silicon Valley, economic development was the driving force for urbanization in the region through the 2000s as technology companies continued to grow and social media began to develop (Kwon and Sorenson 2023). However, the growth of cities can, and often does, lead to the displacement of peoples who have historically inhabited those areas. This struggle between economic development, migration motivated by shifts in capital, and the displacement of previously established communities is often referred to as **gentrification.** As seen in the example of Silicon Valley, gentrification can lead to higher wages in an area; but it also leads to an overall higher cost of living. In particular, property costs can rise as the demand for housing increases. This rise in property values can lead to disparity, specifically between the wealth of people coming into an area compared to people who have historically lived within the community.

World on the Move: 250,000 Years of Human Migration, First Edition. Edward Liebow, James I. Deutsch, Daniel Ginsberg, Sojin Kim, and Caitlyn Kolhoff.
© 2025 John Wiley & Sons, Inc. Published 2025 by John Wiley & Sons, Inc.

In this chapter, we will discuss in greater detail how economic opportunities propel the movements of individuals and households seeking to improve their livelihoods. We will explore how economic development leads to mobility, both by choice and displacement. Moreover, we will see how modern economic development and urbanization has led to a new conceptualization of urban and rural communities.

Patterns of Movement: Demographics

Economic pressures can motivate individuals to migrate to new areas, but there are many nuances of movement related to the social class, perceived career skills, and social identity of people who try to migrate. For example, migrants coming across an international border to perform seasonally limited tasks (such as agriculture) may only be eligible for a temporary work visa, while immigrants with high demand skills recruited by major corporations may be eligible for their own resident visas as well as visas for their families. In this section, we will briefly outline some of the scenarios that have historically related to economically motivated migration.

Under most definitions, a guest worker is a person granted temporary access to work in another country performing tasks the host country is unable, or unwilling, to fill with their domestic labor force. Guest workers are most prevalent in agriculture work, but they can also be found in the industrial and domestic sectors of many countries in the Global North. However, people may also temporarily move within a nation or region in order to earn an income they may be unable to find in their home. For example, many Black residents in the Southern United States and rural, white Southerners from the Appalachian Mountain region moved to Midwestern states during the mid-twentieth century in search for new blue-collar jobs in factories. It was not uncommon for men to move to these areas first to find a job and housing while sending money back to their families. Many ended up moving their whole families up to these new industrial areas, but some families returned to their former homes as industries encountered economic challenges.

The movement of these individuals along the hillbilly highway also illustrates another frequent trend in economic-based migration: the movement of people from sparsely populated rural areas to dense urban centers. People began to migrate from this region to northern, urban-industrial cities in the Midwest manufacturing belt as jobs in agriculture declined between 1900 and 1945 (Fraser 2023). In tandem with the out-migration from the Appalachian region, Black Americans also migrated out of the Southern United States during the early to mid-twentieth century in what is known as the Great Migration. Between 1916 and 1970, six million Black people moved from the rural South to urban areas in other regions of the United States. They moved for economic opportunities as well as to escape the discrimination and violence they were facing in the South. The movement of people from these regions to northern manufacturing cities during the mid-twentieth century remains one of the greatest out-migrations in US history. As we have discussed, **out-migration** is a form of domestic migration where a person moves from one part of their country to another. Globally, in 1950 70% of the world's population lived in rural areas. By 2018, more than half lived in urban areas (United Nations, Department of Economic and Social Affairs, Population Division 2019).

PERSPECTIVE: How Migration Changes All of Us: The Jewish Gauchos and Argentine National Identity, by Judith Freidenberg

Professor Emerita of anthropology at the University of Maryland (USA) and Instituto de Desarrollo Económico y Social (Argentina).

As with the wave of concentric circles created in a pond by throwing a stone, human population movements influence both the social structure and the ideological conceptions of a nation in a territory over time. As new cultural groups move into a territory, established populations change in response. Thus, human displacements create new territories over time. As Appadurai reminds us:

> Histories produce geographies and not vice versa. We must get away from the notion that there is some kind of spatial landscape against which time writes its story. Instead, it is historical agents, institutions, actors, and powers that make the geography. …Each geography is historically produced (2013, p. 66).

In turn, new territories engender a crossroads of people and ideas. The formation of Argentina as a country shows how territories are changed by successive waves of immigration.

Aborigines, the first people to settle in the territory that eventually became Argentina in the nineteenth century, were immigrants themselves who arrived at least 10,000 years ago. Their exact geographical and chronological origins remain uncertain. The next wave of immigration into the territory were Spaniards during the sixteenth century – first as conquerors and later as colonial settlers – who persecuted the sparse and widely distributed aboriginal population, took their land, killed many, and forced others to move or become slave labor alongside Africans forcibly transported to the territory. The theft of land was legalized by the Spanish Crown, which awarded large tracts to the conquering Spaniards.

Central to Argentina's history and national ideology are creoles (*criollos*), the mixed-race offspring of Spaniards, local aborigines, and enslaved Africans. One sub-group of criollo were called *gauchos*, many of whom resisted assimilation to Spanish colonization by choosing to lead a nomadic existence in rural areas. Occasionally, they worked on landowners' ranches and were granted land to build a house, though it was not considered their private property.

Although independence from Spain had been declared in 1810, a constitution was only passed in 1853. By the mid-nineteenth century, Argentina had become a wealthy cattle-raising and exporting country yet was considered uncivilized by a local intelligentsia admiring of Europe. With the enactment of the Immigration and Colonization Law in 1876, the Argentine government sought to attract Europeans as a political strategy to introduce what they called "moral progress," and to diversify the economy through the introduction of agriculture. The government sent delegations to Europe to recruit the immigrants considered desirable, welcomed inquiries from philanthropic associations and civil societies regarding land purchases, and supported landowners willing to lease land to agriculturalists deemed civilized. Eradication policies affected populations considered barbaric, including gauchos and aborigines. The aboriginal population was almost exterminated in a genocidal war in the 1880s, known as the Campaign of the Desert, and survivors were displaced to the mountainous west. The gauchos' lifestyle was seriously compromised by the arrival of European immigration.

Among the newly arrived, so-called civilized groups were the British who, despite their small number, made an outsized impact because they brought capital and new technologies. For example, the British built railroads that cross-cut the territory, facilitating commerce and the export industry. Between the mid-nineteenth century and World War I, millions of other European immigrants settled in rural Argentina on land either leased by the state, individual landowners, or private colonization associations. As the European immigrants came in, the gauchos were displaced, since neither those roving the land and feeding on stray cattle nor those settled in ranches could stay put. Once the land they lived on was sold, they were destitute and had to move to shanty towns or work for the newcomers. In the national discourse at the time the gaucho represented a barbarian, somebody without education and who was uneducable. Their forced displacements, like those of the aboriginal populations earlier, were deemed necessary for the progress of the nation.

The largest European immigrant waves to Argentina between 1880 and 1910 came from Italy and Spain, although about a third eventually returned to their homeland. Eastern and western Europeans settled in agricultural colonies, or *colonias*, closed ethnic communities. Their children assimilated quickly through public schools, military service, and *jus solis*[1] citizenship. Among rural Jewish populations, a new hybrid group emerged: the "Jewish gauchos," as Russian émigré and journalist Alberto Gerchunoff labeled the new generation that mimicked gaucho customs in dress, food, and local dialect. Their parents did not master Spanish upon arrival and were inexperienced in the practice of agriculture in the local environment that demanded skills such as clearing the land for sowing or resisting locust plagues. The local gauchos, with whom they communicated in elementary Spanish and Yiddish, were their teachers and first vehicles to assimilation.

---

[1] *Jus solis* is a Latin term for birthright citizenship, meaning literally "the right of the soil." It is a rule that determines a person's nationality based on their place of birth.

Pepe Soriano and Dora Baret in *The Jewish Gauchos (Los Gauchos Judíos)*, a 1975 film. Source: Wikimedia Commons.

While the Jewish gaucho metaphor epitomizes immigrant assimilation to the host country, placing it in historical context complicates the interpretation. First, an immigrant does not assimilate to a country but to the people and institutions in the locality of residence. The Jewish gauchos of the rural colonies, born in several eastern European countries, learned to live together using a common language, Yiddish; practicing the same religion, Judaism; and responding to the autocratic bureaucracy of the Jewish Colonization Association. Their assimilation to Argentina was eased through the informal learning of local skills from the gauchos and the formal education provided by public institutions (Devoto 2004; Freidenberg 2009). Assimilation is a process that takes place locally and is influenced by current national ideologies. When Gerchunoff published *Los Gauchos Judíos* in 1910 (Gerchunoff 1984), as Argentina celebrated its first centennial, the political climate was anti-immigrant and anti-Jewish. The number of immigrants in the country had grown exponentially – the 1914 census documented that 30% of the total Argentine population was born abroad. Many bilingual schools in the rural colonies were forced to stop teaching foreign languages, and any Jewish teachers in the public school system were dismissed.

Increasingly, however, the symbolic representation of the gaucho had changed. By the centennial of the country in 1910, the gaucho was no longer the barbarian of an earlier time but rather an authentic representative of Argentine identity. In writing this book, Gerchunoff was attempting to show that

> the Jewish colonists had assimilated to this new version of the native of the land. And yet, the Jewish gauchos, while emulating the creole gaucho, had no aspirations to become a landless, poor employee like them. Their upward mobility through commerce, the arts, and the professions suggests that most did not want to stay on the land.
>
> By the 1930s and 1940s the flow of European transatlantic migrations had diminished, partly due to the growing political turmoil in Europe that restricted emigration and partly due to restrictions to immigration policies in Argentina. These trends coincided with the abandonment by immigrant European agriculturalists and their descendants of their assigned lots in the rural areas. One reason was the movement of their children to cities for study or work, which left their parents aging in place and less able to tend to the farms alone. Another was the decrease of state support of agriculture after a military coup in 1930 and the inauguration of a populist government in the 1940s led by a charismatic military leader, Juan Perón. He passed legislation that granted labor rights to rural workers and offered work in factories, which prompted a rural–urban migration to denser population centers, mostly to the capital city but also to smaller cities, towns, and villages. Without capital or human resources transferable to urban life, the rural poor engrossed the population of shanty towns. Older immigrant colonists left and, with little help to work, the farms followed.
>
> Since the mid-twentieth century, most immigration to Argentina originates in Latin American countries, traditionally neighboring ones like Bolivia and Paraguay but more recently Venezuela and Haiti (minor exceptions are Koreans, Senegalese, and more recently, Russians). Yet, while the national origin of immigrants has changed over time, the centrality of immigration in Argentine history and identity (as in many other nations) has not. Too often efforts to define who is us (an Argentine) and who is an other (not an Argentine) are defined by questions and assumptions about who is now an immigrant, who was an immigrant in the past, and who will be an immigrant in the future. It is the movement through time of people (both within and across state borders) that truly helps to understand the emergence and disappearance of national ideological rhetoric and peoples' sense of self and belonging.

Apart from the general economic opportunities, some people moving into the urban centers have done so because cities provide them with a unique opportunity to network with like-minded individuals, acquire specialized resources necessary for their work, or access financial resources concentrated in these areas. These people are sometimes referred to as the "creative class" and include artists, entrepreneurs, scientists, or other people looking to transform their ideas into personal wealth. Under this migration scenario, these creatives are attracted to cities and regions that are diverse, tolerant, and welcoming. Jobs and major firms are then attracted to cities because of the unique workers in their labor force (Borén and Young 2013). For this to occur, these migrants would have to be highly skilled, highly educated, and most importantly, highly mobile. Moreover, they have the ability and resources to pursue these job opportunities.

Because of the diversity within this group, this view on migration also holds that creatives seek out tolerant cities that encourage diversity and have opportunities for a work–life balance that would not be afforded elsewhere. As seen in the introductory Silicon Valley example, an influx of creatives to an area would then lead to an exponential increase in growth and opportunities as companies follow, or are created by, these new migrants.

While some of these descriptions resonate with the dynamics of migration within major cities, the assertions behind the creative class theory have been disputed (Borén and Young 2013). Income is often a larger driver of job selection than amenities within an area, and this view of creative migration does not consider how patterns of movement could change over the lives of creative workers. Specifically, individuals may not remain in these cities as their needs change. For example, members of the creative class who marry or have dependents may move out of high-cost cities in order to achieve a better standard of living for themselves and their families. Another view that explains the various factors and motivations related to economic migration is found in human capital models (Korpi and Clark 2017). This view frames the decision to migrate as an economic choice. That is, a person decides to move based on what they expect to immediately gain from moving, compared with what could potentially be obtained by staying in the new area. In this view, chasing increased earnings would be the goal of migrants, but not everyone is able to translate migration into a higher net income. Earlier research has illustrated that it is often the young, highly educated migrants who see these returns on the decision to relocate for a job opportunity (Korpi and Clark 2017).

What these models fail to highlight is that economic mobility is often tied to many social determinants and motivations that shape and constrain individual choice making. For example, people choose to remain in cities even when the costs of their expenses, like rent, outpace the increase in wages (Korpi, Clark, and Malmberg 2011). There are more factors at work than how much someone could earn. Community, available resources, education level, and social identity can also influence economic mobility. A common thread among all the examples of economic migration we have discussed to this point is the impact of social identity on an individual's ability to move. Specifically, race and ethnicity can play a role in who is able to migrate, how they are able to migrate, and where they can migrate to. Importantly, race and ethnicity also matter when we consider who is displaced by an influx of new residents in an area – as we will see later in our examination of gentrification.

Implications for Places of Origin

As social and economic forces push people out of their old communities, or pull them into new ones, their movement has an impact on their place of origin. These impacts can change based on whether people are leaving for temporary opportunities or uprooting their families. While this chapter has mostly examined how migrants shape the places they immigrate to, it is also important to consider the economic, social, and cultural implications of emigration on places of origin.

One of the most visible impacts of emigration is population loss. The contraction of a rural or urban area can have disastrous consequences for the remaining residents with less social mobility. As young workers leave their place of origin, it reduces the overall size of the workforce. A reduction in population may also lead to stagnation, or even a decrease, in the demand for goods and services in an area (Lianos, Pseiridis, and Tsounis 2023). To explore this concept closer, let's look at how population loss in the city of Detroit has impacted both the housing market and access to educational services.

Issues of race and class were key factors in the out-migration of Detroit. Detroit experienced population growth through 1950. As more Black Americans moved to Detroit during the Great Migration, white Detroiters moved to the suburbs in a phenomenon known as "white flight." White Detroiters searching for a more suburban, spacious lifestyle – or looking to leave the city due to racial tensions – were able to do so through lending programs that were often denied to Black Detroiters. This created a heavily segregated metropolitan area where the urban core was predominantly inhabited by Black residents and the outlying areas were predominantly inhabited by white residents. The population loss in the city of Detroit has continued each decade since the 1950s. More recently, out-migration is happening within the primarily Black American city, which leaves the poorest residents to suffer the consequences (Solomon 2014). The decline in population has led to a diminished tax base, which decreases the available public revenue needed for services such as schools. It has also led to the issue of home vacancies and blight within the city (Solomon 2014).

Abandoned buildings in Detroit, Michigan. Photo by Keen Kris (Wikimedia Commons, CC BY-SA 3.0).

It can be difficult for communities to recover from population loss. Communities must address the population loss itself as well as remediate adverse social, cultural, and economic impacts. Looking at Detroit again, multiple strategies are being implemented to revitalize the city and attract new residents. To address the issue of vacant housing through demolition, Detroit has started blight remediation and rehabilitation programs (Tatum 2022). Specifically, the STEM Entrepreneurial Excellence Program has encouraged Black women entrepreneurs to build their own businesses in the city (Frost et al. 2023). Through economic development and investment from the private sector, the city is aiming to attract both businesses and residents to the city by bringing in new development to the vacant land. The findings of the 2020 US Census demonstrated that the population of Detroit is still decreasing, however, this was challenged by city officials who expressed concerns over undercounting (Cooney et al. 2021). While the challenge was ultimately rejected, it does illustrate there is a concerted effort to work toward revitalization and growth in the city.

Alternatively, emigration can also have positive impacts on a migrant's place of origin, depending on the demographic characteristics of the area and their ties to their community. Reducing the working population alleviates pressure on the domestic labor market. This may result in lower unemployment rates within the country. Migrants may also send remittances, cash or goods sent from their host country back to family, neighbors, and friends in their country of origin. This flow of money through the diaspora network plays an important role in assisting with the financial costs of those who remain in the origin country.

Migrants may also choose to return to their place of origin once they have acquired additional financial means, skills, knowledge, or social capital. This process is known as **return migration** (Organisation for Economic Cooperation and Development 2016). For example, in 2019 diaspora remittances contributed to 16% of the total gross domestic product (GDP) of Kosovo (Organisation for Economic Cooperation and Development 2022), an increase from 9.3% in 2012 (Gollopeni 2016). Tenuous socioeconomic and political situations have led to a large influx of emigration from Kosovo. The payments and goods sent to loved ones within Kosovo from those that have migrated to other nations play an important role in maintaining a stable economy (Gollopeni 2016).

Migration can have both positive and negative effects on the migrant's place of origin. A decreasing population results in a smaller workforce. Depending on the economy of the region, a smaller workforce could further hurt the economy. In cases where there is an oversupply of workers, emigration might actually help. Population loss may result in a reduction in the demand for goods and services, damaging local businesses. Alternatively, international migrants may also help financially support their loved ones who remain home. There is no one way that emigration impacts a region. Social and economic factors all play into how a decrease in population can shape a society moving forward.

Gentrification: Causes and Consequences

Gentrification takes place when higher-income residents move into traditionally low-income communities. While this can increase property values and lead to improved services for neighborhoods, it also has the potential to displace legacy residents and disrupt established cultural patterns. Gentrification takes place in cities and neighborhoods across the globe. This includes any areas in which lower-income, working-class, or marginalized communities are at risk of being pushed out of their communities due to an influx in migration from wealthier people or investors. To understand how these demographic and population changes affect an area, it is useful to explore the history, social, and cultural practices that shaped the communities living there today.

Gentrification is rooted in historical factors related to the development of a community and the cultural makeup of the city or neighborhood. The communities susceptible to gentrification are often those that faced some form of historical discrimination, such as racial, ethnic, or class discrimination. This can take many forms including racism, legalized segregation, and discrimination in housing and lending. For example, the practice known as "redlining" in the United States prohibited lending in neighborhoods deemed risky financial investments, which denied residents access to credit and led to divestment within communities (Richardson, Mitchell, and Franco 2019). Predominantly white suburbs continued to grow as certain residents left urban centers during periods of white flight in the mid-twentieth century. The combination of white flight, discriminatory lending practices, and overall divestment led to predominantly low-income Black communities within urban city centers.

The United States passed the Federal-Aid Highway Act of 1956 (16 USC § 503; 23 USC), which led to the development of interstate highways. The development of these new highways helped people travel between their suburban homes and the urban city centers, but also had devastating impacts on minority communities who lived in city centers bisected by new construction. Highways were not developed with neighborhoods in mind, in fact they often split communities, destroyed homes, and created new impoverished areas within the city (Karas 2015).

Continuous divestment within an area can make it more susceptible to gentrification. Years of divestment have led to lower property values within neighborhoods historically deemed high risk financial investments. Lower-cost homes can be attractive to both homebuyers and real estate investors. Apart from lower-cost housing, changes in societal attitudes and living preferences are also leading to gentrification. While there was once a push to move out of cities to achieve more space and privacy in the suburbs, people are now finding a preference for city living and its unique benefits. Living within the city can allow people to be less car dependent as they may have access to services and public transit in a walkable area (Hjorthol and Bjørnskau 2005). The city may also feel hip and trendy, with access to restaurants, bars, shopping, and other amenities. Additionally, moving from a rural community to the city may give people better access to medical care and social services.

The demographic and economic changes caused by gentrification can have a variety of impacts on the affected communities. First, exploring the economic impacts, gentrification increases the property values and thereby the property tax base of the community being gentrified. A higher tax base provides funds for necessary public services, such as education. However, an increase in property values does not come without other social complications. On the one hand, gentrification can be seen as reinvestment in an area. On the other hand, it may price out the legacy residents from their homes. The increase in tax obligations may place a financial hardship on established homeowners, landlords may pass on their increased costs to their tenants, and renters may face significant increases in their payments as the demand to live in an area increases.

Apart from physical displacement, gentrification can also break up established cultural patterns in a neighborhood. Cultural displacement occurs when areas mostly populated with minorities have their residents replaced with affluent, white gentrifiers (Richardson, Mitchell, and Franco 2019). Mechanisms related to cultural displacement, such as the increase of the cost of living in an area due to new wealthy residents, could make it difficult for former residents to stay in their communities. Moreover, as cultural displacement continues, the new residents in an area will likely have norms, traditions, and even tastes that differ from members of the established community. Independent, community-owned restaurants and grocery stores could be replaced by larger national chains looking to take advantage of increasingly affluent residents. As established residents continue to see their neighborhood change around them, they may no longer feel a sense of belonging or community.

It is possible for new urban development to be done in a way that is sensitive to the culture and existing needs of established residents. Gentrification can lead to integration within communities and an increase in property values for homeowners that are people of color, but more policies might be needed to ensure long-term racial and economic diversity in these neighborhoods (Ellen and Torrats-Espinosa 2019). While additional research is needed to disentangle the net impact of gentrification in light of its potential economic benefits and social costs, it is clear that policies related to encouraging development in urban centers can have an influence on migration.

PERSPECTIVE: Gentrification and Displacement: A Baltimore Case Study, by Matthew Durington

Professor of Anthropology, Towson University (USA)

Gentrification is a complex social and economic process that involves the transformation of a neighborhood or district from a low-income, often deteriorated area into a more affluent and upscale one. This transformation often takes place in waves over time and typically involves the influx of wealthier residents, businesses, and investments, which leads to rising property values, rents, and changes in the cultural and socioeconomic makeup of the area. As property values rise, long-time residents (particularly those from lower-income backgrounds) face displacement due to increasing rents and property taxes. Thus, gentrification, particularly in North America, is dependent on the displacement of historical residents and communities that are often deemed as underserved, aberrant, racialized, and criminalized. Debates surrounding gentrification often revolve around finding a balance between neighborhood revitalization and preserving the social fabric of a community, such as maintaining housing prices for long-time residents. While this balance is aspirational, it is rarely achieved. Although often conceived as a contemporary phenomenon, gentrification relies upon a historical precedent of homesteading (the American West and manifest destiny), forced removal (apartheid South Africa), and urban renewal processes such as highway construction (Corona Queens in New York City). In other words, forced removal and displacement have a deep history with the latest iteration of these processes defined as gentrification.

Contemporary gentrification has evolved in the last several decades to encompass other processes beyond individual housing. In addition to residential areas, gentrification can also encompass large-scale projects by corporations or the revitalization of specific urban zones like waterfronts. Broader gentrification began to be examined in the mid-1980s in terms of societal changes and urban transformation as economies fluctuated in the post-World War II era. Scholars have also linked gentrification to globalization and the impacts of unregulated market forces on urban and societal dynamics. Research has expanded to explore the effects of gentrification on rural settings, new construction projects, and the emergence of super gentrification – a second-generation form of gentrification that excludes both lower- and middle-class residents. Global cities such as New York City and San Francisco are emblematic of super gentrification where all housing is deemed unaffordable to everyone but the super wealthy or international conglomerates. Much of the housing stock in these global cities is not owned by local residents but regarded as an investment opportunity for magnates.

Once a thriving industrial and port center, Baltimore, like many other medium-sized cities in the United States, has faced challenges stemming from post-World War II deindustrialization and the decline of a manufacturing economy. This has led to a significant portion of the urban population moving to the suburbs and beyond, resulting in a decrease in job opportunities and a weakened tax base. In turn, the phenomenon of white flight since World War II has contributed to a racialized perception of the city coded by terms such as "gritty," "dangerous," or even the neutral term "urban." As economic flows have forced the formal economy into decline, an informal economy has emerged, further leading to negative stereotypes of Baltimore as a criminalized city. This perception has disproportionately affected Black men, leading to biased incarceration rates and contributing to unstable housing conditions. The deterioration of urban housing in Baltimore—influenced by historic redlining and absentee ownership—reflects these racial, economic, and demographic changes. The image of semi-abandoned row houses with boarded-up windows has become symbolic of the city's history and a representation of urban decay on a national level. Even broken windows and graffiti have driven criminologists to see these environmental conditions as promoting antisocial behavior. There is an easy explanation for broken windows, litter, and unkempt communities. It is a lack of resources and capital.

The historic Black community of Sharp Leadenhall in south Baltimore is one of the oldest neighborhoods in the city. Throughout its history, Sharp Leadenhall has been a significant hub for African American culture and activism in Baltimore. With the establishment of the Baltimore Abolitionist Society and the African Academy of Baltimore, the community played a crucial role in the nineteenth-century fight against slavery and the advancement of education for free Black people in the postbellum era. Despite its rich heritage and its historical recognition by the City of Baltimore, Sharp Leadenhall has faced challenges in recent decades due to socioeconomic and political pressures, particularly from gentrification. In an oft-repeated process of other North American cities, various urban renewal projects (such as highway construction and real estate development) have contributed to the ongoing gentrification of the neighborhood.

Perhaps the most impactful urban renewal process that has affected this historic neighborhood is highway development in the 1960s, when the city seized property through eminent domain and razed hundreds of homes. As seen in the construction of highways in the northeast corridor of the United States, racialized and underserved communities were specifically targeted in interstate planning. Activists in Baltimore were successful in stopping some highway construction but not completely. The damage to the community was already completed. In the aftermath of efforts to halt highway construction, urban homesteading programs like dollar houses were introduced in the Otterbein neighborhood next to Sharp Leadenhall. In this form of gentrification, individuals outside of the city were incentivized to move in by offering housing for just one dollar, provided they met certain criteria, committed to living there for 18 months, and had substantial savings or income to renovate run-down properties. Although not explicitly racially motivated, the eligibility requirements for this program excluded most of the existing urban residents in these communities who were predominantly renters, leading to another wave of gentrification right next to Sharp Leadenhall. Today, in the twenty-first century, the Sharp Leadenhall community is surrounded by development pressures stemming from this past, and in many ways, community leaders have declared that gentrification has won.

At the turn of the twenty-first century, Sharp Leadenhall gained prominence on real estate speculation maps due to its close proximity to Federal Hill and local sports venues, which were built on the sites of demolished homes of early community residents. Within the relatively short span of five years in the early 2000s, property values in Sharp Leadenhall skyrocketed by over 1,000%.

Simultaneously, the combination of lenient lending practices by financial institutions created an overleveraged housing market that directly contributed to the global economic crisis and subsequent recession in 2008. Baltimore, like many other cities, suffered greatly in the financial aftermath of the housing-based recession, prompting a re-evaluation of the concept of gentrification. As we move further into the twenty-first century, it remains to be seen what types of neighborhoods will emerge from the socioeconomic conditions in cities and what fate awaits historic communities like Sharp Leadenhall. The residents of Sharp Leadenhall find themselves grappling with the preservation of their cultural identity (which is deeply rooted in their historical residency), while simultaneously facing the forces of displacement driven by gentrification.

By 2016 Baltimore's housing stock was overleveraged and underwater due to detrimental financing practices before and after the 2008 housing bubble. Baltimore has consistently deprived Black neighborhoods of capital, effectively stripping residents of the authority to shape their own communities. These challenges have been further exacerbated by the COVID-19 pandemic and its aftermath. Now, over two decades into the twenty-first century, the dynamics of gentrification have undergone a transformation with corporate developers taking on the role of individual gentrifiers. Additionally, the state plays a direct role in fueling this process, while anti-gentrification social movements find themselves increasingly marginalized. These processes are evident in the case of the Sharp Leadenhall community in Baltimore, among others. A significant portion of Sharp Leadenhall was designated for light industrial zoning during the twentieth-century highway development projects. This has hastened major corporate development initiatives under the guise of creating mixed-use developments among high-rise condominiums that mark contemporary gentrification. Like many other cities, Baltimore has supported these efforts to attempt to remedy a weakening tax base and population loss.

So, what happens to neighborhoods like Sharp Leadenhall and other marginalized communities in North America that have gone through various waves of gentrification? Gentrification has not decreased but has undergone a transformation. Developers offer a fraction of new residences as mixed income but seldom fulfill these promises or only make them available as rental properties for current residents. Developers perform negotiations with specific community leaders merely to appease critics or fit tax abatement criteria driven by legislation. In this regard, activism becomes selective as certain community leaders align themselves with development agendas in exchange for favors such as the construction of cultural centers or support for other social programs. The focus of development by cities is no longer centered around ensuring the "Right to the City" for all urban residents. Instead, housing development now reinforces the dominance of developers in the neoliberal era, who possess the financial means to invest when city budgets are depleted. It is difficult to not conceptualize something far more sinister than mere free market practices. One could argue that these processes are built on systems of inequity along race and class lines.

> Yet, residents continue to attempt to exert control over how they are perceived by both external observers and their fellow residents. They may engage in activities such as documenting their histories, fostering solidarity among themselves, organizing festivals and cultural events, advocating for their interests in city council meetings, challenging zoning regulations, demanding improved city services, participating in protests, and forming alliances with like-minded groups across the city, country, or even the globe. The significance of these efforts cannot be overstated, as the very existence of neighborhoods, communities, and the city itself depends on the ability of its inhabitants to demonstrate their value to the world beyond their borders. However, perceptions of gentrification in the city cannot be neatly categorized as solely top-down development schemes or bottom-up activism approaches to confront them. All of these processes intertwine in complex ways, with different groups appropriating the language and ideas of others to serve their own interests. Pressures from the global economy will continue to be felt by local communities broadly, continually changing the conceptualization of gentrification and the literal racial complexion of displacement.

Accommodating Demands in Popular Neighborhoods

As discussed earlier, gentrification can potentially reshape neighborhoods and communities through demographic, cultural, and socioeconomic shifts. Rapid changes in population can also place challenges on the demand for public facilities and services. Cities that have faced decades of divestment are not always able to immediately accommodate the changing needs of their residents. Population changes may also be related to a temporary influx as some regions face gentrification due to tourism instead of permanent residency. This section will explore the role of gentrification in three neighborhoods around the world. Specifically, what strategies have been implemented within these areas to meet the needs of the established community and new people migrating into the neighborhood.

Boyle Heights, East Los Angeles, United States

Los Angeles, California is one of the highest cost-of-living areas in the United States. Boyle Heights in East Los Angeles (LA) is historically a low-income, working-class, Latino neighborhood. The region has a vibrant Mexican American culture that can be seen through its music, art, fashion, and cars. However, as prices continue to rise within Los Angeles, lower-income neighborhoods on the eastern side are attracting new residents and investors interested in urban redevelopment and low property values. From 2000 to 2015 there was a significant increase in the proportion of white-collar workers, disparities in median home prices, and changes in median household income in East LA – three markers indicative of gentrification (Scott 2019).

Prospect of gentrification divides a neighborhood. The student-run *Boyle Heights Beat* reports on divergent views about the potential impacts of gentrification. Source: Photo courtesy of Ted Soqui.

As real estate investors and new residents come into Boyle Heights, it increases the overall property value. These increases can have particularly devastating effects on renters. Historically, a high proportion (80%) of the existing residents of Boyle Heights rented their places of residence. As we have previously discussed, renters are at a significant risk of displacement due to the rising costs of rents and goods related to gentrification. Gentrification within Boyle Heights also presents racial and class conflicts. Legacy Latino/a residents are at risk of being physically displaced by incoming white, middle-class residents. Moreover, their culture could be exploited and commercialized as a marketing tool to attract these new residents and tourists (Ahrens 2015). The increases in cost of living can highlight class differences among higher-income and lower-income Latino/as living in the neighborhood, further placing displacement pressures on the lowest income residents (Ahrens 2015).

The long-time residents of Boyle Heights have pushed back against gentrification. Grassroots activism has sprung up to protest rising rents, the changing cultural landscape, and the use of art to further gentrify the area. Specifically, in 2015 these residents challenged the establishment of a new arts district within their community. Although many would consider the creation of an arts district as a community improvement, this development would also displace approximately two thousand families (O'Brien, Vilchis, and Maritescu 2019). The new development aimed to create over a dozen new galleries in Boyle Heights. While local politicians supported the creation of these galleries, the community felt these were not representative of the neighborhood but rather represented outsider art and artists (O'Brien, Vilchis, and Maritescu 2019).

ECONOMIC DEVELOPMENT AND GENTRIFICATION

Creating a community-based movement to oppose efforts to remove elements of culture is a way long-standing residents can oppose negative implications of gentrification. However, time will tell if the actions taken by the residents of Boyle Heights will effectively mitigate long-term efforts to redevelop their community.

Roma Norte, Mexico City, Mexico

Mexico City is one of the five most populous metro areas in the world, and it is also a prominent example of the recurring impact gentrification and urban planning can have on a city and its individual communities. The area surrounding Mexico City has been attracting migrants consistently since the city's founding, but gentrification and urbanization as we contemporarily understand them has occurred since the 1930s. However, these patterns accelerated after the devastating 1985 Mexico City earthquake.

This catastrophe led to the deaths of thousands of Mexico City citizens and billions of dollars in infrastructure damage. The damage was especially severe in the city center. In response, some of the most influential entrepreneurs in the city were given substantial influence during the revitalization effort. Wealthy investors with the support of government programs, such as Programa de Rescate – a municipal policy within Mexico City that aimed to increase investment and create a true

In Mexico City's Roma Norte neighborhood, a 1920s neoclassical style house sits next to a twenty-first century loft tower. Source: Photo by Francisco Peláez (Wikimedia Commons, CC BY-SA 3.0).

global city – began to transform the city to attract tourists and middle to upper-class residents. The government attempted to balance urban revitalization efforts with the needs of their low-income residents through two municipal policies, Bando 2 and Norma 26. While these policies aimed to place restrictions on urban development and to increase the supply of affordable housing in the center of Mexico City, they were filled with loopholes that led to more middle-class and luxury housing developments (Linz 2021).

While the rebuilding of Mexico City allowed for an influx of economic development, it exacerbated both intentional segregation between wealthy elites and Indigenous communities and inadvertently led to additional inequality between classes. Today, the neighborhoods of the wealthy in Mexico City are absorbing many areas that were formally considered public spaces. While the excluded public petition the government to regain access to these spaces, the national policies of Mexico have created an environment where all land, even spaces formerly considered for the benefit of the public, have been commodified.

Part of Mexico City's gentrification is related to a desire to attract wealthy businesses, migrants, and tourists. In this way, the urbanization and development of the city – especially its central districts – is related to an interaction between policing, economic development, cultural branding, and the resistance of local populations (McDermott 2019). These issues within Mexico City have only become exacerbated as global migration patterns have shifted over time. The region has seen an influx of high-income immigrants retiring or working remotely from the region due to the comparatively lower cost of living within the country. Gentrification and a significant wealth divide within Mexico City contribute to the growing population of people that live in unsanctioned communities on the outskirts of the city (Furszyfer Del Rio and Sovacool 2023).

Bo-Kaap, Cape Town, South Africa

The Bo-Kaap neighborhood in Cape Town, South Africa is in the Cape Malay – or Cape Muslim – Quarter. In the 1700s enslaved persons were brought from around the world to work in the Dutch Cape Colony of South Africa. Many of today's Cape Malay population can trace their ancestry back to the community forced to move to the Cape region during slavery. The emancipation of enslaved persons took place in 1834, at which time the region saw shifts in population demographics as white residents began to move out of the urban areas of the Cape, freeing up land and homes for Black residents. Bo-Kaap became an enclave for newly freed, Black Muslim residents. As the Muslim population grew, so did the number of mosques within Bo-Kaap. This change in cultural beliefs led to architectural changes, such as the residents of Bo-Kaap beginning to paint their homes bright colors (Toffa 2004).

Under the system of strict racial and ethnic segregation known as apartheid (1948–1994), the Muslim South African community was further segregated into separate neighborhoods, including Bo-Kaap. During this era, notorious restrictions were placed

Bo-Kaap neighborhood, Cape Town, South Africa. Photo by K Newman (Wikimedia Commons).

on ordinary freedoms of movement, speech, and livelihoods. The government would not even allow residents to paint their homes. Once apartheid was lifted, residents painted their homes with vibrant colors. Walking through Bo-Kaap today, one would see green, yellow, blue, and pink homes. The colorful homes not only showcase the artistic and cultural expression of the community, but they represent their freedom from both slavery and apartheid (Hutchinson 2006).

This picturesque neighborhood is paved with cobblestone streets, surrounded by brightly colored houses on each side, and has 10 mosques. It is this unique physical and social significance that makes Bo-Kaap attractive to tourists. With the influx of tourism in the region there is a fine balance between historic preservation and tourist gentrification. The South African National Heritage Resources Act of 1999 designated Bo-Kaap as a heritage resource and provides a framework for conservation within the area. Additionally, the UNESCO (United Nations Educational, Scientific and Cultural Organization) Action Plan for the Africa Region provides an outline for the preservation of cultural and natural heritage within Africa (Seepie et al. 2017).

While these preservation frameworks provide a good starting point, they do not completely mitigate the impacts of tourism. In the case of Bo-Kaap, tourists are attracted to the local culture and atmosphere of the community. As pressure to grow the tourism industry continues, it can be difficult to keep the feeling of an authentic community, as opposed to one created to attract tourism.

The three regions explored in this section—Los Angeles, Mexico City, and Cape Town—are all undergoing gentrification. The communities at risk of, or currently undergoing, gentrification all have a history of serving marginalized groups. Each of these areas is facing an economic and demographic shift. However, the reasons for these shifts may vary. In Los Angeles increased pressure on the housing market is resulting in upper and middle-class residents seeking cheaper housing on the eastern side of the city. Natural disasters and weak urban development policies have led to an influx of wealthy residents in Mexico City. Finally, the vibrant culture within the historic neighborhoods in South Africa are attractive tourist hubs. Historic preservation frameworks, municipal protections, and grassroots activism are all ways in which communities and governments are pushing back against gentrification and providing protections for legacy residents. However, even with these efforts, there is a fine balance these communities must strike between economic growth and sustainable development.

Formation and Organization of Informal Settlements

Increased urbanization and migration contributed to the emergence of unplanned or informal settlements. These are defined as unsanctioned settlements not tied to formal land ownership. They encompass squatter settlements, shantytowns, slums, and other forms of unauthorized settlements. As communities face a lack of affordable housing for their poorest residents, informal settlements may emerge as one way to meet the demand for shelter. Growth and movement to urban areas without strong, community-led, urban planning policies has contributed to a shortage of affordable housing within urban city centers. As low-income residents are pushed out of their communities to make space for real estate development or new migrants find themselves unable to afford basic shelter within their new cities, informal settlements are created or expanded. Informal settlements house an estimated 10% of the global population (Welisiejko and Cáceres 2022). Within some cities, the population living in informal settlements is much higher. For example, 25% of the residents in Mexico City live in informal settlements.

Since these settlements are not sanctioned by the public sector, they often lack access to basic services such as water and sanitation (Welisiejko and Cáceres 2022). Substandard and unregulated housing pose safety risks to those living in these settlements. The poor housing infrastructure, overpopulation, and location of the settlements can lead to a variety of negative health consequences. Both communicable and non-communicable diseases, such as cancer and diabetes, remain a threat to the residents. Climate change may exacerbate health inequalities as residents lack shelter and access to services that could help them face climate emergencies (Sverdlik 2011). For example, residents facing extreme heat will be at a higher risk of heat-related injuries without proper shelter and water. Since informal settlements are excluded from the city's urban planning process, they may be placed in areas more prone to natural disasters, such as flooding, fire, and earthquakes. Flooding in particular poses a heightened risk to this group, not only because it can destroy physical infrastructure and property but also because contaminated flood waters bring forth a host of possible diseases and infections.

Discrimination, racism, and classism are all pervasive issues faced by the residents of informal settlements. Discrimination against marginalized members of a community leads to a cyclical cycle of policies that perpetuates a need for informal settlements while simultaneously making it more difficult for those residents of informal settlements to have upward economic mobility. Residents may face stigma and discrimination as a result of living in these settlements. Since these areas are not officially part of the city, they often lack formal addresses that would allow dwellers to join the workforce and obtain identifying documents. Those living in the formal, sanctioned portion of the city may view the informal settlement as a nuisance or a place for the impoverished, further alienating those living within these settlements. Additionally, the informality of their living conditions places residents at higher risks of forced eviction and displacement. Without legal protection and delineated ownership of property, residents face precarious living conditions.

While informal settlements pose risks and challenges to their residents, one must remember that they also provide shelter to the members of a community that have been ignored by government policies and urban planning. These spaces can provide residents with a sense of community and social solidarity. Informal settlements tend to have a highly dense population and close living quarters. This creates conditions in which neighborhoods are more likely to meet and interact with one another (Shehayeb 2009). The bonds they develop with their neighbors can lead to the formation of a cohesive, resilient community (Vertigans and Gibson 2020). While these residents may not have a lot of resources individually, they are able to use their collective power to improve the well-being of informal settlements. Occasionally, this resilience and propensity for collective action can put informal settlements at odds with private and public sector forces looking to develop these areas.

There is great diversity among informal settlements, both in their access to services and their official recognition within their larger communities. While some settlements are seen as a problem that must be corrected through forced removal and urban planning, others have become an essential part of the overall city. Within Rio De Janeiro, Brazil, informal settlements known as *favelas* provide shelter and a sense of community for low-income, working-class Brazilians. Unlike many other informal settlements across the globe, favela residents have access to some public utilities and legal protections.

A *favela* in Rio de Janeiro, not far from the affluent Copacabana beach neighborhood. Photo by Leon Petrosyan (Wikimedia Commons, CC BY-SA 4.0).

Many favelas in Rio De Janeiro have access to running water, sanitation, and electricity (Saborio and Spesny 2019); but access to these services remains lower than for residents of the formal city (Welisiejko and Cáceres 2022). Additionally, many provisions in Brazilian law, such as designating an area as a zone of social interest and protections for favela residents, have created a framework in which the residents living in these informal settlements should be able to remain so long as they are not at physical risk due to land conditions (Vale and Gray 2013). However, despite documented protections, the interests of residents in informal settlements are often at odds with capitalist drives to increase economic development by attracting new industries and tourists.

The informal settlements surrounding the development area for the Olympic Park built for the 2016 Summer Olympic games in Rio De Janeiro were marked for demolition as the games approached. Special statuses preserving communities were revoked, residents were presented with little evidence as to the rationale for their pending removal, and laws were reinterpreted to provide a justification for the redevelopment of a community and the displacement of its residents (Vale and Gray 2013). Many of the structures in these communities were demolished and redeveloped in the lead up to the Olympic games. The Vila Autodromo community formerly housed 700 families, but only 20 houses were constructed for residents who refused to leave their neighborhood (Williamson 2017).

PERSPECTIVE: Cross Locations in the Mediterranean, by Sarah Green

Professor of Social and Cultural Anthropology, University of Helsinki (Finland).

The migrants are not who we think they are, and neither are the hosts, at least not on Lesvos, one of the biggest islands in the Aegean, located less than 30 km (16 miles) from the Turkish coast. About half the island's residents are descended from refugees, forced to leave their homes in Anatolia in the 1920s by the League of Nations, at the end of the conflicts between Turkey and Greece. People on Lesvos say they can still tell the difference between the old refugee families and those who were not refugees, though others deny it; everyone is the same, others say. It depends on what you are looking for, I suppose.

The more recent troubled travelers—those arriving on the island in the first two decades of the twenty-first century and staying until they are processed and sent on to Athens—they are also often being defined by their journey, the one that brought them to the island. The (illegal) rickety boats and dinghies; the (often illegal) rescue missions; the (illegal) pushbacks; the drownings; the endless, interminably slow bureaucracy; and the urgency of the situation without anyone who has authority actually rushing to do anything. It all feels like a mismatch.

So many people have had journeys that are the stuff of Hollywood movies, but few seem to care. Mostly, these people are not seen for who they are, but only for how they traveled: migrant, refugee, from somewhere else, not from here, frequently labeled unwelcome or victim, or both. Yes, that is what these people have been through; but it is not who, or even what, they are. They are not their journey; they are not a flow, a flood, or a foreign problem. Rather than think about who they are, it might be better to think in terms of their relationships with places and people, and the connections and disconnections they have been through.

Many travelers might feel some bond with their fellow travelers, at least temporarily, because of the traumatic events that they went through together to get here; but that is a new layer, a fresh set of relations to add to a lifetime of relations with others, elsewhere, who did not come on that journey but who are still there with the migrants, shaping them and their view of the world. Perhaps, especially, shaping their hopes. Those relations keep them connected with different parts of the world and disconnected from other parts, creating fresh locations where they belong and where they do not belong. But those locations appear just in the memories, bodies, and relations of the travelers. They make up different kinds of maps of the world and in different forms. Political borders are supposed to be static, ideally dividing one side cleanly from the other permanently; in contrast, borders made from people's travels that are layered onto relations, both past and present, those borders are viscerally mobile, shifting with the tides, the winds, and the people as they carve out somewhere to be in the world, for a time. Those borders, and the locations they shape, are processes not things.

The hosts, the locals on Lesvos, have some idea about the migrants' journeys, though the feelings are mixed. The families of many of the islanders have been previously abandoned and betrayed. Athens is far away, and Lesvos is mostly out of sight and out of mind. The islanders are used to that, to being out of sight and out of mind. Even when the Pope and Susan Sarandon and the Archbishop of the Greek Orthodox Church visited Lesvos at the height of the migration emergency in 2015 and 2016, it made a story for a day, and then it was over. Out of sight, out of mind, just like the last time when so many of the islanders' grandparents and great-grandparents arrived—forced out of their homes with nothing—following a brutally violent conflict. Athens did not care very much then, and not much help arrived for the newcomers in the 1920s. They had to fend for themselves. And they did. They managed. That was a long time ago, three or four generations ago, but the traces of betrayal and abandonment remain. People have memories, passed down the generations, and that creates low expectations.

The island survives by producing olives, ouzo, and tourism. The tourist business was doubly hit, both by the COVID-19 pandemic and the publicity about the new migrants and their plight. The media-generated imagery of desperate people arriving on the shore and, even worse, people drowning and washing up on the island's coasts or being found in the water, that imagery did not encourage tourism on Lesvos. The local businesses did not expect help from Athens or the European Union (EU) and did not receive any, most people said. The help, such as it was, arrived late, and it was all for the migrants. That did not go down well in some neighborhoods. The resentment could be heard powerfully through the conspiracy theories that began to circulate about who was gobbling up all the money *this* time. It was not the locals; people were sure of that. It might seem like the resentment was aimed at the new migrants, but that is not entirely right, though it is partly—there were anti-migrant demonstrations on the island. Yet much of the resentment was directed, along with those strong memories of betrayal and abandonment, toward the national and international authorities that had the power to do something. Everyone on the island knew that the migrants did not have the power to do anything.

Or perhaps it was that the migrants had *almost* no power to do anything. The Moria refugee camp (that is what everyone called it, even though not everyone there was an asylum seeker) caught fire during the COVID-19 pandemic shutdown. It was the place where the migrants of the first two decades of the 2000s stayed while they were waiting for the paperwork that permitted them to be put on the ferry for Athens, for the next leg of their journey through the seemingly endless tunnels of stops and starts that is called the EU asylum and migration application process. Moria was the biggest refugee camp in Europe, and it caught fire and was destroyed. Some said it was set alight on purpose by a few of the residents; some said they just went crazy with the waiting and the horrible conditions in the camp. Especially during the COVID-19 shutdown when they were quarantined after some cases of COVID-19 were found in the camp, forcing them to stay in what many described as a terrible placed with inhumane conditions. So, they lit a fire – that is what some people say. Quite quickly, six former Moria camp residents – all from Afghanistan, three of them teenagers – were arrested and convicted of arson in March and June of 2021. But who knows; some people say the trial was a sham. Nothing is ever entirely what it seems in such situations. There's a new place being built now, more sturdy, more formal, a huge place, with international money. There are legal problems with that construction, so it has been slowed down. In the meantime, the migrants are staying in tents, trying to manage, somehow.

The island is not what it seems either, if viewed only from its location as a site for troubled travelers, past and present. In addition to its role as a tourist destination, it is also an important pilgrimage site. Every year in November, people arrive from different parts of Greece (especially Athens) to walk in pilgrimage to Mandamados, to visit the church containing a miraculous icon of the Archangel Michael (called Taksiarchis in Greek). The island is also a particularly important stop off point for migrant birds going to or coming from North Africa, something that regularly attracts bird watchers from all over the world. Those kinds of non-human migrants, the birds, are only of concern when they carry bird flu along with them. That echoes historical controls over the movement of people, goods, and animals across the Mediterranean. The main border-control issues in the past, before nation-states were a dominant form of creating territories in the region, were attempts to stop the spread of disease, plus attempts to control trade in valuable things. Infections and smuggling were the biggest problems facing the border authorities in those days, apart from the occasional invading army or navy. And those issues still matter today and are still controlled, even though they hardly ever attract the kinds of media attention that the human migrants attract. The speed with which the COVID-19 border crossing regulations disappeared is impressive, as is the speed with which all that trouble has simply been forgotten by most people.

The Mediterranean region, perhaps like most places, has always been crisscrossed by different locating regimes – ways to give value and significance to where you are in the world through some kind of logic that gives a relative value to where you are – political, social, religious, financial, linguistic and other ways to give a value to a place and establish how it is connected to and disconnected from other places. And people have been traveling to, from, across, and through these places for millennia. Tracing a few of these journeys and seeing how they fit into the layers of locational logics of where they end up, for a time, might offer a different way to understand what it means to be somewhere in particular, rather than worrying about who people are.

Forced Resettlement and Social Safeguards

Gentrification and urban development can place low-income residents of a community in precarious living conditions. In some cases, these residents may be priced out of their homes, in others they may feel social pressure to leave the neighborhood they once called home. In the most severe cases, residents may face eviction to pave the way for development. Without safeguards in place, economic development can result in the displacement of people. Forced resettlement occurs when people involuntarily move from their homes. This can happen for many reasons including conflict or climate disasters; however, this section will explore development-driven resettlement. Residents of informal settlements are particularly vulnerable to forced resettlement, as they often lack formal, legal ownership of the land they occupy. However, forced resettlement can and does occur to residents in both formal and informal settlements.

Around the world, policies exist that allow governments to seize the private property of citizens and convert it into public property. This land can then either be put to future public use or sold by the state to private enterprises. Within the United States this action is known as eminent domain and is detailed within the US Constitution. Across the globe this practice goes by different terms, such as land acquisition, expropriation, or compulsory purchase. While the terminology varies between nations, the general concept remains the same: governments are able to seize land from their citizens as long as the land is used to benefit the wider public. This practice has been used to open land for infrastructure, business development, public green spaces, and existing neighborhoods. In some instances, this has created iconic spaces like New York City's Central Park. However, these policies were also used to support General Motors's acquisition of land in Detroit for automotive factories (Nader and Hirsch 2004) and the redevelopment of historic *hutong* neighborhoods in Beijing into new commodity housing (Evans 2020). While all three of these projects displaced people, the effects and community implications were dependent upon the type of compensation residents are given in exchange for their holdings. These policies vary greatly across nations and specific circumstances related to the resettlement.

Displacement increases socioeconomic gaps and puts displaced residents at a higher risk of housing insecurity. Removing someone from their home may also mean removing them from their community, their neighbors, their friends, and even family. Evictions can destroy a person's sense of security within their living situation and place them in a precarious environment. Additionally, living under the threat of eviction can negatively impact one's physical and psychological health (Vásquez-Vera et al. 2017).

Social safeguards within development projects do exist to mitigate resettlement and other adverse impacts of urban development. These protections may take the shape of policies, actions, and procedures that are intended to prevent and reduce the harm caused by development projects. This could mean involving the existing community and other stakeholders during the development process (including the early planning stages) or compensating people who are negatively impacted. Social safeguards vary greatly between projects and communities. For example, within the United States, people who have their lands possessed through eminent domain have legal protections and must receive *just compensation*. This standard has been interpreted as the value the land would receive based on its highest and best use (Brinkerhoff 1973). However, these valuations can be disputed between property owners and the government exercising eminent domain. Conflicts can spill over into lengthy legal challenges where marginalized citizens have fewer financial resources than their opposition. In many places experiencing displacement related to land seizure, communities under threat may contact international advocacy organizations in an effort to bring attention to the implications of a development. As we previously explored in our analysis of the Brazilian favelas redevelopment in the lead up to the Rio 2016 Summer Olympics, putting the threat of forced resettlement in the international spotlight can increase the pressure on a government to ensure that their displaced residents receive fair treatment (Ivester 2017).

Future Trends and Challenges

As mentioned at the beginning of this chapter, the global population is becoming increasingly concentrated in urban areas. We have also seen—through the examples of gentrification explored in previous sections—that municipalities have unique approaches to balancing economic development, immigration, and the preservation of existing communities. Here, we will explore some of the emerging global challenges that will impact the relationship between urban economic development and migration. Of those challenges, one of the most immediately pressing concerns is the intersection between climate change and gentrification.

Climate change and economic migration

Climate change has recently emerged as a driving force behind new forms of economic development and gentrification (Lustgarten 2024). As we discussed in talking about the social production of vulnerability in Chapter 6, wealthier residents tend to have homes constructed of higher quality materials that are located in areas more insulated from climate emergencies in comparison to lower-income residents (Mutter 2010). For example, wealthier residents of coastal communities may turn to structural mitigation – changes in the physical construction, engineering, or uses of technology – to mitigate the negative impacts of climate change. This is a development-focused initiative that relies on both innovation and capital investment in the region. Structural mitigation comes at a high cost and can raise the overall cost of living within an area, thus making it an inequitable solution (Gould and Lewis 2021).

Yet, these mitigation strategies may not make all wealthy residents feel their coastal homes are secure from the threat of intensifying storms, floods, and higher temperatures. Many seek refuge in urban areas with higher elevations instead of investing in climate mitigation efforts. While this relocation can be beneficial for the cities attracting economic investment, it can have damaging impacts on existing neighborhoods (United Nations Habitat 2020). As with other examples of gentrification, this climate-driven migration of wealthy individuals can lead to a rapid rise of rents, a change in community dynamics, and a realignment of local urban planning priorities as cities move to accommodate the desires of the new residents.

However, this movement of wealthy individuals from coastal towns can have impacts on their origin communities as well. Lower-income residents in these coastal communities are not as mobile, and the removal of a high-income tax base can mean these legacy residents are at a greater risk of harm due to a lack of available capital for mitigating the impacts of climate change. The gentrification of the higher elevation communities can also make those displaced residents more vulnerable to the effects of climate change. Displacement may result in a lack of adequate housing or relocation to informal settlements. These settlements are often placed in zones that face a higher risk of climate emergencies and have less access to the services needed to combat these issues.

The effects of the changing climate add to the growing socioeconomic divide. The impact of climate gentrification can be seen when looking at the recovery efforts of New Orleans after Hurricane Katrina in 2005. In the 10 years following the storm, the communities that suffered the most damage were also those most likely to be heavily gentrified after reconstruction efforts (van Holm and Wyczalkowski 2019). However, gentrification was less likely to occur in the neighborhoods that had the highest concentrations of low-income, Black residents. This disparity in which areas were gentrified was directly related to how much economic investment neighborhoods received to rebuild their communities. Rebuilding after climate-related disasters can be unequal. In the case of Hurricane Katrina, the redevelopment of New Orleans led to the replacement of the poor by the affluent. Without efforts to prioritize the health of legacy communities during post-disaster rebuilding, it is likely other urban areas will make similar decisions in response to future catastrophes.

Eco-gentrification

Another startling development in gentrification is related to the creation of environmental projects within cities. Although these endeavors are often presented as opportunities to make a community eco-friendlier, the process of redeveloping an area into an urban greenspace can have implications for the surrounding neighborhoods as property values increase. For example, the development of the High Line Park in New York City's West Chelsea neighborhood led to a 35.5% increase in property values and attracted new, high-income residents to the area (Black and Richards 2020). While the High Line Park was created to prevent a historic rail line from being destroyed and was intended to be a community good, the rapid increase in property values has pushed some legacy residents out of the community. The High Line's developers are in great demand to advise on similar projects in cities all over the world, and they are using this opportunity to try to direct cities away from the most serious adverse effects of planned projects (Rigolon and Németh 2020).

ECONOMIC DEVELOPMENT AND GENTRIFICATION

High Line Park, New York City, July 2009. Photo by David Berkowitz (CC BY 2.0).

While the creation of green spaces within urban communities can help mitigate the effects of climate change, it is important to explore the motivations for these projects. One question to ask is, who is the space intended for? Taking the feedback of the existing residents into account and incorporating it into the planning and development phases can help mitigate unintended consequences. The creation of these spaces without protections for the existing community, specifically lower-income residents, can leave gaps for investors to come in and further develop the area with little regard for the needs of the legacy residents.

Conflict, displacement, and economic impacts

Recent conflicts and periods of instability have led to the displacement of millions of people globally. By the end of 2022 approximately 108 million people were displaced due to persecution, conflict, violence, human rights violations, and events negatively impacting public order (United Nations High Commissioner for Refugees 2022). The influx of refugees and asylum seekers related to these problems has strained the economies of neighboring countries. These migrants often find themselves navigating complex regulations related to obtaining housing and employment at some point between leaving their origin community and resettling in a willing host country.

The displacement of people into surrounding countries can have impacts on the economies of those regions. However, research has previously been mixed on whether this influx of migrants has a positive or negative impact on host countries. Many countries limit the legitimate opportunities for economic participation available to refugees. As a result, they often participate in low skill labor. This often puts refugees in direct competition with the most vulnerable laborers in a country (Sarzin 2021). While this displacement of low skill labor may be a short-term consequence of an influx of refugees, allowing resettlement can lead to long-term economic benefits. Such long-term benefits include overall economic growth, innovation, productivity, and structural transformation within the economy (Sarzin 2021).

For refugees and asylum seekers, being resettled within a country can be an opportunity for safety, consistent shelter, and jobs. However, upon arrival in a host country they may find that their economic participation is limited. Countries accepting refugees have a high degree of control over where these individuals are allowed to settle and work. Since these individuals often have limited economic means by the time they reach a host country, they are often at the mercy of the social systems within that state. For example, in the United Kingdom, refugees are dispersed across the country in order to alleviate pressures on immigration hubs. However, this can mean refugees are being placed into neighborhoods that have historically received little economic development (Hill, Meer, and Peace 2021).

While the developers who own property are happy to receive payments related to housing refugees, they may have little incentive to invest in buildings for residents who will only be there temporarily, have little capital, and are unlikely to be afforded the same legal protections of citizens in a country. Therefore, refugees and asylum seekers are still vulnerable to mistreatment even after resettlement. Without enhanced legal protections, there is often little preventing local or national governments from re-placing these migrants in various areas around a community in response to the desires of property managers and developers.

Politics and gentrification

Ultimately, the approaches to economic development and gentrification described throughout this chapter are closely tied to the political influence and social capital of existing residents, local governments, and developers. Public pressure campaigns have successfully brought some of the systemic issues related to gentrification into public discourse. These efforts have led to some municipalities approaching economic development with the needs of the established community in mind. However, the process of gentrifying a community is often unique to each metro area's political landscape.

Ideally, sustainable community development can lead to social, economic, and ecological improvements within an area. Pro-growth, neoliberal policies enacted by a state may advertise themselves as sustainable but, in reality, often prioritize development over societal welfare (Krings and Schusler 2020). The potential impact of a new development project on a community is often only discovered by the residents after plans have already been created by politicians and developers.

Understanding and working to remediate the imbalance in power between planners and the members of a community targeted for gentrification can help lead to more egalitarian community development. For example, historically Black neighborhoods in the United States are often targeted for development with the rationale of improving property values. However, these properties are often undervalued due to the previous, racist, federal housing practices and redlining (Perry, Rothwell, and Harshbarger 2018). While illustrating these differences in value between homes owned by white and Black Americans have led to policy changes, negative perceptions and racial biases are difficult to overcome.

Although laws may change to prevent the future use of discriminatory housing practices, participatory models of community development may be necessary to ensure that marginalized groups have their voices heard in development projects. Community-based development initiatives are one way to approach balancing economic desires with the needs of the community. This model of development brings the residents of a community into the stages of the development process and allows them to help shape the project. One example of a community-based approach is the use of **inclusive development**. This process for development accounts for individual experiences and identities of each community member and engages them in the revitalization process (United States Agency for International Development 2023). Inclusive development can also be used in international development and urban planning efforts to mitigate negative impacts on the residents.

Chapter Summary

We will continue to see migration away from rural areas as cities around the world grow and expand through urbanization. This migration may lead to the displacement of existing residents who can no longer afford to live within the community or feel as though they no longer belong in it. Gentrification occurs as higher-income residents move in and new types of businesses develop, which changes the demographics and characteristics of a neighborhood. The impacts of gentrification are mixed. This process can both positively and negatively impact communities; however, the negatives often fall on existing residents while the benefits are passed on to municipalities through economic development. The influx of income can stimulate the economy and lead to needed tax dollars, which can then be used to expand social services within the region. Yet, these improvements can also result in a higher cost of living, unaffordable rents for legacy residents, and a shift in the character of the community.

Urban and economic development projects must account for the needs of the residents living in the affected communities. Attracting new residents and growth to these areas can play an important and sometimes vital role in stimulating the economy, but it is important that these efforts do not negatively impact legacy residents. Balancing historic preservation, affordable housing, and economic development can be a challenge. Therefore, it is important that social safeguards are put in place to protect low-income and marginalized communities. Incorporating residents early in the planning process and throughout all stages of development can help to balance both the economic interests of the project and the needs of the existing community.

Review Questions

1. What are some of the ways in which economic development leads to mobility, either by choice or displacement? What happens to places of origin when migrants leave in search of economic opportunities?
2. Gentrification takes place in cities and neighborhoods all over the globe. What is it, and what are some of the main causes of gentrification?
3. If governments around the world can seize land from some of their citizens for uses that benefit the wider public, what safeguards (if any) do you think are needed to protect the interests of people displaced by such seizures?

References

Ahrens, M. 2015. "Gentrify? No! Gentefy? Sí!": Urban redevelopment and ethnic gentrification in Boyle Heights, Los Angeles. *Aspeers* 8: 9–26. https://doi.org/10.54465/aspeers.08-03

Appadurai, Arjun. 2013. *The Future as Cultural Fact: Essays on the global condition*. New York: Verso.

Black, K J, and M Richards. 2020. Eco-gentrification and who benefits from urban green amenities: NYC's High Line. *Landscape and Urban Planning* 204(6): 103900. https://doi.org/10.1016/j.landurbplan.2020.103900.

Borén, T, and C Young. 2013. The migration dynamics of the "creative class": Evidence from a study of artists in Stockholm, Sweden. *Annals of the Association of American Geographers* 103(1): 195–210. http://www.jstor.org/stable/23485235.

Brinkerhoff, A T. 1973. Eminent domain: Proving highest and best use of undeveloped land in Utah. *Utah Law Review* 1973(4): 705–717.

Cooney, P., Farley, R., Jubaed, S., et al. 2021. Analysis of the Census 2020 Count in Detroit. Poverty Solutions. University of Michigan. Retrieved from: https://sites.fordschool.umich.edu/poverty2021/files/2021/12/PovertySolutions-Census-Undercount-in-Detroit-PolicyBrief-December2021.pdf

Devoto, Fernando. 2004. *Historia de la Inmigración en la Argentina*. Buenos Aires: Editorial Sudamericana.

Ellen, I G, and G Torrats-Espinosa. 2019. Gentrification and fair housing: Does gentrification further integration? *Housing Policy Debate* 29(5): 835–851. https://doi.org/10.1080/10511482.2018.1524440.

Evans, Harriet. 2020. *Beijing from Below: Stories of marginal lives in the capital's center*. Durham, NC: Duke University Press.

Fraser, M. 2023. *Hillbilly Highway: The transappalachian migration and the making of a white working class*. Vol. 1. Princeton: Princeton University Press.

Freidenberg, Judith. 2009. *The Invention of the Jewish Gaucho: Villa Clara and the Construction of Argentine Identity*. Austin, Tx: University of Texas Press.

Frost, S L, Y Jung, M Rencher, and D Batts. 2023. Re-centering race in emancipatory entrepreneurship: Black female tech founders, money, and meaning in a Detroit-based incubator program. *Journal of Business Anthropology* 12(2): 114–137. https://doi.org/10.22439/jba.v12i2.7065.

Furszyfer Del Rio, D, and B Sovacool. 2023. Of cooks, crooks and slum-dwellers: Exploring the lived experience of energy and mobility poverty in Mexico's informal settlements. *World Development* 161. https://doi.org/10.1016/j.worlddev.2022.106093.

Gerchunoff, Alberto. 1984. *Los Gauchos Judíos*. Buenos Aires: Aguilar.

Gollopeni, B. 2016. Kosovar emigration: Causes, losses and benefits. *Sociologija I Prostor* 54(3): 295–314. https://doi.org/10.5673/SIP.54.3.5.

Gould, K A, and T L Lewis. 2021. Resilience gentrification: Environmental privilege in an age of coastal climate disasters. *Frontiers in Sustainable Cities* 3. https://doi.org/10.3389/frsc.2021.687670.

Hill, E, N Meer, and T Peace. 2021. The role of asylum in processes of urban gentrification. *The Sociological Review* 69(2): 259–276. https://doi.org/10.1177/0038026120970359.

Hjorthol, R J, and T Bjørnskau. 2005. Gentrification in Norway: Capital, culture or convenience? *European Urban and Regional Studies* 12(4): 353–371. https://doi.org/10.1177/0969776405058953.

Hutchinson, M. 2006. *Bo-Kaap: Colourful Heart of Cape Town*. New Africa Books.

Ivester, S. 2017. Removal, resistance and the right to the Olympic city: The case of Vila Autodromo in Rio de Janeiro. *Journal of Urban Affairs* 39(7): 970–985. https://doi.org/10.1080/07352166.2017.1355665.

Karas, D. 2015. Highway to inequity: The disparate impact of the interstate highway system on poor and minority communities in American cities. *New Visions for Public Affairs* 7: 9–21. https://www.ce.washington.edu/files/pdfs/about/Highway-to-inequity.pdf, accessed 13 Feb 2024.

Korpi, M, W A V Clark, and B Malmberg. 2011. The urban hierarchy and domestic migration: The interaction of internal migration, disposable income and the cost of living, Sweden 1993–2002. *Journal of Economic Geography* 11(6): 1051–1077. http://www.jstor.org/stable/26162584.

Korpi, M, and W A W Clark. 2017. Human capital theory and internal migration: Do average outcomes distort our view of migrant motives? *Migration Letters: An International Journal of Migration Studies* 14(2): 237–250. https://www.ncbi.nlm.nih.gov/pmc/articles/PMC5604464.

Krings, A, and T Schusler. 2020. Equity in sustainable development: Community responses to environmental gentrification. *International Journal for Social Welfare* 29: 321–334. https://doi.org/10.1111/ijsw.12425.

Kwon, D, and O Sorenson. 2023. The Silicon Valley syndrome. *Entrepreneurship Theory and Practice* 47(2): 344–368. https://doi.org/10.1177/10422587211050892.

Lianos, T P, A Pseiridis, and N Tsounis. 2023. Declining population and GDP growth. *Humanities and Social Sciences Communications* 10(1): 1–9. https://doi.org/10.1057/s41599-023-02223-7.

Linz, J. 2021. Where crises converge: The affective register of displacement in Mexico City's post-earthquake gentrification. *Cultural Geographies* 28(2): 285–300. https://doi.org/10.1177/1474474021993418.

Lustgarten, Abrahm. 2024. *On the Move: The overheating Earth and the uprooting of America*. New York: Farrar, Straus and Giroux.

McDermott, J. 2019. Towards an icon model of gentrification: Global capitalism, policing, and the struggle for iconic spaces in Mexico City. *Urban Studies* 56(16): 3522–3539. https://doi.org/10.1177/0042098018813065.

Mutter, J. 2010. Disasters widen the rich-poor gap. *Nature* 466: 1042. https://doi.org/10.1038/4661042a.

Nader, R, and A Hirsch. 2004. Making eminent domain humane. *Villanova Law Review* 49: 207–232.

O'Brien, K, L Vilchis, and C Maritescu. 2019. Boyle Heights and the fight against gentrification as state violence. *American Quarterly* 71(2): 389–396. https://doi.org/10.1353/aq.2019.0033.

Organisation for Economic Cooperation and Development. 2016. The Development Impact of Migration in Origin Countries. In *Perspectives on Global Development 2017: International Migration in a Shifting World*. Paris: OECD Publishing. https://doi.org/10.1787/persp_glob_dev-2017-11-en.

Organisation for Economic Cooperation and Development. 2022. Labour Migration in the Western Balkans: Mapping patterns, addressing challenges and reaping benefits. Global Relations Policy Insights, OECD Publishing, Paris. https://www.oecd.org/south-east-europe/programme/Labour-Migration-report.pdf

Perry, A, J Rothwell, and D Harshbarger. 2018. *The Devaluation of Assets in Black Neighborhoods: The case of residential property*. Brookings Institution. https://www.brookings.edu/wp-content/uploads/2018/11/2018.11_Brookings-Metro_Devaluation-Assets-Black-Neighborhoods_final.pdf.

Richardson, J, B Mitchell, and J Franco. 2019. *Shifting Neighborhoods: Gentrification and cultural displacement in American cities*. National Community Reinvestment Coalition. https://ncrc.org/wp-content/uploads/2019/03/NCRC-Research-Gentrification-FINAL.pdf.

Rigolon, Alessandro, and Jeremy Németh. 2020. Green gentrification or 'just green enough': Do park location, size and function affect whether a place gentrifies or not? *Urban Studies* 57(2): 402–420. https://doi.org/10.1177/0042098019849380.

Saborio, S, and S Spesny. 2019. Favelas. In A M Orum, ed. *The Wiley Blackwell Encyclopedia of Urban and Regional Studies*. Oxford: Wiley Blackwell Publishers. https://doi.org/10.1002/9781118568446.eurs0094.

Sarzin, Z. 2021. *The impact of forced migration on the labor market outcomes and welfare of host communities* [reference paper]. Reference Paper for the 70th Anniversary of the 1951 Refugee Convention. https://www.unhcr.org/people-forced-to-flee-book/wp-content/uploads/sites/137/2021/10/Zara-Sarzin_The-impact-of-forced-migration-on-the-labor-market-outcomes-and-welfare-of-host-communities.pdf

Scott, A J. 2019. Residential adjustment and gentrification in Los Angeles, 2000–2015: Theoretical arguments and empirical evidence. *Urban Geography* 40(4): 506–528. http://dx.doi.org/10.1080/02723638.2018.1500253.

Seepie, Z., Mwasinga, B., De Almeida, P., and Ntanzi, N. 2017. Bo-Kaap: City diplomacy stakeholders in urban regeneration heritage precincts. City Diplomacy Papers: Volume 1. South African Cities Network.

Shehayeb, D. 2009. Advantages of Living in Informal Areas. In R Kipper, and M Fischer, eds. *Cairo's Informal Areas between Urban Challenges and Hidden Potentials*. Norprint SA. pp. 34–43.

Solomon, L D. 2014. *Detroit: Three pathways to revitalization*. Routledge. https://doi.org/10.4324/9780203793374.

Sverdlik, A. 2011. Ill-health and poverty: A literature review on health in informal settlements. *Environment and Urbanization* 23(1): 123–155. https://doi.org/10.1177/0956247811398604.

Tatum, J. 2022. *Examining Detroit's vacancy rate drop*. Citizens Research Council of Michigan. https://crcmich.org/examining-detroits-vacancy-rate-drop

Toffa, T. 2004. Cape Town Bo-Kaap: The architecture of identity. In A. Malan, ed., Vernacular Architecture Society of SA: Workshop II pp. 16–35.

United Nations, Department of Economic and Social Affairs, Population Division. 2019. World Urbanization Prospects 2018: Highlights (ST/ESA/SER.A/421).

United Nations Habitat. 2020. *World cities report: The value of sustainable urbanization*. https://unhabitat.org/sites/default/files/2020/11/world_cities_report_2020_abridged_version.pdf

United Nations High Commissioner for Refugees. 2022. Global trends: The forced displacement in 2022. https://www.unhcr.org/global-trends-report-2022

United States Agency for International Development. 2023. *Inclusive Development: Additional help for ADS 201*. https://www.usaid.gov/sites/default/files/2023-10/USAID-ID-Hub_ADS-201-AH-Document_Oct-2023_1.pdf

Vale, L, and A Gray. 2013. The displacement decathlon. *Places Journal*. https://doi.org/10.22269/130415.

van Holm, E J, and C K Wyczalkowski. 2019. Gentrification in the wake of a hurricane: New Orleans after Katrina. *Urban Studies* 56(13): 2763–2778. https://doi.org/10.1177/0042098018800445.

Vásquez-Vera, H, L Palència, I Magna, C Mena, J Neira, and C Borrell. 2017. The threat of home eviction and its effects on health through the equity lens: A systematic review. *Social Science & Medicine* 175: 199–208. https://doi.org/10.1016/j.socscimed.2017.01.010.

Vertigans, S, and N Gibson. 2020. Resilience and social cohesion through the lens of residents in a Kenyan informal settlement. *Community Development Journal* 55(4): 624–644. https://doi.org/10.1093/cdj/bsz012.

Welisiejko, S, and B Cáceres. 2022. *Informal Settlement: No longer invisible*. Global Steering Group. https://gsgii.org/wp-content/uploads/2022/05/informal-settlements-report-2022.pdf.

Williamson, T. 2017. Not Everyone Has a Price: How the small favela of Vila Autódromo's fight opened a path to Olympic resistance. In A Zimbalist, ed. *Rio 2016: Olympic Myths, Hard Realities*. Washington, DC: Brookings Institution Press. pp. 57–95. https://library.oapen.org/bitstream/id/65b71478-c1a2-4cc0-bcce-c95c84cbbaa0/644222.pdf, accessed 13 Feb 2024.

9

Enslavement and Coercion

When discussing migration, it is important to recognize that people do not always move by choice. While forced migration can occur for a variety of reasons (as discussed in prior chapters), such as fleeing conflicts or environmental disasters, this section will delve specifically into the movement of people due to enslavement and coercion. Throughout history individuals have been removed from lands they had previously called home. For many readers, the first example that springs to mind is likely the transatlantic slave trade of the seventeenth to nineteenth centuries. Africans were forcibly captured, removed from their homelands, and resettled in captivity across the Caribbean and the Americas. Others may picture Native Americans being forcibly removed from their ancestral territories and resettled in reservations. History is filled with examples of how disparities in power between groups of people can lead to coercion, enslavement, and forced migration.

These coercive movements of people persist today. In this chapter, we will explore historical and global perspectives on enslavement. Specifically, we will focus on the motivations for, and lasting repercussions of, these acts. To do this, we will examine both historical cases of enslavement and coercion around the world while taking a deeper dive into the history of the transatlantic slave trade and its lasting impacts. We will close this chapter with a discussion on modern-day forms of human trafficking and the effectiveness of anti-trafficking efforts at local, national, and international levels.

World on the Move: 250,000 Years of Human Migration, First Edition. Edward Liebow, James I. Deutsch, Daniel Ginsberg, Sojin Kim, and Caitlyn Kolhoff.
© 2025 John Wiley & Sons, Inc. Published 2025 by John Wiley & Sons, Inc.

Global Perspectives on Enslavement

Enslavement is not unique to one point in history, one geographic location, or a specific cultural group. While different cultural groups justified this exploitation in different ways – such as using it as a form of criminal punishment, to collect on debts, or rationalizing through religious ideology – the act of enslaving humans is driven by power dynamics. At its core it is a process that removes the agency of the people that are enslaved by brute force, restricting their freedoms, movement, and ability for self-determination. Slavery allows one group to economically profit from the labor of another. To better understand the different global perspectives on enslavement over time, let's explore three examples of slavery throughout history: ancient China, Barbary piracy, and Native American groups.

Ancient China

Records of the practice of slavery can be found in the material artifacts of ancient civilizations. Ancient Greece is often noted when discussing early documented practices of enslavement. Approximately 15–30% of the population was enslaved (Vujčić 2021). However, it is important to understand that forced labor was practiced throughout many early civilizations, one such case being ancient China. Unlike the ancient empires of the Romans or Greeks where status as a slave was distinguished through a codified legal framework, disentangling the practice of slavery in Chinese history has been more challenging (Crossley 2011).

Prior historians have identified the practice of treating certain humans as "dominated non-persons" who held status below that of the common, ancient Chinese citizen based on interpretations of legal documents that date back to the Qin dynasty (221–206 BCE) (Yates 2002). In these documents, clear distinctions can be drawn between citizens based on their social status. Members of the aristocracy are clearly delineated in these texts from the rank-and-file citizens; however, both of these groups had standing higher than prisoners incarcerated for short periods of time and enslaved people – who were referred to as "socially dead" even though they were not physically deceased (Yates 2002).

Enslaved people were known as "*nubi*," and were forced to work in both government positions and private households. The penal system of ancient China allowed the government to place those convicted of a crime into conscripted labor. Those enslaved by the central government often served in operations and infrastructure roles, such as building palaces, tombs, roads, and bridges (Scheidel 2013). Apart from those within the penal system, people were enslaved through human trafficking as well as coercion through bonds and debts (Venters 2022). While no large uprising of nubi are documented, literary and legal source materials document the ways in which they were able to demonstrate resistance to their enslavement. Theft, work abstention, suicide, and murder are all documented ways in which ancient Chinese enslaved persons resisted (Venters 2022). Legalized forms of forced labor continued throughout much of ancient, medieval, and imperial China.

After nearly 2,000 years the Qing Dynasty made the buying and selling of people illegal in China in 1910. While efforts to abolish slavery within China had been made before, these efforts did not have lasting impacts. The motivation of the Qing Dynasty was not necessarily to provide freedom to those that were enslaved under the previous policies. Rather, their goal was to improve China's international reputation through the abolition of slavery to ensure they would be seen as more modern and civilized when compared to European imperialism (Ling 2021). While the effects of the abolition were not immediate, this did create a government stance against the practice of enslavement and codified punishment for those who continued to enslave others. However, the story does not end here. Issues of forced labor and coercion have continued to affect China up to the present day. This will be addressed later in this chapter during the exploration of modern-day human trafficking.

Barbary coast pirates (sixteenth to eighteenth centuries)

The Barbary coast is a historical region of North Africa that borders the Mediterranean Sea. This region makes up today's Morocco, Algeria, Tunisia, and Libya. The region probably gets its name from the Berbers, a large cultural group that has occupied this territory for at least 10,000 years. The Mediterranean basin was a bustling region for trade, and this sea trade brought with it opportunities for piracy and privateering from the sixteenth to eighteenth centuries. While many friendly commercial activities were conducted in the region (as well as beyond to the English Channel) the practices of taking captives, trading enslaved people, and piracy were also common during this period. Piracy existed both with the North African communities and Europeans, with each group targeting others due to religious and regional differences (Matar 2001). Few groups in the region would amass a more infamous reputation for piracy, raiding, and enslavement of sailors and coastal villagers than the Barbary coast pirates.

While no concrete figures have been tabulated regarding how many Europeans were enslaved in North Africa between the sixteenth to eighteenth century, estimates are as high as 1 to 1.2 million (Davis 2003). While Barbary pirates conducted raids across Europe, their presence was well known and visible throughout Britain. The British published informational pamphlets and hosted plays that told of horrific encounters and enslavement in the Ottoman Empire. Occasionally these performances would include formerly enslaved British men (Styer 2014). Crews and passengers captured by North African pirates would be brought back to the Barbary coast to be sold into slavery or ransomed. Those captured faced difficult conditions. Privateers would subject their prisoners to torture to extract information about wealthy passengers and the location of valuable goods. Additionally, privateers felt these stories of torture could help hasten payment of ransom (Matar 2001).

While some sailors were ransomed from the Barbary privateers, many of the enslaved people in Barbary did not have the financial means or status to buy their freedom. Those who remained in North Africa for the remainder of their lives would die of maltreatment, disease, or malnutrition. Enslaved people were put to work in a variety of positions, which could range from "cruel enslavement to well-paid positions and from professional labor to an ambassadorial opportunity" (Matar 2001). It was also not uncommon for enslaved people in the Barbary to convert to Islam as a way to obtain preferential treatment (Davis 2011).

By the 1700s the paying of ransoms had significantly reduced the population of enslaved people on the Barbary coast. Many of these ransoms were paid by churches throughout Europe, where parish collection boxes and associations developed in an effort to free victims. Little is currently known about the impact Barbary raids had on the potential depopulation of coastal areas surrounding the Mediterranean or the impoverishment caused by kidnapping the primary wage earners of families (Davis 2011). However, the institutionalization of slavery and piracy by the states on the Barbary coast illustrates the economic and political impact these practices can have within a region. Slavery, and the threat of enslavement, by Barbary privateers allowed leaders of these states to bolster their economies through ransoms and treaties with neighboring countries.

Native American groups

In the Americas, Native American groups engaged in acts of slavery and were also enslaved by European colonizers. Native American groups rooted the practice of slavery in cultural contexts (Reséndez 2021). Therefore, the motivations for enslaving people varied greatly between Indigenous societies. While the Iroquois took captives from other tribes to replace warriors killed in combat, the tribes of the Pacific Northwest exchanged enslaved peoples as a way to finalize marriages among their elite. A well-known example of slavery among the Indigenous communities in the Americas may be seen in the Aztecs and the Maya, who each used captives as sacrificial offerings.

The motivations and acts committed pre-European contact differed from those committed after European colonizers arrived in the Western Hemisphere (fifteenth century). Europeans introduced an institutionalized and systematic form of slavery, rooted in a racial hierarchy. At first, some Indigenous communities were part of this activity and provided captives to arriving Europeans. Over time, this changed the function of slavery in the Americas from culturally specific to a more economically based practice. Native American enslaved persons during the early colonial period may have served as guides or intermediaries for new arrivals. However, enslaved Indigenous persons in the early European colonies often performed intensive manual labor for their masters, such as mining or farming cash crops like tobacco and sugar.

It is estimated that between 2 and 5.5 million Native Americans were enslaved between the time Christopher Columbus arrived in 1492 and the late nineteenth century when slavery was finally abolished everywhere in the Americas (Reséndez 2021). Native Americans were not only used in domestic slavery within the colonies established in the New World but also shipped to Europe and North Africa where they were sold at slave markets. As Indigenous peoples attempted to stand up to colonizing

Europeans, they were aware that these actions could lead to their enslavement and forced migration (Fisher 2017). However, the eighteenth-century trade in enslaved Native Americans began to decrease on the Atlantic coast of the present-day United States as African slavery increased.

Through the exploration of enslavement across cultures, time, and regions, it is possible to see that the practice of forced labor is not isolated to one particular group. While the motivations and specific practices may vary, enslavement and coercion have been used by dominant groups to enforce a power structure over others for as long as humans have existed. However, none of these systems had the level of scale as the transatlantic slave trade. Although this formalized system of exchanging humans for goods only lasted for approximately 250 years, it had profound socio-cultural impacts that continue to be felt today.

The transatlantic slave trade (seventeenth to nineteenth century)

The transatlantic slave trade saw the forced migration of 12.5 million enslaved Africans to the Americas (Eltis 2007). This was a large-scale, global form of slavery in which multiple countries participated in the buying and selling of humans. While many historic instances of enslavement have been explored in prior sections, the foundation of the transatlantic slave trade started within the interactions between European traders and African kingdoms.

Established in the thirteenth century, the Kingdom of Kongo ruled much of central Africa, the area spanning from present-day Gabon to Angola and the Democratic Republic of Congo. The Kingdom of Kongo was the center of a vast trans-African trading network through the 1600s, which included goods such as textiles, ivory, pottery, and metals. While there are few definitive accounts of the practice of slavery in the Kingdom of Kongo prior to European contact, it is believed that the practice did exist among the Kongolese (Heywood 2009). This enslavement was typically related to captives taken in battle during Kongolese conflicts with other regional powers. However, the dynamics of slavery within Kongo would change after they encountered Portuguese merchants.

In 1483 the Portuguese landed in the Kingdom of Kongo. Motivated by the desire to locate shorter spice trade routes from Africa to India, they began to search along the coast of West Africa for a sea passage to the east (Newitt 2004). Portuguese merchants quickly began to trade goods and form alliances with the Kongolese. Slavery became an integral part of foreign trading for the Portuguese, and by the 1560s Portuguese merchants, priests, Kongolese kings, and others involved in foreign trading would convert all trade goods into enslaved people (Heywood 2009). Men often outnumbered the number of women sent from central and West Africa to the New World. Some researchers have attributed the higher rates of male enslavement to European ideology around the division of labor and the idea that able-bodied men would be better suited for harsh labor on plantations (Domingues da Silva 2017). However, others have attributed these differences to the higher value of female labor within African society

ENSLAVEMENT AND COERCION

(Domingues da Silva 2017). This illustrates how both economic conditions and gender ideology within both European and African societies shaped the demographics of enslaved populations during the transatlantic slave trade.

Merchants used a **triangular trade** route between Africa, Europe, and the Americas to transport goods and newly enslaved Africans between these regions. Each leg of the triangle represents a different part of the exchange system. Textiles, alcohol, and manufactured goods were sent from Europe to Africa. During the second leg of the trip, the goods are replaced with newly enslaved Africans who are then sent to the Americas. After being emptied of their human cargo, merchant ships would leave on the third leg of the trip from the Americas to Europe with raw materials, sugar, tobacco, and cotton. It was prior to this second leg that captive Africans would be forced to march anywhere from a couple to hundreds of miles to the Atlantic Ocean and the waiting ships (Mustakeem 2016).

The brutal sea journey across the Atlantic, from Africa to the Americas, was known as the Middle Passage. The voyage could take several months to complete. People were chained and branded, then packed tightly into the vessel with no space to move. The purpose of these trips was to transport as many humans as possible, with some trips carrying hundreds of people at a time. The poor conditions led to disease and starvation during the journey. Ship captains, knowing they were paid based on the number of humans they delivered alive, would weigh the risk of disease from overpacking the ship against the risk of delivering fewer people overall due to underloading. Regardless of the approach taken by the captains, the journey was ruthless. By the end of the transatlantic slave trade, it was estimated that 15% of Africans did not survive the Middle Passage (Davis 2006).

Augustus Earle, *Capoeira, Brazil*, 1822, watercolor, 16.5 x 25.1 cm, National Library of Australia, object no. 134509842.

Men and women practice capoeira in Florianopolis, Brazil. Photos by Ed Liebow.

Enslaved central Africans taken to Brazil brought martial arts and ritual dance traditions with them. They and their descendants developed these traditions into Capoeira de Angola, a practice that honors its African roots.

Upon their arrival to the New World, between 90 and 95% of enslaved African people, or approximately 10 million, were transported to either present-day Brazil or the Caribbean to work as laborers on plantations (Eltis and Richardson 2010; Eltis, Lewis, and Richardson 2005). Others were taken to British colonies in North America.

The plantations in the United States were often significantly smaller than those in Brazil and the West Indies. Conditions in the United States also led to an increase in the number of enslaved people from births over multiple generations of enslavement. Conversely, other areas in the Americas had death rates so high that their slave populations could not be sustained without the import of new enslaved people from Africa. By the 1850s most enslaved people in the United States were multiple generations removed from their African ancestors.

While transportation to the New World came with its own dangers, enslaved people in the Americas were also subject to inhumane living and working conditions. Poor nutrition led to many contracting diseases such as rickets, pellagra, and tetany. Blindness, bowed legs, and abdominal swelling were also common among enslaved populations (Resnitriwati 2020). The harsh labor and malnutrition that enslaved pregnant women were subjected to also impacted the health of their infants. An estimated 50% of infants born into slavery died within their first year (Owens and Fett 2019). Moreover, infant children of enslaved people had high death rates due to chronic undernourishment, respiratory diseases, and dysentery.

On January 1, 1808 the transatlantic slave trade was made illegal in the United States. Other countries across Europe passed similar laws in the first decades of the 1800s. However, this change in legislation did not immediately result in the end of the transportation of enslaved Africans to the United States, South America, or the Caribbean. The illegal transportation of people across the Middle Passage continued through the middle of the nineteenth century. Approximately 25% of all enslaved people sent to colonies in the Americas traveled the Middle Passage in the final six decades of the transatlantic trade; however, a vast majority of these captives would travel from Africa to either Brazilian or Cuban plantations (Meredith 2014).

A variety of factors led up to the end of the transatlantic slave trade. Abolitionists around the world felt a strong moral and ethical motivation to end slavery. In the United States societies such as the Quakers and the American Anti-Slavery Society formed with the goal of immediately ending slavery. Notable abolitionists like Frederick Douglass traveled around the world pressuring countries to end their participation in the slave trade. Pressure from the international community, including from nations who had already abolished slavery within their own societies, played a role in delegitimizing the formal industries that had developed around the slave trade – such as the construction of purpose-built slave transport ships. The United States Civil War provided a tipping point where the remaining holdouts participating in the illegal trade of Africans capitulated to international pressures.

The defeat of the Confederate States of America led to a series of constitutional reforms aimed at reconstructing race relations in the United States. However, it would be another hundred years before anti-segregation acts and the work of civil rights leaders would create a sense of legal equality for Black Americans. The impact of slavery continues to cause intergenerational trauma in descendant communities. Despite progress, issues of systemic and institutionalized racism frequently occur, and political discourse has grappled with how descendants of slavery survivors should receive reparations for their family's forced relocation and dehumanization.

PERSPECTIVE: In the Face of Forced Migration – Gullah People, Language, and Culinary Agency, by Antoinette Jackson

Professor and Chair, Department of Anthropology, University of South Florida (USA)

Gullah communities are concentrated in the Sea Islands along the Southeast Atlantic coast of the United States. Gullah people are descendants of enslaved Africans who were forced to labor on the numerous rice, indigo, and cotton plantations primarily located along the coast of North and South Carolina, Georgia, and Florida. They brought technological skills in rice and indigo production and demonstrated resilience in the face of enslavement and its long-term consequences as underscored, for example, in the development of their language and communication system. Gullah people and their active persistence in practicing and maintaining cultural traditions are to be acknowledged as integral to America's story. The preservation, protection, and promotion of Gullah cultural heritage is now formally authorized by US law – the National Heritage Areas Act (Pub. L. 109-338, 32 Stat. 388, 2006) that authorized the establishment of the Gullah Geechee Cultural Heritage Corridor, was signed into law in 2006.

Gullah is both a language and the name of the people who speak the language. In her book, *Making Gullah,* Cooper (2017) highlights the import of the construction of identity and meaning of Gullah (developed by previous writers, scholars, and researchers) in establishing expectations and norms. She posits the importance of knowing the social, historical, and political influences that operate in the construction of the word "Gullah" and the ways in which these influences impact how we derive our knowledge of this community. In this discussion of Gullah, I draw upon the seminal work of scholars who have spent extensive time developing a knowledge of Gullah people and communities as researchers and through lived experience. I do this to contextualize the history and heritage of Gullah people and communities in the face of forced migration and enslavement.

Linguist Turner (1949) has done an extensive study of the Gullah language, and his fieldwork and scholarship have done much to inform the field on the origins and structure of the Gullah language. The creation of Gullah Creole represented a considerable effort on the part of enslaved Africans to establish both a communication system and a community under the abusive and disorienting conditions of the American chattel slavery system. For example, Africans (primarily from areas along the West Coast of Africa extending from Senegal to Angola) were enslaved and shipped directly to Charleston, South Carolina beginning in 1670. The largest percentage of Africans in South Carolina and Georgia were acquired from Angola, Senegambia, and the Windward Coast – including Sierra Leone (Littlefield 1991). By the year 1720, African descendant people were the majority in South Carolina, comprising over two-thirds of the population; plantation populations on the Sea Islands were, in most cases, over 90% African. Such conditions created an environment that fostered the development of communities and language structures that were highly influenced by African cultural and linguistic patterns.

Turner's research of the Gullah people and language extended over a period of 15 years in which he spent time directly recording the speech patterns of people in the communities of coastal and mainland South Carolina and Georgia. His work linguistically confirms the tendency exhibited by South Carolina slave owners to select from specific populations of Africans based on observed ethnic tendencies and observed technical competence. His findings illustrate that the Gullah lexicon not only contains a large proportion of English words but also contains words found in multiple West African languages, such as: Wolof, Malinke, Mandinka, Bambara, Fula, Mende, Vai, Twi, Fante, Ga, Ewe, Fon, Yoruba, Bini, Hausa, Ibo, Kongo, Umbundu, Kimbundu, and others. Each of these languages is spoken in the areas from which Africans were primarily enslaved and brought to America (Turner 1949).

Turner selected people who were native members of their respective communities and collected phonograph recordings, created autobiographical sketches and narratives of life experiences, including recollections of slavery, religious experiences, and methods of planting and harvesting crops. He was able to gain access to a level of knowledge on the Gullah language that had been unobserved by previous researchers. He reported that:

> … when talking to strangers the Gullah Negro is likely to use speech that is essentially English in vocabulary. When he talks to his friends, however, or to members of his family, his language is different. My first recordings of the speech of the Gullahs contain fewer African words by far than those made when I was no longer a stranger to them (Turner 1949, p. 12).

As a result of his position of familiarity and acceptance within the Gullah communities in which he worked, Turner was able to acquire an extensive list of Gullah words, sentences, names, and expressions of African origin. He compiled a list of approximately 1,000 personal names used by Gullah – explaining that most Gullah people switch between two names. The personal names that he recorded are considered nicknames, or basket names, and are used exclusively by the Gullah at home or among friends. These names are primarily of African origin with most of the words on Turner's list specifically reflecting Yoruba origin. Examples of some of these names and meanings follow: (1) *ade biyi* is a Yoruba feminine name meaning "the crown has begotten this"; (2) *ago'go* is a Yoruba masculine name meaning "a bell or clock"; and (3) *be'randa* is a Wolof feminine name meaning "a long pole used for propelling a boat" (Turner 1949).

Turner has done an impressive job in documenting Gullah language and dissecting it linguistically. His work underscores the tremendous creativity of Africans in the face of forced migration, particularly in terms of the ability to create effective modes of communication through the development of a common language that bridged the many ethnic groups enslaved and brought to the Sea Islands. Turner's work has informed the field and opened the door for further research on

Gullah and its West African language connections. It remains one of the most comprehensive studies of Gullah Creole in the United States documented today.

In addition to these distinct language and communication patterns, evidence of other norms (such as foodways and culinary expertise) practiced in the face of enslavement, remain relevant to the history and heritage of Gullah and other Southeast coastal communities today. For example, in terms of food production, Africans were critical to all aspects of food security on South Carolina rice plantations. Specifically, African knowledge of and expertise in growing rice is well documented (Carney 2001; Fields 2008; Jackson 2012). They prepared the fields, sowed the seed, harvested the crop, processed the grain for market export (i.e., winnowed, hulled, and milled), and controlled and managed the hydraulic irrigation system on which the entire system of rice production was based. Most importantly, Africans (mainly African women) were intimately involved in food security at the household level.

In South Carolina, African women toiled in the fields and performed all functions essential to the production of rice. In addition, they prepared food for themselves, their families, and labored in European households and kitchens throughout the Americas, producing many outstanding dishes that have become essential parts of southern cuisine and cuisine around the world. It is these women that Karen Hess speaks of in her book, *The Carolina Rice Kitchen* (1991). Hess details the history of rice preparation in the kitchens of South Carolina and acknowledges the culinary expertise of African women. According to Hess, African women out cooked the French in the preparation of rice dishes, starting with the most basic of rice dishes – the pilau (Hess 1991, p. 37). Vertamae Smart-Grosvenor (1937–2016), who authored several books on African American cooking and grew up steeped in the traditions of Gullah people, writes:

> And speaking of rice. I was sixteen years old before I knew that everyone didn't eat rice every day. Us being geechees, we had rice every day. When you said what you were eating for dinner, you always assumed that rice was there. That was one of my jobs too. To cook the rice. A source of pride for me was that I cooked rice like a grown person. I could cook it till every grain stood by itself (Smart-Grosvenor 1992, p. 6).

Nikky Finney, another South Carolina native, writes in her book entitled, *Rice* (1995):

> In the 1960's, as a girl growing up in the Palmetto state, there was always a punch bowl of rice on the dinner table. In my own house today, we eat rice daily, never tiring of it. I hold this tradition of rice culture and diet to be sacred (Finney 1995, p. 11–12).

And the 2021 Netflix series *High on the Hog: How African American Cuisine Transformed America* – based on the similarly titled book by Harris (2012) – chronicles the development of African American cuisine and its African origins.

> Africans relied on their ability to improvise throughout much of their period of enslavement in America. In the case of South Carolina, southern cooking is culturally grounded in the cultivation and consumption of rice. Rice was not only food but also a way of life. African descendant people and members of Gullah communities throughout the Sea Islands are renowned for the centrality of rice, the craft of sweet grass basket sewing, and the oral tradition of Gullah as linguistic creation and practice. In 2006 then President George Bush, signed into law the National Heritage Areas Act, which authorized the establishment of the Gullah Geechee Cultural Heritage Corridor. This law, which was championed by Representative James E. Clyburn (D) of South Carolina, instructs the US Secretary of the Interior to oversee the implantation of the Gullah Geechee Cultural Heritage Corridor to help preserve, protect, and promote this endangered cultural group and their communities (Jackson 2012).

The impacts of the transatlantic slave trade are also still felt in African countries of origin. More than half of the enslaved people forcibly brought to the Americas between 1502 and 1888 came from central Africa. This large-scale removal of people created a rupture in central African societies. Areas of the African continent that had the largest amounts of forced emigration continue to have worse economic outcomes than their neighbors (Nunn 2017). The legacy of colonialism lives on in today's systems, policies, and societies. Political borders drawn by colonial empires remain in place in much of Africa, despite African nations regaining their independence from these empires in the 1950s. This continues to split ethnic groups across national borders within Africa (Michalopoulos and Papaioannou 2016).

Burundian refugees fleeing political violence arrive in Mboko, Democratic Republic of the Congo. Source: Photo courtesy of United Nations High Commissioner for Refugees, © UNHCR/Federico Scoppa.

Contemporary Forms of Human Trafficking

Although formalized slavery has largely been abolished globally, illegal trade in humans continues to take place in every region of the world today. Like the ways in which slavery existed in past societies, contemporary enslavement continues to exist through debt bondage, forced labor, forced marriage, and human trafficking. There are an estimated 50 million people living in some form of modern slavery (International Labour Organization 2022). To explore how modern forms of enslavement impact human migration, we will now take a deeper look at the issue of human trafficking.

Human trafficking is a form of modern slavery that occurs when people are forced into labor or sexual exploitation through coercion, direct violence, or manipulation. While trafficking can be part of other forms of contemporary slavery, it specifically involves the recruitment, transportation, and harboring of people (United Nations 2000).

Although victims can be of any race, gender, or ethnicity, women and children are at the highest risk for trafficking (United Nations Office on Drugs and Crime 2022). Displaced persons and migrants are also at an increased risk of becoming victims of human trafficking. For example, human smugglers may promise migrants safe transportation across borders, only to place them in a debt bondage leading to forced labor. While not all victims of trafficking migrate long distances between their homes and their point of exploitation, it is becoming increasingly common for victims to move long distances, harkening back to the journeys made during the transatlantic slave trade (Shelley 2010).

Human trafficking is an economically motivated crime. It has become one of the fastest growing transnational crimes as an influx of global migrants and a shrinking of trade barriers have led to a high supply, and demand, for smuggled individuals (Shelley 2010). This increased movement of people allows for illegal trade in persons to hide within migrations. Globalization has affected the supply chain for trafficking by establishing wealth disparities, which further marginalizes rural communities. The demand for trafficked labor has increased in today's global economy as exploited labor allows producers to develop cheaper, lower-cost goods (Shelley 2010).

Human trafficking often falls into two broad categories: labor exploitation and sexual exploitation. These are not mutually exclusive, as sexual exploitation may also overlap with labor, as seen in the cases of forced prostitution. Labor exploitation and forced labor can take place in both commercial and domestic environments. It is inclusive of those forcibly working in agricultural settings or domestic servitude and more dangerous work conditions, such as manufacturing, mining, and soldiering.

Three contemporary examples of labor exploitation can be seen in (1) North Korea's government sanctioned trafficking of its citizens, (2) child labor in Ghana, and (3) domestic servitude in France. First, the North Korean government has historically trafficked their own citizens to other countries as a way to obtain foreign currency and finance their internal operations. The People's Republic of China is one area in which North Korean migrants are working in conditions of forced labor. These victims of trafficking are often found within the hospitality, manufacturing, and cyber operations industries (United States Department of State 2022).

Domestic trafficking of children is a significant problem within Ghana, particularly within the cocoa production and fishing industries. In the Lake Volta region children are forced to work on fishing boats in hazardous conditions. Issues of endemic poverty create situations where families can be easily coerced into providing their children to traffickers, or in some cases, parents themselves are willing trafficking participants (Challenging Heights 2022). Working conditions on the boats make it difficult, if not impossible, for children to continue their education. Further, their physical and mental wellbeing is challenged as they face difficult working conditions, abuse from their traffickers, and being away from their families.

Labor exploitation can also take place within private residences in the form of domestic servitude. It can be difficult to detect when domestic servitude occurs because it happens within the privacy of one's home. For example, if a trafficking victim is forced to work as a nanny, it is possible they would not have access to leave the premises or interact with the outside world. Thus, not only would they have little opportunity to report they needed help but others in their community may not see signs of abuse. In France, domestic servitude accounts for approximately 10% of all trafficking cases. Women and children are primarily the victims of this type of trafficking within France. While this form of trafficking frequently goes unnoticed, it is often linked to families who bring relatives from foreign countries to work within their households and exploiting their labor (United States Department of State 2022).

The International Labour Organization (ILO) estimates that about 6.3 million of the 27.6 million human trafficking victims are trafficked for the purpose of sexual exploitation and acknowledges that labor and sexual exploitation can be – and often are – intertwined (International Labour Organization 2022). Sex trafficking is when humans are coerced, forced, or misled into providing sexual services. This can include the forced prostitution of adults and children, forced marriage or bridal trafficking, and sex tourism.

Sex tourism, travel with the purpose of engaging in commercial sex, is a growing industry that plays upon wealth gaps between victims in low-income nations and the tourists of high-income nations. This reflects a larger issue within sex trafficking, where the women and children trafficked tend to come from poorer nations and are trafficked within the low-income nation or to high-income nations (O'Brien 2009). The issue of child sex tourism is a persistent problem within Brazil. Foreign tourists, many of whom are from Europe and the United States, travel to engage in commercial sexual acts with minors. Child sex tourism is a common problem in the resort and coastal areas where tourists frequent (United States Department of State 2022).

Fraud or coercion may be used to deceive someone into migrating for the purpose of marriage. While not all forced marriages are the result of human trafficking, migrants may be particularly vulnerable to the situation of forced marriage. Specifically, migrants may be coerced into entering a new country for the purpose of forced marriage. They may face pressure from not only the traffickers but also their families to migrate for the purpose of marriage to help their families financially

(International Labour Organization 2022). Once within their new country it can be difficult for migrants to receive the legal services and counseling to assist them with ending a forced marriage. These challenges are exacerbated by the dual stigmatization of both sex trafficking and migration.

People subjected to forced marriage are also vulnerable to domestic servitude, where they work within their households with little or no compensation. There are often intersections between labor and sexual exploitation. Similar methods of recruitment are used in both types of exploitation, such as fraud, force, and coercion. Victims of each type of exploitation can be pressured using debt bondage and involuntary servitude. At their core, each type of exploitation allows a trafficker to benefit from the labor of the person being trafficked. In some cases, this is the sale of commercial sexual services (as seen with prostitution) or domestic labor (as seen with forced marriages).

Human trafficking, for both labor and sex exploitation, takes place in all regions of the world today. The mobility of people and money, increasing inequality between men and women, and the marginalization of rural communities all increase the supply and demand for trafficked persons. The buying and selling of people remains a lucrative industry that generates an estimated $150 billion in global profits for traffickers annually (International Labour Office 2014; United States Department of Homeland Security 2022). Human trafficking has devastating impacts on the physical and mental health of those that are trafficked. Moreover, communities where trafficking is prevalent often face social and economic impacts. The remaining sections of this chapter will focus on dispelling common myths around human trafficking, identifying anti-trafficking efforts, and exploring the overall consequences and effects of both modern and historical enslavement and coercion.

Dispelling Misconceptions About Human Trafficking

Many misconceptions and stereotypes surround human trafficking, and these misconceptions often impact the ability to effectively act on this issue at an individual and national level. Specifically, when many people envision trafficking their mind may go to media representations, where a defenseless woman is kidnapped, or political discourse that paints the problem of trafficking as an international issue. In fact, victims of human trafficking come from multiple genders, are found in high- and low-income countries, and trafficking can occur within legal industries. Most alarmingly, it can often be difficult to create clear distinctions between victims and perpetrators under existing legal frameworks.

For example, within the United States, protections for victims of human trafficking can vary greatly between states. Survivors of human trafficking are often arrested for offensives they committed as a result of their victimization. Even if they have escaped trafficking, arrest and court records related to these offenses may still follow. New York was the first state to pass a law giving survivors of trafficking a mechanism to remove these incidents from their criminal record. Following that law's enactment in 2010, states across the United States have passed similar legislation; however, many of these may either have stipulations that make the process of clearing a criminal record difficult or are too narrowly tailored (Marsh et al. 2019). This can be seen in the differences between Michigan and Nebraska's trafficking victim relief laws.

As of 2019, survivors of trafficking in Michigan who petition for the removal of charges are required to pay filing fees and have their behavior and conduct since their conviction reviewed by a court. While they may appear to be reasonable conditions on first read, these requirements mean that victims of human trafficking have to demonstrate that they deserve to have their records cleared. Moreover, the financial requirements can be burdensome for survivors when the criminal record could prevent them from entering a career after their victimization (Marsh et al. 2019). Conversely, Nebraska allows survivors to have all offenses committed as a result of trafficking vacated without a hearing (Polaris Project 2019).

While many of these state laws still have room for improvement, it is important to note there is currently no law in the United States that offers criminal-record relief to victims of human trafficking who commit a *federal* crime. Therefore, the only avenue currently available for vacating charges received by survivors who are charged at the federal level is a presidential pardon. Although law enforcement agencies, lawyers, and judges are actively working to address human trafficking, many trafficking survivors are frequently arrested, prosecuted, and convicted for acts they committed during their victimization (Marsh et al. 2019).

Apart from the criminalization of human trafficking survivors, other misconceptions around *who* is a victim of human trafficking exist. While women and girls are disproportionately impacted by human trafficking, men and boys can also be trafficked. There are regional differences in the profiles of who is trafficked and for what purposes. For example, women and girls are more often trafficked for sexual exploitation within the Americas. There are higher rates of forced labor trafficking among men in Europe, the Middle East, and North Africa, as well as the trafficking of boys into criminal activity (United Nations Office on Drugs and Crime 2022). Furthermore, lesbian, gay, bisexual, transgender, and queer (LGBTQ) persons are particularly vulnerable to trafficking. LGBTQ persons face higher rates of poverty and discrimination both of which are risk factors for trafficking. Systemic discrimination against the LGBTQ community not only places them at a higher risk of becoming the victims of human trafficking but it also can make it more difficult for survivors to receive legal support (Mooney 2020).

One of the most pervasive myths about human trafficking is that it always begins as a physically violent crime. Not all traffickers kidnap or physically assault their victims as a means of recruiting them. In fact, many traffickers use more nuanced and manipulative methods of coercion, fraud, and threats to recruit. This psychological violence can often play a larger role than overt physical violence during the initial stages of recruitment. Traffickers are able to identify and target vulnerabilities within their victims to better control them. For example, a trafficker may target people who are seeking stable employment or shelter and promise to provide these things. In reality, they are providing fraudulent job offers with little or no pay and exploiting the labor of their victims. They may also use promises of love and romance to control victims and to convince them to work for them.

As with previously discussed forms of enslavement, unequal power dynamics play a large role in modern-day human trafficking. Power dynamics can provide insight into how traffickers are able to both recruit and maintain control over their victims (Kim 2011). Traffickers leverage their positions of power over their victims to manipulate or coerce them into working for them. Social power in this case is derived from an exploitation of the victim's socioeconomic status, history with abuse or violence, and support from their community or social networks (Preble and Black 2020).

It is common for traffickers to use seduction, grooming, and excessive displays of affection to recruit victims. To better understand how power dynamics are used in combination with romance to control people, let's examine the loverboy method of recruitment used by pimps to force young people into prostitution or other forms of sexual exploitation. Within this method the trafficker forges a false romantic relationship with their prospective victim using seduction, manipulation, and violence (Government of the Netherlands 2011). This allows them to have their trust and to be able to isolate victims from any support systems they may have. The trafficker may promise that they will be together forever or that they will support them unconditionally, when in reality the end goal is to control them. What appears to be a loving relationship for the victim quickly turns into one of psychological and potentially physical abuse. Loverboy pimps operate domestically, trafficking people within their own countries, and internationally, moving victims across national lines as part of wider criminal networks.

Another misconception about trafficking is that it only exists within so-called illegitimate industries or quasi-legal spaces. People are trafficked into all types of industries. Forced labor can happen in an individual's private homes, small local stores, farms, tourist locations, Fortune 500 companies, and more. Understanding that people's labor can be exploited in any environment is important to help prevent, identify, and stop this type of abuse from continuing.

Anti-trafficking Efforts

In this chapter, we have talked at length about various systems of slavery, but little attention has been paid to the work of advocates who actively work against institutionalized enslavement. Counter-trafficking efforts are taking place at international, regional, national, and local levels. These efforts take the form of legislation, conventions, humanitarian organizations, and grassroots activism.

United Nations declarations, conventions, and treaties

Founded in 1945 the United Nations (UN) is a non-governmental organization (NGO) made up of representatives from countries all over the world. Broadly, the UN charter outlines the international body's areas of focus as maintaining international peace and security, protecting human rights, delivering humanitarian aid to areas of need, supporting sustainable economic development, and upholding international law. These charges are directly related to a core document of the UN: the Universal Declaration of Human Rights (UDHR).

Initially developed in 1948, the UDHR is a set of provisions that UN members consider to be fundamental human rights that should be universally protected. The document specifically illustrates the UN's opposition to slavery within article four of the UDHR:

> No one shall be held in slavery or servitude; slavery and the slave trade shall be prohibited in all their forms (United Nations 1948).

Over time, additional provisions and conventions ratified by the members of the UN have further codified acts of human trafficking as violations of international law. Specifically, in December 2000 the UN affirmed the Protocol to Prevent, Suppress and Punish Trafficking in Persons, especially Women and Children (UN TIP Protocol). This supplement to the UN Convention against Transnational Organized Crime functions as a legal framework for member states to ratify at a national level. The TIP Protocol is seen as a foundational piece of international law that effectively created standards for what acts should fall under the crime of trafficking. Critically, this protocol also outlines the severity of punishment that traffickers should receive for these acts.

International protections for child victims of human trafficking can be found in the UN's Convention on the Rights of the Child, with the Optional Protocol on the Sale of Children, Child Prostitution, and Child Pornography (OPSC). The OPSC outlines calls for nations to adopt effective legislation to prosecute child traffickers and encourages international collaboration in combating this issue. Furthermore, the OPSC reinforces the rights of children who have been victimized by sexual and labor exploitation. It outlines the safeguards nations can put in place for survivors during the criminal justice process and rehabilitation and reintegration services.

National initiatives

While human trafficking is a global crime and an international, united response is imperative, it is important that countries adopt their own laws and statutes to combat sexual and labor exploitation based on their unique challenges. Domestic laws strengthen the international statutes through enforceable laws and the expansion of services to survivors. Let's explore key pieces of anti-trafficking legislation in the United States, Japan, United Kingdom, and Sudan. Each of these countries are included among the 180 signatories to the UN TIP Protocol.

United States of America

Within the United States, the Victims of Trafficking and Violence Protection Act of 2000 (TVPA) (Pub. L. 106-386, 114 Stat. 1464) aims to combat sexual and labor exploitation as well as provide resources and support to victims. The issue of human trafficking began to gain wider attention within the United States in the 1990s. However, at that time the United States did not have strong tools to combat trafficking domestically or abroad. Finding a solution to address human trafficking was a priority for both the Clinton administration and the 106th Congress (Miko 2004). It was through this work that the TVPA was developed.

The TVPA operates on a three P's framework: prevention, protection, and prosecution. The prevention arm focuses on strategic interventions to deter trafficking, such as economic alternatives and public awareness campaigns. The TVPA discusses the uses of microcredit lending programs, job and skill training, programs targeted toward increasing women's economic participation and decision making, and programs designed to educate on the harms of trafficking. It also suggests the use of grants issued to non-governmental organizations that can be used to advance women's educational, social, political, and economic capital within their home nations (Victims of Trafficking and Violence Protection Act of 2000).

The protection piece of the TVPA focuses on the identification of trafficking victims, both US nationals and victims in other countries. This section also aims to expand victim protection services, such as legal aid, and safeguards from further violence as well as immigration status. Finally, the TVPA aims to create pathways for strengthening prosecution and punishment of traffickers. This is not only accomplished through a review of the US criminal code but also through a push for international partnerships to assist with anti-trafficking efforts globally (Victims of Trafficking and Violence Protection Act of 2000).

Apart from the prevention, protection, and prosecution framework, the act included both oversight and specific immigration pieces to assist with the enforcement of its protocols. The Interagency Task Force to Monitor and Combat Trafficking, a cabinet-level group of federal agencies, was also created as a result of the TVPA. They are responsible for responding to issues of human trafficking in alignment with the policies outlined in the TVPA. Furthermore, the act created the T-nonimmigrant status visa, a temporary visa that allows trafficked persons to remain and work within the United States. Since its initial adoption into federal law in 2000, the TVPA has been amended and reauthorized six times to better address the ever-changing climate of human trafficking within the United States.

United Kingdom
On March 26, 2015 the United Kingdom passed into law the Modern Slavery Act 2015 (c. 30). This landmark anti-slavery and anti-trafficking law, similar to the TVPA, aims to increase awareness, aid in preventing, and increase prosecutions of modern slavery and exploitation. The Modern Slavery Act places particular emphasis on the role that businesses play in trafficking and emphasizes the risk of exploitation within the global supply chain. Additionally, the act created the Independent Anti-slavery Commissioner, an appointed position responsible for overseeing matters related to slavery and trafficking within the United Kingdom. Since the United Kingdom comprises England, Wales, Scotland, and Northern Ireland, the act is written to accommodate the

unique situations of each individual country. For example, the section on maritime enforcement covers variations of enforcement power in relation to ships within each part of the United Kingdom.

The Modern Slavery Act is an important step in combating slavery in the United Kingdom; however, the act has been criticized for its lack of emphasis on victim's rights and enforcement. The Modern Slavery Act does not have a provision for general civil remedies for victims. However, it does allow courts to issue reparations during convictions or confiscation orders. Furthermore, rooting out misconduct within the supply chain relies on self-reporting and audits (Mantouvalou 2018). This system places power in the hands of the commercial entities that may be partaking in the abuse.

Japan

Unlike the United States and the United Kingdom, Japan does not have a comprehensive domestic law that addresses human slavery. Instead, they rely on their existing domestic welfare, immigration, and labor laws to cover the prosecution of these crimes. Forced labor, including sexual labor, is criminalized under both the Employment Security Act and the Labor Standards Act. Japan is both a destination and transit country for labor and sexual human trafficking. People from other regions of the world travel to Japan with the promise of employment or marriage. These migrants are vulnerable to forced labor or sex trafficking. For example, Japan's exploitative work-study contracts place international students at a higher risk for trafficking (United States Department of State 2022).

Crimes against children do receive some additional protections under Japanese laws. In 1999, Japan enacted the Act on Regulation and Punishment of Activities Relating to Child Prostitution and Pornography and the Protection of Children. While not specific to victims of trafficking, the act does prohibit and prescribe penalties to those that engage in the commercial sexual exploitation of minors (Japan 1999).

Japan also has a National Action Plan to address human trafficking, initially adopted in 2004 and most recently updated in 2022. The plan outlines a strategy for the prevention of trafficking, eradication of trafficking, and protection of victims. It also highlights the need for international cooperation between the Japanese government, NGOs, and other origin–destination countries (Ministry of Foreign Affairs Japan 2004). The overarching aims of the action plan are reflective of the three P's framework.

Sudan

In Sudan, human trafficking has historically been prevalent in militias, agriculture, mining, and sex work. Instability within the country has often made it difficult to dedicate adequate resources to anti-trafficking measures. However, Sudan has taken recent steps to prevent domestic trafficking and the movement of trafficked victims through the country. For example, the 2007 Sudan Armed Forces Act imposes criminal penalties on anyone recruiting children into military roles, forcing citizens into sexual or labor-based slavery, or coercing civilians into prostitution (United States Department of State 2023). The government has also collaborated with international organizations to bring an end to trafficking rings within the country.

Yet, the legal framework and lack of resources dedicated to anti-trafficking efforts within Sudan can make it challenging to obtain a clear picture of their effectiveness. While anti-trafficking laws exist, the government of Sudan did not report providing any anti-trafficking training to judges, prosecutors, or law enforcement officers between 2021 and 2023. The government also reported identifying significantly fewer trafficking victims during 2021–2023 than in the period prior to 2021 (United States Department of State 2023). However, there was an increase in awareness workshops and programs organized by the government across the country aimed at bringing awareness to trafficking. Many of these interventions occurred in primary and secondary schools, which could help mitigate the recruitment of child soldiers and the likelihood of adolescents becoming victims of trafficking. While anti-trafficking governmental organizations are meeting regularly within Sudan, they frequently report not having the necessary resources to investigate and prevent human trafficking.

While each of these countries has made efforts to reduce human trafficking, the process of developing legal frameworks and putting them into practice can be challenging. Through these examples, we can see that the struggle against human trafficking is often an *iterative* process. While initial policies may lead to some success, governments often re-evaluate and modify frameworks in response to changes in trafficking. However, being aware of the evolutions in human trafficking within a country and having enough political capital to change and revise longstanding policy can be a daunting task. Although none of these strategies have completely eliminated trafficking within their respective nations, the goals of bringing attention to trafficking and increasing penalties for those who choose to enslave others can help mitigate the negative consequences of enslavement and coercion.

Consequences of Enslavement

Enslavement is an insidious crime that has impacts on a victim's physiological and physical health, the communities in which they live and are trafficked within, and long-lasting intergenerational impacts on survivors and their families. Slavery and trafficking create conditions of abuse and exploitation that place people's physical health at risk. Victims of trafficking may endure not only physical violence but also be subject to dangerous living conditions and occupational hazards.

Trafficking can also take a toll on one's mental wellbeing, creating issues of post-traumatic stress, depression, and anxiety. Social stigmas against trafficked persons and the types of work that they may be trafficked into, sex work in particular, may lead survivors to fear coming forward. This fear of coming forward can prevent traffickers from being brought to justice; however, forcing survivors to document their trauma in an identifiable, publicly accessible forum can lead to their revictimization.

While prosecution and protection efforts have improved in the last 60 years, focus and attention should be placed on the mental health care afforded to trafficking survivors.

Enslavement also has devastating impacts within communities. Policies and procedures rooted within a society that support the prioritization of one or more racial groups over others can create the conditions in which marginalized victims are overlooked and modern slavery exists. These practices place marginalized communities at risk for trafficking and can make it more difficult for them to receive protection from the legal system if they become victims of trafficking. For example, the United States' predatory and exclusionary lending practices keep minority communities from building generational wealth. Practices like redlining, unequal access to government services, and exclusion from entering white-collar jobs based on race can be difficult to overcome (United States Department of State 2021). Denying these communities access to wealth can make them more susceptible to traffickers that promise access to labor, housing, or financial stability in exchange for their human capital.

At its most severe, the trafficking of a people out of a region can lead to a decimation of their cultural practices. For example, in the late nineteenth and early twentieth century the children of Native Americans in the United States and Canada were systematically removed from their homes and placed within industrialized boarding schools to anglicize reservations. Within these buildings the cultural practices of tribes were intentionally stripped away and replaced with mandatory English lessons and Christianity. Native children who did not adhere to lessons were severely punished physically, leading to death in some cases. The children that survived these harsh conditions returned to their families unable to speak their native languages and fearful to participate in cultural traditions. The memory of these events within the collective tribal culture can lead to intergenerational trauma. While some traditions and customs have been preserved, others have likely been lost forever (Sebwenna-Painter, Beckstein, and Kraus 2023).

Chapter Summary

In this chapter we have explored global perspectives on enslavement, identified the long-lasting impacts that slavery can have, and examined the influence of modern slavery on migration. Throughout history forced migration has removed people from their native lands, eviscerated historical traditions, and separated families and communities. Slavery is not unique to one region of the world or one point in time. It takes place in every nation and is still happening today. Just as they were centuries ago, humans continue to be trafficked domestically and internationally for the purposes of labor and sexual exploitation.

There are active efforts being made in the fight against human trafficking. Through international conventions (such as the UN TIP Protocol) and nation-specific laws aimed at prevention, protecting victims, and punishing those that engage in trafficking, countries are developing a better understanding of the unique impacts of modern slavery on their communities. However, additional legal protections are often needed as trafficking continues to evolve. Apart from legislation, active efforts are being made to educate the public about the risks and misconceptions of human trafficking. Dispelling harmful stigmas can help survivors and provide pathways for reintegration.

Review Questions

1. Enslavement is not new, nor is its history restricted to one portion of the planet. Why do you think slavery has been such a widespread and persistent feature of human history?
2. What are some examples of international, national, and local counter-trafficking efforts? To what extent are any of these efforts effective? If there is room for improving the effectiveness of these efforts, where would you want to see attention focused in the near term?
3. Antoinette Jackson's "Perspectives" piece about the African-descended Gullah people of South Carolina focuses on their resilience and retention of cultural cohesiveness in the face of forced migration and enslavement. What combination of cultural institutions and legal protections has helped contribute to Gullah resilience?

References

Carney, Judith A. 2001. *The African Origins of Rice Production in the Americas*. Cambridge, MA: Harvard University Press.

Challenging Heights. 2022. *Children hidden in plain sight: A report on the state of child labour in the fishing industry of Ghana*. https://cdn.modernghana.com/files/610202233312-wbrevihuto-challenging-heights-june-2022-report-version-12a.pdf, accessed 13 Feb 2024.

Cooper, Melissa L. 2017. *Making Gullah: A history of Sapelo Islanders, race, and the American imagination*. Chapel Hill: University of North Carolina Press.

Crossley, P. 2011. Slavery in Early Modern China. In D Eltis, and S Engerman, eds. *The Cambridge World History of Slavery*. Cambridge: Cambridge University Press. pp. 186–214. https://doi.org/10.1017/CHOL9780521840682.010.

Davis, David Brion. 2006. *Inhuman Bondage: The rise and fall of slavery in the New World*. New York: Oxford University Press.

Davis, Robert C. 2003. *Christian Slaves, Muslim Masters: White slavery in the Mediterranean, the Barbary Coast, and Italy, 1500–1800*. New York: Palgrave Macmillan.

Davis, Robert C. 2011. *British slaves on the Barbary Coast*. https://www.bbc.co.uk/history/british/empire_seapower/white_slaves_01.shtml

Domingues da Silva, D B. 2017. *The Atlantic Slave Trade from West Central Africa, 1780–1867*. Cambridge: Cambridge University Press. https://doi.org/10.1017/9781316771501.

Eltis, D. 2007. *A Brief Overview of the Trans-Atlantic Slave Trade*. Voyages: The trans-atlantic slave trade database. https://www.slavevoyages.org/voyage/essays#interpretation/overview-trans-atlantic-slave-trade/introduction/0/en/.

Eltis, D, F D Lewis, and D Richardson. 2005. Slave prices, the African slave trade, and productivity in the Caribbean, 1674–1807. *The Economic History Review* 58(4): 673–700. https://doi.org/10.1111/j.1468-0289.2005.00318.x.

Eltis, D, and D Richardson. 2010. *Atlas of the Transatlantic Slave Trade.* Yale University Press. http://www.jstor.org/stable/j.ctt5vm1s4.

Fields, Edda. 2008. *Deep Roots: Rice Farmers in West Africa and the African Diaspora.* Bloomington: Indiana University Press.

Fisher, L D. 2017. "Why shall wee have peace to bee made slaves": Indian surrenderers during and after King Philip's War. *Ethnohistory* 64(1):91–114. https://doi.org/10.1215%2F00141801-3688391.

Government of the Netherlands. 2011. *Comprehensive action plan on the issue of 'loverboys' action plan 2011–2014.* https://rm.coe.int/168063219d05/31/2017

Harris, Jessica B. 2012. *High on the Hog: A culinary journey from Africa to America.* New York: Bloomsbury Publishing.

Hess, Karen. 1991. *The Carolina Rice Kitchen: The African connection.* Columbia, SC: University of South Carolina Press.

Heywood, L M. 2009. Slavery and its transformation in the Kingdom of Kongo: 1491–1800. *The Journal of African History* 50(1): 1–22. http://www.jstor.org/stable/40206695.

International Labour Office. 2014. *Profits and Poverty: The economics of forced poverty.* Geneva: International Labour Organization. https://www.ilo.org/wcmsp5/groups/public/---ed_norm/---declaration/documents/publication/wcms:243391.pdf.

International Labour Organization. 2022. *Global Estimates of Modern Slavery: Forced labour and forced marriage.* Geneva: International Labour Organization. https://www.ilo.org/wcmsp5/groups/public/---ed_norm/---ipec/documents/publication/wcms:854733.pdf.

Jackson, Antoinette T. 2012. *Speaking for the Enslaved: Heritage interpretation in antebellum plantation sites.* New York: Routledge.

Japan. 1999. Act on Punishment of Activities Relating to Child Prostitution and Child Pornography, and the Protection of Children. *Act No. 52 of May 26, 1999.* https://www.japaneselawtranslation.go.jp/en/laws/view/2895/en, accessed 13 Feb 2024.

Kim, Kathleen. 2011. The coercion of trafficked workers. *Iowa Law Review* 96: 409–474. https://papers.ssrn.com/sol3/Delivery.cfm/SSRN_ID2079316_code332621.pdf?abstractid=1710282&mirid=1.

Ling, B. 2021. Chapter 8 The Abolition of Slavery, Constitutional Reforms, and Modernity in late Qing China. In R Allen, ed. *Slavery and Bonded Labor in Asia, 1250–1900.* Leiden, The Netherlands: Brill. https://doi.org/10.1163/9789004469655_010.

Littlefield, Daniel C. 1991. *Rice and Slaves: Ethnicity and the slave trade in colonial South Carolina.* Champaign: University of Illinois Press.

Mantouvalou, Virginia. 2018. The UK Modern Slavery Act 2015 three years on. *The Modern Law Review* 81(6): 1017–1045. https://doi.org/10.1111/1468-2230.12377.

Marsh, E., Anthony, B., Emerson, J., Mogulescu, K. (2019). State report cards: Grading criminal records relief laws for survivors of human trafficking. Polaris Project. Retrieved from: https://polarisproject.org/wp-content/uploads/2019/03/Grading-Criminal-Record-Relief-Laws-for-Survivors-of-Human-Trafficking.pdf

Matar, Nabil. 2001. *Piracy, Slavery, and Redemption: Barbary Captivity Narratives from Early Modern England.* New York: Columbia University Press.

Meredith, Martin. 2014. *The Fortunes of Africa: A 5000-year history of wealth, greed, and endeavor.* New York: Public Affairs.

Michalopoulos, S, and E Papaioannou. 2016. The long-run effects of the scramble for Africa. *American Economic Review* 106(7): 1802–1848. https://doi.org.10.1257/aer.20131311.

Miko, F. 2004. Trafficking in women and children: The U.S. and international response (Report No. RL30545). Washington, DC: Congressional Research Service, The Library of Congress. https://www.everycrsreport.com/files/20040326_RL30545_7e071628f6800fea1d9ea2e05cd773f6e0347745.pdf

Ministry of Foreign Affairs, Japan. 2004. *Japan's actions to combat trafficking in person*. Retrieved from: https://www.mofa.go.jp/policy/i_crime/people/pamphlet.pdf

Mooney, Claire. 2020. Overrepresented yet overlooked: LGBTQ survivors of trafficking and the imperative for the nordic approach to sex trafficking laws in the United States. *Cardozo Journal of Equal Rights and Social Justice* 26(2): 261–282. https://www.cardozoersj.com/_files/ugd/a6e465_361efa0f34264edab09fc085c8773625.pdf.

Mustakeem, Sowandé M. 2016. *Slavery at Sea: Terror, sex, and sickness in the Middle Passage*. Champaign: University of Illinois Press.

Newitt, M. 2004. *A History of Portuguese Overseas Expansion 1400–1668*. New York: Routledge.

Nikky, Finney. 1995. *Rice*. Toronto: Sister Vision.

Nunn, N. 2017. Understanding the long-run effects of Africa's slave trades. In S Michalopoulos, and E Papaioannou, eds. *The long economic and political shadow of history, 2*. CEPR Press. pp. 36–48.

O'Brien, Cheryl. 2009. An analysis of global sex trafficking. *Indiana Journal of Political Science*: 7–19. https://www.semanticscholar.org/paper/An-Analysis-of-Global-Sex-Trafficking-O%27Brien/6ceeca2106ff8fb8a751a34383d98ab4f978dda6.

Owens, D C, and S M Fett. 2019. Black maternal and infant health: Historical legacies of slavery. *American Journal of Public Health* 109: 1342–1345. https://doi.org/10.2105/AJPH.2019.305243.

Polaris Project. 2019. Criminal records relief for trafficking survivors: Nebraska. Polaris Project. Retrieved from: https://polarisproject.org/wp-content/uploads/2019/10/2019-CriminalRecordRelief-Nebraska.pdf

Preble, K M, and B M Black. 2020. Influence of survivors' entrapment factors and traffickers' characteristics on perceptions of interpersonal social power during exit. *Violence Against Women* 26(1): 110–133. https://doi.org/10.1177/1077801219826742.

Reséndez, A. 2021. *Perspective: The other slavery*. Smithsonian Institution. https://americanindian.si.edu/sites/1/files/pdf/seminars-symposia/the-other-slavery-perspective.pdf.

Resnitriwati, C. 2020. The agony of the slaves as described in Frances Ellen Watkins Harper's the slave auction. *Endogami: Jurnal Ilmiah Kajian Antropologi* 4(1): 133–138. https://doi.org/10.14710/endogami.4.1.133-138.

Scheidel, Walter. 2013. Slavery and forced labor in early China and the Roman world. Princeton / Stanford Working Paper in Classics SSRN 2242322. https://papers.ssrn.com/sol3/Delivery.cfm/SSRN_ID2242322_code896702.pdf?abstractid=2242322&mirid=1

Sebwenna-Painter, K, A Beckstein, and S Kraus. 2023. Psychological impacts of historic loss and current events surrounding American Indian boarding schools. *American Indian and Alaska Native Mental Health Research (Online)* 30(2): 1–21. https://coloradosph.cuanschutz.edu/docs/librariesprovider205/journal_files/vol30/30_2_2023_1_sebwenna-painter.pdf.

Shelley, L. 2010. *Human Trafficking: A global perspective*. Cambridge: Cambridge University Press.

Smart-Grosvenor, Vertmae. 1992. *Vibration Cooking or The Travel Notes of a Geechee Girl*. New York: Ballantine Books.

Styer, Cate. 2014. *Atlantic Slaveries: Britons, Barbary, and the Atlantic World*. In D' Maris Coffman, Adrian Leonard, and William O'Reilly, eds. *The Atlantic World*. New York: Routledge. pp. 172–186.

Turner, Lorenzo Dow. 1949. *Africanisms in the Gullah Dialect*. Chicago: University of Chicago Press.

United Nations. 1948. Universal Declaration of Human Rights. https://www.un.org/en/about-us/universal-declaration-of-human-rights

United Nations. 2000. UN General Assembly, Protocol to Prevent, Suppress and Punish Trafficking in Persons, Especially Women and Children, Supplementing the United Nations Convention against Transnational Organized Crime. https://www.ohchr.org/en/instruments-mechanisms/instruments/protocol-prevent-suppress-and-punish-trafficking-persons

United Nations Office on Drugs and Crime. 2022. *Global Report on Tracking in Persons 2022*, (United Nations publication, Sales no.: E. 23. IV. 1). https://www.unodc.org/documents/data-and-analysis/glotip/2022/GLOTiP_2022_web.pdf

United States Department of Homeland Security. 2022. *Countering human trafficking: Year in review (October 2020–September 2021)*. DHS Center for Countering Human Trafficking. https://www.dhs.gov/sites/default/files/2022-02/CCHT%20Annual%20Report.pdf.

United States Department of State. 2021. *Acknowledging Historical and Ongoing Harm: The connections between systemic racism and human trafficking*. https://www.state.gov/acknowledging-historical-and-ongoing-harm-the-connections-between-systemic-racism-and-human-trafficking/

United States Department of State. 2022. *2022 trafficking in persons report*. https://www.state.gov/wp-ontent/uploads/2022/10/20221020-2022-TIP-Report.pdf

United States Department of State. 2023. *2023 trafficking in persons report: Sudan*. https://www.state.gov/reports/2023-trafficking-in-persons-report/sudan/#:~:text=Due%20to%20the%20years%20of,forced%20labor%20and%20sex%20trafficking

Venters, Laurie. 2022. Lightening bonds: Servile resistance in early imperial China. *The Historian* 84(2): 262–289. https://doi.org/10.1080/00182370.2023.2217635.

Victims of Trafficking and Violence Protection Act of 2000. Pub. L. No. 106-386, 114 Stat. 1464. 2000. https://www.govinfo.gov/app/details/PLAW-106publ386.

Vujčić, Nemanja. 2021. A numbers game: The size of the slave population in classical Athens. *Zbornik Matice srpske za klasične studije* 26(23): 87–112. https://reff.f.bg.ac.rs/bitstream/handle/123456789/4360/A_Numbers_Game_The_Size_of_the_Slave_Pop.pdf?sequence=1&isAllowed=y.

Yates, Robin D S. 2002. Slavery in early China: A socio-cultural approach. *Journal of East Asian Archaeology* 3(1–2): 283–331. https://doi.org/10.1163/9789004346611_020.

Section 5

Where Are We Going?

Today, we are at a crossroads. The decisions we make about migration now will affect the futures of millions of people. Will we adapt to the changes that migration brings and find ways to live together? Or will we resist change and allow our differences to divide us? Even considering the tension between structure and agency, by being informed citizens we can make a difference in where we are going, no matter where we are from.

Source: Photo by Nito (Shutterstock).

World on the Move: 250,000 Years of Human Migration, First Edition. Edward Liebow, James I. Deutsch, Daniel Ginsberg, Sojin Kim, and Caitlyn Kolhoff.
© 2025 John Wiley & Sons, Inc. Published 2025 by John Wiley & Sons, Inc.

10
National and International Policy

National and international policies concerning migration and immigration are set by governments and intergovernmental organizations. Although they differ considerably depending on specific circumstances of geography and history, these policies have a common goal to protect the rights of migrants, refugees, asylum seekers, and others on the move while properly anticipating the public benefits as well as burdens placed on public facilities and services that result from the movement of individuals, households, and communities.

Protecting the rights of migrants has not always been the focus of migration policies. As Glick Schiller points out (2021), a complex of "migration regimes" arose with the emergence of nation-states to reinforce the accumulation of wealth by dispossession. Empires built on raiding, warfare, and conquest displaced people and "divided people into differing legal statuses, with varying rights to mobility including slaves, ordinary subjects, nobles, bureaucrats, colonists, soldiers, religious practitioners, and traders" (Glick Schiller 2021, p. 4). It is really only since the mid-twentieth century that the migration goals began to shift toward protecting the rights of migrants.

International Policies

No international institution has the binding authority to enact and enforce global policies concerning transnational migration. However, the United Nations (UN) offers standards with which participating nation-states agree to comply. Foremost among these are the standards embodied in the UN Declaration of Human Rights (and upheld by the UN Commission on Human Rights) and the Sustainable

World on the Move: 250,000 Years of Human Migration, First Edition. Edward Liebow, James I. Deutsch, Daniel Ginsberg, Sojin Kim, and Caitlyn Kolhoff.
© 2025 John Wiley & Sons, Inc. Published 2025 by John Wiley & Sons, Inc.

Development Goals, created by the UN Conference on Sustainable Development in 2012 (and upheld by the UN Development Programme). An additional UN agency, the International Organization for Migration (IOM), provides advice on migration policy, works to develop the resilience of people on the move (especially those in vulnerable positions), and maintains an extensive information clearinghouse that helps member states in their quest to improve migration governance.

Human rights of migrants in UN declaration

As noted, in 1948 the UN issued a Universal Declaration of Human Rights, a precedent-setting document that recognized the inherent dignity and "equal and inalienable rights of all members of the human family" as "the foundation of freedom, justice, and peace in the world." The Declaration goes on to say that these rights should be "protected by the rule of law." It follows logically that if these are universal rights, then they apply to migrants and displaced persons. However, the articles make specific reference to people on the move, with human rights–based migration governance to protect migrants' rights in transit, at international borders, and in the countries to which they move.

Migration and sustainable development agenda

In 2015 the UN completed a lengthy consultative process and issued a set of global goals that together aim to end poverty and hunger around the world, ensuring that people everywhere have an equal opportunity to fulfill their individual potential in a healthy environment (United Nations Department of Economic and Social Affairs 2015). This set of goals is known as the *2030 Agenda for Sustainable Development Goals*, and migration governance is seen as essential to the achievement of all 17 goals. As acknowledged by the IOM, "migration is a global phenomenon affecting all countries worldwide, and its effective governance needs global partnerships and both a 'whole of government' and a 'whole of society' approach if we want to make the most of its benefits." The goals are summarized in Figure 10.1, along with ways in which the IOM relates migration to each.

The UN International Organization for Migration and regional agreements

Along with the *2030 Agenda for Sustainable Development Goals*, the UN has been working to craft a worldwide agreement on migration. In 2018 a Global Compact for Migration (United Nations International Organization for Migration 2018) was completed, but mobilizing any implementation of the principles embodied in this global compact has been challenging. Although non-binding, this compact is designed to support international cooperation and offer a comprehensive menu of policy options for individual countries to employ in tackling international migration issues. The IOM offers useful resources to help with the health and safety of people on the move

NATIONAL AND INTERNATIONAL POLICY

Figure 10.1 Migration and the 2030 sustainable development agenda. Source: United Nations International Organization for Migration 2020. https://publications.iom.int/books/iom-institutional-strategy-migration-and-sustainable-development, accessed 20 Dec 2023.

(particularly in a post-COVID-19 world) and with building government capacity by strengthening passport and visa systems, immigration systems, border management systems, migration intelligence systems, management of operational data, and administrative workforce development.

More promising is the recognition of regional and bilateral agreements that spell out processes and mechanisms for smaller groups of countries to cooperate on protecting the rights of migrants while properly anticipating how migration changes places of origin, destination, and places in between. Regional cooperation frameworks are important because of the magnitude and direction of movement and the forces that are driving such movement. In the Americas, for example, the countries that extend from Venezuela to the United States form a major corridor for migrant movement. People from Venezuela and Central American countries like Guatemala, Costa Rica, Honduras, and El Salvador are generally aiming to reach the United States, eventually. And there are also large numbers of people who come from war and conflict zones outside the region who pass through Central America and Mexico on their way to the United States–Mexico border region. As it has become more difficult to enter the United States, more people are settling in Mexico. A regional policy framework that includes all of these countries can protect the rights and safety of migrants and asylum seekers, while also investing in development and the communities through which people are routed while on the move.

In South Asian countries and the oil-rich countries of the Persian Gulf, more than 10 million temporary contractual workers from Bangladesh, India, Pakistan, Sri Lanka, and Nepal have been actively recruited to work overseas in construction, small factories, domestic services, and agriculture. Most migrant workers from this region work in countries belonging to the Gulf Cooperation Council (GCC; Bahrain, Kuwait, Oman, Qatar, Saudi Arabia, and the United Arab Emirates) or in Malaysia. As Aarthi and Sahu note, "the GCC states share a standard regulatory institutional mechanism to manage transnational labor migration" (2021, p. 411). This mechanism is based on a sponsorship (*kafala*) system that places the financial and legal responsibility with the sponsor and, in effect, creates a dependency on the sponsor that leaves workers "vulnerable to exploitation, low wages, delay in payment and nonpayment of wages. . . .. Migrant workers are only required to work for their sponsor and cannot switch employers without the written permission of the sponsor" (Aarthi and Sahu 2021, p. 418). This arrangement restricts the immigrants' integration into Gulf State society and makes it all but impossible for these migrant workers to become citizens. With pressure from non-governmental organizations like Human Rights Watch and the International Labour Organization, reforms have been implemented since 2010 that offer some greater protections from sponsor exploitation.

To easily move across international borders within a region requires that individual countries' laws and regulations are well aligned with one another and with regional agreements. This requires compromise and giving up a certain amount of national government authority in deference to regional accommodation. Where such accommodation is observed, it will likely look like the European Union, where freedom of movement and the ability to work, attend school, or receive social service benefits are open to all who live within any of the cooperating countries. One can also see a similar arrangement in the six countries of the East African Community[1] and the 15 member states of the Economic Community of West African States[2].

These processes and mechanisms for regional cooperation are often not spelled out in a stand-alone agreement on migration. Instead, they are included as migration-related provisions in preferential trade agreements. Such agreements, like those among European Union nations or the North American Free Trade Agreement, may facilitate the international mobility of service providers and workers, protect the rights of migrants, and place controls on unauthorized trans-border migration (Lavenex, Lutz, and Hoffmeyer-Zlotnik 2023). A comprehensive data source has been developed in recent years that captures migration-related content of these trade agreements: the Migration Provisions in Preferential Trade Agreements (MITA) dataset (2023). As Lavenex and her colleagues point out, the use of trade agreements to shape migration is selective and tends to involve arrangements between high-income countries and large emerging economies with a focus on highly skilled migrants linked to investment and multinational corporations – the types of migrants that are of interest in high-income countries and therefore less politically controversial.

The migration-related provisions in trade agreements focus only occasionally on migrant rights. Where they exist, which is almost exclusively in agreements that involve at least one of the 38 Organisation for Economic Cooperation and Development (OECD) countries[3], they emphasize non-discrimination and the portability of social security benefits to a greater extent than offering commitments to protect refugees.

The role of border walls in international migration and immigration policy

In 2022 the American Anthropological Association released a report that was commissioned to document the history and global proliferation of border and security walls as well as the impacts of these walls (American Anthropological Association 2021). Such impacts include the displacement of native peoples; increasing militarization that forces migrants, refugees, and asylum seekers to take more dangerous routes; the division of communities and families; an increase in violence and death; and the adverse effects of wall construction on archaeological and cultural heritage sites.

The Association report observed that fortified, lengthy walls have been built for thousands of years, but it is only relatively recently that their specific purpose was to create a physical barrier to crossing a national border. The earliest walls in history were originally built not for military purposes or as marking political borders but to help

---

[1] For member states of the East African Community, see https://www.eac.int/.
[2] For member states of the Economic Community of West African States, see https://www.ecowas.int/.
[3] For a list of OECD Members and Partners, see https://www.oecd.org/en/about/members-partners.html.

control the movement of animals, to aid hunting, and to protect agricultural fields by holding back herds of small animals.

Walls were eventually built and maintained to serve many purposes – to mark boundaries, prevent attacks, safeguard sovereignty, control infectious diseases, stabilize economies, and shore up political alliances. In recent years the idea has been reinforced that walls are erected in dangerous places and invested with symbolic meaning, claiming that they serve national security interests by controlling the free movement of people.

Border walls have become a prominent focus in the world today. At the time of the fall of the Berlin Wall in 1989, there were only about 15 border or security walls in place or under construction globally. In contrast, by 2022 there were more than 70 walls, with additional ones proposed. The longest physical border wall, still under construction in 2024, lies between India and Bangladesh (3,268 km or 2,031 miles) (World Population Review 2024b).

Although migration has been a fundamental element of the human condition throughout history, walls are built mainly as barriers to control the mobility of people and commerce. Virtual walls (advanced technological surveillance systems) add another barrier layer. However, with very few military exceptions, no wall achieves complete closure. Despite the physical danger and material barriers, people have always found a way under, over, and through the walls. Decades of anthropological and archaeological research clearly demonstrate that walls do not work at preventing movement, but they do succeed at deepening discrimination and intensifying social and cultural divisions.

Walls are symbols. They stand for an enclosed inside that is separated from and protected against an uncontrolled or threatening outside. Walls are usually proposed in times of manufactured crisis, which easily slips into racism. Once established, walls enhance perceived racial divisions by segregating individuals, communities, and regions.

Walls perpetuate inequalities, where the privileged and essential workers pass. Those who are not allowed and cannot pass face the payment of large sums to human smugglers and often the physical risk of death and injury in dangerous routes around walls.

Walls have devastating consequences for environmental and cultural resources. They disrupt the movement of animals, destroy habitat through construction activities, and wipe out plants and wildlife by rechanneling or blocking the flow of surface water. Walls destroy some sacred sites and landscapes and obstruct access to others.

Walls have adverse impacts on human rights. They prevent people from gaining a livelihood, fleeing from religious persecution and war, and they place people at risk of injury and death when they encounter barriers and intensive enforcement zones. When people wait in camps and towns for a chance to move lawfully through checkpoints, they find themselves in the midst of danger and extreme exploitation.

Based on these well-documented harms, the Association called on the global community to seriously consider the likely adverse consequences associated with the formation of border walls, call into question the stated purpose of walls, and appeal for further research on those who shoulder the baleful burdens created in the name of benefits that walls purportedly confer.

PERSPECTIVE: Border Walls and Security Policy, by Miguel Díaz-Barriga and Margaret Dorsey

Professors of anthropology, University of Richmond (USA)

The fall of the Berlin Wall in November 1989 and the subsequent reunification of Germany were met with a mixture of anxiety and hope. For many this was a moment to celebrate, since we could now build a bright future based on the promises of globalization and a world without walls. The Cold War had ended. New communication and technological advances signaled increased global economic integration and cooperation. Free trade agreements blossomed. Europe began a process of economic and political integration as well as opening borders between countries. Pundits and politicians planned on redirecting funding from Cold War militarization to economic development and social welfare projects. This peace dividend would create a more equitable world. Within anthropology, scholars explored how social movements – now free from the shackles of Cold War conflict – could emerge as creative sources for new forms of politics and citizenship. Anthropologists examined how activist groups in countries emerging from Cold War–based civil wars (such as in Nicaragua, El Salvador, and Guatemala) proposed novel plans for economic development and social justice.

Amidst these struggles for social change, the inequalities hardened due to a constellation of economic policy changes that we call "neoliberalism" – eliminating price controls, deregulating capital markets, lowering trade barriers, and other means of reducing state influence on the economy. In addition, peace dividends did not materialize and authoritarian rule gained a new license. In much of the world the promises of globalization and neoliberal economic growth never materialized and political repression reigned. In some countries, the drug trade has become a dominant economic force and a source of violence and terror for the population. Free trade agreements upended rural life in countries like Mexico where the 1994 North American Free Trade Agreement led to the unemployment of at least six million small-scale farmers. Dispossessed people – in the face of these inequalities, repression, and violence – sought a better life by migrating. Anthropologists understand that migration is another example of a social movement. Anthropologists, as this volume shows, have actively theorized and documented the causes and consequences of migration while advocating for migrant rights. Anthropologists have accompanied migrants on their journeys, served as expert witnesses on asylum cases, and helped migrants escape from detention centers.

The current appetite for border walls is a symptom of the global misery caused by poverty and political repression. In 1989 only 15 countries were divided by border walls and most of these walls were built because of international boundary disputes, not for keeping out migrants. These older walls included buffer zones between North and South Korea, Morocco and Western Sahara (now annexed by Morocco), the United Kingdom and Spain in Gibraltar, and Greece and Turkey in Cyprus. After 1989, nation-states began to build walls not to defend against foreign armies but to limit the mobility of so-called non-state actors – undocumented migrants, smugglers, and terrorists. By 2024 over 70 walls separate countries. Examples of contemporary border walls include not only the increasingly tense border between the United States and Mexico (1,193 km or 741 miles) but also Spain and Morocco (23 km or 14 miles), and Israel and the West Bank (690 km or 429 miles). Fifty of these walls were constructed following September 11, 2001, including Botswana with Mozambique (690 km or 300 miles), Bulgaria with Turkey (130 km or 81 miles), and China and North Korea (1,414 km or 879 miles). Greece has built a wall on its border with Turkey (201 km or 125 miles), and Turkey has built a wall on its border with Syria (829 km or 515 miles) to stop migrants fleeing the Syrian civil war. The Iron Curtain has become the wired curtain with Finland (200 km or 124 miles), Norway (200 m or 650 feet), Poland (190 km or 118 miles), Estonia (137 km or 85 miles), Lithuania (547 km or 340 miles), and Latvia (130 km or 81 miles, with 167 km or 104 more miles planned) building walls on their borders with Belarus and Russia[4]. Ukraine is now planning on building a fence along its border with Belarus.

The wired curtain not only refracts political tensions between states but is also a reaction to the weaponization of migrants. In retaliation to European Union sanctions, Belarus has allowed thousands of Middle Eastern migrants to amass at its borders with Poland, while Russia has pushed migrants to its northern borders with Finland and Norway. Belarusian troops have mistreated amassed migrants, even beating them, and the UN has characterized migrants' living conditions in Belarus as "intolerable" (Traugott 2021). European government officials have charged Belarus and Russia with state-sponsored human trafficking. Dispossessed migrants are now political pawns.

All indications are that the tragedy of border wall construction will continue unabated well into the future. At least 10 more countries are in the process of building or planning to build walls, including on the Belize–Guatemala, Costa Rica–Nicaragua, Dominican Republic–Haiti, and Chile–Bolivia borders. Countries that once fought civil wars over social justice are now the targets of walls or building their own walls. Many countries, such as Greece and the United States, are expanding and fortifying their walls. Excluding island nations, over half of the world's countries have border walls. At this rate, almost the entire world will be walled in the next 20 years.

Border walls have promoted human suffering by intensifying socioeconomic inequality, restricting access to resources, and fostering a cycle of division,

---

[4] For a complete list of border walls see, World Population Review 2024. Countries with Border Walls. https://worldpopulationreview.com/country-rankings/countries-with-border-walls, accessed 11 Mar 2024.

mistrust, violence, and fatalities. Border walls have become sites where state violence is normalized. Heavily armed security agents from a number of countries – including Hungary, India, Israel, Spain, and the United States – patrol border fortifications employing deadly force. Security forces have detained, beaten, and shot migrants as well as protestors who approach walls. Border security forces, for instance, at the Indo-Bangladeshi boundary have practiced a shoot-on-sight policy, killing over 1,000 migrants from 2000 to 2015 (Jones 2016, p. 61). Macedonian paramilitary forces have violently turned back migrants gathered at its border fence. The Israeli Defense Forces regularly employ tear gas and deadly force to disperse Palestinians protesting the Israel–West Bank wall. Agents from Spain's Guardia Civil regularly beat and severely injure migrants as they attempt to scale the border fence that surrounds the Spanish exclaves of Ceuta and Melilla in Morocco. Moroccan security forces have destroyed migrant camps outside of Ceuta and Melilla, beaten migrants, and deported migrants to the Algerian border, leaving them in the desert. In the United States, the US Border Patrol has killed over one hundred people in the last decade, including the shooting of six people in Mexico. An ex-internal affairs chief of the US Customs and Border Patrol has described how Border Patrol agents have and continue to commit acts of violence with complete impunity (Flores and Drake 2020).

By violently defending their borders, nation-states have also transformed seas and deserts into death zones. Border walls and fortifications have funneled migrants seeking a better life into treacherous landscapes. In the United States, over 800 migrants died – mainly from dehydration and exposure – while trying to cross into the United States in 2021 (Garsd 2023). Since 1998, over 8,000 migrants have died while trying to enter the United States (Barros 2023). In the Mediterranean – in the face of increased border security and walls – over 8,000 migrants have drowned over the last three years (2021–2024) (United Nations International Organization for Migration 2024). Since 2014, over 29,000 migrants attempting to cross into Europe have died or vanished in the Mediterranean (United Nations International Organization for Migration 2024). Boats in distress, as evidenced by the number of shipwrecks, disappear without any survivors. Hundreds of human bones have been found on the shores of Libya, a point of departure for migrants crossing the Mediterranean (United Nations International Organization for Migration 2024).

To make matters worse, countries have enacted laws and practices that either outlaw or hinder attempts to aid migrants. In the United States, the US Border Patrol regularly pours water out of plastic jugs left for migrants while arresting people suspected of aiding migrants. Countries in Europe have interfered with the work of humanitarian organizations attempting to save migrants in distress at sea. A 2021 report by the UN, *Lethal Disregard: Search and Rescue and the Protection of Migrants in the Central Mediterranean Sea*, charges European countries with failing to assist migrants in distress while targeting humanitarian organizations (United Nations Office of the High Commissioner for Human Rights 2021). Amidst this suffering, European countries are now considering building water walls. Greece is considering the construction of a wall in the Aegean Sea made of pylons and nets that will stop migrants sailing from Turkey (Digidiki and Bhabha 2020).

Walls are a global surrender. Walls do not resolve the issues of violence, poverty, and social injustice that fuel migration and political conflict. Walls exacerbate the inequalities that produce migration and heighten political tensions. Walls refract efforts at international cooperation into policies based on militarization, surveillance, detention, and death. Walls absolve countries from their responsibilities to work with their neighbors to resolve social, economic, and political issues. As US Congressman Raul Grijalva notes about the US–Mexico border: "This wall is an admission of defeat by this Administration and the Congress in the face of an important public policy challenge." The IOM notes: "Leaders need to step up and offer a new narrative that puts the fundamental rights, needs and vulnerabilities of everyone on the move at the center of migration policy instead of the overarching focus on reducing the number of arrivals" (Ambrosi 2017). Migration scholars agree.

In our own work we have documented the devastating impacts of border walls not only on migrants but also US border residents who are enmeshed in the wider politics of walls, militarization, and surveillance. Our research highlights how border walls not only aim at keeping people out but also imprison the people they are meant to protect (Díaz-Barriga and Dorsey 2020). The rights of both citizens and non-citizens are under attack under the logic of nativism and militarization. We are among a growing group of anthropologists focused on the horrors of walls. In 2017 we introduced a resolution at the American Anthropological Association (AAA) to condemn border wall construction[5]. This resolution led to the formation of an AAA task force that, through a consideration of border walls globally, critically assessed how border walls are implicated in death and violence and called for the AAA to act through its lobbying and public-facing efforts (American Anthropological Association 2021).

As we face the proliferation of border walls, scholarship is also reshaping itself as we seek to –as in Alisse Waterston's powerful words – find light in dark times (2020). We have opened the doors of migration researchers to contemplating future(s) and utopian possibilities. One of these futures is (re)exploring the possibilities of and advocating for a world without walls – a world in which violence is not normalized and people, including dispossessed migrants, are treated with dignity. As committed scholars we will not surrender.

---

[5] A copy of the resolution can be found at https://www.academia.edu/35336343/2017_Resolution_Against_Global_Proliferation_of_Border_Walls.

National Immigration and Migration Policies

The first sections of this chapter have focused on policies and strategies that shape international migration, that is, movement across national borders. But movement *within* national borders is also shaped by public policy. In the United States, for example, public investment in urban industrial development, combined with the persistence of Jim Crow laws in the American South, led to the Great Migration when about six million Black people moved from the rural South to cities in northern, midwestern, and western states over the period 1910–1970. In an equally large movement of people within the US borders, mid-twentieth century public investments in a national interstate highway system have resulted in the relocation of households in urban areas and enabled urban sprawl.

In the Peoples' Republic of China, twentieth century rural-to-urban migration has been observed on an unprecedented scale. Beginning in 1978, the Reform and Opening-up national policy led to market-oriented reforms, the de-collectivization of agriculture, and relaxing restrictions on internal mobility. In turn, hundreds of millions of rural workers moved to cities to pursue employment opportunities. The market reforms led to rapid economic growth, with the conversion of agricultural land to urban settlements and extended investment in transportation infrastructure. Between 1950 and 2023, the percentage of China's population living in urban areas increased from about 11% to almost 65%, and as of 2023, China had 65 cities with more than a million people (World Population Review 2023).

PERSPECTIVE: Principles for Equitable and Effective Migration Policy Reform

In February 2018 the American Anthropological Association (AAA) put forward a series of principles for national migration policy reform that scholarship shows would achieve equitable and effective outcomes.

Many anthropologists spend their professional lives studying migration, displacement, immigration, border communities, guest workers, security and refugee issues. Based on their scholarly expertise and the lived experience of both anthropologists and the communities with whom they live and work, the AAA offers these principles for equitable and effective immigration policy reform in the US.

US national policies should provide:

- A path to citizenship for all who are living here, contributing to society, and wishing to become citizens. This includes Dreamers and those enrolled in the US government's Deferred Action for Childhood Arrivals (DACA) or Deferred Action for Parental Accountability (DAPA), but may also include their parents, minors, undocumented members of mixed households, students, and others.

- Adequate and consistent protections for the integrity of families and family groups throughout the immigration process.
- Equitable opportunities for all, regardless of religion or country of origin, who wish to seek US residency and citizenship.
- Consistent and rigorous measures to prevent discrimination against LGBTQ persons seeking US residency and citizenship as well as discrimination against women seeking equal opportunities and rights to work.
- An effective system for dealing with refugee and asylum requests, for the humane treatment of refugees and asylum seekers while awaiting a hearing, and consistent assurance of due process throughout the hearing process for detention and deportation.
- Clear and consistently enforced protections for guest workers, unaccompanied minors, and other vulnerable populations subject to exploitation or abuse.
- Sensitivity to the human costs of displacement, the division of families, and deportation to locations where individuals lack family or other support networks.
- Thoughtful and thorough measures to protect the privacy of all individuals and prevent improper use of information recorded as part of the customs, immigration, and naturalization process.
- An effective, equitable, and consistent border enforcement program, with appropriate oversight and accountability for enforcement actions and the humane treatment of immigrants at our borders.
- Clear and consistently enforced standards that prevent state and local authorities from undertaking illegal enforcement practices, including racial profiling.
- Attention to and respect for the interests, values, and concerns of border communities.

Policies at the national level concerning immigration and migration generally stand on their own, rather than being embedded in trade agreements or other policy mechanisms. **They usually serve several purposes, including:**

- Countering population decline.
- Addressing population aging.
- Meeting labor demands.
- Safeguarding employment opportunities for nationals.
- Promoting integration of immigrants.
- Policies to permit remittances or encourage investment by diaspora.
- Asylum and sanctuary from violence and conflict.
- Temporary protected status.

Since the beginning of the twentieth century, it has been quite common to see national immigration control enshrined in law and regulation. The general purpose has been to define some groups of international migrants as undesirable, either because they are seen as threatening the economic livelihoods of existing residents or they threaten to destabilize the existing balance of political power. In both cases, exclusionary laws make it possible to deny lawful entry to members of such groups. In the United Kingdom, for example, the 1905 Aliens Act (5 Edw. 7. c. 13) made it legal to deny entry to people who appeared to lack financial self-sufficiency, had health problems (and therefore would be needing public assistance), or who had a criminal record (Bashford and Gilchrist 2012). This law grew out of political pressure in response to Britons objecting to the large number of Polish and Russian Jews that began arriving in England in the 1890s to avoid persecution by the Russian empire (Wray 2006). The main concern prompting this exclusionary law appears to have been a perceived threat to the livelihoods of existing residents.

Similarly, Honig (2016) documents the parallel cases of two West African countries, Ghana and Côte d'Ivoire, in the post-colonial period from the late 1960s to the 1990s. Both countries had prosperous coffee and cocoa production industries, and both had sizable immigrant populations from neighboring West African countries like Burkina Faso, Mali, Guinea, Togo, and Nigeria. Ghana issued an expulsion order in 1969 that targeted immigrant traders, most of whom were from Nigeria, Burkina Faso, or Togo. Importantly, the Ghanaian government focused on non-citizens in the commercial sector and did *not* seek to exclude agricultural workers, who made up the majority of non-citizens at the time. By contrast, tensions built up in Côte d'Ivoire until the national parliament passed land reform legislation in the 1990s that said only Ivorian citizens could own land. This went against existing land-use agreements between Ivoirians and foreigners and led to violence against migrants, especially in the coffee and cocoa producing regions. Primarily affected were immigrants from Burkina Faso, Mali, and Guinea. Honig's careful analysis concludes that "it is not the social but the economic position of immigrants that drives the choice of exclusionary policy" (2016, p. 532).

In the United States, the earliest history of international immigration involved the coercive trafficking of enslaved people from Africa and the Caribbean until the early decades of the nineteenth century, followed by a surge of people fleeing Europe from religious and political persecution, crop failures, and pursuing the economic opportunities presented by increased industrial manufacturing and the conquest of Indigenous lands east of the Mississippi River. An 1848 discovery of gold in California led to a large number of immigrants arriving from China. As Marinari observes:

> during the second half of the nineteenth century, immigration to the United States shifted away from northern and western Europe to southern and eastern Europe, Asia, and Mexico. These immigrants belonged to a movement of millions of migrants around the globe who left their countries to escape stagnant economies, political unrest, persecution, and the pressures of population growth, and to take advantage of the demand for unskilled labor in rapidly industrializing nations such as the United States (Marinari 2022, p. 271).

Up until 1875, nearly all immigrants were admitted to the United States upon arrival. The Immigration Act of 1875 (Section 141, 18 Stat. 477) in effect excluded Asian women, who were characterized as coming to the US for "lewd and immoral purposes." In 1882 the Chinese Exclusion Act (Pub. L. 47-126, 22 Stat. 58) then restricted access by Chinese men.[6] These two laws were followed by 60 years of further restrictions placed on foreign nationals, including a national-origins quota system instituted in 1924 that remained in place until 1965.

After the bombing of Pearl Harbor and US entry into World War II, the US president authorized the infamous round-up and internment of more than 100,000 Japanese Americans who lived within 100 miles of the Pacific coast, regardless of their citizenship status. At least two-thirds of these people were US citizens. Executive Order 9066[7] was only ended by a US Supreme Court decision in December 1944, but many who were incarcerated in the internment camps lost their homes, businesses, and property. Eventually, in 1990 surviving internees began to receive individual redress payments and an official letter of apology from the US government.

After the end of World War II, restrictions began to ease somewhat, with the establishment of a guest-worker visa program, exceptions to the national-origins quota system, and increased accommodation of refugees and asylum seekers. In 1965 a major change was instituted in eligibility criteria that replaced the national-origins quota system with a system based mainly on family unification, employment, and refugees. Up until 2001, specific accommodations were added to receive refugees and asylum seekers from various conflict zones in Southeast Asia, Latin America, and the Caribbean.

Major Policy Instruments	Summary
Nationality Act of 1790 (Pub. L. 1-3, 1 Stat. 103, Ch. 3)	First law to define eligibility for citizenship by naturalization and establish standards and procedures by which immigrants could become US citizens, limited to "free white persons."
Alien and Sedition Acts of 1798 (Pub. L. 5-58, 1 Stat. 570; Pub. L 5-66, 1 Stat. 577, 50 USC 3; Pub. L. 5-74, 1 Stat. 596)	Deportation laws targeting persons deemed political threats to the US.
Slave Trade Act of 1803 (2 Stat. 205, Ch. 10)	Stops the importation of enslaved persons from Africa, went into effect in 1807.

---

[6] An act to execute certain treaty stipulations relating to the Chinese, May 6, 1882; Enrolled Acts and Resolutions of Congress, 1789-1996; General Records of the United States Government; Record Group 11; National Archives (https://www.archives.gov/milestone-documents/chinese-exclusion-act).

[7] Executive Order 9066, February 19, 1942; General Records of the Unites States Government; Record Group 11; National Archives. https://www.archives.gov/milestone-documents/executive-order-9066.

Major Policy Instruments	Summary
Indian Removal Act of 1830 (Pub. L. 21-148, 4 Stat. 411, Ch. 148)	Authorized the confiscation of Native lands from North Carolina and Georgia and directed their forced removal to the "Indian Territory" west of the Mississippi River.
Treaty of Guadalupe Hidalgo of 1848 (February 2, 9 Stat. 922, TS 207)	Ended the Mexican–American War, annexed a major portion of northern Mexico (present-day California, Nevada, Utah, most of Arizona, and the western parts of New Mexico and Colorado), and conferred American citizenship on Mexicans choosing to remain in the territory.
Supreme Court Passenger Cases of 1849 (48 US 283)	Determined that the federal government, and not state or local governments, have the authority to enact and enforce immigration restrictions.
Burlingame–Seward Treaty of 1868 (https://history.state.gov/milestones/1866-1898/burlingame-seward-treaty)	International agreement that guaranteed rights of free migration to Chinese citizens to help construction of the transcontinental railroad, which depended heavily on Chinese labor.
Naturalization Act of 1870 (Pub. L. 41-254, 16 Stat. 254)	Extended naturalization rights to include "aliens of African nativity and to persons of African descent," excluding rights to other immigrant groups of color.
Page Act of 1875 (Pub. L. 43-141, 18 Stat. 477, Ch. 141)	Vaguely worded restrictions placed on immigrants but targeting specifically Chinese women.
Angell Treaty of 1880 (https://immigrationhistory.org/item/angell-treaty-of-1880/)	Updated the 1868 Burlingame Treaty with China and tightened restrictions on migration of Chinese workers.
Chinese Exclusion Act of 1882 (8 USC 7)	Targeted Chinese immigrants and represented the first law that specifically targeted a group by race and ethnicity for limiting entry and denying eligibility for citizenship.
Immigration Act of 1882 (Pub. L. 47-376, 22 Stat. 214)	Increased the list of persons who could be excluded to cover "convicts," "lunatics," and "those likely to become a public charge."
Immigration Act of 1891 (Pub. L. 51-551, 26 Stat. 1084, Ch. 551)	Authorized creation of the Immigration Bureau and centralized enforcement of immigration laws in one agency.
US v. Wong Kim Ark, 1898 (169 US 649)	Supreme Court case established the birthright citizenship precedent, that anyone born in the United States is a citizen by birth, regardless of their parents' status.

(Continued)

Major Policy Instruments	Summary
Immigration Act of 1903 (Pub. L. 57-162, 32 Stat. 1213, Ch. 1012)	Identified anarchists as targets for exclusion from US residency.
Extension of the Chinese Exclusion Act, 1904 (33 Stat. 428)	Extended in perpetuity the Chinese exclusion laws.
Expatriation Act of 1907 (34 Stat. 1228, Ch. 2534 §2)	Stripped citizenship from US-born women when they married noncitizen immigrant men.
Alien Land Laws of 1913 and 1920 (*Oyama v. State of California,* 332 US 633)	California state legislation that barred "aliens ineligible for citizenship" from owning or leasing lands, upheld by the US Supreme Court as constitutional.
Immigration Act of 1917 (Pub. L. 64-301, 39 Stat. 874)	Commonly known as the Barred Zone Act for creating a zone from the Middle East to Southeast Asia from which no immigrants were allowed to enter the United States; it also introduced a literacy test intended to reduce European immigration.
Emergency Quota Act of 1921 (Pub. L 67-5, 42 Stat. 5)	Fears of the spread of radicalism and increased immigration after World War I prompted Congress to enact this "emergency" measure imposing specific limits on immigration.
Cable Act of 1922 (8 USC 9 §§367–370)	Restored citizenship to US-born women who had married noncitizen husbands.
Immigration Act of 1924 (Pub. L. 68-139, 43 Stat. 153)	Commonly known as the Johnson–Reed Act, this established quotas based on immigrants' national origins and remained in effect for the next 40 years.
Undesirable Aliens Act of 1929 (45 Stat. 1551, Ch. 690)	Commonly known as Blease's Law, this act criminalized crossing the border outside of an official port of entry. It was mainly designed to restrict immigration from Mexico.
Tydings–McDuffie Act of 1934 (Pub. L. 73-127, 48 Stat. 456)	Granted the Philippines independence and effectively imposed immigration restrictions on Filipinos, who had previously been able to move freely as US nationals from a US colony.
Bracero Agreement of 1942 (Exec. Order 9213, 7 FR 6063)	This agreement authorized Mexican workers, all men without other household members, to work on short-term contracts on farms and wartime industries. After World War II ended, the program continued in agriculture until 1964.

Major Policy Instruments	Summary
Executive Order 9066, 1942–1945 (7 FR 9107)	The president authorized rounding up and incarcerating all Japanese Americans living within 100 miles of the Pacific coast, regardless of their citizenship status. This order was ended by Supreme Court decision in December 1944.
Repeal of Chinese Exclusion, 1943 (Pub. L. 78-199, 57 Stat. 600)	China was a US ally in the Pacific theater during World War II, prompting Congress to repeal the Chinese Exclusion laws and placing China under the same immigration restrictions as European countries.
War Brides Acts of 1945 and 1946 (Pub. L. 79-271, 59 Stat. 659, 8 USC 232–236; Pub. L. 79-471, 60 Stat. 339)	Exceptions were granted to national origins quotas to accommodate marriages involving World War II soldiers and veterans who wished to bring foreign-born spouses back to the United States.
Luce–Celler Act of 1946 (Pub. L. 79-483, 60 Stat. 416)	Extended naturalization rights and immigration quotas to Filipinos and Indians as wartime allies.
Displaced Persons Act of 1948 (50 USC §§1951–1965)	Authorized admissions for refugees from Europe and permitted asylum seekers already in the United States to normalize their status.
Immigration and Nationality Act of 1952 (8 USC §§1101–1483)	Commonly known as the McCarran–Walter Act, ended racial restrictions on citizenship but expanded immigration enforcement.
H-2 Guestworker Visa Program Immigration and Nationality Act of 1952 (§214)	Created a non-immigrant visa category, H-2, authorizing the recruitment of foreign farmworkers on a temporary basis.
Refugee Relief Act of 1953 (8 USC 12)	Expanded the number of refugee visas authorized by McCarran-Walter.
International Adoption Act of 1961 (Immigration and Nationality Act Amendments of 1961, 8 USC 1101 §2)	Added an exception to national origin quotas by classifying international adoption as a form of family reunification.
Immigration and Nationality Act of 1965 (Pub. L. 89-236, 79 Stat. 911)	The Hart–Celler Act set forth the main principles still in effect today, applying a system of preferences for family reunification (75%), employment (20%) and refugees (5%). It also capped immigration from Latin America for the first time.

(Continued)

Major Policy Instruments	Summary
Cuban Adjustment Act of 1966 (Pub. L. 89-732, 79 Stat. 919)	Authorized permanent status for anti-communist Cubans who fled to the United States after Castro's revolution.
Indochina Migration and Refugee Assistance Act of 1975 (Pub. L. 94-23, 89 Stat. 87)	After the Vietnam War ended, authorization for the admission and resettlement of refugees from Vietnam and other Southeast Asian countries.
Immigration and Nationality Act Amendments of 1976 and 1978 (Pub. L. 95-571, 90 Stat. 2703; Pub. L. 95-412, 92 Stat. 917)	Quotas for Western Hemisphere countries were increased in 1976, and a worldwide annual ceiling of 290,000 was established by Congress in 1978.
Refugee Act of 1980 (Pub. L. 96-212, 94 Stat. 102)	Authorized greater flexibility in the number of refugees that could be admitted, depending on worldwide circumstances, after consultation between the president and Congress.
Immigration Reform and Control Act of 1986 (8 USC 12 §§1101–1151)	Amnesty was granted for established residents, increased border enforcement, placed enforcement responsibility with employers, and expanded the guestworker visa program.
Immigration Act of 1990 (Pub. L. 101-649, 104 Stat. 4978)	Revised the 1965 law by creating the H-1B visa program for skilled temporary workers, with provisions to allow conversion to permanent status, and created a visa lottery for people unable to enter through the preference system.
Chinese Student Protection Act of 1992 (Pub. L. 102-404, 106 Stat. 1969)	Authorized permanent legal status for Chinese students living in the United States after the Chinese government crackdown on student protests in Tiananmen in 1989.
Nicaraguan Adjustment and Central American Relief Act of 1997 (Pub. L. 105-100, 11 Stat. 2193)	Authorized Salvadorans, Guatemalans, and Nicaraguans who had fled violence and poverty in their homelands to request asylum and remain in the United States.
Haitian Refugee Immigration Fairness Act of 1998 (Pub. L. 105-277, 112 Stat. 2681)	Authorized Haitian nations who had been residing in the United States to request asylum and remain in the United States.
Enhanced Border Security and Visa Entry Reform Act of 2002 and the Homeland Security Act of 2002 (Pub. L. 107-173, 116 Stat. 543; 6 USC 1 §101)	After the September 11, 2001 attacks, these acts authorized expanded budgets and enforcement powers and moved immigration enforcement to a new cabinet-level agency.

Major Policy Instruments	Summary
Secure Fence Act of 2006 (Pub. L. 109-367, 120 Stat. 2638)	Authorized the Secretary of Homeland Security to beef up border operations, including an expansion of existing walls, fences, and surveillance.
Deferred Action for Childhood Arrivals (DACA) Policy of 2012 (June 15, 2012 Memorandum from Janet Napolitano, Secretary, DHS, to David V. Aguilar, Acting Commissioner, US CBP, et al.)	A Department of Homeland Security policy that provided work authorization and protection from deportation for people who arrived in the United States as children prior to June 2007. This policy was later expanded to include the parents of children who were either citizens or lawful permanent residents.
Muslim Travel Bans of 2017 (27 Jan and 6 Mar) (Exec. Order 13769, 82 FR 8977; Exec. Order 13780, 82 FR 13209)	A series of executive orders prohibiting travel and refugee resettlement from predominantly Muslim countries, eventually upheld by the Supreme Court.

PERSPECTIVE: Birthright Citizenship and Policy, by Leo R. Chavez

Professor of anthropology, University of California-Irvine (USA)

Birthright citizenship is based on the principle of *jus soli*, "the right to soil," which means that anyone born on US territory is a citizen. They are born into the nation, which is derived from *nascere*, "to be born." Currently, 33 countries and two territories guarantee unrestricted birthright citizenship (World Population Review 2024a). Most of these countries are in the Americas (Colombia being the exception), but Chad, Tanzania, and Lesotho on the African continent also have unrestricted birthright citizenship. Other countries typically granted citizenship only through the principle of *jus sanguinis*, or "by blood," meaning that at least one, or sometimes both, parents must be citizens. However, due to the increased migration over the last 50 years (especially to industrialized nations with low-birth rates) many countries that did not see themselves as a nation of immigrants are now among the 33 nations that allow some form of restricted birthright citizenship.

The Fourteenth Amendment to the US Constitution guarantees citizenship to those born in the United States: "All persons born or naturalized in the United States, and subject to the jurisdiction thereof, are citizens of the United States and of the State wherein they reside."

At the time (in 1868), the Fourteenth Amendment's guarantee of birthright citizenship was meant to correct a great wrong, the denial of citizenship to the US-born children of African American slaves. At long last, the Fourteenth Amendment guaranteed the children of African slaves a place in the nation as citizens by birth. Of course, the privileges of citizenship for African Americans were later diminished by Jim Crow laws that undermined their equal rights to education, voting, and a myriad of infringements on everyday ways to participate in the social life of the nation (Gates 2020).

Up until the Fourteenth Amendment, citizenship applied mainly to white Americans. Native American, Black, and Asian people were not included. The first naturalization act, passed in 1790, made any free, white adult alien (male or female) who had lived in the jurisdiction of the United States for a period of two years (increased to five years in 1795) eligible for citizenship. The Chinese Exclusion Act of 1882 made explicit that state and federal courts could not grant citizenship to Chinese resident aliens[8]. Many opponents of the Fourteenth Amendment argued that it would grant citizenship to people who had been deemed unworthy of citizenship, particularly the children of non-white immigrants (Wydra 2009).

Not long after passage of the Fourteenth Amendment, nativists raised challenges to birthright citizenship, particularly for the children of Chinese immigrants. Given the racial restrictions on citizenship, nativists began to question why US-born Chinese should receive birthright citizenship given their parents' status as unwelcome immigrants barred from US citizenship. On March 28, 1898, the US Supreme Court answered that question in the case of the *United States v. Wong Kim Ark* (US Supreme Court 1898). In deciding the case, the Supreme Court went to great lengths to make clear that the phrase "under the jurisdiction thereof" meant that at moment of Wong Kim Ark's birth in the United States both he and his parents were subject to the laws and authority of the United States and its government, and thus the Fourteenth Amendment guaranteed him birthright citizenship.

By deciding that Wong Kim Ark was a citizen by birth, as guaranteed by the Fourteenth Amendment, the US Supreme Court made it clear that citizenship was a birthright not limited by race or parents' political status (Justia 1898). The Court's decision thus attempted to assure that children of stigmatized immigrant groups would not become a caste of internal minorities without citizenship, perhaps for generations (Gerstle 2001). The Court also made it

---

[8] An act to execute certain treaty stipulations relating to the Chinese, May 6, 1882; Enrolled Acts and Resolutions of Congress, 1789-1996; General Records of the United States Government; Record Group 11; National Archives; https://www.archives.gov/milestone-documents/chinese-exclusion-act.

clear that while Congress has the power to regulate naturalization, the Fourteenth Amendment did not confer upon Congress the authority to restrict birthright citizenship.

The nineteenth and twentieth centuries witnessed high levels of immigration, and birthright citizenship was a way of incorporating the children of immigrants and their families into the nation. Citizenship by birth made the New World, including the United States, different from the Old World, where blood ties determined who was French, German, and many other nationalities. In the United States, fears of demographic change fueled nativist ideologies that blamed new immigrants from southern and eastern Europe and Asia for reducing the relative numbers of Americans of white, northern European heritage. Nativists, such as Lothrop Stoddard and Madison Grant, blamed stigmatized racial and ethnic groups for "diluting the 'blood' of the nation" (Chavez 2017; Grant 1916; Stoddard 1920). They also accused immigrants of introducing strange new cultural beliefs and behaviors that would irrevocably alter what it means to be American. Such fears continue in contemporary political discourse that proposes an end to the Fourteenth Amendment and birthright citizenship.

Since 1991, there have been at least seven bills introduced into the US Congress to deny birthright citizenship to the children of undocumented parents, the most recent in 2023. Some states, such as Texas in 2023, have introduced their own bills to disqualify from citizenship those children whose parents are not citizens of the United States. Some politicians have even made ending birthright citizenship a part of their presidential campaign promises. However, many, if not most, Americans believe birthright citizenship is a positive aspect of American law and American values.

In the early 2000s, anchor babies emerged in public discourse to provide a face to children for whom birthright citizenship is said to be a bad idea. The term "anchor babies" refers to the children of undocumented immigrants and is used to raise questions about their legitimacy as citizens. Although born in the United States, these children were said to be part of their parents' conspiracy to take advantage of the United States. When they turned 21 years of age, the anchor babies would be able to sponsor their parents for citizenship. Although sponsoring immigrants is costly and it is unclear how many children actually sponsor their parents' legalization, even the possibility of sponsorship makes these US-born children undeserving of citizenship, according to some who favor restricting immigration.

Birthright citizenship for the non-white children of immigrants is also a talking point for white nationalists and their concern for white decline and white replacement, echoing nativist beliefs of the nineteenth and early twentieth centuries (Chavez 2021). In this view, birthright citizenship and anchor babies are blamed for a foreign invasion of the United States and the cause of demographic change. For some, this threat is great enough that they are willing to jettison the constitutional guarantee of citizenship by birth for children born in the United States.

> Most legal scholars agree that birthright citizenship is enshrined in the Fourteenth Amendment of the US Constitution. Keeping the debate on birthright citizenship alive may make good political fodder, but at what cost? The rhetoric over birthright citizenship stokes anger by falsely blaming immigrants for having too many children, who, even if they are born in the United States, are part of an invasion and reconquest of America and therefore undeserving of citizenship. Can birthright citizenship weather this round of nativism and furor over immigration and demographic change? Birthright citizenship may be facing its toughest challenge in over a century.
>
> Eliminating birthright citizenship would create new problems. It would result in the legal construction of a group of US-born, nationality less outcasts living in the United States. Denying birthright citizenship to those who would almost certainly continue to live among us would render them the most liminal and miserable subjects in the nation. It is unlikely they would leave the country of their birth to return to their parents' country of origin. Children of these US-born non-citizens would also be denied citizenship by birth, a process of exclusion that could continue for generations. What we would then have in America is a social caste from which thousands or even millions of people cannot escape. Social stigma is often ascribed to castes who are viewed as abject people lacking full membership in society. Is this not exactly the situation for which the Fourteenth Amendment was needed in the first place?

After the September 2001 terrorist attacks, US policies concerning international immigration shifted to emphasize national security concerns. Immigration policy enforcement was concentrated in the newly formed US Department of Homeland Security agencies, physical barriers and surveillance technology were authorized along the US–Mexico border, and with the Trump administration's election, border wall construction was accelerated and heated anti-Muslim rhetoric was translated into exclusionary policies.

Specific policies shaping the size and composition of immigrants coming to the United States from other countries form only part of the international immigration experience. Other policies concerning education, health care, housing, and labor also have a material effect on immigrants once they have arrived in their new homes. Language learning services, multilingual and multicultural curricula, access to healthcare in a system that depends heavily on employer-provided insurance, eligibility to work and change employers under various visa programs all affect the livelihoods, well-being, and integration of immigrants into the host society.

PERSPECTIVE: Forced Out – Migrant Mothers on the Move, by Susan J. Terrio

Professor Emerita of anthropology, Georgetown University (USA)

Since 2012, thousands of Central American mothers have sought protection in the United States as the rates of abuse and murder of women exploded, incidents of extortion and killing by criminal groups soared, and the rule of law disintegrated. The violence and corruption that are forcing women to migrate make home, in the words of poet Warsan Shire, "the mouth of a shark."

The story of a Salvadoran woman I call "Teresa" is all too typical. Home became the mouth of a shark for her when the principal of her high school coerced her into having sex with him when she was 15 and he was 41. Teresa lived with her grandparents, who accused her of lying about the principal until she got pregnant. They refused to involve the police because domestic violence laws were typically ignored. Instead, they demanded that the principal support Teresa and the baby. When Teresa's daughter was born, he paid the bills but expected the sex to continue. When Teresa declared her independence by finding work and winning a school scholarship, he stalked and threatened her.

Seeing no way out, Teresa left her daughter with her grandmother and headed north on a journey where she nearly died twice – once when she fell from a moving cargo train in Mexico and again when she was abandoned by a smuggler in Arizona's Sonoran Desert. US Border Patrol agents saved her life but transferred her, in shackles, from the hospital to an immigration prison where the conditions were horrible, and the guards were abusive. On her first day there, they confiscated Teresa's pain medications and sent her to solitary confinement. Her offense had been to violate the prison prohibition on physical contact. She had hugged a friend from home.

Teresa thought that she had escaped the mouth of a shark when she passed her credible fear interview for asylum in prison and was released. She skipped her hearing in immigration court because she had no attorney and was afraid the judge would deport her. She settled in Virginia, worked two jobs, and borrowed over $9,000 to hire smugglers to bring her daughter over the southern border. Later she discovered that because she missed her immigration court hearing, the judge issued a deportation order rendering her ineligible for legal status.

If Teresa had had legal representation, she could have applied for asylum within one year of arriving in the US as required by law. Her attorney could have argued for asylum based on the sexual abuse she suffered as a minor in her home country. With a grant of asylum, she would have been on a path to US citizenship.

Interviews conducted with Central American migrants by researchers and the United Nations High Commissioner for Refugees (UNHCR) revealed that 85% of these women faced extreme levels of violence on a near-daily basis. They experienced threats, extortion, and assaults from transnational and local criminal groups alongside life-threatening and degrading forms of domestic violence at home. Criminal groups were just the public face of corruption. They worked hand in hand with local officials, police, and criminal groups. Sixty percent of the women reported rapes and assaults to the police or prosecutors but received little or no protection. This explains why 40% never reported harm to the police (United Nations High Commissioner for Refugees 2015a).

Teresa had no good choices – either remain in El Salvador at the mercy of a sexual predator or begin a perilous trek north that lasted months and would keep her in debt for years. Such journeys always take longer than migrants plan and many have to work or beg to survive. Some are assaulted or robbed, and they often go hungry. If they are lucky, they find smugglers who can be trusted, and they cross the border without being apprehended. If they are not lucky, they can drown crossing the Rio Grande, die in the desert, or get caught, detained, or deported by US immigration authorities.

Making it across the border without being caught is just the first of many challenges. Without legal papers they have to share apartments with other undocumented relatives and work long hours in unskilled jobs – washing dishes and cleaning houses – in order to pay expenses. They must send money to support the children they left behind and repay the smuggling loans they made. Many mothers promise to bring their children over right away, but it almost always takes much longer than they thought. They make so little, expenses are so high, and the smuggling fees for their children have skyrocketed. Often, years go by before they could try to get them to the United States.

Their kids say that home is the mouth of a shark when they have to leave behind the grandmother who became a parent to them after their mothers left. They never forget that they nearly suffocated in the back of a trailer truck on the journey north. Or that they were terrified when immigration agents caught them and handcuffed them. They did not understand why US Border Patrol agents put them in freezing cages and sent them to a government shelter when they have a mother here. They feel safer in the United States, but they miss hanging out with their cousins and families back home. After years of separation, they are angry because they say that their mothers abandoned them. They insist that they did not really care about the clothes, or the school money sent from the United States. They just wanted their mother to be with them. They say that the United States is not what they imagined. English is hard, the schools are different, the workload is heavy, and it is tough to make friends. The country is full of poor people and tough neighborhoods. Then they stick the knife in. They say that the worst part is that their moms are always working and once again they spend hours alone at home.

In 2017 life got much harder in Fairfax County, Virginia where the mothers I interviewed live (Terrio 2024). In a tense environment of enhanced enforcement operations, these women had to continue to go to work, shop, and get their children to school. There was widespread fear every time a mother's workplace was raided, she was detained after a traffic stop, or abruptly deported after appearing for a routine check-in with US Immigration and Customs Enforcement (ICE). On days when ICE stationed their vehicles outside public schools, their children were forced to hide at home. They saw first-hand what happens when a parent is deported. Families are shattered, they face hunger and risk a plunge into homelessness.

In the twenty-first century a widespread – if heavily debated – consensus has emerged that many migrants, including asylum seekers, do not deserve protections under immigration law or have the right to access public goods like decent housing, safe work, or public education.

Increasingly, destination countries like the United States, Australia, and countries in western Europe are preemptively barring asylum seekers from entering their territories or imposing increasing restrictions on asylum claims without the benefit of a court hearing.

In response to migration spikes at the US southern border beginning in 2012, both the Obama and Trump administrations shifted from humanitarian approaches to intensified enforcement and deterrence measures. First, in 2014 President Barack Obama increased deportations and expanded family detention in private prisons – in which due process protections were violated, parents and children were systematically mistreated, and medical care was woefully inadequate. Then, beginning in 2017, President Donald Trump's family separation policy tore families apart by sending parents to jail and detaining children alone. Many of them were under five years old and held in appalling conditions in packed, freezing cages or repurposed warehouses. In the same year, the Trump administration ended asylum protection for migrant women fleeing gang and domestic violence.

The Biden administration has reversed some of the draconian immigration restrictions of the Trump era. It ended mass worksite raids as well as long-term family detention. It closed two notorious immigration prisons, one in Georgia and one in Massachusetts, because of flagrant civil rights violations. However, under political pressure to crack down on the undocumented migrants entering the United States, the Biden administration supported a proposed Senate border bill that would substantially increase the standard of evidence needed to win asylum, expand detention facilities, and permit summary deportations of migrants (Factcheck.org 2024).

Despite the enhanced enforcement policies, migrants fleeing violence in their home countries continue to come. In the first three months of fiscal year 2024, immigration authorities apprehended 639,675 migrants, the highest monthly figure in 21 years. Of that number, 325,739 were single adults; 35,118 were unaccompanied minor children; and 268,818 were families. When home is the mouth of a shark, survival is the only thing that counts (United States Customs and Border Patrol 2024).

Policies Concerning Movement in Response to Climate Change

In the coming decades, we can expect that flooding, wildfires, coastal storm surges, and extreme weather events like hurricanes, cyclones, and tornados will increase in frequency and intensity due to climate change. Because we have seen higher concentrations of people living in coastal areas around the world, we also expect that coastal cities and settlements will be especially vulnerable to these climate hazards. Moving people out of harm's way is a likely policy choice when these hazards pose too great a risk. But it is also necessary to anticipate the adverse impacts of relocating vulnerable populations, with special attention to the loss of livelihoods and cultural heritage.

The UNHCR has developed a useful guidance document for planned relocation in the context of climate-related risks and hazards (2015b). Acknowledging that planned relocation is a measure of last resort, the guidance identifies the situations in which planned relocation may be appropriate, spells out measures that ought to be taken to ensure that relocated persons have their rights protected, and lists the specific responsibilities that governments have for protecting these rights.

In the United States, more than 70 Alaska Native villages are in coastal areas that have been made more hazardous due to the effects of climate change (United States Department of the Interior 2020). With polar ice caps melting, the sea ice that used to serve as a near-shore buffer from severe storms is gone, and coastal villages are now more vulnerable to serious storm damage. As a matter of policy, the US government is making sizable grants available to help fund the ongoing efforts of some of these villages to relocate to safer ground. Villages like Newtok and Napakiak in western Alaska were slated to receive about $25 million each in 2023; other tribes in the lower 48, like the Quinault Nation, have received the same amount to relocate their capital city, Taholah, so it is out of the way of sea level rise, storm surges, and flooding.

PERSPECTIVE: Climate Change–driven Migration, by Elizabeth Marino[a], Chantel Comardelle[b], and Dennis Davis[c]

a Professor of anthropology, Oregon State University-Cascade (USA)
b Tribal Executive Secretary, Isle de Jean Charles band of Biloxi-Chitimacha-Choctaw Tribe (USA)
c Iñupiat photographer (USA)

Climate Change, migration, and trope

In 2024 climate change–driven migration (climate-driven migration) is a framework used to discuss the flow of people that are temporarily or permanently migrating from one location to another – and have a climate signal in their decision to move. These mobilities – of people, materials, ideas, and cultures – are influenced by disasters (Curtis, Fussell, and Ward 2015), agricultural changes or collapse (Falco, Galeotti, and Olper 2019), and other changes that have, in turn, been influenced by the anthropogenic release of greenhouse gasses. These migrations and mobilities are worrisome because social scientists have demonstrated that forced migrations can have lasting negative social impacts on migrating communities (Cernea 1995); and estimates for the number of people who may face migration as an outcome of climate are growing (Hauer, Evans, and Mishra 2016). An anthropology of care centers demands for action, attention, policy, and financial support for frontline communities, often from the Global South (Bank and Fröhlich 2018) or overburdened communities within the Global North (Farrell et al. 2021), who are being forced to move as an inequitable experience of climate change.

Climate-driven migration (often referred to as managed retreat) is also an increasingly well-worn trope deployed by scientists, government planners, and climate change activists to demonstrate the seriousness of human-caused climate change (Maldonado, Marino, and Iuakea 2020). As an author on the *Fifth National Climate Assessment*, Elizabeth Marino (one of the authors of this essay) was instructed by the science communication specialist who gave media training to always give a "what and why it matters" in response to journalists' questions. The example she gave was that sea level rise is occurring, and why it matters is because it will "force millions of people to migrate." As a trope, climate-driven migration has been used to explain why natural science research on climate change is important and to express the criticality of climate change within slow-moving political systems. It is colloquially deployed as the "why" for the t-shirt slogan "Time to Panic."

These tropes are powerful and at their zenith justify social and political intervention and, in some cases, social engineering. In Harris County, Texas (home to Houston), *mandatory* buyouts, as opposed to *voluntary* buyouts, are being enforced for the first time as a hazard mitigation strategy offered by the state. The book *Nomad Century* goes so far to suggest a governed, orderly, and (do not forget) forced abandonment of the middle latitudes (Vince 2022). The relocation of many families off of Isle de Jean Charles, Louisiana, has been touted by the state as a success (https://isledejeancharles.la.gov), despite being objected to by tribal leadership (Jessee 2022).

As a trope, climate-driven migration reinforces state authority through an epistemologically western construct of a destructive wilderness lashing out against agentless communities. It justifies the über-agency of a self-identified elite – western scientists and Global North governments – with oversight and informational aid from a high-powered group of tech entrepreneurs (Kinstler 2019). It moves the places, people, and relationships impacted by changing weather and coasts from the *governance of neglect* (Marino 2015) to the *governance of for-your-own-good* (Jerolleman et al. 2024). Whether empathetic or xenophobic, climate-driven migration narratives are discursively constructed as a threat to security (Walters 2010) and a reason to *act* (Gebre and Melaku 2024).

Climate-driven migration – the epistemological, material, and discursive mess that it is – will likely be a critical driver of social organization and governance for the coming century.

In search of beauty

Humans have moved over landscapes in the Arctic and the south bayous of Louisiana for hundreds and thousands of years. While long-distance and permanent migrations are present in the archaeological record and oral traditions, the seasonal round along the western coast of Alaska and the heavy reliance on the marshland in southeast Louisiana are perennial features of life. Flexibility to changing coasts was, and is, built into habit, architecture, economy, and relationships in both places (Davis and Marino 2023). The social–ecological reciprocity of land, animals, and people included the capacity to change when circumstances called for change – to move back, to move sideways, to retreat, and to return. The point here is not to idealize Indigenous relationships to land but to emphasize that the epistemological and material systems of movement visible in Iñupiat and Biloxi-Chitimacha-Choctaw histories are foundationally different and more flexible than the narrow discourse of water driving people away.

Dennis Davis and Chantel Comardelle, two of the authors on this essay, are Indigenous artists and photographers from Shishmaref, Alaska and Isle de Jean Charles, Louisiana, respectively. Both communities have been called poster children for climate-driven migration; and both communities have confronted permanent migrations because of repetitive flooding. Dennis and Chantel are also collaborators on a research project on climate change–driven migration and adaptation to repetitive flooding. As part of that collaboration, they created a traveling photograph exhibit and short film that highlight their vision of the communities they come from, the traditions they uphold, and the migrations they now face because of changing ecological features, including larger storms and erosion. The art exhibit is divided into five categories of photos: Beauty, The Past, Subsistence and Life, Climate Change, and The Future.

The exhibit is a clap back to the climate change–driven migration narrative that is foregrounded in popular discourse. Instead of zeroing in on a hazard and subsequent movement from an increasingly uninhabitable place, the photos in the exhibit approach climate-driven migration through a different epistemological lens. Here, artists and community members identify the cultural needs that constitute a beautiful life; remember the past they have inherited; identify critical, material, subsistence needs and lifeways; and then move to focusing on changing conditions and the future. It is a holistic, relational, and flexible orientation to change, landscape, and society. It engenders a narrative of continuation and love, not interruption and fear. It focuses on rootedness – even amidst uprooting.

The property regime

Our collaborative project also made clear that one reason the epistemological vision of migration embodied in Chantel and Dennis's photographs is difficult to achieve is because the property regime, including property law, does not support that kind of flexibility (Jerollerman et al. 2024). When property lines are rigid and fixed, it is very difficult for movement to be iterative. When houses are immobile and state infrastructure investment is competitive, rural and neglected places become legible only in their cost–benefit uninhabitability. It is no surprise to anthropologists that when we ignore policy drivers and focus on the ecological drivers alone, we misinterpret social phenomena for natural ones. In this case, the term is *climate-driven migration,* not a compounding driver of history, environment, law, and oppression.

Our research team has only begun to map out the policy environment of climate-driven migration (https://blogs.oregonstate.edu/adaptationlaw). We have only started to understand how property law and its constituent corollaries in regulation, guidance, and bureaucratic precedent shape the migration choices communities and individuals have when they confront ecological shift. We do not yet understand the complex and compounding influence that zoning laws, development regulations, and legal limits to just compensation have on adaptation possibilities and migration choices (Jerolleman et al. 2024, p. 131). What we do know is that these policy landscapes are complex, dynamic, and predictive of harm (Marino et al. 2022). We also know that they are ethnocentric (Marino 2018) and grossly understudied in the climate-driven migration literature.

A Conclusion

Humans alter and are subservient to the earth and sea. We have now altered the composition of the atmosphere, and we are being moved by the agentive forces of storms, erosion, weather, wind, and water. Climate-driven migration is not merely a social construct. The water is rising; and we are bearing witness to dramatic changes in the way that rising is altering the land. The epistemological tools we use, as we decide how to respond to those alterations, will be all-important in creating the future. As anthropologists we know the infinite multiplicity in ways that humans may respond to ecological pressures. Whether governance and property regimes are flexible enough to allow for a diversity of adaptive responses is unknown.

250   NATIONAL AND INTERNATIONAL POLICY

This is a winter snowstorm. All the water that is there on the ocean, it is supposed to be frozen, but it is not and you have a big storm coming. This is beautiful, but it is also dangerous. This was in October – right at the beginning of the storm season; if the ocean is frozen, then the waves cannot cut into the permafrost and cause erosion and flooding. If the water is not frozen, then it is dangerous. Source: *The Calm Before the Storm,* photo by Dennis Davis.

Chapter Summary

Policies aim to protect the rights of people on the move while properly anticipating the impacts on public facilities and services that result from this movement. At the international level, recognizing and protecting human rights are a central focus, and the governance of migration is seen as a key element in achieving the global *2030 Agenda for Sustainable Development Goals.*

Regional agreements, which are often embedded as provisions in more encompassing trade or security agreements, spell out processes and mechanisms for groups of countries to cooperate on protecting the rights of migrants while properly anticipating how migration changes places of origin, destination, and places in between.

National policies usually serve a number of purposes, regulating the international and internal flow of people to meet labor demands, protecting people from natural hazards, promoting the integration of immigrants in their new homes, and offering asylum and sanctuary from violence and conflict on a permanent or temporary basis.

Review Questions

1. What are the two general objectives of most national and international immigration policies? Why do you think these two objectives are sometimes viewed as mutually exclusive?

2. What were the main findings from the 2022 report by the American Anthropological Association about the role of border walls in international migration policy? Why do you think nation-states continue to build border walls if, as Miguel Díaz-Barriga and Margaret Dorsey write in their "Perspectives" piece, a well-documented effect of border walls is to promote human suffering?
3. With many countries facing the unavoidable impacts of climate change in coming decades, what do you think the main policy objectives should be to mitigate (or avoid altogether) the harmful consequences of climate-related, forced migration and displacement?
4. What are some of the current arguments in favor of, or opposing, birthright citizenship in the United States? What are your thoughts on the merits of these arguments?

References

Aarthi, S V, and M Sahu. 2021. Migration policy in the gulf cooperation council (GCC) states: A critical analysis. *Contemporary Review of the Middle East* 8(4): 410–434. https://doi.org/10.1177/23477989211028748.

Ambrosi, Eugenio. 2017. The Unbearable Lightness of Leadership. *EU Observer* (republished in the *United Nations International Office on Migration*). https://euobserver.com/opinion/139507, accessed 11 Mar 2024.

American Anthropological Association. 2021. *Anthropology and the Proliferation of Border Walls*. Washington, DC: American Anthropological Association. https://americananthro.org/wp-content/uploads/aaa-the-proliferation-of-border-and-security-walls-task-force.pdf, accessed 11 Mar 2024.

Bank, André, and Christiane Fröhlich. 2018. *Forced Migration in the Global South: Reorienting the Debate*. (GIGA Focus Global, 3). Hamburg: GIGA German Institute of Global and Area Studies – Leibniz-Institut für Globale und Regionale Studien. https://nbn-resolving.org/urn:nbn:de:0168-ssoar-57809-3, accessed 6 Apr 2024.

Barros, Aline. 2023. UN Agency: US-Mexico Border Is World's Deadliest Land Crossing for Migrants. Voice of America News (4 Oct 2023), https://www.voanews.com/a/iom-us-mexico-border-the-deadliest-land-crossing-in-the-world-/7297145.html, accessed 11 Mar 2024.

Bashford, Alison, and Catie Gilchrist. 2012. The colonial history of the 1905 Aliens Act. *Journal of Imperial and Commonwealth History* 40(3): 409–437. http://dx.doi.org/10.1080/03086534.2012.712380.

Cernea, Michael M. 1995. Understanding and preventing impoverishment from displacement: Reflections on the state of knowledge. *Journal of refugee studies* 8(3): 245–264. https://doi.org/10.1093/jrs/8.3.245.

Chavez, Leo R. 2017. *Anchor Babies and the Challenge of Birthright Citizenship*. Stanford, CA: Stanford University Press.

Chavez, Leo R. 2021. Fear of White Replacement: Latina Fertility, White Demographic Decline, and Immigration Reform. In Kathleen Belew, and Ramón A Gutiérrez, eds. *A Field Guide to White Supremacy*. Berkeley: University of California Press. pp. 177–202. https://doi.org/10.1525/9780520382534-015.

Curtis, Katherine J, Elizabeth Fussell, and J Jack DeWaard. 2015. Recovery migration after Hurricanes Katrina and Rita: Spatial concentration and intensification in the migration system. *Demography* 52(4): 1269–1293. https://doi.org/10.1007%2Fs13524-015-0400-7.

Davis, Dennis, and Elizabeth Marino. 2023. Representation and Luck: Reflections on Climate and Collaboration in Shishmaref, Alaska. In Susan A Crate, and Mark Nuttall, eds. *Anthropology and Climate Change*. 3rd ed. New York: Routledge. https://doi.org/10.4324/9781003242499.

Díaz-Barriga, Miguel, and Margaret E Dorsey. 2020. *Fencing in Democracy: Border Walls, Necrocitizenship, and the Security State*. Durham, NC: Duke University Press.

Digidiki, Valileia, and Jacqueline Bhabha. 2020. Greece's Proposed 'Floating Wall' Shows the Failure of EU Migration Policies. *The Guardian* (7 Feb 2020). https://www.theguardian.com/commentisfree/2020/feb/07/greece-floating-wall-eu-refugees-migrant-policy, accessed 11 Mar 2024.

Factcheck.Org. 2024. Unraveling Misinformation About Bipartisan Immigration Bill. https://www.factcheck.org/2024/02/unraveling-misinformation-about-bipartisan-immigration-bill, accessed 15 Feb 2024.

Falco, Chiara, Marzio Galeotti, and Alessandro Olper. 2019. Climate change and migration: Is agriculture the main channel? *Global Environmental Change* 59: 101995. https://doi.org/10.1016/j.gloenvcha.2019.101995.

Farrell, Justin, Paul Berne Burow, Kathryn McConnell, et al. 2021. Effects of land dispossession and forced migration on indigenous peoples in North America. *Science* 374(6567): eabe4943. https://doi.org/10.1126/science.abe4943.

Flores, Andrea, and Shaw Drake. 2020. Border Patrol Violently Assaults Civil Rights and Liberties. American Civil Liberties Union (24 July 2020). https://www.aclu.org/news/immigrants-rights/border-patrol-violently-assaults-civil-rights-and-liberties, accessed 11 Mar 2024.

Garsd, Jasmine. 2023. Desperate Migrants Are Choosing to Cross the Border through Dangerous U.S. Desert. National Public Radio (3 May 2023). https://www.npr.org/2023/05/03/1169010633/desperate-migrants-are-choosing-to-cross-the-border-through-dangerous-u-s-desert, accessed 11 Mar 2024.

Gates, Henry Louis Jr. 2020. *Stony the Road: Reconstruction, White Supremacy, and the Rise of Jim Crow*. London: Penguin Books.

Tefere Gebre, and Nicole Melaku. 2024. Climate migration is our new reality and new responsibility. The Hill. https://thehill.com/opinion/energy-environment/4435928-climate-migration-is-our-new-reality-and-new-responsibility Accessed 6 Apr 2024.

Gerstle, Gary. 2001. *American Crucible: Race and Nation in the Twentieth Century*. Princeton: Princeton University Press.

Grant, Madison. 1916. *The Passing of the Great Race or The Racial Basis of European History*. New York: Charles Scribner's Sons.

Hauer, Matthew E, Jason M Evans, and Deepak R Mishra. 2016. Millions projected to be at risk from sea-level rise in the continental United States. *Nature Climate Change* 6(7): 691–695. https://doi.org/10.1038/nclimate2961.

Honig, Lauren. 2016. Immigrant political economies and exclusionary policy in Africa. *Comparative Politics* 48(4): 517–537. http://www.jstor.org/stable/24886186.

Jerolleman, Alessandra, Elizabeth Marino, Nathan Jessee, et al. 2024. *People or Property: Legal Contradictions, Climate Resettlement, and the View from Shifting Ground*. New York: Palgrave Macmillan. https://doi.org/10.1007/978-3-031-36872-1.

Jessee, Nathan. 2022. Reshaping Louisiana's coastal frontier: Managed retreat as colonial decontextualization. *Journal of Political Ecology* 29(1): 277–301. https://doi.org/10.2458/jpe.2835.

Jones, Reece. 2016. *Violent Borders: Refugees and the Right to Move*. London: Verso.

Justia.com. 1898. US Supreme Court: *United States v. Wong Kim Ark, 169 U.S. 649* (1898). http://supreme.justia.com/us/169/649/case.html#715, accessed 15 Feb 2024

Kinstler, Linda. 2019. Big tech firms are racing to track climate refugees. *MIT Technology Review*. https://www.technologyreview.com/2019/05/17/103059/big-tech-firms-are-racing-to-track-climate-refugees, accessed 6 Apr 2024.

Lavenex, Sandra, Philipp Lutz, and Paula Hoffmeyer-Zlotnik. 2023. Migration governance through trade agreements: Insights from the MITA dataset. *The Review of International Organizations*. https://doi.org/10.1007/s11558-023-09493-5.

Maldonado, Julie, Elizabeth Marino, and Leslie Iaukea. 2020. Reframing the language of retreat. *Eos 101*(10.1029). https://doi.org/10.1029/2020EO150527.

Marinari, Maddalena. 2022. The 1921 and 1924 immigration acts a century later: Roots and long shadows. *Journal of American History* 109(2): 271–283. https://doi.org/10.1093/jahist/jaac232.

Marino, Elizabeth. 2015. *Fierce Climate, Sacred Ground: An Ethnography of Climate Change in Shishmaref, Alaska*. Fairbanks: University of Alaska Press.

Marino, Elizabeth. 2018. Adaptation privilege and voluntary buyouts: Perspectives on ethnocentrism in sea level rise relocation and retreat policies in the US. *Global Environmental Change* 49: 10–13. https://doi.org/10.1016/j.gloenvcha.2018.01.002.

Marino, Elizabeth, Alessandra Jerolleman, Nathan Jessee, et al. 2022. Is the Longue Durée a legal argument?: Understanding takings doctrine in climate change and settler colonial contexts in the United States. *Human Organization* 81(4): 348–357. https://doi.org/10.17730/1938-3525-81.4.348.

Migration Provisions in Preferential Trade Agreements (MITA) Dataset. 2023 *Zenodo* https://doi.org/10.5281/zenodo.7837954

Schiller, Nina Glick. 2021. Migration, Displacement, and Dispossession, in *Oxford Research Encyclopedia – Anthropology*. https://doi.org/10.1093/acrefore/9780190854584.013.205

Stoddard, Lothrop. 1920. *The Rising Tide of Color Against White World-Supremacy*. New York: Charles Scribner's Sons.

Terrio, Susan. 2024. *Forced Out: Migrant Mothers in Search of Refuge and Hope*. New York: New York University Press.

Traugott, David. 2021. Belarus and the Weaponization of Migrants: The engineering of a crisis in Eastern Europe. *Transatlantic Policy* (7 Dec 2021). https://www.american.edu/sis/centers/transatlantic-policy/articles/20211207-belarus-and-the-weaponization-of-migrants.cfm#:~:text=Throughout%20November%2C%20thousands%20of%20Middle,and%20lines%20of%20razor%20wire, accessed 11 Mar 2024.

United Nations Department of Economic and Social Affairs. 2015. *Transforming Our World: The 2030 Agenda for Sustainable Development*. https://sdgs.un.org/sites/default/files/publications/21252030%20Agenda%20for%20Sustainable%20Development%20web.pdf, accessed 12 Oct 2023.

United Nations High Commissioner for Human Rights. 2021. "*Lethal Disregard*": Search and Rescue and the Protection of Migrants in the Central Mediterranean Sea. https://www.ohchr.org/sites/default/files/Documents/Issues/Migration/OHCHR-thematic-report-SAR-protection-at-sea.pdf, accessed 11 Mar 2024.

United Nations High Commissioner for Refugees. 2015a. *Women on the Run: First-hand accounts of refugees fleeing El Salvador, Guatemala, Honduras, and Mexico*. https://www.unhcr.org/us/media/women-run, accessed 15 Feb 2024.

United Nations High Commissioner for Refugees. 2015b. *Guidance on Protecting People from Disasters and Environmental Change through Planned Relocation.* https://www.unhcr.org/media/planned-relocation-guidance-october-2015, accessed 19 Oct 2023.

United Nations International Organization for Migration. 2018. Global Compact on Migration. https://refugeesmigrants.un.org/sites/default/files/180713_agreed_outcome_global_compact_for_migration.pdf, accessed 12 Oct 2023.

United Nations International Organization for Migration. 2020. *Institutional Strategy on Migration and Sustainable Development,* https://publications.iom.int/books/iom-institutional-strategy-migration-and-sustainable-development, accessed 20 Dec 2023.

United Nations International Organization for Migration. 2024. *Missing Migrants Project Database.* https://missingmigrants.iom.int/, access 11 Mar 2024.

United States Customs and Border Patrol. 2024. Border Encounters by Component. https://www.cbp.gov/newsroom/stats/southwest-land-border-encounters-by-component, accessed 15 Feb 2024.

United States Department of the Interior. 2020. *Informational Report: The Unmet Infrastructure Needs of Tribal Communities and Alaska Native Villages in Process of Relocating to Higher Ground as a Result of Climate Change: Fiscal Year 2020.* Albuquerque, NM: Department of the Interior, Bureau of Indian Affairs, Office of Trust Services, Tribal Climate Resilience Program. May, 2020. https://www.bia.gov/news/unmet-infrastructure-needs-tribal-communities-and-alaska-native-villages-process-relocation, accessed 23 Oct 2023.

United States Supreme Court. 1898. United States v. Wong Kim Ark. In *169 U.S. 649*: Cornell University Law School: Legal Information Institute.

Vince, Gaia. 2022. *Nomad Century: How Climate Migration Will Reshape Our World.* New York: Flatiron Books.

Walters, William. 2010. Migration and security. In J Peter Burgess, ed. *The Routledge Handbook of New Security Studies.* New York: Routledge. pp. 217–228. https://doi.org/10.4324/9780203859483.9.

Waterston, Alisse. 2020. *Light in Dark Times: The Human Search for Meaning.* Toronto: University of Toronto Press.

World Population Review. 2023. Population of Cities in China 2023. https://worldpopulationreview.com/countries/cities/china, accessed 19 Oct 2023.

World Population Review. 2024a. Countries with Birthright Citizenship 2024. https://worldpopulationreview.com/country-rankings/countries-with-birthright-citizenship, accessed 15 Feb 2024.

World Population Review. 2024b. Countries with Border Walls. https://worldpopulationreview.com/country-rankings/countries-with-border-walls, accessed 11 Mar 2024.

Wray, Helena. 2006. The aliens act 1905 and the immigration dilemma. *Journal of Law and Society* 33(2): 302–323. https://doi.org/10.1111/j.1467-6478.2006.00359.x.

Wydra, Elizabeth. 2009. Birthright Citizenship: A Constitutional Guarantee. *American Constitution Society for Law and Policy Briefs 2007-2011,* May. Page 4. https://www.acslaw.org/wp-content/uploads/2018/05/Wydra-Issue-Brief.pdf.

11
At A Crossroads

Human population movement is not new. People have been on the move for all of human history and across the entire planet. Practically everyone, everywhere, has a migration story somewhere in their family history. Our movement has been propelled by curiosity, the pursuit of livelihoods, flight from violence and conflict, changing environmental conditions, or forced by coercion and enslavement.

We are inclined to think about migration in exceptionalist terms, meaning that the patterns and processes we see unfolding today are unprecedented, unusual, and problematic. If you take away nothing else from this book, you should be able to challenge this exceptionalist viewpoint and note that the nature and extent of human population movement today is not at all unusual. Rather, it is a demonstrable extension of trends that have been with us for a very long time.

Another important observation that we would like you to consider is the ever-unfolding, self-correcting nature of systematic research on migration. As new evidence is produced from archaeology, genetics, linguistics, cultural anthropology, and environmental science, we are constantly updating our understanding about early population movements, the reasons people move, and the changes that mobility brings to how we live, whether we are among those who move or those who stay.

We have seen convincing evidence about the routes that human population groups followed when dispersing from Africa, first to the Arabian Peninsula and then from there to Europe, Asia, Australia, and the Pacific Islands. Based on recent findings, we now believe that this dispersal and geographic expansion appear to have taken place in waves, rather than all at once. The timing of these waves of movement coincides with major global climate changes, which resulted in changes in the ranges of vegetation and wildlife as well as fluctuations in sea levels that, in turn, made it possible to cross territories

World on the Move: 250,000 Years of Human Migration, First Edition. Edward Liebow,
James I. Deutsch, Daniel Ginsberg, Sojin Kim, and Caitlyn Kolhoff.
© 2025 John Wiley & Sons, Inc. Published 2025 by John Wiley & Sons, Inc.

that had at times been submerged. It is also likely that humans had become accomplished seafarers as long as 50,000 years ago, which enabled them to cross open waters and settle in Australia and, by 30,000 years ago, the Japanese archipelago. Later nautical accomplishments enabled exploration and settlement of vast stretches of the Pacific Islands, well before the Mediterranean and transatlantic voyages of recorded history.

Some of the widely prevalent patterns that we have discussed are worth emphasizing. First, migration is selective. Not everyone in a particular locale is equally likely to move to another place. Vulnerability to hazards and economic uncertainty is socially produced, and while war and conflict may have broad impacts over a geographic region, those who seek to flee may be those more likely to have the resources or social connections to aid in their flight.

Second, the largest movements of people in human history have involved the growth of cities, which is largely a result of people moving from sparsely settled rural and frontier areas to create larger, more densely settled places. Other important processes of human population movement have included colonization, enslavement and human trafficking, and movements in response to changing environmental conditions. Many researchers think the latter will accelerate in scale and pace in coming decades due to global climate change. We point this out to challenge the narrative that migration is a destabilizing force, and that migrants are "the other," somehow set apart with their essential humanity discounted or dismissed altogether.

We believe that humanity is at a crossroads. The spread of COVID-19 beginning in 2020 shows us how interconnected places are to one another, regardless of how distant and disconnected they might have seemed. The inevitability of people on the move in such an interconnected world means greater numbers of people from diverse backgrounds encounter and interact with one another, which heightens the need—as anthropologist Ruth Benedict once said—to make the world safe for cultural difference.

It is only a relatively recent phenomenon that national and international policies have shifted. Where earlier policies served to protect the concentration of wealth by various forms of dispossession and displacement, we now see a greater emphasis placed on protecting the rights of people on the move while properly anticipating the impacts on public facilities and services that result from this movement. As we have noted, at the international level, recognizing and protecting human rights has become a recent central focus, and the governance of migration is seen as a key element in achieving global sustainable development goals. Over the past four decades, regional agreements—which are often embedded as provisions in more encompassing trade or security agreements—spell out processes and mechanisms for groups of countries to cooperate on protecting the rights of migrants while properly anticipating how migration changes places of origin, destination, and places in between. National policies usually serve a number of purposes, regulating the international and internal flow of people to meet labor demands, protecting people from natural hazards, promoting the integration of immigrants in their new homes, and offering asylum and sanctuary from violence and conflict on a permanent or temporary basis.

Index

American Anthropological Association
  collaboration with Smithsonian   1
  principles for equitable and effective migration policy   236–237
  task force on border walls   225, 230
American Community Survey   20
Archaeological evidence   13–14, 66, 70–71, 98–99, 100
Armenia   52, 127–128, 154
Aswan High Dam, Egypt   124
Asylum seeker   8, 188

Barbary Coast   38, 196–197
Beringia crossroad   39–45
Biloxi–Chitimacha–Choctaw Nation, United States   45
Biological evidence
  genetic evidence   18–19, 55, 59, 64, 89, 94–97, 99
  skeletal evidence   14, 65, 70–71, 81–83, 134
Birthright citizenship   162, 232, 239–242
Border walls   225–230, 235
Britain's Migration Museum, immigration narrative   3
Byzantine Empire   38

Chain migration   8, 153
Circular migration   8
  Ethiopian migrants   131–133

European guest workers   131
Gulf Cooperation Council   134, 224
Climate migration   8, 29–30, 176, 184, 185–187, 246–250
Colonization   27–28, 38–39, 161–163, 256
  historical examples and enduring impacts of   38, 45, 48–49, 51–52, 83, 120–123, 142–145, 148–150, 204
  Terra nullius, concept of   27
Creation stories   63–65
Crossroads concept, the   34–60
  Bantu trade routes   47–48
  Beringia crossroads   39–45, 126–127
  Boyle Heights neighborhood   52–54, 153, 173–175
  Central Africa crossroads   45–49
  "crossroads," narrative device   3, 35
  East Los Angeles crossroads   49–55, 153, 173–175
  Mediterranean basin crossroads   35–39, 181–183, 196–197
  Tongva/Gabrielino tribal territory   51–52
Crash (film)   23–24
Crete   36
Current Population Survey   20

Definitions of key terms   8–10
  asylum seeker   8
  chain migration   8

World on the Move: 250,000 Years of Human Migration, First Edition. Edward Liebow, James I. Deutsch, Daniel Ginsberg, Sojin Kim, and Caitlyn Kolhoff.
© 2025 John Wiley & Sons, Inc. Published 2025 by John Wiley & Sons, Inc.

Definitions of key terms (cont'd)
  climate migration 8
  displacement 8
  emigration 8
  immigrant 8
  internally displaced persons 8
  internal migration 8
  international migration 8
  irregular migration 9
  labor migration 9
  lifetime migration 9
  migrant flow 9
  migrant 9
  migrant stock 9
  migration stream 9
  mover 9
  net migration 9
  place of destination (arrival) 9
  place of origin (departure) 9
  place of transit 10
  refugee 10
  remittances 10
  return migration/migrant 10
  short-distance (local) mover 10
  xenophobia 10
Department of Homeland Security 20, 207, 235, 242
  Office of Immigration Statistics 20
"Deserving" and "undeserving" immigrants 21–22
Diaspora 117–120, 127–129, 154, 167, 237
Displacement 8, 25–32, 107, 125–126
  internally displaced persons (IDPs) 8, 133–134

Economic development, forced relocation and 124–126
  Aswan High Dam, Egypt 124
  Sardar Sarovar Dam, India 124
  World Bank, environmental and social standards 125
Economic migration 49, 165, 185, 224
Enslavement 4, 14, 28, 38, 45–48, 148, 154, 161, 171, 176–177, 194–218, 231–232
  Ancient China 195–196
  Barbary Coast 38, 196–197

  consequences of 200–204, 213–214
  Gullah Resilience, case study 201–204
  Native American groups 197–198
  transatlantic slave trade 48, 198–204
Ethiopia 131–133

Favelas, Rio de Janeiro, Brazil 179–180
Forced Relocation 108, 115–200, 252–255
  Armenian genocide 154
  Guatemalan Indigenous women case study 117–120
  Japanese Americans in World War II 115–116
  Japanese in Japan in World War II 129–130
  Miao (Hmong) fleeing the Vietnamese War 130
  Native Americans 120–121
  Pakistan and India, partitioning of 122
  Palestinian resettlement (Nakba) 121–122
  Rohingyas 122–123
Foreign immigrants, categories of 19–20
France's National Migration Museum, narrative framework 3

Gauchos, Jewish, Argentina 161–164
Genetic evidence, migration research 18–19, 55, 59, 64, 89, 94–97, 99
Gentrification, forced relocation and 124–126, 168–175
  Bo-Kaap, Cape Town 176–177
  eco-gentrification, High Line case study 186–187
  Roma neighborhood, Mexico City 175–176
Geological nomenclature 72–73
Gran Torino (film) 130
Guest Workers
  European guest workers 176, 179
  Mexican guest workers 204
  South Asian guest workers 31

Heyerdahl, Thor hypothesis 87
Hmong, Cambodia and Vietnam 130
Human evolution 66–69

Human Rights, UN Declaration of 209–210, 220–222
Human trafficking 205–215
  prevention initiatives, Japan 212
  prevention initiatives, Sudan 212–213
  prevention initiatives, United Kingdom 211–212
  prevention initiatives, United States 210–211
Hunting and gathering, and migration 25, 36, 41, 75

Immigrating foreigners, categories of 19–20
Informal settlements, formation and organization of 178–180
  Favelas, Rio de Janeiro, Brazil 241–242
  social safeguards, World Bank 246–247
Internal migration, definition 8
International migration, global trends 35, 255–256
International Passenger Survey 23

Jebel Faya site, United Arab Emirates 81

Kindertransport 22, 125
Kongo Kingdom, Central Africa 47–48

Lampedusa, Italy 39
Language and migration 141–158
  creole languages 20, 148–149
  diaspora languages 154
  English language, history of 145–147
  glottochronology 147
  language change, phylogenetic approaches 147–148
  lingua franca 149
  linguistic evidence 14–16, 40, 84–85, 86, 94, 100
  markers of identity and heritage 153–154
  pidgin 14
  place in citizenship, education, employment 151–152
  trade jargon 149–150
Lesvos, Greece 181–183

Marine isotope stages, dating technique 70, 73–74
Measurement and data sources 13–24
  administrative statistics 16–18
  census data 17
  estimating migration in history and prehistory 13–16
  international migration data sources 18–20
  passenger statistics 16
  population registers 16
  special survey data 17–18
  visas and work permit data 16
Megacities 110–115
Migration policies, international 221–230
  border walls 225–230
  border walls, American Anthropological Association Statement on 230
  International Organization on Migration 8, 21, 222
  migration provisions in preferential trade agreements dataset 225
  regional agreements 224–225
  regional agreements, East African Community 225
  regional agreements, Economic Community of West African States 225
  regional agreements, European Union 224
  sustainable development agenda 222–223
  UN Human Rights Declaration 209–210, 222
Migration policies, national 231–245
  birthright citizenship 162, 232, 239–242
  migration policy and climate change 246–250
  national policy, Côte d'Ivoire 238
  national policy, Ghana 238
  national policy, United States 238–245
Misliya Cave complex, Israel 26, 70, 81–82
Mobilities studies 10–13
Museum exhibitions
  British Migration Museum 4
  "crossroads," narrative device 47–48
  French National Immigration Museum 3

INDEX

Museum exhibitions (cont'd)
   Smithsonian American History Museum   4
   World on the Move exhibition   1–6, 35

Nautical navigation, Pacific Islanders   86–87
Neanderthals, human encounters with   70–71
Net migration, definition   9

Origin stories   86–88
Ottoman Empire   36, 38, 121, 128, 154, 196
Out of Africa, migration models   63–77
Overseas Filipino Workers (OFW)   24–25

Paleoenvironmental evidence   40, 71, 81, 84–86, 95
Philippines   24–25
Prehistoric dispersal and expansion   70–71
   Americas   92–104
   Andaman Islanders   84
   Arabian Peninsula   71–72
   Arroyo Seco site, Argentina   98–99
   Australia and New Guinea   85–86
   Clovis, New Mexico   97–98
   Cooper's Ferry, Idaho   99
   Crete   36
   Gondwana   85
   Homo floresiensis   83
   Huaca Prieta site, Peru   98
   Japanese archipelago   84
   Jebel Faya, UAE   81
   Jebel Irhoud, Morocco   70
   Jwalapuram site, Jurreru River Valley, India   111
   Lapita cultural complex   86–87
   Middle Son River Valley, Madhya Pradesh, India   83
   Misliya Cave complex, Israel   26, 70, 81–82
   Monte Verde site, Peru   98
   Neanderthals, cohabiting with   70–71
   ocean navigation, Polynesian   86–87
   Pacific Islands   80, 86–87
   Paisley Cave, Idaho   99
   Ranis site   82
   "regional continuity" model   84–85
   Sahul landmass   67, 85
   Salkhit, Mongolia   83
   Southeast Asia   84–85
   Sunda land mass   66, 78
   Taiwan   39, 84, 88
   Tianyuan Cave   83
   Toba volcanic eruption event   83
   White Sands, New Mexico, United States   94–95, 100
Push/pull factors, drivers of migration   107–109

Refugees   10, 118–120, 236–237, 239–245
Remittances   10, 25, 131, 167, 237
"Replacement" model   85
Retirees   2, 24, 110
Rohingya, Myanmar   23, 122–123

Sardar Sarovar Dam, Narmada River, India   124
Selective movement   24–25, 225
Settler colonialism, forced relocation and   27–28, 120–122
   Palestinian resettlement   121–122
   partitioning of Pakistan and India   122
   Rohingya displacement, Myanmar   23, 122–123
Shire, Warsan, poet   134, 243
Smithsonian Center for Folklife and Cultural Heritage   1
Social production of vulnerability, migration context   107–138
South Asian guest workers   134, 224
Sustainable Development Goals, Agenda 2030   221–223

Terrebonne Parish, Louisiana, United States   53
Transatlantic slave trade   48, 198–204

Undocumented migration   20
United Arab Emirates   24
Urbanization   25–27, 110–115
   China, rural to urban migration   112–115
   megacities   115
   Mesoamerica   26, 96
   Mesopotamia   26, 110–111

Vikings   38
Vulnerability, social production of   107–138

World Bank Environmental and Social Standard   124–125

Xenophobia   10, 117–120, 152, 239–242, 256